MW00911214

The.
Mission2

The inside story of Geelong's
2007 & 2009 AFL Premierships

By Scott Gullan

The Mission2

Published by:
Weston Media & Communications
Melbourne
Ph: 0423 074 391

Copyright © 2009 ˙

All rights reserved. No part of this publication may be reproduced, stored in a retrieval system or transmitted in any form by any means without the prior permission of the copyright owner. Enquiries should be made to the publisher.

Every effort has been made to ensure that this book is free from error or omissions. However, the Publisher, the Author, the Editor or their respective employees or agents, shall not accept responsibility for injury, loss or damage occasioned to any person acting or refraining from action as a result of material in this book whether or not such injury, loss or damage is in any way due to any negligent act or omission, breach of duty or default on the part of the Publisher, the Author, the Editor, or their respective employees or agents.

The authors and publisher expressly disclaim all and any liability to any person, whether the purchaser of this publication or not, in respect of anything and of the consequences of anything done or omitted to be done by any such person in reliance, whether whole or partial, upon the whole or any part of the contents of this application.

ISBN 978-0-646-50203-8

Cover and page design by Spike Creative Pty Ltd.
Prahran, Victoria. Ph: (03) 9525 0900.
www.spikecreative.com.au

Photographs: Reg Ryan, courtesy Geelong Football Club, AFL Photos
Printed by Trojan Press

About The Mission2

In March, 2008, the first edition of *The Mission* was published, encapsulating Geelong's remarkable run to the 2007 premiership.

Now, some 18 months later, author Scott Gullan has added more than 100 new pages on the two seasons since – the disappointment of the 2008 campaign, which fell at the final hurdle, to the glory of securing the 2009 premiership.

Gullan also has added footnotes to the first edition content, ensuring a fresh take on the events that dramatically changed the history of a football club.

About the author

Scott Gullan is an award-winning sports writer for Melbourne's *Herald Sun*. He has covered AFL football, Olympic Games, Commonwealth Games and world athletics championships over the past 17 years.

His first book was the best-selling autobiography with Olympic champion Cathy Freeman, *Cathy, Her Own Story*.

He lives in Geelong with his wife, Tess, and son Noah.

Acknowledgements

In 2006, after reading yet another brilliant sports book by acclaimed American writer John Feinstein, the idea of doing a behind-the-scenes expose of an AFL club was born. It was more a 'Why hasn't it been done here before?' thought than anything, and when I started to investigate it with Geelong I received a positive response.

Brian Cook, Kevin Diggerson and Mark Thompson were quite receptive. Before anything could get off the ground, the 2006 season turned into a disaster and the idea was put well and truly on the backburner.

Mid-way through 2007 it came back. As the streak gathered momentum, discussions started again with Diggerson and then Cook. They saw the vision and understood what a great story they had happening around them: 44 years since the last premiership, and one of the greatest seasons of football ever played.

It was potentially a great story waiting to be written. They both deserve a lot of credit for making *The Mission* and *The Mission2* coming to life.

Cook's support for both projects from day one to the final sign-off was the key to everything. Diggerson's strategic manoeuvring throughout the process was invaluable, along with his organising of interviews and fact-checking at any time of the day or night. His assistant, Sarah Birch, also went above and beyond to ensure the interview process ran smoothly.

This is very much a players' book. I thank every one of them for giving me their time and I think they got as much enjoyment out of re-living the best year of their lives as I did in hearing about it ... warts and all. Their honesty was an integral part in the telling of the real story behind two premierships in three years.

In particular, I'd like to thank the two leaders, captain Tom Harley and vice-captain Cameron Ling. They got the ball rolling and it was their attention to detail which helped enormously.

The support of the coaching staff was much appreciated with Ken Hinkley, Brendan McCartney, Brenton Sanderson, Leigh Tudor and Thompson all giving their time, while Neil Balme and Steve Hocking played key roles in the final product. President Frank Costa, vice-president Gareth Andrews and recruiting manager Stephen Wells also gave crucial insights.

Producing two books in such a small space of time is a difficult exercise and that's where James Weston (or "John", as he has become known) took control. From our initial meeting when I went to him seeking advice on how to get such a book published, he embraced the concept. It has been an enjoyable journey.

There are many people who have helped in different ways, including the Mithens for the use of the Lorne writing retreat – again – Ondrej Foltin for his planting of the seed, my mother and father for the late-night spelling checks … amongst other things … while my in-laws, John and Fran, gave up a lot to cover my absence on the home front.

Getting a book written requires the author to extract himself from normal life. This could not have happened without the support of my two best friends, my wife Tess and son Noah, who put up with a lot but make everything worthwhile – all of the time.

Introduction

"To achieve this is massive. We hadn't won one for 44 years, the club was broke, nearly out of the competition, had a terrible stadium. We recruited young people who we trained up, we played a gritty style of footy."

– Geelong coach Mark Thompson

Every step Mark Thompson took around the Palladium Ballroom it happened. A kiss, a hug or an outstretched hand would be coming his way; some were friends, some were recognisable faces but many were complete strangers. Each one came with the same message: "Thank you".

Most had tears in their eyes. He had certainly shed a few of his own in the past five hours since what he'd once regarded as mission impossible was achieved: a Geelong premiership. A lot of people in the room had waited 44 years for this moment; Thompson had only been part of it, as coach, for eight years but he was quickly getting an understanding of the enormity of the situation.

He knew it would be big. He had been here on three previous occasions as a player with Essendon, the last time as captain. But this was different. On the stage, president Frank Costa was holding court. He was the man who had appointed Thompson and who had stood by him during the dark days of the previous 12 months.

"Mark has proven to be a fantastic builder from scratch," Costa was telling the 1500-strong crowd. He then proceeded to reel off some of his favourite statistics about the high turnover of players in the early days and how Thompson had predicted back then that the club would be ready to win a flag in 2006-07.

"Good things happen with good people coming together and working," he continued. "We have got a terrific group of young players who have played with such courage and determination this season. I heard as I was driving here this evening on the radio that they are now saying that this team has produced the best full year of effort of any team in the history of senior football in Australia."

Standing next to Costa, with his arm around him, was Brian Cook. It had been a massive year for the chief executive and he was ready to start celebrating the record-breaking 119-point Grand Final humiliation of Port Adelaide. His much-lauded review of the club's football operations had been seen as the catalyst for the team's stunning turnaround this season.

That was the majority view, not Cook's. After the applause had died down, following his introduction, Cook set the record straight. "Some people have said the review was the major reason for things to happen around this place, that is so wrong," he said. "The reason why we performed well this year is because the players and the coaches and the changes came from the changeroom."

When it was Thompson's turn to take to the microphone, he had one intention: he wanted his team up there with him. It hadn't been about the individual all year at Geelong; it had been about the hard work of an extraordinary group of people that had brought the premiership cup to this great club.

First he called up his assistant coaches. Ken Hinkley, who had gone through the heartache as a player in three losing grand finals for the Cats, then Brendan McCartney, his loyal lieutenant who had been next to him for the entire journey, and Brenton Sanderson, the recently retired defender who had returned to Skilled Stadium this year and been a revelation.

Then there was VFL premiership-winning coach Leigh Tudor, player development manager Ron Watt, assistant football operations manager

Steve Hocking and fitness coaches Paul Haines and Dean Robinson. Physiotherapist Nick Ames was called up along with recruiting manager Stephen Wells, doctor Chris Bradshaw and even video co-ordinator Eugene Dickinson.

Thompson explained Neil Balme's absence. The football operations manager had woken up sick on the morning of the game, had battled through the day but was now at home in bed. He then motioned to the people assembled on the stage and said, "We have come together every day for the last six months. We turn up to work and it is a professional environment, dynamic, it takes a lot of work, co-ordination, administration and these guys here together have helped Geelong win a premiership, the first one in 44 years."

He then asked the three assistant coaches for some quick words. All they wanted to talk about was Thompson. "To do the job he does and also to trust us to do the job we do, we couldn't get it done without his trust. It is a vital part of the success of the club," Hinkley said.

Sanderson summed it up for everyone: "I absolutely love him. I loved playing for him and I love working for him."

Later, after the players had hoped on a bus with the premiership cup to head back to Geelong, and the party at Crown Casino was starting to wind down, Thompson had more time to reflect. An inner peace had come over him. "This is the hardest football club in Australia to win a premiership at, no question, you can do a lot right and then have a little moment, little moments where it doesn't work exactly the way you want it to work and it can fall apart," he said.

"So to achieve this is massive. We hadn't won one for 44 years, the club was broke, nearly out of the competition, had a terrible stadium. We recruited young people who we trained up, we played a gritty style of footy. I had done it from Melbourne, not being a Geelong person, so there was the travel and everything else that had gone on.

"It is just huge, just huge."

Then it hit him.

"This has been the best night of my life."

chapter 1
September, 2006

"I will do an extensive review and it won't be based on perception as most seem to be. I want to collect evidence, not simply collect opinion."

– Geelong CEO Brian Cook

The rhythmical sway of the palm trees and the sun beating down on his back was just the tonic for Mark Thompson. He had needed an escape after the most trying year of his career, and Hamilton Island in Queensland's Whitsundays was the perfect choice.

While the surroundings were intoxicating and, more importantly, thousands of kilometres away from Geelong and AFL football, Thompson wasn't able to fully let go. He had a lot on his mind and a crucial decision to make.

The season had been a disaster. After winning the NAB Cup and being installed as flag favourites after round two, the Cats had self-destructed. This was supposed to be their premiership window. Instead, everything Thompson had built up since he took over in 2000 was fracturing. It finally ended with a disappointing loss to Hawthorn and tenth place on the ladder, although the coach had at least seen some rays of light over the last couple of months.

That meant nothing to an increasing band of critics which, significantly, included some club board members. For the first time, Thompson was wondering if it was all worth it. Was he better to just walk away? He had always said that he wasn't a career coach and he'd know when his time was up[1]. Maybe, it was now. "I really didn't think I could be bothered doing it," was how he summed up his feelings.

Back in Geelong, Brian Cook was coming to the end of a searching review of the club's football operations. It had started before the end of the season and, while it was multi-faceted, ultimately it would decide whether Thompson saw out the final year of his contract. Cook, who had led West Coast to two flags in the 1990s and was regarded as the best CEO in the business, couldn't have envisaged what he was getting himself into when he told the board he was the man to put the microscope over the only part of the club which wasn't performing.

"I have had two or three incidents in my life in footy which have been really hard. That's one of them," he would say afterwards. "In fact, that is probably the toughest. It took a lot out of me, it really did. I wouldn't do it again."

The problems started when the Cats lost seven of eight games to virtually rule themselves out of the finals before the mid-year break. Cook knew a review of some description was required at the end of the season but the urgency and importance of the exercise went up a notch when a challenge to the board by former club director Denis McMurrich began to gain momentum.

McMurrich had confronted the executive team with a list of requests and conditions. At the top was a review of the football department and the coach. In truth it was more like a demand, given McMurrich had indicated he had enough signatures to force an extraordinary general meeting to make it happen. Faced with a political mess, Cook suggested to president Frank Costa that they needed to get in first.

---

1. In October, 2009, Thompson confirmed that 2011 would be his final season. "I just signed for two years and that's it," he told the *Herald Sun*. "And the club pretty much knows that."

"We thought it would be best if we come up with our own review before this guy gets legs," Cook said. "People who aren't politically astute saw that as a bit weak and asked why don't we take this guy on and tell him to get stuffed. To me it was going to be inevitable that there was going to be some analysis of what we were doing, so let's get out there early and carry out the review."

The August board meeting was a hot one. The idea of a review was welcomed. But who to do it? That was the topic of debate. The two football directors – former centre half-forward Gareth Andrews and legendary goalkicker Doug Wade – had been the most vocal that changes had to be made. Each was evidently keen to have a significant influence on the review. This set alarm bells off for the chief executive. The review had to be free of any agendas, and the idea of bringing in outside consultants also didn't appeal, so he put up his hand and argued that he was capable of doing it on his own. The board remained unconvinced, and worried about Cook's independence.

"I think I can remain as independent as possible," Cook told them. "I will do an extensive review and it won't be based on perception, as most football department reviews seem to be. I want to collect evidence, not simply opinion."

On August 16, the club released a statement saying Cook would co-ordinate a review which would look at football administration, all coaching areas, medical and sport science, welfare, list management, player leadership and recruiting. No timeline was given. Cook wanted to be thorough and, more importantly, he also needed the hysteria to die down.

Over the next month the chief executive conducted 43 interviews – most lasting over two hours – and spoke to more than 60 people. It included one-on-one chats with players to group discussions with the player leadership group, all the coaches individually, some support staff as well as many influential people in the football world including leading commentators and player managers.

While he tried to keep it as confidential as possible, that was unlikely given how wide the net was spread, plus the overwhelming media attention. The press had a whiff of a possible sacking; Thompson was forced to have his future discussed daily in the papers and on talkback radio, while still trying to keep his focus on coaching the remaining games of the season. "The fact I interviewed so many people, including player managers, meant that some of the stuff got out and it just steamrolled," Cook said. "It was really quite unfair, particularly on Bomber (Thompson) and he had to live with it every day for six to eight weeks.

"I know he tried to get away but it was just impossible. I felt terrible. I was trying to independently review a department and there was leakage from the interviews I was carrying out. But to do it properly I had to interview all of these people. There was no stopping. The issue was whether I should have interviewed player managers but they gave me bloody good feedback; these guys deal with every club, they compare how their players have been treated from one club to another and what their players are saying to them."

The most valuable information came from the players, in particular the leadership group, and resulted in 80 per cent of Cook's eventual findings. The bottom line was that Thompson was a great coach and he just needed to get back to doing just that: coaching.

"The one that got me was the healthy relationship Mark had built between the individual players and himself had dissipated. That was the issue," Cook said. "Trying to identify the reasons for that was really difficult because they all said, to a man – everyone I interviewed, the 60 people – everyone said, 'This guy can coach, and he is great one-on-one but he is not doing enough of that anymore.'

"So early in the piece it became obvious this guy was a good coach and if he wasn't staying it would be for some reason other than his coaching ability, which would be crazy."

The lobbying of board members was starting. Andrews' phone hadn't stopped ringing since the Hawthorn debacle a week earlier. He had even attended a meeting with 10 influential supporters at the Botanical Hotel in Melbourne - they were calling for change, and not just the coach.

Cook knew a lot was going on behind the scenes when he arrived at Costa's house in Geelong on Thursday, September 14, 2006, for a briefing with the board. While the media had Andrews and Wade pegged as the anti-Thompson movement, there were a couple of other lower profile board members who agreed that there needed to be more debate over the coach's position and the structure of the football department.

For the first time in Costa's reign, the board was split. After Cook provided an update on the progress of the review, it was decided he would be given extra time to come up with different scenarios for a new football department. At this point the job was still Thompson's but there was a consensus that new faces and new ideas were desperately required at several levels.

A week later, after wading through hundreds of pages of notes, the 70-page 'Cook Report' was ready. It made 30 recommendations relating to the senior coach and his role, general manager of football operations and his role, assistant coaches and their roles, captaincy and on-field leadership, expanded role of player leadership group, a new high performance department and an increase in the volume and intensity of training.

Cook found that Thompson needed to get back to more one-on-one coaching; he needed to go back to what he was good at and remove everything else that had distracted him over the previous year. He had to get out of administration, get out of recruiting, get out of fitness, get out of IT and concentrate on coaching. Coach the coaches, coach the players and get back to enjoying the job.

A key was to build a support network around Thompson which would enable this change to take place. The key member of the support network would be the general manager of football operations. This position would be beefed up, with the person to sit above the senior coach in the club hierarchy. Thompson would be answerable to him, too, instead of only the CEO. A nationwide search for the right person to fill this important role would begin immediately through head-hunting firm Slade Consulting. Garry Davidson, the long-time football manager, would not have his contract renewed.

An overhaul of the coaching structure was desperately needed. Freshness and new ideas were required, with a change in roles for Ken Hinkley (forwards) and Brendan McCartney (backs), who had worked the same zones for a long time. Midfield coach Andy Lovell, who was coming out of contract, was to be replaced[2].

---

2. In the three years since, the coaching panel has been remarkably stable: the sole addition has been retired Brisbane Lions star Nigel Lappin, the only departure VFL coach Leigh Tudor to St Kilda.

Tom Harley was to be appointed captain, replacing Steven King. It was vitally important that the right player leadership group was installed and, while Harley was a player not naturally blessed, he had made it to the top through character and attitude. "He has great values," Cook said. "The more you put those people into leadership positions the greater the opportunity you have of developing a good culture."

The player leadership group needed to have more responsibility, a wider operation and more depth. They should have input into match selection, in list management and in how the coaches are performing.

Steve Hocking was to be appointed assistant football manager, concentrating on high performance. He would be in charge of finding new fitness staff and co-ordinating the medical / fitness areas. One of the issues identified midway through the season as a factor in the disappointing performances was the players' fitness. A consultant in physiology, Simon Sostarich, had been introduced to assess training loads and intensity. He compared the 2006 pre-season to the previous two pre-seasons and calculated that the players were 50 per cent down on the workload in the running area.

Other recommendations covered a host of areas, including increasing the recruitment resources and the change in size and cancellation of some meetings (this, in particular, surprised Cook, who had spent a week sitting in on all the football department meetings).

Before he could present the finished product to the board, Cook rang the coach in Hamilton Island to ask him one simple question. He knew how much Thompson was hurting, so he needed to be certain that he still wanted the job. "Bomber, you just have to decide whether you want to do this," Cook said down the line. "After all that has happened, do you still want to do this?"

Luckily for Cook and the Geelong Football Club, Thompson had been mulling over some advice he had received from his close circle of confidantes. One of those was Geelong fanatic (and Victoria's attorney general) Rob Hulls. "I have a group of people who I talk to, three blokes in particular, and he (Hulls) is one of them." Thompson said. "I met him in a pub in Essendon one night and he is one of these smart people I speak to who have followed Geelong. The reason why I decided to stay was I liked the club, I liked the players and I thought they had potential. I knew we were better than that and I knew there were reasons why we didn't perform that way this year.

"People were sitting there just pointing the finger but I was given some great advice. I was basically told that: 'At the moment everyone is blaming you. If you walk away you will prove them right. So you might as well go and stick your head down and, if you think you are any good at it, go and do it your way.'"

By the time Cook rang, Thompson had made up his mind. He was scheduled back in Melbourne that weekend to watch Geelong's reserves side play in the VFL Grand Final and it was agreed that he would front the board at 7am on the Sunday before the game. The message was quickly relayed to Costa by his CEO. The relationship between the three men – Costa, Cook and Thompson – had been the envy of many, and the triumvirate was seen as the driving force behind the extraordinary turnaround of the club. A sign of the respect was that they all operated on handshake agreements, not signed contracts.

Throughout the angst and furore surrounding his club, Costa had been unwavering in his support of Thompson and he was determined to stick strong. "The whole thing was very hard on Mark Thompson," Costa said.

"Mark felt he was really put under the microscope. There was a lot of pressure from the media wanting me to sack Mark Thompson but I wouldn't be a party to that. What I was worried about was that he was knocked off his normal equilibrium. That was Mark's seventh year and in the first six he had been fantastic. That is why I stuck by him because I knew what had happened.

"There were many things that added to the damage. One of those was the fact that Mark was going through a separation from his wife and kids at the end of 2005 and, over the next few months before the footy season started, he left home."

Ascertaining if Thompson's battery was re-charged was a key part of his appearance at the 7am meeting, held at a secret location in the

Melbourne city offices of law firm Harwood and Andrews. Those present were Costa, Cook, Andrews, Wade, Nick Carr – who was the managing director of Harwood and Andrews – Alastair Hamblin and Greg Hywood. The remaining board member, Helene Bender, was overseas.

"Did he have the passion to pick up this ball and run with it after all he had been through?" was the question Costa wanted answered. "After the toughness of the review, we needed to know if he could give this board 100 per cent confidence that he would take the ball and run with it under the new structure."

It was obvious from the moment Thompson entered the room that he meant business. He sat down and immediately stared every board member in the eye and said: "We have all had a very bad year."

His message was clear. The time for finger pointing was over. Everyone from the president, CEO, senior coach to the 40th player on the club's list had contributed in some way to the mess. For the next hour Thompson shot straight from the heart, his passion for the task ahead and commitment in his plan plain to see.

"We are going to change the way we play footy," he declared.

Thompson's coaching philosophy had centred around defensive, hard, tough, accountable football. It followed from his playing days, when he had been a hard-nosed back pocket with Essendon. But the game had changed recently, getting significantly faster. That fact, combined with the team's fitness problems, had left Geelong floundering. "This game plan is not going to be without risks," Thompson explained to the board. "We are going to be running straight and fast from the backline; we are going to come into the centre corridor as fast as we can and then deliver the ball into the forward line quickly.[3] Any time we lose possession the resultant turnover is going to hurt us. They are going to come back and kick goals but we have the players to make it work."

When he left the room, Thompson didn't know whether he'd saved his job. He didn't have to wait long, however. Cook rang shortly afterwards with the good news. After everything that had unfolded over the previous

---

3. Thompson delivered on the attacking gameplan. In 2006, the Cats averaged 90 points per game. Across 2007-09, they averaged 114ppg.

few months, the board didn't even vote on the senior coaching position – it was obvious from the discussion around the table that everyone was now convinced Thompson had the fire in his belly to turn things around.

Cook then had the unenviable task of calling those who would no longer be part of the GFC. He found the call to Davidson the toughest. The pair had become very close over the journey. Harley, who had been one of three vice-captains, had to be informed of his promotion, while King, who had already told his teammates he was stepping down, was also on Cook's list to call.

Coincidentally, the pair had planned to travel together to the VFL Grand Final. The new skipper was in his car en route to pick King up when his mobile rang. "This is a strictly confidential phone call," Cook told him. "Providing you accept, I would just like to congratulate you on being the new captain of Geelong."

For a moment Harley was lost for words: "Of course, I accept," he blurted out. Cook then explained that Harley could tell no one because he was still trying to find King. "No worries, I won't tell anyone," Harley said.

When he got to King's house, his friend's phone rang and it was Cook. Harley said he would wait outside in the car. When the big ruckman returned, nothing was said straight away but, a few minutes into the journey, King – who thought Harley knew but wasn't quite sure – went fishing.

"Mate, I think the club might have made a decision with the captaincy," he said.

The look on Harley's face immediately told the story. King, whose four-year reign as skipper had been ruined by injury, leaned over and the pair shook hands.

"Well done, mate," the now former captain said.

And with that, a new era was born.

chapter 2
A new beginning

"Everyone was pretty embarrassed. We said to each other, well, you might only get one crack at it ... if it is not this year then half of us wouldn't be here any more."

– Steven King

T om Harley had put plenty of thought into his maiden captain's address to club faithful at the Carji Greeves Medal presentation night. For the previous week he had tossed around ideas but in the end figured it was just easy to speak from the heart.

"I went along to the (2006) Grand Final and found myself feeling a little bit uncomfortable, uneasy and envious of the two teams (West Coast and Sydney) that played," Harley said. "Aside from the obvious talent on the park I saw two teams that were so united, team-orientated and committed to winning that nothing was going to stand in their way. I must admit when I walked away from the game I was a bit emotional because I saw the reason why you play (this game). I thought to myself, 'This is where we need to be'.

"I would love nothing more than the players from other clubs to be envious of the Geelong Football Club, and we need to gain the respect of the football world. We fought too bloody hard to gain it and it's so quickly lost. We need that passion, spirit, honesty and trust, and, most importantly, the respect among ourselves to regain it."

Cameron Mooney admired his mate's passion but he wasn't a believer. In fact, when the season had finished he'd actually spoken to his manager about leaving. "I said to him, 'Is there anything on the table anywhere else?'" Mooney said. "It was probably only because I had a year to go on my contract that I stayed. It was basically seven years of work and all of a sudden it just fell apart and I'm like: 'You're kidding.' It was just so bad, I thought if that is the best we have got then we're stuffed."

There were others around the room also questioning their future. Andrew Mackie, the Cats' first-round pick in the 2002 national draft, had started to emerge as a player in the second half of the season and had caught the attention of Port Adelaide. The Power came knocking with a very lucrative offer to return home.

James Kelly was wondering whether this would be his last Geelong best and fairest count. While he'd once been rated ahead of Gary Ablett and Jimmy Bartel, the talented midfielder had lost his way – badly – and played three of the last four games in the VFL. Already he'd read his name in the papers as one of the likely key players in the trading period, which started in four days' time.

Yet for Paul Chapman, who would that evening win his first best and fairest award, the new skipper's speech had moved him. It was exactly the same way he felt, so to hear it come from another teammate gave him hope. The mood was certainly a lot more bouyant the following week when the team – including Kelly, who every club had asked about but been rejected by Thompson – flew to London to play an exhibition game against Port Adelaide.

Opinion was divided as to whether the trip was a good or bad thing. It turned out to be a winner in several ways. Harley saw it as a great opportunity to bond the group; a chance to escape the hell of the previous few months. In London they would be able to breathe, relax and have fun without that feeling of someone watching your every move, which is how life in Geelong can be for an AFL footballer.

The hierarchy saw it as an opportunity for players and officials to analyse other professional sporting operations. New club doctor Chris Bradshaw had previously worked with English Premier League football side Fulham, so he arranged for a guided tour of its facilities and seats for the club's Monday night game against Charlton.

Harley and media manager Kevin Diggerson also got the chance to look around EPL powerhouse Arsenal's facilities and found the experience quite inspiring – particularly an engraving they came across in one of the club's corporate rooms. "Embossed in gold in a granite floor was, *Victory grows from harmony*," Harley recalled. "It just struck a chord with me, just with life in general. If you are not happy with something then your life is going to suck. As a footy team I figured we needed to fall in love with each other all over again."

Across town, another group of Cats, including McCartney and defenders Josh Hunt, David Johnson and David Wojcinski, were spending the day with rugby team the London Wasps. What was eye-opening was the level of professionalism compared to Skilled Stadium. "We thought we were pretty professional but going there and watching them, they were just so professional at everything they did," Wojcinski said. "They are not cracking it that they have to be there all day at training. It's their job, they have weights in the morning, then have lunch, then have to be out on the track in the afternoon. It made us realise that these blokes are professional and this is what we need to be."

A second soccer game was placed on the schedule after ruckman Brad Ottens managed to scalp tickets to a Euroleague showdown between Chelsea and Barcelona. A dozen Cats hence found themselves standing amongst the Spanish team's supporters in the terraces at Stamford Bridge.

The trip also gave Cook and Thompson the chance to interview Brenton Sanderson about the vacant assistant coach's position. Since retiring at the end of 2005, Sanderson had worked as development coach with Port Adelaide – indeed, he was in London with the Power – but he was interested in returning. A meeting was arranged in a coffee shop around the corner from the team's hotel.

"When I left Geelong I was always hoping that I would come back, whether it was five years or 10 years or whatever," Sanderson said. "Because I had just finished playing I wasn't sure if coaching would be something I was even interested in. I went to Port, which for me was sort of going home because I grew up in Adelaide, and watched from a distance as Geelong had their year in 2006. Obviously still my heart was very much with Geelong but I had a great year at Port and I loved working there as a development coach, mainly working with the first- to fourth-year players.

"Some people thought I was crazy wanting to go back after the year the club had, and after the review, because it didn't seem like the best place to be. But I was still very close to the playing group, I loved playing under Bomber and I thought it would be great to work with him because we had all been chasing this 44-year dream."

Thompson loved Sanderson as a player during his 199-game career at Geelong (he played six games with Adelaide in 1992-93 and four with Collingwood in 1994), where he won a best and fairest and had been vice-captain. Yet he was worried Sanderson might still be too close to the players. "I was happy he went away to Port Adelaide but in saying that, when we interviewed him … the fact he had seen another club operate, he realised some of our boys have got a lot more work to do and I think he is ready to tell them," Thompson said.

Sanderson was particularly tight with Harley, Mooney, Matthew Scarlett and Max Rooke. He rang all of them when he applied for the job and asked how they would feel having one of their best mates coaching them. "They were all great," he recalled. "They said if we do something wrong then you are going to give us a serve and we respect the job that you have got. They encouraged me to do it. Once I heard that I was ready to take it on."

A trip which initially looked like a being an untimely distraction for Geelong actually ended up being a positive on a number of fronts – they won the game at The Oval by 20 points and gained an assistant coach in the process.

Melbourne Cup eve, 2006. It wasn't the normal surroundings for the start of pre-season training, and this would turn out to be anything but a normal day. The baseball fields in Waurn Ponds, on the outskirts of Geelong, was where players and media assembled to welcome the beginning of a new year.

New faces were abundant. Neil Balme, the two-time Richmond premiership player and former Melbourne coach, had left Collingwood to take on that new, pivotal role of general manager of football operations. Paul Haines, an assistant fitness adviser at the Adelaide Crows, and Dean Robinson, the strength and conditioning coach from NRL club the Manly Sea Eagles, had been appointed to jointly run the fitness department. Sanderson was present, as was another ex-player, former Tiger turned physiotherapist Duncan Kellaway, who was part of the new medical structure.[4]

Given it was Cup eve, the expectation of the small media contingent for Thompson's first press conference of the season was at the lower end of the scale. A token: "*So you're happy the review is over?*" question was lobbed his way.

What happened next sent shockwaves through the corridors of power at Skilled Stadium.

"The whole process was pretty crappy, to be honest, I didn't really approve it," Thompson said. "I was lucky it fell my way and we sorted a few things out, but as a club, I think we still have a bit of work to do. I haven't got a problem with the findings but just the process I was filthy on. Too long, too public. It is pretty embarassing for everyone at the footy club (but) saying that, it is a good result now ... I think everyone was embarrassed, I was embarrassed, all the other coaches were, the players were."

Diggerson, who had been trying to put a positive spin on the club's affairs for the past couple of months, was standing a few metres away from the press conference chatting with Balme. He didn't hear Thompson unload. When told about the outburst after the coach had wandered off to join in training, Diggerson's jaw dropped. "He said what?"

Yet Thompson's words were brutally honest and provided insight into how he and his team were going to attack the year. Honesty and confrontation would become the motto of the pre-season. Vice-captain Cameron Ling,

4. Just as the coaching panel has remained stable, this entire off-field group was unchanged from 2007-09.

who like a number of the senior players had arrived at pre-season training the fittest he'd ever been, could already sense a different feel about the place. "It was a real breath of fresh air having the new people there," Ling said. "There was this burning desire never to have a year like we had just had. We had never doubted we had the players to be right up there, it was just a matter of fixing a few things up."

King thought a lot of players had started to see the writing on the wall. "Everyone was pretty embarrassed and we said to each other that you might only get one crack at it," he said. "And it got to a stage where if it is not this year then half of us wouldn't be here any more."

"Everyone had just had enough of being mediocre," was utility Joel Corey's take on the situation.

The coaching staff also sensed something good was brewing. "I'm sure they were tired of letting each other down," McCartney said. "I'm sure they were tired of the criticism of the club and I was sure they'd had enough of being an average club."

It didn't take long for Balme to pick up on it. "You could immediately smell that these blokes are ready to do something, they are ready," he said. "What is it? I don't know, but they were begging for some sort of organisational change to say, 'Okay, let's go, let's do this'."

Leadership had long been seen as Geelong's Achilles heel, much to Harley's angst. "It seemed that every team has a catch cry when they lose a game," he said. "Essendon have got a lack of leg speed; Geelong's is that their leaders didn't stand up, they have got poor leaders. I was a part of that group with Scarlo, Kingy, Moons, Lingy and we were just offended by it. I mean, what does leadership look like? We are not all Wayne Careys and strut and stuff, and I think footy has moved on since then."

Progress had been made in that department, courtesy of a program run by former assistant police commissioner Bill Kelly. However, in what would be reflected upon as one of the most important decisions of the year, Balme decided to ramp this focus up, bringing in *Leading Teams*, a company run by renowned leadership expert Ray McLean. McLean was the man responsible for creating Sydney's much-lauded 'Bloods' culture, which was the cornerstone of the Swans' 2005 premiership success.

Balme had met him during his time at Collingwood and had been impressed (although the program was short-lived as key Magpies officials did not embrace it.) McLean's co-founder in *Leading Teams*, Gerard Murphy, had been communications manager at Melbourne Football Club for five years; he was the man assigned to work with Geelong. "I knew Murph reasonably well and I knew Ray McLean very well," Balme said. "I just knew how dynamic they were at it and I knew they took any risk out of it. I didn't want to miss the opportunity, you could just see that the players were ripe."

The leadership group was determined by a player vote. King and Scarlett both withdrew from the ballot. Max Rooke was the new face elevated into the group to join Harley, Ling, Mooney, Chapman and Corey. Then, in December, Murphy walked into Skilled Stadium for the first time. Mooney wasn't impressed with what he saw. "He walked in and, as you do as a group, you are all very sceptical about it," he said. "He started talking and talking and talking and you're thinking, 'Just shut up, mate'."

Mooney would soon change his tune.

"Player number 111457. Joel Selwood, Bendigo Pioneers." Stephen Wells did his best to hide a smile as he read out Geelong's first pick in the 2006 national draft. Sitting next to him, Neil Balme was doing the same. At the table behind, Wells' assistant recruiter, John Peake, and Mark Thompson were nodding in approval. "I'm very happy with that," the coach said with his own big smile.

It had been an anxious few minutes for the Cats' recruiting guru. Wells had come to the draft determined to get either Selwood, who was the younger brother of West Coast's Adam and Brisbane's Troy, or a local boy from Torquay named Travis Boak, with selection No.7.

He figured it would most likely be Boak as he doubted whether Selwood would last. But just before he sat down in the Victory Room at Telstra Dome, Wells had heard that Port Adelaide was hot for Boak with its No. 5 pick. This left Hawthorn at No. 6 as the only stumbling block. They had shown interest in Selwood but also in Mitch Thorpe, a tall, strapping forward from Tasmania.

As soon as Chris Pelchen, Hawthorn's recruiting manager, started reading the number out for their selection, Wells knew it was Thorpe, not Selwood. And he knew the Cats had got away with one. Again. Twelve months earlier, Selwood would have likely gone No. 1 but he had been too young to be eligible for the draft. A knee injury had restricted him to just three games in 2006; consequently, he had dropped off the radar for many. Yet Geelong had followed his progress and concluded that the kid had a long AFL career ahead of him.

The word that Joel was the best of the Selwood dynasty had been out for a couple of years. Given that Adam had run fifth in the Eagles' best and fairest in a premiership year, it was a fairly big statement. But Joel's deeds as part of the Australian Institute of Sport squad and on an under 16 tour of Ireland had recruiters drooling. "He was destined to be a top quality AFL player as a 16-year-old," Wells said. "He went to Ireland and was the best player there. He then played in the under 18 national championships in 2005 and played really well, earning All-Australian selection. The next year he fronted up and could only play three games so I can completely understand why people had concerns about taking him."

Fifteen minutes later after securing Selwood, Wells experienced similar pleasure when announced to the room: "*Player number 111734. Tom Hawkins, Melbourne Grammar*".

The fact it was the No. 41 selection and not No. 1 had caused dissension for months, and was one of the reasons why the father-son system was changed for 2007. Hawkins, the son of 'Jumpin' Jack Hawkins, who had played 182 games for the Cats between 1973-81, was a monster of a kid who had dominated school footy playing for Melbourne Grammar. Given Geelong's long-time drought of key forwards, big Tom, who stood at 197cm and 105kg, had been on Wells' radar for three years. He knew he had another father-son steal and the rest of the football world had got to see that at the national under 18 championships in June.

This had been Hawkins' biggest test. He had really only played against other school teams, and had just a handful of TAC games (the elite under 18 feeder competition) to his credit. Taking on the best in the country was a different story but it took just one game for the media hype to explode. The headlines simply told the world what Wells already knew: 'Cats' new Judd' and 'Brown clone: Cat father-son pick likened to Lions champ'.

"He was a genuine player," Wells said. "You wouldn't have been surprised if he was called out as No.1 pick because he is a powerful key position player with great skills. We were fortunate that he had only ever wanted to play for Geelong because of his father's fantastic career here."

The drafting of the Tomahawk, as he would soon become known, made it five father-son selections in six years. There were now six on the Cats' list: Matthew Scarlett, Gary Ablett, Nathan Ablett, Mark Blake, Tim Callan and Hawkins. It had been a gold mine for Geelong, perhaps off-setting the fact that Wells, who had been in charge of recruiting since 1994, had never had a pick before No. 7. Unlike some of their main rivals, such as St Kilda, West Coast, Hawthorn and Collingwood, the Cats had never had the luxury of a priority pick or a sniff at the No. 1.

Wells and Thompson had basically re-built the entire list from the moment the coach walked in. Twenty-two players were shown the door in their first 12 months. The 1999 November national draft, which came just a month after the new coach's appointment, proved a good launching pad with the selections of Joel Corey (No.8), Paul Chapman (31), Cameron Ling (38), Corey Enright (47) and Cameron Mooney (as part of the Leigh Colbert trade to the Kangaroos).

Corey had been a standout for Western Australia in the national championships and had already played senior football. Chapman, according to Wells, was a lot like he is today: rough and ready. "He was a hard nut who had fantastic skills," he said.

"It had been a tough year for Chappy and his family as his brother had died but I remember spending some time with him and his parents out at their home. Paul expressed to me that he was really going to appreciate the opportunity."

The visit to the Ling family home in Geelong had also been interesting. The whole family were mad Cats fans – Cameron had gone to renowned local football school, St Joseph's, and was playing at full-forward for the Geelong Falcons. "I went around to Lingy's place before the draft and his mother wanted me to promise that we'd draft him. I couldn't promise anything, you never can, but she didn't really want to hear that," Wells said. "But Lingy had shown fantastic endurance in the beep test at the draft camp and we saw him play a couple of games in the midfield with the Falcons and do well. It was no surprise he had more strings to his bow than full-forward."

Enright was an old fashioned draft smoky. He was the Cats' seventh and final pick that year; Wells recalls sitting with Peake and Thompson and saying, "Why don't we take a punt on someone who might be able to offer us something different?" Enright hailed from Kimba in South Australia, a dot on the map halfway between Adelaide and Perth. It was the same small town in which the Wakelin twins, Shane (Collingwood) and Darryl (Port Adelaide), had grown up. Enright hadn't appeared at any of the underage carnivals but played a couple of games for Port Adelaide in the under 19s, plus reserves, which is where Wells' team spotted him. "When a guy like Corey comes along, rangy, running ... such a natural footballer but he had been under-developed because he'd played in the country," Wells said.

"He was a guy with special qualities who, with work, might just turn out to be something."

Mooney had played in a Grand Final with North Melbourne in his 11th game. He only received a handful of minutes on the ground and didn't touch the ball. Thompson had been an assistant to Denis Pagan that year at North, so when Leigh Colbert – who had been named Geelong captain in 1999 missed the entire season due to injury – decided he wanted to go to Arden St, a deal was done for the young tall forward and draft picks.

After trading away most of their picks in 2000 – a bad mistake in hindsight – Thompson and Wells hit the road in the lead-up to the 2001 draft. They interviewed parents, teachers and coaches of all potential draftees with Thompson on the lookout for kids with good character. On the football side of it, he wanted hard players who, more importantly, could kick it well. "What Mark was good at was judging people and their character, so we travelled the countryside talking to people and finding out all those sorts of things," Wells said.

While that year's draft would become known as the super draft because of the hype surrounding the top three priority selections – Luke Hodge

(Hawthorn at No.1), Luke Ball (St Kilda No.2) and Chris Judd (West Coast No.3) – it would also prove to be a bonanza for the Cats.

All eight players selected in the 2001 draft played senior football in 2006 – Jimmy Bartel (No.8), James Kelly (17), Charlie Gardiner (23), Steve Johnson (24), Gary Ablett jnr (40), Henry Playfair (41), Matthew McCarthy (69) and David Johnson (81).

Bartel was another local who had dominated for the Falcons and was always going to be a fantastic AFL player. The biggest danger to the Cats had been West Coast, who had pick No.6. "We were very excited Jimmy was still there because West Coast in particular had shown a lot of interest in him, a real lot, " Wells said. "There was a definite concern Jimmy would be gone but they ended up taking Ashley Sampi, who had been the best under 16 player I have ever seen at the national carnival in Tasmania the year before. He had been just sheer brilliance."

There was also a bit of luck with Kelly. A broken thumb caused him to miss a fair chunk of the second half of the preceding season. Wells thinks this eroded his stock a few spots. "Mark really liked him from the vision we'd showed him," he said of Kelly. "He played a bit taller than he is and was a good midfield type. If he had played all year and played really well then he would have probably gone a bit earlier."

During the season Wells had taken Thompson to a trial game for Vic Country at Windy Hill. Bartel was playing, as was Gary Ablett Jnr and a Wangaratta kid named Steve Johnson. "I said to Mark, 'Have a good look at Steve Johnson, at times he looks like he's a bit slow but we don't think he is,'" Wells said. "He just kicks goals when he shouldn't kick goals." Thompson had one look at him in a passage of play and said simply, "He's not slow."

The cache of talent could have even been scarier had everything gone completely to plan at the 2001 draft table. While Bartel and Kelly were the prioritised 'fingers crossed' propositions as they easily might have been selected earlier, the next two picks were pencilled in for a big strong hulk of a boy from Warrnambool named Matt Maguire, then Johnson. "I rang Matt Maguire's (house) that morning and they said no-one else had spoken to him," Wells recalls.

"St Kilda had played their cards very close to their chest and jumped in ahead of us and got Matt at pick 20."[5]

While they may have lost that one, history would show it had been an inspired morning's work for Wells and his team.

5. Ironically, through the end of season 2009, Maguire had not played since Round 7, 2008, and was stranded on 99 games when delisted by the Saints after 2009, having missed the Grand Final against Geelong. A badly broken leg and later complications derailed Maguire's career.

chapter 3
Wakeup calls

"We used to laugh, joke about it, 'Hey Moons, suspended again, you idiot'. It got to the point where no one pulled me up ... when they did it struck home a bit."

– Cameron Mooney

At 6am on December 23, 2006, Steve Johnson got out of bed at his family home in Wangaratta. It was a beautiful morning in the northeast Victorian town and he had a long bike ride planned. He once again found himself on a rehabilitation program after yet another post-season surgery, this time on his knee.

Johnson had been warned by the fitness staff and coaches before he left on the Christmas break: stay off the drink and be diligent with his program. He knew he needed to get the extra work in so he could catch up to the rest of the team, and figured an 80km ride would more than fulfil that criteria.

When he returned, Johnson felt on top of the world. The knee was coming along a treat, so when he headed around to a friend's house for a barbecue, he felt he'd earned a nice cold beer on this hot, sunny afternoon. The first one went down well. So did the next. A few more beers and a lot of laughs later, the group decided to head to the pub.

Johnson had already shown he was an old-school style of footballer; he loved to play it hard on and off the field but, when his friends wanted to head across the road to a different pub, he pulled the pin. The bike ride had taken its toll, and the sun and alcohol didn't help. So he hailed a taxi and headed to another mate's house but, when the taxi driver dropped him at the Munce St address, there didn't seem to be much happening. No-one answered when he knocked on the front door. Johnson went around the back to see if anyone was there. There wasn't, but the outdoor setting next to the pool looked inviting, so he sat down and waited for his mate to arrive home.

The next thing Johnson remembers is someone shoving him hard in the shoulder. He opened his eyes and found two policeman forcibly trying to get him out of the chair. "What are you doing here?" they kept asking. "I'm waiting for my mate to come home," Johnson said.

"He doesn't live here any more," they informed him. With that, the two policeman started dragging him down the driveway, and Johnson crashed face-first into the ground. He tried to cushion the fall but the police had his arm pinned behind his back. "You don't have to cuff me," he screamed. "Why don't you just let me walk home?"

With blood streaming from his face, Johnson was loaded into the back of the divisional van. He was taken to the police station and charged with being drunk in a public place. For four hours he stayed in the cells and was still in shock when he was released at 6am.

As he went to leave the station, the sergeant on duty warned him that they could have also charged him with trespassing and resisting arrest. Johnson argued it had been an innocent mistake and he'd just been trying to protect himself. They then both agreed to keep the incident quiet.

When he finally got home, his parents were horrified by the full story and took photos of the injuries to his face and wrists. They were determined to take the matter further but Johnson simply wanted the whole thing to go away. He knew that if the football club found out he was, in football terms, dead.

Geelong media manager Kevin Diggerson was just getting into the swing of things again after the New Year break when his telephone rang. It was a Channel 7 reporter claiming Steve Johnson had been arrested in Wangaratta on Christmas Eve. He'd heard nothing about it and, given it was nine days ago, he figured the club would have heard something if the claim was accurate.

He thought it was probably another hoax. Like the Christmas Day one he had to deal with involving Gary Ablett jnr: someone had rung newsrooms claiming that Ablett had shattered his arm at 4am on Christmas morning and had been rushed to hospital for surgery. Diggerson rang Ablett and found him happily enjoying Christmas lunch, limbs intact.

The difference in this case was that the scenario was quite believable. Johnson had a reputation for attracting trouble and had several "priors". In August 2005, he and Andrew Mackie had broken a curfew after the latter's 21st birthday and been arrested for being drunk in a public place. In December 2003, Johnson broke his ankle jumping over a fence at the Torquay hotel after a big night out. He had numerous complications with the injury and it remains a troublesome remnant of a forgettable action.

Diggerson walked into Neil Balme's office and told him about the phone call. He was already thinking strategy – if it turned out to be right, it was only 11am and they had plenty of time before the evening news bulletin. Balme rang Johnson, who fessed up straight away and tried to explain why he hadn't told anyone about it.

The frustration for Balme was that the club had enjoyed such a positive start to the pre-season; the leadership program was working well and the vibe was good. This scandal was going to hurt, he thought, as he hit the phones to inform the club's hierarchy of the news.

The majority view was that this was the final straw for Johnson. Three months earlier he'd been close to leaving the club, offered as tradebait to both Collingwood and Essendon. Each came very close to doing a deal before being scared away by the medical reports on his ankles.

"Initially I thought, 'That's it'," Thompson said. "But once I heard the story it wasn't as bad as I thought. He only fell asleep in someone's backyard. However, it was more about his reputation, the club's image and everything else, so it was hard to take from that perspective. We just wanted to change and that took us straight back to where we'd been."

Ken Hinkley was shattered. He had taken Johnson under his wing and had formed a very close relationship. "I had defended him a lot and I felt I had really been let down," he said. "I wondered why I had tried so hard and I thought he would probably now end up out of the club."

Brian Cook was enjoying the second day of his holiday in Bali when Balme called. It was the last thing he wanted to hear but it was a situation he knew had to be thought through properly. "We need time to think about this," he said. A statement was released at 5pm confirming the incident, Balme saying the club was "bitterly disappointed" in the delay over being informed. "We expect to be in a position to announce any sanction on Tuesday, January 9. Until such time the club will not speculate as to any potential penalty."

The Johnson stuff-up spread like wildfire through the playing group. "That's it, he is gone now," was Cameron Mooney's reaction. Even the guys he was close to, like Cameron Ling, were starting to lose patience. "Stevie is a mate and I was pissed off given the number of times I have gone into bat for him," he said.

King rang captain Harley, who was on holiday with his girlfriend, Felicity, and her family in Lake Conjola, on the south coast of New South Wales. "Did you hear about Johnno?" King said.

"No, what's happened," the skipper responded. His heart sank as the story unfolded. As soon as he hung up, Balme rang. "We're just finding out all the details at the moment," he said. Harley was fuming. While they were at different ends of their careers and were very different people, he and Johnson had been close since sharing a room together on a footy trip in 2002. But Johnson had continued to push buttons and while the veteran defender had previously shrugged it off, this time it had gone too far. "I thought, 'I couldn't give a shit about him now, he has run his race'," Harley said.

Balme and Gerard Murphy organised a leadership meeting but Harley was unable to get back, so he was placed on conference call. "I said to my girlfriend's parents, 'Do you mind if I just use the phone for 20 minutes?' Three hours later I got off the line," he said.

Johnson was in the meeting and spoke of his remorse. He copped it from every angle as the leaders made their point, none more strongly than Harley, who found that (given he wasn't face-to-face) it was easier to unload with both barrels. He ended his spray with: "Johnno, I'm really disappointed and I feel I can't trust you any more."

The barrage from his teammates made everything suddenly hit home. Johnson was in tears as he left the meeting with the realisation that his AFL career could be minutes away from being ended. There was certainly division in the leadership group about what to do. Balme was asked if the club could delist him and he confirmed it was within its rights to do so. This was debated strongly, with Balme and Murphy walking through all the other options. "We just said there are two ways you can go with this bloke," Balme said. "You can burn him and no-one gets anything, you get nothing or you can help him but make it that he really has to do something to get your help."

Ling wanted to help. "We looked at it and said, 'If Stevie goes now he ends up in a pub in Wangaratta pissed off his head for the next 30 years telling everyone how good he could have been'," he said. "We didn't want that to happen. So we talked about what is the most important thing in his life – it's footy, he loves footy, he just wants to play and it is everything to him. So let's take away what is the most important thing in his life and make him realise just how important it is to him. To do that we had to banish him from his teammates and from the footy club, make him appreciate what he had and make it his call whether he wants to keep it."

The details of his punishment were thrashed out. Johnson would be suspended indefinitely with the ban not reviewed until round six. He would be kept away from the main playing group, training and playing only with the club's VFL team. He would have to do the majority of his fitness and recovery sessions away from Skilled Stadium. Effectively, Johnson had been suspended until May, meaning he had four months to prove to his teammates that he wanted to keep playing. He was shocked when informed of the decision given he thought this misdemeanour was on the minor scale. He was also informed that if there was even a slight slip-up then it was all over.

The next week Harley addressed the entire playing group and told them of the penalty. Johnson was then asked to speak to the team. He apologised and accepted the suspension, saying he would train and play hard in the VFL. "But if you want me to show you I am serious and I want to get back, I'll do anything," Johnson said. He then paused slightly and looked around the room. "I will not touch another drink of alcohol until the whole season is over, not one drink." The 23-year-old didn't believe he had a drinking problem yet he had realised that every time he had got into trouble alcohol was involved.

President Frank Costa had been invited down to sit in on the session and was impressed with what he had witnessed. "I was sitting there thinking this was powerful," he said. "This responsibility had been taken on by these young blokes and they are prepared to be this disciplined with a teammate who has done the wrong thing. Then the teammate has copped it on the chin, accepted it and said on top of that he wouldn't touch a drink at all. I just thought, 'Wow, this is good'."

Opinion was divided as to which way it would go. Harley wasn't convinced Johnson had it in him to turn things around. "To be honest a lot of us thought, 'He's going to blow it'," he said. Hinkley, while still very upset, backed his man. "He is such a strong bastard with such a strong belief in his own ability," he said. "If anything it would make him go harder and stronger and almost want to show people that he could do this. He would be thinking, 'You think I can't, you think I am a weak individual that's going to melt away into another glass of beer'."

Charges resulting from Johnson's arrest were dropped after Johnson engaged a lawyer to explore his legal options. He then began to train fanatically. He started boxing training five times a week, changed his diet, lost 5kg and set about improving himself as a person. He sought counselling and even started a job in real estate. "I wasn't really developing as a person," Johnson said. "I was still living like I was an 18-year-old from Wangaratta."

After a month he figured it was time he made contact with Harley. "He had been the hardest on me, he was the one who drove it more than anyone," he said. "I was pissed off with him but in the end I thought it's not going to work unless I have got a relationship with him. He's going to be captain of the footy club and I can't be hating him.

"I also wanted him to know that I was getting on with things, I wanted to know if there was anything else they wanted me to do. I didn't want them to hand down the suspension and still have a grudge against me."

Harley had also been thinking it was time to build a bridge. A meeting at the Club Cats bistro was organised. When Johnson sat down it was already obvious to the skipper that all the stories he'd been hearing about his training were on the money. "Already physically he had changed, his face, he was just ripped," Harley said. They had a very honest discussion, and Johnson again apologised for letting his friend down. After an hour they stood and shook hands. Harley left knowing something very special was happening.

"It's pretty hard sitting in front of 40 guys and basically get told what a wanker you are, it is really tough." Matthew Scarlett's typically honest description of his peer assessment summed it up perfectly. The program introduced by leadership consultant Gerard Murphy was designed to generate a change in the culture of the club, in particular the workings of the team, and the full-back was a key player.

Scarlett had always struggled with the notion of being a role model. Despite being arguably the club's best player and one of the oldest at 27, he preferred to stay out of the spotlight. He rarely gave interviews and lived by the mantra that actions speak louder than words. Scarlett was the type of person who only saw black or white, nothing between. This had caused problems within the team, particularly with younger players coming in – they didn't know how to handle Scarlett's gruff and dismissive nature. While he wasn't anywhere near Steve Johnson in the bad boy ratings, he'd had his share of run-ins with management over his after-hours activities.

Scarlett had always been a bit different, from the moment he walked into Skilled Stadium as a father-son selection in the 1997 national draft. His dad, John, or "Gunner" as he was known, was an uncompromising defender himself playing 183 games for the Cats between 1967-77. Matthew, who actually barracked for Essendon as a kid, was by no means a star junior, more a solid performer for the Geelong Falcons. He certainly had the breeding to make it as an elite defender, and not just on his dad's side – his second cousin on his mother's side was Carlton great Bruce Doull.

That explains a lot. Doull, whose trademark was a greying beard and the navy blue and white headband which kept his thinning long hair in place, was an intensely private person. Scarlett also very much kept to himself when he first started to the point where, legend has it, the coaching staff and most of the playing list were unaware that he and his partner, Jodie Nankervis (daughter of Cats legend Bruce), welcomed a daughter, Tayla, into the world. The story goes that Scarlett, then 18, had to ask to leave training to attend the birth.

Despite the couple since parting, he has played an active role in his daughter's upbringing, and Scarlett now has another daughter, Charlie, with his partner, Milla, whom he married late last year

He played his first game as a raw 19-year-old in 1998. Coach Gary Ayres brought him off the bench to play on a rampant Matthew Lloyd. The Essendon star ended the day with six goals and Scarlett was dropped the next week. He didn't get another look-in until the following year when Ayres did it again, plucking him out of the reserves to play on Lloyd.

The arrival of Thompson came at the perfect time for him, though a bit of luck helped kickstart his career. The new Cats coach had told him that he was behind a couple, including Hamish Simpson, in the pecking order. Scarlett bluntly told the coach he didn't agree but, fortuitously (for Scarlett), an injury to Simpson on the eve of the 2000 season saw him given an opportunity.[6] He and the Cats have never looked back. He was second in the best and fairest in 2001 and then took out the Carji Greeves medal in 2003. He also earned All-Australian selection in 2003-04 and represented Australia in the international rules series.[7]

By this stage Scarlett and his big mop of black curly hair had developed a cult following with the cheer squad selling "Matty" wigs for $25 a pop at Geelong's home games (naturally, this didn't sit well with him; he promptly

6. Traded from Port Adelaide for pick 37, Simpson was delisted by the Cats after season 2002. He played 19 games and averaged 8.8 disposals.

7. Scarlett earned his fifth All-Australian selection in 2009. At Geelong, only Gary Ablett Snr (8) has earned the honour more times.

took to his own hair with a pair of kitchen scissors). He is a favourite of Thompson's and the respect goes both ways with Scarlett actually tracking down the mobile phone number of *Herald Sun* chief football writer Mike Sheahan late one night to throw his support behind the embattled coach when speculation about the latter's future was at its hottest in the 2006 post-season. "I like his honesty, he plays to win, and he is the best defender I have seen," notes Thompson, who is not known for hyping his players.

Harley knew his good friend was open to the change which the peer assessments were helping to generate. "He (Scarlett) has had a glittering individual career but he just wants to win," he said. "What's the point of being best and fairest and All-Australian if you play in a side that is useless? His evolution started before all this leadership stuff came in, he came to a point where he said, 'I am sick of losing, I want to play in winning sides'. I just think he has grown up, he is the ultimate family man now, he's got two kids and is married."

Given his influence in the changerooms there was a feeling that if Scarlett embraced the peer assessments it would go a long way in selling it to the group. As part of the procedure, a player has to write down what he thinks his teammates will say of him. Scarlett got almost every point right; more importantly for Murphy, he took it on the chin.

"Mine was a lot of off-field stuff," Scarlett said. "They wanted me to be more disciplined. When I am at training I am very professional and hard on guys to do the right thing. I am hard on everyone to train the way we play and I guess they just wanted me to be disciplined off the field. There was also a bit of a respect issue there with me and a few of the other players but it's all fixed up now.

"You have to just take it on board, look them in the eye and promise that you are going to change the way they want you to because it will help the team."

Mooney was the second player up after the new captain – the players decided who was assessed first – to take part in an exercise which involved the playing list being split into six groups. Each group then worked out a number of points between them that they wanted to raise with the player.

Nothing personal allowed. If they thought the guy was an idiot that was irrelevant; if he was a distraction, that was a different matter, for everything was linked to the team's goal of winning games and the premiership. It was constructive feedback aimed at helping that player contribute to that goal. There were rules to the procedure. The player being assessed sitting out the front but on the same level as the rest of the team; eye contact was mandatory and the use of humour was banned.

Opening the lines of communication was vital, according to Ling. "We just didn't talk," he said. "Communication within the whole club had to change. It really just wasn't good enough and we're not just talking about Bomber and the players. Whether it was marketing and the players, the board and the coaches, coaches and coaches, players and players, the whole communication was crap."

Mooney was told he didn't spend enough time with the young players – the same point which had been made to Scarlett. Yet the biggest statement from his teammates centred around on-field discipline issues which had resulted in him collecting an AFL record four suspensions the previous season. "I knew it was coming but to actually hear it is the hard thing," he said.

"Like I said to the boys afterwards, 'Where was this six months ago, you weak pricks?'

"The whole thing is we used to laugh, joke about it, like, 'Hey Moons, suspended again, you idiot'. It got to the point where no-one pulled me up on it because we were laughing about it. When they finally did it struck home a bit."

The clearing of the air was powerful on many levels and for many people. Gary Ablett was told he didn't work hard enough. It completely caught him off guard given he had become one of the side's prime movers.

"You can continue the way you are going with this talent – and you are a very, very good footballer and you could have a 15-year career at Geelong being a very good player – but you will never achieve greatness," the players told Ablett.

"Or you can push yourself to the absolute limit, which might shorten your career, but you will be great, you will become a champion. We want you to become our Chris Judd. He is the same age as you and we believe you have probably got more talent."[8]

Ablett was clearly stunned by the assessment and needed 24 hours to get his head around it. He initially thought he was getting picked on. "I used to think I trained quite hard but I didn't realise I wasn't in their eyes," he said. "It is tough when you hear things about yourself that you thought you were doing well but the group didn't think that was the case."

Jimmy Bartel described his assessment as "the most nerve-racking thing you ever want to go through". They wanted him to be more vocal, share his game knowledge and step up to being more of a leader.

"Brutal" was the word James Kelly used to sum up his time on the chair. "I actually wanted, for my own development, to get done and be one of the early ones," he said. "But then when you sit down on a chair in front of all your mates, at eye level with eye contact, you instantly start sweating and your face goes red. You think you know yourself and you know your teammates pretty well but then you start to think about whether there is stuff they'll say that you're not expecting."

Kelly was told to respect the game more and take it more seriously. "In 2006 I sort of floated along a little bit to my detriment," he said. "For a long time I used to hear Bomber (Thompson) say: 'You have to always respect the game'. I never really understood what it meant. I thought I respected the game because I know it is a hard game but I never really understood how hard it was until 2006. That was a real wake-up call."

Andrew Mackie was told he wasn't putting in enough work but the one assessment which was a reflection of most of the list was that of speedster David Wojcinski. When he plays well, Wojcinski, who had been at Geelong for eight years, is up and bouncing around the club. When he doesn't get a kick he is a totally different character. The highs and lows were too extreme and affected his life.

Wojcinski not only agreed with the feedback but he expanded about his feelings and made a lasting impression on many of his teammates. After he had finished, a number of players put up their hands and said: "It's great

---

8. Ablett's numbers 2007-09: 29.8 possessions and 4.0 tackles per game, 27 goals per season. Judd: 25.6, 3.8 and 15.

to hear Bomber (Wojcinski) talk like that because that's exactly how I feel."

Some of the staff were put through their paces by Murphy, even the coaches. Later, Thompson was peer assessed by the players. This was seen as critical to the concept because if the senior coach didn't believe in it then it could easily fall apart. Thompson told the group about how when he was playing it was worlds apart; the guys who he played with were so much different than those he now coached. It was a completely generation removed and his former teammates were entirely "results based". They were driven to win and that's why they became great Essendon teams.

He said where he had struggled as a coach was that players who get drafted now – the Generation Ys – are so much more "relationship based". They all want to have relationships with the coaches and it had been difficult for him to get used to because his own experiences were from this exceptional bunch of Essendon players who had a completely different mindset.

By this time the changes in the coach were already obvious to the players. There was more one-on-one time and he wasn't locked in his office staring at a computer screen … basically the players' picture of him in 2006. When he wasn't the star of the session, Thompson would often just sit in, watch and listen. He liked what he saw.

"Things we had been wanting to do, and the good teams do, is actually try and challenge each other and talk honestly with each other and that's what we did," he said. "It's pretty hard to cop, it's intimidating sitting in front of all your teammates and hearing it but I watched it and thought this is good. This is exactly what good teams do."

chapter 4

Attack, or die

"Bomber was copping it, there was talk he was going to go at the end of 2006 ... but he backed us in to play this style. That's hit and miss, and if it's miss he is probably minus a job."

– Andrew Mackie

Mark Thompson fell into coaching half-way through the 1996 season, talked into taking on a temporary role by Essendon coach Kevin Sheedy. Twelve months earlier, the three-time premiership player was ready to call it quits at 31 and after 194 games.

But Sheedy, who started his coaching career at Windy Hill the same day Thompson started in the under 19s, stressed to him the importance of reaching the 200-game milestone. Thompson conceded, but gave up the captaincy and managed eight more games to get to 202 before a broken arm ended his playing career.

Coaching certainly wasn't on his agenda. Getting back to his electrical business and spending time with his three young children was what he had planned. "I didn't think I would ever go down that path," he reflected. However, circumstances – and the persistence of his long-time mentor – again intervened. Mark Williams, an assistant to Sheedy, had returned to Adelaide mid-season in 1996 to pursue his (ultimately successful) goal of coaching Port Adelaide. Sheedy wanted Thompson to take Williams' place as reserves coach.

Thompson agreed, but only for the rest of the year. He steered the reserves into the grand final. Sheedy set to work on him again, and two years later Thompson was still there. But in 1999 he found himself in the middle of a boardroom battle to oust Sheedy. Some board members wanted Thompson to be senior coach – in his discomfort, Thompson told Sheedy, then after 18 years at Windy Hill he walked, taking an assistant's role at North Melbourne under Denis Pagan. Twelve months later he was a senior AFL coach, having rejected approaches from Richmond and Hawthorn to take on Geelong.

Not bad for a self-confessed "lazy kid", a Carlton supporter who often had to be dragged down to training at Airport West by his mates. Back then he already had his nickname … it was actually "Bomba", a Tarzan-imitating jungle boy on television. It had come about because of his penchant for climbing, be it onto the roof or up a tree, and usually to fetch a ball he or his older brother, Steven, had deposited up there. The nickname somewhat understandably morphed into "Bomber" when he started playing at Essendon.

Both his parents worked full-time with his father, Bruce, a butcher in Puckle St, Moonee Ponds. His mother, Trisha, also worked for Tip Top Bakeries. He soon realised he wasn't destined to be an academic so he left Niddrie High School at the end of Year 11 to begin an electrician's apprenticeship. After stints doing electrical fitting at Ansett and plumbing at the Gas and Fuel Corporation he took up an offer to earn his ticket with an Essendon electrician. Hence, he could be close to Windy Hill, where he had been invited down to train with the under-19s.

Yet his boss wasn't really understanding about the demands of playing football. After four years, Thompson was faced with an ultimatum to choose his job or football. So at the age of 21, he started his own business, Bomber

Thompson Electrics, which still operates today under the guidance of his brother. Throughout his time coaching Geelong, Thompson has maintained that he could easily go and do something else, maybe even go back on the tools. This had often been misinterpreted as a lack of passion for the job, a line some critics have used often. Another has been the fact that he never moved his family to Geelong, instead preferring the daily commute from Melbourne.[9]

The local paper, the *Geelong Advertiser*, has had a love-hate relationship with the club in recent times. One of its columnists wrote an article questioning what Thompson had done for the city of Geelong. The basis of the column was that he doesn't help the local economy because wasn't spending any of his money there; wasn't buying his groceries or paying for his kids to go to school in the area.

While a coach needs resilience in any environment, nowhere moreso than Geelong. Yet these sort of attacks didn't even register on the 2007 Thompson register. He was a man on a mission and he needed the pieces of the jigsaw in his head to come together to complete a premiership picture. "When I started to coach I had this picture of how I wanted [the team] to play and I have never deviated from it. I just have never been able to achieve it," he said.

The first step was fit players. He hadn't needed to receive the results of the expert analysis of the team's fitness data to know that his side hadn't been fit enough in 2006. The NAB Cup victory had camouflaged a problem when then came to a head in the opening month of the season when long-time fitness and conditioning coach Loris Bertolacci left the club.

The Cats tried to play catch-up, putting the players through a mini pre-season during the middle of the year, but the damage had been done. As centre half-back Matthew Egan said: "It was only my second year and I hadn't had a real feel of what we should be doing," he said. "But there were times when you think surely this isn't what it is supposed to be like, pre-season wise. I still remember looking back on it saying, 'I never really did a gruelling, hard session'.

9. Thompson eventually moved to Geelong. He owns land between Geelong and Torquay and intends developing the project when he finishes coaching.

"During the year I noticed playing on certain players I couldn't keep up with and I'm sure a few people felt like that in the end."

Steve Hocking, who was the back pocket in the 1989 and 1994 Grand Final sides, was given the task of finding part of the solution to the coach's problem. Cameron Falloon, who had taken over after Bertolacci left, had taken up an offer from the Western Bulldogs so a new fitness team had to be built from scratch. There were more than 30 candidates but a blind recommendation from a contact at Port Adelaide had Hocking on a plane. All he had been told from the source was that the "young bloke at the Crows was very good".

That "young bloke" was 26-year-old sports science graduate, Paul Haines. Hocking arranged to meet him in Glenelg for lunch but, when he stepped off the plane, there was Haines waiting to pick him up. That summed up his enthusiasm for the task, plus his personality: over-the-top but infectious.

Hocking also liked another strong candidate. Dean Robinson, a 33-year-old former champion steer wrestler who was then working with National Rugby League team Manly, had sent in his CV. While it went against convention and was definitely a risk, the idea of joint heads of the fitness department was starting to form in the mind of the Cats' assistant football operations manager.

Robinson's lack of AFL background appealed to Hocking. He had new ideas and a different way of doing things so, in October, the board received the recommendation to appoint Robinson as strength and rehabilitation manager, and Haines fitness and conditioning manager. Everything they did went through Hocking, the same reporting line as the medical team. Everyone was on the same page – the fitness staff, the doctors, the physios, the massage staff. Most importantly, these were no longer Thompson's problems.

Between Balme and Hocking, who Thompson had brought back to the club in 2004 in a part-time basis on the match committee, the coach estimated they took away 40 per cent of the "rubbish" (read: non-core coaching duties) he had been dealing with the previous season. "I knew what I needed to do and the review just confirmed that," Thompson said. "Balmey took a lot of the stuff away, a lot of the work away as did "Hock" with all the new fitness appointments and straight away there was a freshness. The coaches sat down and talked a lot about trends in the game. What's happening? What do you think the style of play is going to do this year? Is it going to work? We had lot of meetings and by the time the players got back we were ready with how we wanted to play and train."

The coaching panel had been given a significant shake-up. Hinkley and McCartney had both become "too protective" of their areas. Their attachment to specific players clouded their decision-making. Thompson wanted them to be more inclusive of the entire team, so their roles were changed. While former player Leigh Tudor continued as VFL coach, Sanderson coming in, along with experienced campaigner David Wheadon, who joined the club in a part-time capacity as skills / development coach.

Hinkley was put in charge of attack; not just in the forward line, but in all facets of the game. He would also take over opposition analysis during the season. Sanderson came in as the defence coach, not just the back six, which had become the norm, but focussing on defensive pressure in all positions. Stoppages were McCartney's new domain, not just dealing with midfielders but all around the ground.

"I thought it was remarkable how brave [Thompson] was," McCartney said. "With all that had happened, it was him who had copped all the scrutiny, not us. But we were part of it and we all had to take responsibility for what had happened that year. It was so brave that he actually gave us more responsibility, he re-jigged the coaching staff and said, 'Go and do it'. Not everyone would have done that.

"I have seen coaches at this level, under pressure, go into themselves. We went the other way and Bomber was strong with what he wanted and put it in place. What he did well was identify what was needed in the organisation and that was to have us all mix through different areas. It gave the three assistants the chance to flourish in their jobs, a chance to really develop as people and coaches."

McCartney had certainly come a long way since his days at Ocean Grove, 30 minutes down the road past Geelong, where he became a local coaching legend by winning four consecutive premierships from 1994-97. During this time he met Jeff Gieschen, who was an assistant to Gary Ayres at Geelong. When Gieschen earned the senior job at Richmond in 1998 he hired McCartney as assistant / development coach.

St Kilda coach Ross Lyon was also on the coaching panel at the time. "[Geischen] wanted a younger coach to look after their younger players," McCartney said of his role at Punt Road. "He had a choice of some big names who had left the game but he didn't want that, he just wanted a down-to-earth person who could communicate. It was obviously a big step going from training two to three times a week to six times a week, two or three sessions a day. There was obviously more strategy than in local footy and more resources but the game is still the same. If you don't go hard at the ball, if you don't put pressure on the opposition, if you don't kick it well then you are going to lose. It is the same everywhere." Gieschen's stint at Richmond lasted only two years and McCartney left concurrently, joining Geelong and Thompson, who he had impressed while coaching against him in the reserves back in 1999.

Hinkley came from the other end of the spectrum. He had been a star half-back flanker during the Cats' glory years under coach Malcolm Blight. The skinny kid from Camperdown won the best and fairest in 1992, was a two-time All-Australian and co-captain with Gary Ablett and Garry Hocking in 1995. He finished third in the Brownlow Medal in 1992 and was later made a member of Geelong's Hall of Fame. After retiring in 1996 after 121 games (he played 11 games for Fitzroy 1987-88), Hinkley returned to Camperdown where he coached back-to-back premierships (1999-2000) before in 2001 joining Blight for his infamous single season at St Kilda. A detour through Geelong side Bell Park to coach the 2003 premiership led Hinkley back to the Cats.

He drew on that experience at St Kilda as the Cats approached a critical 2007 season. "Footy is so volatile," he said. "I was at St Kilda when Blighty lost his job and to worry about what is going to happen doesn't do anyone any good. You are better off just going about and doing what you know you should do. The feeling was this is going to be our last year … this is going to be the roll of the dice and we might as well roll the whole lot. If we are going to go down, we are going to go down our way."

During the coaches' pre-season "think tank", Hinkley and Sanderson did their projections of what was required. Their analysis of the numbers found that Geelong needed a considerably higher percentage to be a top four side. The highest the Cats had been rated in scoring in the competition over the previous decade had been sixth. Only one team in the past 11 years had won the flag with an attack outside the top four (Sydney in 2005). "To win a flag we need a much higher percentage," Hinkley said. "Which means we have to attack, we actually have to score. So we had to find a way to create a belief that we had to score more without also becoming a leaky boat."

All summer the training was focussed on risk-taking and carrying the ball. Players jumped at the opportunity to be part of creating a new Geelong way of playing. "What frustrated the players in 2005-06 was that we changed our game plan week in, week out," skipper Tom Harley said. "As a playing group we just said give us something and we will do it. We will train it up and we are going to play our way and try to do it the best we can. If that doesn't deliver us a flag, who cares, as long we give it a go because what we had been doing wasn't going to get us there."

There was a new level of professionalism about training. A lot of the changes were results of McCartney's October visit to American National Football League club the Baltimore Ravens. Closed training sessions, filming of the sessions, streamlining the information flow to players and moving their day off to Tuesday were some of his key introductions.

"There was a professional atmosphere there which rubs off after a while," McCartney said. "Moving the day off to early in the week on a Tuesday meant that the weekend's game ended on Monday and you started on the new game on Wednesday. It meant that there was no lingering, whether it had been a great win or a bad loss because that was dealt with on the Monday, Tuesday was a day off and then Wednesday we had moved on. It also gave time for the coaches to get their teeth into the next opposition so when the players walked in on Wednesday all the information was there."

The players' week was a lot more structured. Each player knew exactly where they were supposed to be and at what time. "Everything just worked," Kelly said. "You knew your massage was at this time and you had to be at the pool then, it made a huge difference and made actually concentrating on training and working hard a lot easier."

More importantly, according to McCartney, there was nowhere for players to hide. "There were no loop holes anywhere," he said. "There was no way out. So if there was a swim they swam, if there was a stretch they stretched, if there was a recovery, or protein supplements to take, they took them.

"There were no questions. You just did what was required and if you didn't do it you were accountable to the whole group which was very strong."

The first major beneficiary of the new environment and attacking game style was Andrew Mackie. After struggling to find his niche, a home was found at half-back following a conversation Hinkley had with recruiting manager Stephen Wells, who had shocked many by taking the skinny kid from Adelaide at No.7 in the 2002 national draft.

"I was talking to Wellsy and he said we don't have a defender who can attack well enough, maybe it's an attacking player who just has to defend adequately," Hinkley said. "I had played half-back in a similar sort of way and straight away I thought of Mackie because for a while I thought he was a wingman. We always knew he could run, he has got a massive engine and beautiful skills but he was just too light and at the start of his career he'd been forced into the forward line where he was getting monstered."

Mackie began his campaign to move further away from the goals midway through 2006. "Before I got drafted I was half-back, wing or ruck-rover, but then I'd come to Geelong and been pigeon-holed at half-forward," he said. "When the team is not winning it is a hard position to play because the ball is not down there, someone's job is to play on you and it is hard to get in the game. Then pretty much you are out of the side if you lose. So I was nagging Kenny, saying 'Get me up on the wing'. Half-way through 2006 was the turning point for me because I played some alright games towards the second half of the year on the wing."

He was grateful for Thompson's new philosophy. "Bomber was copping it, there was talk he was going to go at the end of 2006, get the boot, but then he backed us in to play this style. It would have taken a lot of courage," Mackie said. "That's hit and miss, and if it's miss he is probably minus a job." It certainly hit in the club's first official match of the 2007 season on Sunday, February 25 when Geelong hosted Richmond in the opening round of the NAB Cup. A larger than expected crowd showed up, forcing officials to open the gates during the first quarter with 15,000 people – 7000 more than predicted – packing the terraces of Skilled Stadium.

By the time most got to their seats, the game was already over with the Cats' quicker, play-on at all costs style dominating the Tigers. The quarter-time lead was 35 points; it blew out to 77 before ending up as a 43-point victory on the strength of 20 goals being kicked. "It's been a long time since we kicked 20 and we did it through run and through hardness and tackling the ball off the opposition; we were pretty pleased with the effort," Thompson noted.

Brad Ottens, coming off his first full pre-season in years, had been the star kicking four goals in the first half. Wojcinski's rebound from half-back was a highlight while Selwood's first appearance in the blue and white hoops was more than promising. The only concern was Darren Milburn going to hospital after being accidentally kicked in the head. Next was a trip to Darwin to play Port Adelaide. "Worst flight I have ever had," Thompson recounted. "It took us 14 hours to get to Darwin and we were sitting on the tarmac for three hours because of a tropical cyclone." Conditions didn't improve for the game, which went to overtime. Power star Chad Cornes then missed a goal from the goalsquare in the dying seconds to hand Geelong the victory. It came at a cost though: goalsneak Stokes would that week receive a four-week suspension under the AFL's new crackdown on head-high contact.

The NAB Cup semi-final was played at Telstra Dome against Brisbane. Geelong lost – a lacklustre first half was followed by a much improved third quarter – but Thompson was happier than normal about a loss because he'd seen something which he knew would stand his team in good stead. As expected, Brisbane had flooded across half-back in an attempt to de-rail the Cats' fast and direct game style. Instead of making counter-moves in the coach's box, Thompson deliberately sat on his hands and left it up to the players to figure out a way around the Lions defensive tactics.

"I had got some good advice that if you are going to play a certain style of footy then just play it," Thompson said. "If the opposition are going to try and stop it, well, just do it better. Still play the way you want to play but just get better at trying to beat those tactics. It might cost you a game or two along the way, but in the long run it will make you a better football team."

chapter 5

The Captain's curse

"He is called Gary Ablett, who was regarded by lots as the greatest player ever. For God's sake, he is actually called that. It has been amazing what he has done."

– Ken Hinkley on Gary J nr

The curse at Geelong has been a favourite subject of the media for years. Every time a new one gets appointed the curse and its victims are dragged up. Tom Harley knew all about it.

He knew Steven King's reign had been a write-off because of injuries; he knew Ben Graham's three-year stint had been unsuccessful, accelerating his venture into gridiron; he knew Leigh Colbert had quit the club while skipper, never actually captaining a game because he'd blown his knee out not long after his appointment.

Then there was champion midfielder Garry Hocking, who had two attempts. The first lasted a few months because, frankly, he couldn't handle the attention that came with it. Barry Stoneham's stint was ravaged by injury, while the great Gary Ablett Snr had failed miserably and, in 1995, he was actually one of three who had a crack at the job.

When Harley's knee blew up after the second NAB Cup game, he naturally started to feel nervous. He sat out the following week's semi-final but he was determined to lead the Cats out in round one of the home and away season against the Western Bulldogs. "The pre-season feedback on my gig was, he's making all the right sounds, he has looked after the Johnson situation, he is a solid citizen, he is fit now but he hasn't played a full season in three," Harley said. "The captain's curse kept getting brought up and I was desperate to be there in round one for what I thought would be the highlight of my career, leading the team out."[10]

Seven minutes into the game, the curse struck. Harley went to spoil Brad Johnson in a marking contest and badly damaged his finger. "I looked down and my finger was just limp," he said. A trainer tried to "put it back in", but it wouldn't go; Harley played the quarter out and, to make matters worse, Johnson was carving him up. At the quarter-time break he was taken to the rooms. "I made a vow to myself that I wasn't going to have any pain-killing injections yet there I was in the first quarter of the first game getting jabbed up in the finger," Harley said.

He went back out with his hand half-numb and continued playing but the day went from bad to worse. Johnson had five goals by half-time and the Bulldogs led by 22 points. The positives for the Cats were there: an ominous look to a forward line featuring Nathan Ablett and Cameron Mooney; dash off half-back from Corey Enright and David Wojcinski, and Cameron Ling's blanketing job on key Bulldog Scott West. But they were butchering the ball with turnovers, a sin against the pace of the Bulldogs, and by three quarter-time the margin was out to 37. Some late goals cut it back to 20 by the final siren but Johnson had eight goals and Harley's captaincy debut had been a shocker.

The next morning he fronted up to the specialist for scans on the finger.

---

10. Of the 22 that ran out in Round 1, 2007, no less than 16 remained to play in the 2009 premiership. Two of the absent six that day were Steve Johnson and James Kelly, who were injured. The others: Josh Hunt, who missed the entire 2009 with injury, Nathan Ablett retired, injury prematurely ended Matthew Egan's career and Brent Prismall and Charlie Gardiner have since been traded.

"You have blown it apart and you're out for six weeks," the surgeon said. Cursed, indeed. As he was going under the knife, the match committee was sharpening one of its own at the selection table. Josh Hunt and Kane Tenace paid the price for the round one loss, youth being introduced courtesy of Tom Hawkins and Travis Varcoe, who made their debuts against Carlton on Easter Saturday evening at Telstra Dome. The opening goal gave a clear indication of what was to follow. Full-back Matthew Scarlett ran off Carlton's star full-forward Brendan Fevola and delivered a great pass on the outside of his boot, hitting the chest of a leading Nathan Ablett. By half-time the margin was 32 points.

Varcoe, wearing the famous No. 5, provided the highlight of the second quarter. His first AFL game had taken a lot longer than expected given that three years earlier he had been regarded as one of the best juniors in the country. But a foot injury had ruined a year of his football, and the South Australian was ignored until the Cats swooped with their first-round selection (No. 15) in the 2005 National Draft. The lightning quick Aborigine was given the honour of wearing Gary Ablett Snr's number – out of commission since Ablett's retirement a decade earlier – after his two sons indicated they had no intention of making it their own. Aboriginal star Polly Farmer, rated alongside Ablett as the best players to wear the blue and white hoops, had also worn No. 5 during the 1960s.

Initially plagued by the foot problem at the start of 2006, Varcoe ended up playing 15 VFL games, including the Grand Final, and showed flashes of brilliance. But he hadn't been on coach Thompson's radar early in the pre-season; Thompson actually had to be talked into playing him against Brisbane in the NAB Cup semi-final. Two goals in the third quarter of that game electrified the crowd and thrust the 19-year-old's name into the mix, his unpredictability and pace both appealing assets. Fittingly, it was a piece of magic that earned Varcoe a goal with his first kick in the AFL. After fumbling an earlier opportunity, he grabbed the ball at a ball-up, dummied to kick as a Carlton player attempted to dive over his boot and then waltzed into an open goal.

The opening four minutes of the third quarter were a snapshot of the way the Cats had trained all summer to play. Nathan Ablett lead out from centre half-forward, grabbed the ball, handballed to Jimmy Bartel, who off-loaded to Mooney for a goal in the opening 30 seconds. A minute later the brothers Ablett combined, Gary executing a sublime pass – which he adjusted at the last second – to the chest of his younger brother on another lead up the centre corridor. Nathan off-loaded to Mooney, who ran past, took a bounce and drilled his fourth for the night. The flying Wojcinski strutted his stuff next, intercepting an errant Carlton handball on the wing and exploding away, taking three bounces to goal from 35 metres. From the next centre bounce the Cats again went forward, Nathan Ablett roving the pack to kick a brilliant left-foot snap from 30 metres. Four goals in four minutes and the game was over. A 14-goal second half blew the final margin out to 78 points; Mooney and Nathan Ablett kicked five goals each, while Hawkins (three goals) and Varcoe (two) showed plenty in a forward structure that looked its most potent for years.

The Ablett boys provided the game's memorable moment. Half-way through the final quarter Nathan tapped a bouncing ball to himself and fired off a handpass to Gary, who returned the favour. With a burst of speed which highlighted his improved agility, the youngest of the clan ran towards goal and casually snapped over his shoulder. The late, greatly respected Clinton Grybas, in the Foxtel commentary box, nailed the call perfectly when he said: "It's like it's in the backyard, and Nathan says, 'I'll kick it!'"

The sight of the 196cm youngest Ablett roaming centre half-forward, receiving it lace-out from his older brother – who was close to best-on-ground that night – was one of modern football's great stories, one of great patience and persistence. During their father's wonderful career, the pair were always loitering in the changerooms and all of Gary Snr's teammates have their own Gary Jnr and Nathan story. They were wild boys who followed their dad around everywhere, even on the team bus, and back then were already showing signs of being more than handy at the game. Both lived with their mother, Sue, and two sisters in Jan Juc – she had separated from Gary when the boys were quite young – and played junior football at Modewarre. Gary Jnr took the traditional pathway, coming through the ranks with the Geelong Falcons and representing Vic Country in the national under 18s championships, where he immediately showed he was an AFL footballer in the making. "He was an outstanding team player," Stephen Wells recalled. "He would have twice as many handballs as he would kicks because he wanted to bring other people into the game."

Ken Hinkley played with Gary snr and has been a confidante for the oldest son. He is the one Gary Jnr trusts and talks to about the pressures involved in following in his father's footsteps. "People who say they have had pressure on them to play the game, this kid has got the same name," Hinkley said. "He is called Gary Ablett, who was regarded by lots as the greatest player ever. For God's sake, he is actually called that. It has been amazing what he has done because he got pressure from the very first game he stepped into the club, they put a good player to sit on him."

As for Nathan, he was, to use Wells's words, "a little less conventional". Nathan's stint at the Falcons lasted until Christmas before he headed back to Modewarre under 18s. Several times the Cats recruiter ventured out to watch him and each time he came back convinced he had everything required to make the grade.

"It was obvious he had all the ability in the world," Wells said. "Nathan was a big kid who was running around in the ruck, he was virtually pacing himself through the game in that he would influence the game almost whenever he wanted to. But he was happy to share the glory ... happy not to play a dominant role.

"He was covering the ground as a ruckman, winning ruck contests, tapping the ball both hands, finding it at ground level and doing all the team things like shepherding, blocking and creating space. If there was a marking contest he would mark it. He was a beautiful kick and kicked left foot nearly as much as his right. The kid had serious talent."

However, Nathan already was showing signs of not wanting to join his brother. While Gary Jnr learnt to cope with the attention that came with his name, Nathan had walked off in the middle of a game when he noticed a newspaper photographer had turned up to take photos of him. Every attempt by the football club to make contact was rejected. Thompson and Wells had got to know him a bit as they played indoor soccer against him a couple of times – one night he had actually filled for their team – but still they couldn't nail him down.

Frank Costa, who had helped out Gary Snr – "he was a hero of mine" – along his troubled journey and also knew Sue, had travelled down to see Nathan several times without any luck. Finally, a meeting was arranged at Skilled Stadium with Nathan, Sue and the Ablett family's manager, Michael Baker, sitting down with Costa, Cook and Thompson. Baker, who no longer manages the family's affairs, would later tell Costa that just before they were about to go into the meeting Nathan had said there was "absolutely no way on earth" he was going to sign with Geelong. The meeting was going along those lines early. "He was as shy as buggery, I had never met anyone like him, because you would have to drag words out of him," Costa said.

Eventually, Costa struck a nerve. "I'd gotten nowhere with anything else so I looked Nathan straight in the eye and said, 'Nathan, I'll tell you something, if you change your mind and sign with Geelong, the first two years you are playing you won't get big money, you will get good money but at the end of those two years you'll get a contract which will be good money. If you look like you are going to go on at that point, I know your brother will be going on and you will both be on good money, well, then I will be back. I'll be back because I will be expecting you and your brother to do something towards helping this lady gain independence, to have a nice decent home on her own and she can cut back from two jobs a week to one job if she wants to do it and have a decent life. Because she has spent her whole life looking after you guys.'"

With that, Nathan reached over, grabbed a pen and signed the draft form which would see him become a Geelong player at selection No. 48 in the 2004 national draft.[11]

The club initially took a *softly, softly* approach with him because his body was still developing and he'd never trained properly in his life. But raw talent still saw him play four games in his first season (2005) and seven the following year. VFL coach Leigh Tudor remembers fondly the first game Nathan played in the reserves. "He had kicked a couple a goals and then he called the runner over and said, 'Ask Leigh if someone else can have a turn

---

11. Ablett played 32 games for the Cats, his last being the 2007 Grand Final before turning his back on the game. In November, 2009, he met with the Gold Coast franchise to discuss the option of playing VFL football.

at kicking goals," he said. "So I told him, 'You kick one more goal for us, I'll put you on the ball.'"

His teammates often joked about "Nathan's world", as he would regularly produce the bizarre and unexpected. Before a VFL final game at Port Melbourne, a club official was driving to the ground at around 1.30pm when he saw Ablett walking out of the ground dressed in his full kit. "We had played a game at Port Melbourne earlier in the year and normally we do our stretches about half-an-hour before the game and Nathan decided he wanted some room so he went for a walk himself and found a park somewhere nearby to do his stretching," Tudor explained. "It worked for him, he came back at the right time and then had a good game so when we were playing the final at Port Melbourne he went and did the same thing."

Before another game he was discovered at the bottom of the plunge pool next to the locker room – the coach who was looking for him actually thought he was in trouble because he'd waited there 30 seconds and he still hadn't surfaced. Ablett would often be found sleeping in the players' lounge and would regularly be there late at night (on one occasion he saved the place from burning down when he discovered a stove had been left on).

Officials never knew what to expect; one thing they did know was that performances like the one against the Blues were only the tip of the iceberg. But, as if on cue, the following week against Melbourne at the MCG he produced another surprise. After complaining of slight soreness, Nathan got through the first warm-up on the ground but after the team ran out, and with just a handful of minutes before the opening bounce, he withdrew. Joel Selwood, who had been the emergency on standby for any late mishaps, had just started munching on a Mars Bar in the stand when his phone started ringing.

"It was Kane Tenace and he said, 'You'd be getter down here, mate, because you're playing,'" Selwood recalled. "Lucky I just had a Mars Bar, a few of the other boys had ordered a pie and I nearly did the same. So I got down there, got stripped and was on the ground within the first 15 minutes."

Ablett's absence didn't hurt the Cats as another young father-son prodigy stole the spotlight that day. After kicking the opening goal of the game,

Tom Hawkins took over the "G" in a mesmerising 10-minute burst in the second quarter. The 18-year-old kicked three goals, his strong leading and booming kick igniting comparisons to the great Tony "Plugger" Lockett. The first came after a trademark Wojcinski four-bounce run and pass to Brent Prismall, another impressive Geelong midfield prospect, who chipped it to the goalsquare. Hawkins jumped over Demon Nathan Carroll, took the mark and casually strolled into an open goal.

Three minutes later, defender David Johnson directed a perfect pass to the leading Hawkins, who converted from 50m. He repeated it again three minutes later, marking on the lead and unleashing a thumping drop punt from 45m. Radio commentator Rex Hunt even declared at half-time that such was the Tomahawk's dominance that Fred Fanning's 18-goal record was under threat. However, the youngster spent a lot more time on the bench in the second half and didn't add to his tally, a move some observers even ridiculously suggested was a ploy by Thompson to rein in the hype.

While Hawkins dominated the talk, it overshadowed a clinical display from the Cats, who had 10 goalkickers on the day. Prismall booted three, while the usual suspects in Bartel, Chapman, Ling and G Ablett ensured victory No. 2 to the tune of 52 points.

Thirty-nine goals in two weeks – Geelong's new attacking style was ticking over a treat. But even five days before his side's round four clash with Hawthorn, Thompson was predicting it wouldn't be making the journey with them to Launceston on the Sunday.

In round one, the Hawks had been ridiculed for being part of one of the worst games in years, when they only kicked two goals to three-quarter time at the Gabba, against Brisbane. While they'd beaten Melbourne and the Kangaroos since, their high-possession, chip-backwards flooding style was the complete opposite to the Cats of '07.

"It will probably be more of an ugly game than it will be a fashionable, pretty game because that's just the way Hawthorn tends to set up and we need to set up that way," Thompson predicted at his weekly Tuesday press conference. "We probably won't win the game kicking 18, (or) 16 goals – we might hopefully win the game by kicking a lot less. It might end up being a 10-goal-all game because of the way Hawthorn play."

His opposite number, Alastair Clarkson, used this veiled criticism to motivate his players. Combined with a typically windy day at York Park, it ensured the Cats were in for a hard day at the office. This was obvious from the start with Geelong's first goal – Ling on the run from 40 metres – not coming until the eight-minute mark. The ensuing arm wrestle had the Cats just in front by four points at three-quarter time but the vaunted forward structure of Mooney, N Ablett and Hawkins still hadn't bothered the scorers. Hawthorn's big guns Shane Crawford and Luke Hodge were seeing plenty of it, while Gary Ablett (two goals), Ling and Bartel were holding their own. Yet the momentum, and the wind, was with the Hawks in the final term. A mistake by Steven King (playing his first game for the season after yet another injury interruption) and missed chances by Mathew Stokes, also making his debut for '07 after a four-week suspension, and Mooney in the dying minutes conspired to produce a four-point loss for the Cats.

Thompson had been right with his prediction. The final scoreboard? Hawthorn 10.16.76 defeated Geelong 9.18.72. As the Geelong contingent boarded the plane to leave Launceston, there was an all-too-familiar feel amongst the group. Another interstate trip, another loss and another game they should have won. Another 2006?

chapter 6

Time for the Truth

"We had promised each other we weren't going to keep doing those things. Everyone just spoke up, a lot of things were said that had never been said before, very honest stuff."

– Matthew Scarlett

Mark Thompson couldn't believe what he was seeing. It was happening again. Why now? Why the first home game of the season? Why against the Kangaroos? After all the summer work and positive talk, surely this team was now beyond this. In his eight years at Skilled Stadium, this sort of *disinterested* performance would pop up maybe three times a year. He knew it happened at other clubs, but it happened way too often, and at the most inappropriate times, at Geelong.

A two-goal deficit at quarter-time blew out to 33 points at the half. It wasn't just the coaches and fans who were in shock, but also the players. "I was just watching them tear us apart," Mooney said, "and no one was doing anything. All of a sudden it seemed like 2006 again."

While his more senior teammates were fumbling and standing back, it was left to 18-year-old Joel Selwood, playing just his fourth game, to lead the way. He threw himself at every contest, often taking on two or three Kangaroos because that was the way he'd been brought up. He wasn't aware of the *Geelong way*.

"I had heard about the old Geelong but I didn't know what that was," he said. "Playing that day I sort of got a bit of a taste of it and it just wasn't fun football." What frustrated Thompson nearly as much as the pathetic start was how his players decided to flick the switch in the second half. Ling went forward and kicked three goals and, when Bartel kicked his third from 50 metres out – near the boundary line – the margin was 10 points with three minutes left. Mooney, who had already kicked three, had a shot with 90 seconds left to get them within a kick. It missed.

A Kangaroos goal just before the siren made it official: 16 points at the finish. Adam Simpson had finished with 41 possessions, Brent Harvey had kicked three goals and Daniel Wells had played perhaps his best game ever. Walking off, all David Wojcinski could think about was the nightmare of the previous season. "I just thought, 'Well, I hope we're not going down this path again.'"

Josh Hunt, who had been dropped again after the Hawthorn loss, was in the stands and had left his seat five minutes before the siren to avoid what had become a very angry mob. "I thought there would be blokes' heads on stakes down Moorabool Street, that's how filthy the people were," he said.

It was matched by the feeling in the changerooms. All support staff were kicked out of the meeting room as Thompson, his coaching staff and the players shut themselves away and put everything on the table. Instead of launching into a tirade, the coach was calm and calculating. "Unless some of you change, you are going to lead unfulfilled football careers," Thompson said. "If you want to finish your career like that, that's okay, but you'll be disappointed and have regrets for a long time."

Then it started. Players began speaking up. No one was spared. Personal attacks were delivered but what was most startling thing was the honesty in their eyes and their voices. "It was pretty cold, but direct," Bartel recalled.

"A few things were said which weren't very nice," Egan added.

The players were urged to look at Darren Milburn. He'd given his heart and soul to the football club for almost 200 games but he was going to be denied the one thing he kept playing for – a premiership – because the culture of the team hadn't changed in the 12 years he'd been there.

They weren't playing as a team and were wasting the talent sitting in the room. "There is no way we can go down this road again," Joel Corey said. "We are a joke if we keep doing this. We are too good to be not doing something."

Thompson asked the group what it wanted him to say in his press conference. He was sick of trotting out the same old story. They agreed he should say they hadn't respected the game or the opposition and that it was mentally weak to come out and play the last 40 minutes like they'd wanted to win the game. When Thompson left the room, Scarlett took the floor. "Do you realise if we don't keep winning we could have a new coach?" he said. "You know Bomber could get sacked, that sort of stuff does happen."

Outside, Brian Cook was sitting in a corner by himself, away from board members who were circling with intent. "I am looking at the directors and they were very unhappy. Understandably," he noted. "I was thinking, 'What role do I play here?' I wasn't sure what to do. I could go over there and join in or do nothing, I chose to do nothing." Frank Costa soon came over and tapped him on the shoulder. "I want to have a chat to you," Costa said to Cook, who then joined the group. A couple of the board members were wanting to develop a media position but Cook wouldn't have a bar of it.

"Do you believe in where we are going?" he asked them. "Do you believe in your executive? Do you believe in your coach? Do you believe in the players?" Cook wasn't totally sure himself but at least he had bought some time. He knew all the changes that had been made – the new fitness staff, new leadership method and game style – would take that time to come together. Or not. "If it didn't come together we were gone," Cook said. "I had already said this to the board that maybe we have all had our day, maybe the pain threshold of our supporters had been surpassed and maybe they need to think about someone else."

Club director Gareth Andrews had played in the 1974 Richmond premiership team alongside Neil Balme after he'd left Geelong. He had been part of the hiring process to bring Balme to the Cats because he knew

Balme's wealth of knowledge would be of great value in a supporting role to Thompson. Right now, he needed to talk to his friend. He was getting an awful sense of deja vu about this season. Balme saw him coming and said straight away: "Don't worry, mate. We are going to be a good side."

"What makes you say that?" Andrews asked.

"These boys can play," Balme said.

"Gee, I hope they do it soon," Andrews said, though he was encouraged by the conviction in his premiership teammate's voice.

After 45 minutes, the players meeting ended. Scarlett walked out convinced something had clicked inside that room. "In the past I have walked out of those meetings thinking it is just another useless meeting, we have said it all before and nothing has changed," he said. "But I knew this one had actually hit home. For some reason walking out I knew and probably everyone else knew that things were going to change. This time we had promised each other we weren't going to keep doing those things. Everyone just spoke up, a lot of things were said that had never been said before, very honest stuff."

Kelly also sensed it.

"It wasn't a meeting full of buzz words," he said. "You go into those meetings and hear we have to got to be 'committed' and all those cliche sort of words. You walked out of that meeting and you could see in the boys that it actually meant something."

The club's media policy after a loss dictated that a senior player front the press along with the coach. Tom Harley did not play, so media manager Kevin Diggerson went in search of a replacement. When he walked into the spa room he found Paul Chapman and Mooney. Given Mooney had done it a week earlier in Launceston, Chapman – who along with Selwood and Bartel had been one of the few good players – was the man. As Diggerson escorted him out to the waiting reporters, he was slightly apprehensive about what might happen.

On and off the field, with Chapman there was no holding back. He would be brutally honest. And he was. A transcript of Chapman's candid assessment of the team's performance is as startling as it is blunt.

"We're picking and choosing when we want to play. There are no excuses," Chapman said. "Our first half was pretty bad and our second half was very good so it's not a matter of just being flat on the day or not being hard or not using the ball well, because we showed that we can do that in the second half.

"You'd have to say it's individual blokes. I think, at the moment, we've probably got some passengers and we can't afford to carry them. We need 22 blokes who are going to live your values and die for your team. If you think about it, it's war, it's our little war. I know it's not, it's only a game of footy. But we need everyone to contribute and you can't have blokes picking and choosing and deciding when they want to go and when they don't want to go.

"It's not just this year and it's not just last year, it's been around for a while and it's something that we're going to have to change as a side. You can't just be happy playing, getting your money and having a good lifestyle or whatever it is. You've got to go out there and do everything you can to win, and that's what it's about.

"It does make you angry. I reckon we're a good side, but we're not a great team. We've got heaps of talent, probably right up there in the league I reckon, but just playing as a team – coming to play week in, week out – is probably one of the hardest things we've got to get our heads around and not pick and choose, just do it."

That sentiment was the focus of another team meeting the following day. It had been called by the leadership group and was driven by Harley and Ling, who were concerned the confidence of the group was wavering and that some guidelines into how they prepared for games had to be set down.

They gathered in a large circle and Ling started asking questions. "When you go into a game, what do you think about? Do you go into the game thinking I want to have 25 possessions and kick three goals?" he asked the group. "Because if you do, one week you might but the next five weeks you might not. You have to change that mindset, what I have done over my whole career is know that the result takes care of itself if I play a certain way. I play well when I do my three "focus areas" well. They are the most simple, basic kids' footy sort of things but when I do them well, I play well. So if you focus on the process, the result will take care of itself."

The players were then asked: "Hands up ... who goes into the game just hoping they will play well to stay in the team?" Ling couldn't believe it. Not one hand went up. "Well, that is a load of bullshit. When I first started my career, for the first 80 games that is all I thought about." About 30 players then put up their hands. A few were asked what they needed to do to play well and stay in the team. The answers were all very similar: tackle hard, be aggressive around the ball and strong over the ball.

From this discussion, several areas were nominated for the whole team to focus on for each game. Each quarter these measures would be reviewed, instead the focus being on the scoreboard. "If we beat the opposition in those areas then we win the game," Ling said.

Out of that also came a pledge to stick to the gameplan they had trained to perfect all summer and to refine the *Geelong way* of playing. Max Rooke also came up with the idea of presenting an award each week to the player who best epitomised the team ethic. After every game there would be a ceremony (the winner received a Quiksilver gift pack). There would also be a focus on ensuring that, win or lose, every Monday would be the same. A stranger could walk into the club and not be able to tell if the team had won or lost.

Earlier in a leadership meeting, Mooney had questioned whether they were good enough to win the premiership. This had troubled Harley, Ling and Chapman, in particular, who wanted to get a feel from the rest of the group. "Hands up if you think we are absolutely good enough to win a premiership," Ling said. "No bullshit, not that you want to win one but you truly *believe*."

Most hands went up. Each player was asked why. The reasons they were a good team were outlined. They were then asked to raise their hands if they had played in the 2002 VFL premiership. About a dozen had. Then those who had played in the narrow preliminary final loss to Brisbane in 2004? About 20 hands raised. A few more were added when it was the turn of those who were part of the 2006 NAB Cup premiership team.

"We've done it before, we have got some quality players so there's no reason why we can't do it again," Chapman said. Those who had doubts when Ling had initially asked the question were starting to be swayed by the mounting evidence. Thompson, who had been quietly observing, then put his hand up. "I really believe we are (ready)," he said.

Ironically, just as Thompson and his players were thinking premierships, a betting agency had installed the Geelong coach as favourite to be the first AFL coach sacked in 2007.[12]

12. For the record, three coaches were marched that season: Fremantle's Chris Connolly and Denis Pagan at Carlton were sacked late in the season while, in July, Essendon legend Kevin Sheedy was informed that his contract would not be renewed in 2008.

chapter 7

Step One

*"I think the public has probably got this
perception that I am just this pure party
animal that doesn't care about the footy.
Footy means more than anything to me."*

– Steve Johnson

Every Wednesday night over the summer months, Geelong's Victorian
Football League team invites one of the local sides to training. An
obviously good public relations exercise, it is also about trying to find a
player or two for the squad's top-up list, as the best and fairest winners from
the different leagues in the area also receive an invitation to try out.

Generally, there are up to 50 players at these sessions and, in 2007, there
was also a celebrity. Steve Johnson was the star attraction and many of the
local boys spent most of the time engrossed with his sideshow rather than the
actual training. "Steve was all the rage at the time, all the news, so we've got
40 or 50 blokes there and they are all sort of watching him," VFL coach
Leigh Tudor said. "Every kick he did he was hitting blokes on the chest
and then he would go, 'Watch this Lurker', and he took the ball and ran to

the boundary line and kicked a goal straight through the middle, post high. He'd then look around to see all the boys going, 'Oh my God, did you see that?' He loved it, he was in his element."

Showboat, maybe. Well, definitely. Yet from the minute Johnson started his suspension, Tudor was impressed by the way he attacked his training. "We made it fun for him but he really trained hard and knuckled down," he said. "He didn't miss a session and it was the most I have seen him run (and) I have been at the club three years."

Two months into his ban, Johnson was invited back to train with the senior team after convincing the leadership group of his commitment. It was also to get him into groove with the Cats' new playing style and have him ready to go in round six. After watching the Kangaroos debacle and, having seen what Johnson was doing at VFL level, Tudor knew it was a matter of bringing him straight back in.

"He really had a strong mindset to give off as many goals as he could," he said. "He kicked a couple of bags as well but he was pretty much playing as a ruck rover. For him to play like he had in the midfield in the VFL you could just see that he was going to be a very hard man to stop in the AFL as a forward."

The four months in Siberia had been a humbling experience, such that Johnson often found himself hiding out in his house. "I felt pretty embarrassed," he said. "I would walk past people and think that they were looking at me, thinking: 'You're this drunken idiot'. I think the public has probably got this perception that I am just this pure party animal, a pisshead, that doesn't care about the footy. Footy means more than anything to me. People close to me know how much that hurts when you take footy away from me. That's why with the suspension there wasn't any fine or anything. They thought, 'We'll take footy away from him and let's see how he copes with that.'

"Looking back it is probably the best thing they could have done for me. I have got so much more to offer so it really hit home a bit when I realised it could have been the end."

The return of Johnson was the feelgood story Geelong desperately needed. Behind closed doors, though, the players and coaching staff were confident a statement was going to be made in the Sunday twilight game against Richmond at Telstra Dome. Joel Selwood's performance against the Kangaroos had stung a lot of the senior players. Joel Corey said he was embarassed by how the rookie had shown up the rest of the team and Brenton Sanderson (in his review of the loss) had made a highlights package of Selwood to screen to the rest of the group.

They were also shown the half-time interview by Kangaroos midfielder Daniel Harris as he was leaving the ground: "We came down here with a focus to be harder and lower than Geelong and we think we have been that," Harris said.

That was like a red rag to a bull for the likes of Corey, Bartel, Chapman, Scarlett and Ling, who prided themselves at playing it hard and tough. "We review the game as coaches individually, it takes about five hours," Sanderson said. "You go through slow motion of the game and you put it into movie segments. It made you sick watching it.

"We showed edits of players not playing the way we wanted to play and Joel Selwood was just outstanding that day. He played the game of his life in his fourth game of AFL footy. He was the one guy that played like a Geelong footy player that day. I think the guys were embarrassed by their performance and wanted to take it out on Richmond the next week."

When Tom Harley sat down for his morning coffee and the Sunday papers, he almost choked when he saw a double-page feature in the *Sunday Herald Sun*. The headlines screamed. *"DOUBLE STANDARDS AND INFLATED EGOS"*. The article attacked Geelong's culture and quoted a number of former players, including rover David Spriggs (who had been off-loaded to Sydney and then subsequently sacked), Aaron Lord and Derek Hall, who'd only been around for one year of Thompson's reign. When he got to the rooms before the game, the story was the talk among the players. "We were just that focussed," said Harley, who was still out injured. "It could have been Essendon of 2000 that day, we would have beaten anyone."

Wooden spooner Richmond of 2007 was hardly Essendon of 2000. After 13 minutes, it was seven goals to nil; three already to Chapman.

Importantly, one of those goals had been scored by the new face in the team wearing No. 20 … at the 10-minute mark, Gary Ablett had roved a ball-up and handballed to Steve Johnson, who ran in from 30 metres to announce his return to the football world.

At quarter-time the margin was 55 points. Another 10 goals in the second quarter stretched it to 107 points. Eight goals in the first 19 minutes of the third quarter, including three to Hawkins, had Geelong on track to break its own league scoring record of 37.17 (239), set against Brisbane at Carrara in 1992. Their tally at three-quarter time was the highest in VFL / AFL history, 29.9 (183), with the lead now 144 points. It was as close to perfection on a football field that you could get and even the players recognised it. "About half-way through the third quarter I sat back for about five minutes and sort of watched the game a bit," James Kelly said. "I was thinking, this is perfect."

The old record prevailed, but not by much. The Cats kicked 35.12 (222) to win by a whopping 157 points, Richmond's biggest loss in its 100-season history. It was the eighth highest score in the history of the game, yet not one Geelong player kicked more than four goals. Chapman, Hawkins, Nathan Ablett and half-back Andrew Mackie kicked four; Gary Ablett, Travis Varcoe and Ling three; Johnson and Mooney a pair each. Ablett was best afield with 32 possessions but you could have raffled it … Corey, Mackie, Chapman and even young ruckman Mark Blake were in the top handful of players on a bizarre night.

The biggest positive for the coaches and the leadership group was that the focus going into the game had nothing to do with a goal frenzy but had been about getting back to basics: defensive pressure and tackling. "We went out in the first quarter to be physical, to get two or three tackles each," Jimmy Bartel said. "It sounds like the smallest goal but we wanted to hunt them, wherever the ball was … we didn't care if we were out of position because we just wanted to make it three on one."

Ling said the amazing performance reinforced that what they had discussed during the week actually worked. "We focussed on the basic areas and look at the result," he said. "We won by 157 points. I think that showed guys that it worked."

Brendan McCartney described it as the perfect wakeup call. "Average teams don't score 35 goals in a game and score them like that," he said. "It showed them, and everyone, that the talent was there."

Thompson immediately threw forward after the game. The undefeated reigning premiers, the West Coast Eagles, were coming to Geelong in a week's time. That would be the real test, although Bartel already had one on his hands.

Bartel had gone back with the flight of the ball in a marking contest late in the second quarter against Richmond and copped a knee in the stomach from Tiger big man Matthew Richardson or teammate Matthew Egan. When he went in at half-time, he began vomiting blood. He tried to drink some water but it wouldn't stay down, so he decided he would have to play out the rest of the game without having a drink.

At the end of the match he was doubled over in the rooms with crippling stomach cramps. "It was that painful, as if it was going to rip me in half," Bartel said. "It took me forever to leave the rooms. The doctor said, 'Go home. If there is something wrong, give us a call.'

"I got 10 minutes down the highway and I was just pissing out sweat. The doc then said go straight to St John of God Hospital and I spent the night there. It turned out that when I got hit straight down the middle, it actually pushed my bowel and my organs around to my spine, pushed everything back."

After gaining a clearance to play the following week, the medical staff wanted Bartel to wear a guard. He declined for vanity reasons: "That would look stupid." That's the Bell Park boy in a nutshell. There aren't many harder and tougher players in the competition, as teammates testify. "He is one of the most competitive people you would ever meet," Ken Hinkley says.

"Even at training his teammates used to get shitty on him because he smashes in and they would say he goes too hard, he goes too far. You think he is going a bit far but you can't stop it because he doesn't care. When we get the marking bag out he would try to take the mark of the year at training. With any of that sort of stuff he just pushes it to the limit."

It was no surprise to Hinkley to watch as Bartel, six days after leaving hospital, was best-on-ground as the Cats dismantled West Coast. From the opening bounce he was everywhere and, along with Gary Ablett, he helped inspire a five-goal third quarter which set up a crucial victory.

Ablett broke free of the clutches of Adam Selwood (teammate Joel's older brother) to kick two goals as the Cats seized on the ruck dominance of Mark Blake and Brad Ottens; admittedly, no small thanks to Eagles star Dean Cox's late withdrawal. Scarlett was dominating Quinten Lynch and setting up numerous attacking moves while the two big talls Mooney (four goals) and Nathan Ablett (three) were dangerous. Johnson (two) was typically, well, freaky.

While Corey took on the task of trying to control Chris Judd, Ling had latched onto Daniel Kerr and shut him down. In the corresponding match last year, Geelong had led by 54 points early in the third quarter but were overrun by a Kerr-inspired Eagles, who stole the round 10 match by three points.

Ling wasn't going to let that happen again and, after having just 10 possessions in the first half, Kerr didn't touch the ball after the long break.

It was a heroic return for Ling in front of his home crowd as he had strangely copped the brunt of a lot of criticism for the previous year's debacle. The likeable red-head, who is probably the friendliest and most approachable footballer in the business, became the scapegoat in the fans' eyes. Renowned as the premier tagger in the league, he had been forced to change his role due to the state of the team and combine his bread and butter with trying to be a creative midfielder. The plan backfired. Suddenly there were fears in the outer that the game had passed him by, as he was seen to be too slow for the modern game.

Thompson couldn't believe the personal attacks. Before the start of the season he had gone on record and told everyone to lay off Ling, all the while recognising that he could fend for himself. "He is an incredibly strong human being," he said. The coach got to see this first-hand during the 2001 pre-season. Ling had played 10 games in his first year, mainly at half-forward, but after resident tagger Carl Steinfort was traded to Collingwood he was called in for a heart-to-heart.

With a queue of forwards ahead of him, the coach suggested he should look at a midfield run-with role, so Ling began his transformation. With fitness freak Spriggs, he ran every day, took up boxing and found a job as a brickie's labourer, working five hours a day to harden his body. When Ling fronted for round one in 2001, he had lost eight kilograms and was a different player. "It was quite extraordinary," Thompson said.

"It was pretty extreme," Ling said. "I suppose I tried to prove a point, too, that I could lose the weight and get fit."

Overcoming adversity was nothing new in his family. The then 19-year-old didn't have far to look for inspiration – his father, Linton, lost his right hand at 18 when, as an apprentice butcher, he caught it in a mincer. The handy footballer had been trying out for the Geelong under 19s and had also shown plenty of cricket ability. Four years later, bowling left-arm spin – he is a natural right-hander – Linton Ling took seven wickets for the Geelong City seconds and made 80 not out.

For the next 20 years, Ling Snr defied his handicap to bamboozle the town's best grade cricketers. He only hung up his whites after fulfilling a dream of playing in the same cricket team as sons David and Cameron, even changing clubs to ensure it happened. "If you think about what he did, it's pretty amazing," Cameron said.

Ling's leadership qualities were noted very early by Thompson and after just three seasons and 44 games he was made deputy vice-captain in 2003. He won the best and fairest award in 2004, having been runner-up the previous two years. And six years after his fitness revolution, the 26-year-old is still the hardest runner at the club.

He puts a lot of his amazing stamina down to the amount of time he spends in the ocean near his home in Torquay, following his second love, surfing. But it is his mental strength which continues to amaze his coach and frustrate opponents like Kerr.

With the Eagles star under Ling's lock and key, the Cats cruised home to win by 39 points. It was a decisive performance and one that had Cook, and many others, starting to believe the on-field side of the operation was beginning to seriously find its feet. "I saw what the players did pre-season, these guys were on a mission," he said. "The tempo at training had gone up

30 per cent and I thought, 'This is great, this is fantastic, at least we're going to give ourselves a chance'.

"After round five I doubted it. After round six against Richmond I was hoping it wasn't just a flash in the pan. But when we played West Coast, with the ability they had, I knew we were onto something then. I knew we had the ability and we were starting to show it."

chapter 8
The front office

"In the event that this level of capital is not available, we believe a number of combined factors will result in the club being unable to compete in the AFL in the short to medium term."

– KPMG 1999 report on the GFC finances

Frank Costa was doing the rounds of the radio boxes two hours before kick-off at Skilled Stadium. The Fremantle Dockers were out on the ground having a walk around, already looking like they'd rather be back in the sunshine of Perth than going into battle in the wind and rain that had blown in from Victoria's western district.

The Cats president was his usual jovial self; the familiar, gravelly voice spruiking his beloved team and the city of Geelong across the airwaves. But the one question every radio station wanted to know was this: was he going on? Costa, 69, had indicated the previous season that he was likely to move on for family reasons at the end of 2007.

"I promised Shirley," Costa said in a nod to his wife – and the mother of his eight daughters – who had ridden the ups and downs of a reign which began in 1998, and the club on its knees. While he was explaining the reasons behind the decision, across the other side of the ground at the official luncheon Brian Cook was instigating a plan to try and change Costa's mind. Cook's wife, Annette, arranged for the two couples to catch up for lunch the next day at a local restaurant, Bellbrae Harvest.

Cook had made up his mind that if Costa went, so did he. Yet he was worried what that would mean to the football club, for he saw plenty of unfinished business. Plans for a new grandstand and a gaming facility in Point Cook were at crucial stages and already there were people positioning themselves to challenge for the presidency should Costa go. This, of course, would mean more upheaval and a messy election later in the year. Plus, thought Cook, if anyone deserved to be president when Geelong broke its 44-year-old premiership drought it was Frank Costa.

The president had been a lifelong Geelong fan and remembers the 1951-52 and 1963 triumphs ... plus the heartache of 1967, 1989, 1992 and 1994-95. From an early age he realised the fortunes of the football team greatly affected the morale of the city. "I have always made the statement that the Geelong Football Club is the soul and the spirit of our town and our community," Costa said. "When Geelong Football Club was succeeding in its endeavours the town was up; when it failed it was down.

"I got my first realisation of this when I was an 11-year-old selling *Heralds* and *Sporting Globes* on Saturday night on the street corner. I used to double my order when Geelong won and sell every paper, but I would go back to my traditional order when we lost and take half the papers back to the depot."

Costa's grandparents were Sicilian immigrants who moved to Australia in the 1880s. His great-uncle established the Geelong Covent Garden in 1888 – a produce grocery he ran until 1934, when he turned it over to Costa's father. In 1959, aged just 21, Frank and his brother Adrian took over the business.

They commenced wholesaling and, under the guidance of Frank, developed the business to the point where it is now the largest service wholesaler of fruit and vegetables in the country, with annual turnover approaching the $1 billion mark. In 1997, Costa was awarded the Order of Australia Medal for services to youth and the community.

His involvement with Geelong began as a long-time member of the Pivots coterie group. He was a driving force behind the R.J Hickey Trust, which was established 20 years ago to fund the construction of the Hickey Stand (now the Doug Wade Stand). Costa was invited to join the board as marketing director in 1997; he became vice-president in 1998 and took over the presidency in December of that year. Nothing happens in Geelong without Costa's fingerprints on it.

The enormity of the man's influence is something which shocks outsiders, according to media manager Kevin Diggerson. "You don't realise, until you get here, how big Frank is," Diggerson said. "I'm sure people involved in other clubs think Frank's a fruit-and-vege bloke and no big deal but he is as big a deal as there is in this town. His realness is great, there is nothing phoney, he is very genuine. He loves the club and loves the people."

When Costa returned from his media commitments, Shirley informed him of his Sunday lunch date. "We have got nothing on, so is that okay?" his wife asked. "No worries," Costa said. He didn't give it another thought as he sat back and watched his team chalk up its third win in a row and move into third place on the ladder. The match started in identical fashion to the Cats' previous outing, with Nathan Ablett kicking the opening goal. The Cats then piled on six straight to lead the Dockers by 16 points at the first break. It was 29 at half-time, James Kelly playing his best game for the season while Bartel and Wojcinski were seeing plenty of it.

The unheralded Matthew Egan was in the process of taking another big scalp, this time Fremantle captain Matthew Pavlich, while Steve Johnson (four goals) had the Dockers defenders running in circles. An early final quarter surge by the visitors – veteran Peter Bell freed Ling's clutches for three quick goals – made the game interesting, but this new Geelong team had shown it could find another gear when pressured. End result? An easy 25-point victory.

Cook didn't wait long to reveal his true intentions at lunch. While the ladies were talking at the other end of the table, he looked his president straight in the eye. "Are you bloody fair dinkum about pulling out at the end of the year?" Costa was surprised with the question. "Brian, I have been telling you all year that I am. I promised Shirley that."

"You are bloody mad," Cook said.

"What do you mean I'm mad?" Costa asked.

"You will lose me, I'm telling you right now I'm not staying and forget all about your new stand, you're not going to get it."

The president was rattled ... which is saying something. "What do you mean I'm not going to get the new stand?" Cook explained that the local federal member of parliament, Stewart Macarthur, had told him on Friday that if the rumour was true – that he and Costa were leaving – the Federal Government was unlikely to approve a grant for the new stand, for the football club didn't have a stable, tried and true management team.

"They just won't do it," Cook said. "So you had better find yourself a new CEO and forget about your bloody stand."

"Don't say that," Costa said.

"I'm telling you this is how it is."

Costa knew his CEO wasn't joking. He also knew it was a decision which was out of his hands. "Well then, Cooky, you had better get down and say something to that lady at the other end of the table because I can't have either of those two things happening."

Cook went over to confront Shirley; Costa smiled. The pair had been through a lot since he'd managed to convince Cook to leave Perth, such that he would often refer to his CEO as "the best recruit the Geelong Football Club has ever had in its 148-year history".[13]

Brian Cook was first mentioned to Costa at a dinner party, not long after he took over the presidency. He was at the home of good friend and AFL Commissioner Craig Kimberley, who had also invited the league's CEO, Wayne Jackson, over for the evening. Before the group had sat down, Costa said: "Listen, I have got a problem and I need some expert advice. I need to know the best sports administrator in this country."

He added. "I don't know the people in this industry, you guys do. The second best won't do, either."

Kimberley and Jackson took about a minute to come up with their

13. Cook and Costa date their pairing as president/CEO back to 1999. The next longest pairing in the AFL is that of Sydney, whose Chairman Richard Colless and CEO Myles Baron-Hay began their partnership in the latter half of 2003.

answer: Brian Cook. They told the new Geelong president that Cook had picked West Coast up from absolute oblivion, won two premierships and turned them into a financial power. "But why in the hell would he leave what he has got going so well and come to a basket case like you have got down there?" Kimberley said. "I don't know ... but we're going to try," Costa replied.

They got lucky. Cook was having problems with an Eagles board which had changed considerably in recent times. He had three children living in Melbourne and had flown cross country to visit 25 times in the previous 12 months. Perhaps the idea was not so ridiculous.

Cook was born in Scotland. He had been a handy Australian rules footballer – he was also a star junior boxer – starting his career in division two with Box Hill in the Victorian Football Association. He did not play in a winning team there for two years, then went to Hawthorn where he spent 1975-76 in the reserves. He wore No. 35 with the Hawks (the same number Gary Ablett wore when he began his then-VFL career at Glenferrie).

In 1977, Cook transferred to Melbourne and made his debut against Collingwood on the Queen's Birthday at the MCG, in front of 60,000. He only played four games as a centreman because, if he played one more, the Demons would have been up for a bigger transfer fee. The following year he returned to the VFA and played with Caulfield before former Hawthorn teammate Brian Douge lured him over to Western Australia, where Douge had been appointed coach of Subiaco. It was a move which would change the course of Cook's life; he completed a Master of Education (leisure studies) at the University of WA and on the football front joined East Perth.

After six games he – and East Perth – figured out that he was no longer up to the grade, although he played in a reserves premiership in 1981. He then moved into coaching and took East Perth to another reserves flag in 1983. A move to Canberra to coach Ainslie was next, however it only lasted a year. (Cook jokingly claims to be the only coach never to make a Grand Final – they got knocked out in the preliminary final – with the club, which had historically dominated the ACT league).

While in Canberra he became national sports research co-ordinator with the Australian Sports Commission. He returned to Perth in 1986, becoming general manager of the WA Football Development Trust, and then became chief executive of the WA Football Commisson. They were the major owner of the West Coast Eagles, so in 1990 it became a dual role and he was installed as the football club's CEO.

The club went through a period of unprecedented success. Mick Malthouse arrived as coach and drove the Eagles to the preliminary final in his first year and the Grand Final in 1991. The following season came premiership success, ironically over Geelong, and West Coast repeated the feat against the Cats two years later. During this time Cook oversaw the redevelopment of Subiaco Oval and turned the club into a financial power, collecting more than $27 million in profit before he struck problems with that new board in 1998. Put simply, he got caught in a power struggle and knew it was the end of the road for him in Perth. Enter Frank Costa.

There is no better salesman of his football club and town than Costa. His passion for the task was obvious from the moment he and Cook met. After meeting with the Geelong board – which also interviewed Greg Swann, the former Collingwood CEO who in 2007 moved across to Carlton – Cook agreed to take on what looked like a monumental challenge to resurrect the league's only country-based team.

Costa knew things were bad but he had no idea the depth of the problem which Cook began to uncover on a daily basis. "I remember his first month, the poor bloke, it was worse than I thought it was," Costa said. "I didn't mislead him because I didn't know it was that bad, I had told him what I thought was wrong. Every day he would ring me up as he would be finding another skeleton in the cupboard or in a draw. After a month he rang me up and said, 'Frank, I think I have got the skeletons out. You had better come down and I'll show you the full picture'."

It wasn't pretty. The club was looking at a $1 million loss to add to increasing debt problems, which had reached $5.1 million (not including the bank overdraft) and were rising by the minute. The stadium was falling down, the club owed the social club around $1 million and the Australian Tax Office was owed close to the same figure. Plus, there were creditors of almost $2 million. The club therefore had a liability problem of close to $10 million and by Cook's estimate was inches away from toppling over.

Transparency was one of the key planks in his philosophy for a successful business, and Costa still vividly recalls sitting in his new CEO's office and being told Cook wanted to air the club's dirty linen. "He sat me down and said we had to tell our two partners," Costa said. "I said, 'Who do you mean?' He said, 'The AFL and the bank.' When he said the bank, I turned white."

One of the first initiatives Cook had implemented was employing accounting firm KPMG to do a full assessment of the operation. Four months later, KPMG delivered its report declaring Geelong was in serious danger of extinction. *"GFC will not emerge from its current position unless it receives a capital injection in the region of $3-4 million,"* the report stated. *"In the event that this level of capital is not available, we believe a number of combined factors will result in the club being unable to compete in the AFL in the short to medium term."*

A strategy to switch banks was instigated. The club owed $5.1 million to the Bank of Melbourne, which had already been burned by the demise of Fitzroy. Little wonder it agreed to accept 55c in the dollar. Overnight, debt reduced from $5.1 million to $3 million ... the size of the new loan courtesy of the Cats' newest partner, the Bendigo Bank. There was one snag: the new bank would not agree to part with its money unless the club's board, which had come into power on the Costa ticket in 1999, acted as guarantor for the first $1 million of the debt.

Plus, there remained a major problem with cash flow, or lack of it. Cook went to the club's sponsors and pleaded for an early advance. Long-time sponsor Ford agreed to provide $500,000 ahead of schedule, as did several others, including club patron Alex Popescu, who had from time to time been forced to fund the payroll. The end result was a $1 million injection.

On top of this, Cook had to deal with the departure of senior coach Gary Ayres. He still had a year to run on his contract but came in asking for an extension. If not offered, Ayres would leave to replace Malcolm Blight in Adelaide, exactly what he had done at Geelong five years earlier. The CEO advised him to take up the Crows position. Then Leigh Colbert, who had been appointed captain for the 1999 season but hadn't played a game because of a serious knee injury, decided he wanted out, pushing for a trade to North Melbourne.

The ship still faced rough seas, but was at least salvaged for the time being. Cook then went about setting up the resurrection by upgrading the stadium. First, the AFL had to be lobbied to give the Cats a guarantee of at least seven games a year at Kardinia Park. They did, and backed it up with a $2 million grant to help with the $28 million ground development proposal. After ticking the League off their list, the Cats turned to the City of Greater Geelong ($6 million), the State Government ($13.5 million) and Federal Government ($2 million) to get the project up and running. The club made up the difference of $4.5 million, most of the funds coming from money owed to it from the sale of Waverley Park.

On May 1, 2005, Cook's dream became a reality when the new Hickey Stand opened. Two years later, as he and Costa lunched in a regional winery, and the club has more than 30,000 members (compared to 19,000 when Cook started) and was on target for a $1 million-plus profit.

The drive down to the Costa holiday home in Airey's Inlet was a quiet one. Shirley had yet to utter a word about her discussion with Cook. Finally, Frank said: "Shirley, don't give me an answer now, tomorrow is Monday, I can change a couple of things around in my diary and I'll take the morning off and we'll go for a nice walk along the cliff face. Then we'll come up to Truffles and have a cup of coffee. When we're doing that you can tell me what you want to do." Nothing else was said for the rest of the night, nor during the lovely stroll along the beach in the morning. Once at the coffee shop, he could resist no longer. "You would have thought about it ... what do you think?" Frank asked. "Well, I know how much you love the football club," Shirley said. "There is no way I can say no. But there will be one very, very serious condition."

Frank braced himself. He had no idea what was coming next. "I don't want to go to all of those functions, I am functioned out," she said. "I have been doing this for nine years. I want to spend time here at Aireys and with my grandchildren." A smile broke out on the president's face and the Costas embraced. "It's a deal," he said.

chapter 9

Restoring the balance

"When you are not playing it is really hard. Winning is bittersweet, you do go on a self-preservation mode. You start to think, 'Where am I going to fit into this side?'"

– Geelong captain Tom Harley

Tom Harley had survived his first game for six weeks unscathed, albeit in the VFL. His injured finger had stood the test in defence; Harley took a few contested marks and generally felt good about the whole experience. Even though he was captain of the club, he understood the need to get a match under his belt before stepping back into the senior team.

Harley had played reserves before but always only for a week to gain match fitness on his way back from injury. In his nine years at Geelong he had never been dropped or left out of the side if he was available. Harley was thinking about that record as the team's preparation for the next weekend's clash against Port Adelaide at AAMI Stadium started to take shape.

Nothing had been said, but the skipper started to have an uneasy feeling. Maybe he was searching for things that weren't there but he was sure the coaches, particularly Thompson, seemed a bit evasive. In truth, during his extended time on the sidelines he had moments where he started to wonder where he was going to slot back into the side.

"When you are not playing it is really hard. Winning is bittersweet, you do go on a self-preservation mode," Harley said. "You start to think, 'Where am I going to fit into this side?' I actually switched myself off the internet and newspapers and all that kind of stuff because it seemed as far as anyone was concerned I didn't deserve a spot in the team."

His instincts were right. In what all the coaches described as the toughest decision the match committee had faced, they decided to leave the captain out and go with Josh Hunt, who was considered the perfect match-up for Port's dangerous forward, Brett Ebert. Harley was devastated. To make matters worse, the VFL had a bye that week, so he flew to Adelaide with the team and sat in the coaches' box during the game. "I tried to be upbeat but I had cheersquad members telling me, 'Oh, gee, you're not going to get back in this side'. I just felt like chinning them," he said.

What he saw from the box didn't help. The Cats were awesome in the first half, kicking 13 goals to two to defy the wet and wintry conditions. It was the best hour of football for the season, according to the coach. "Outstanding," Thompson assessed.

Port Adelaide had one of the best midfield combinations in the competition, yet on this day the Burgoyne and Cornes brothers were thrashed by the likes of Bartel, Corey and G Ablett, who were unstoppable as they fed off Ottens' domination in the ruck. Ling kept Peter Burgoyne in check, Wojcinski and Milburn rebounded at will and Max Rooke kicked three goals. The eight-goal second quarter finished with two exceptional goals from Bartel: the first was classic wet weather football with the Cats' hard man fighting for the ball in a pack, taking one step and unloading a 55-metre torpedo which sailed through. At the next bounce, Bartel accepted a handball from Selwood and again nailed the shot from similar distance.

In the stands, vice-president Gareth Andrews was quickly becoming a believer. "I could not believe what we did in that quarter," he said.

"We bottled them up so badly they didn't know where to go. The lead was 71 points at half-time but it was just the way they handled the ball on a really slippery day. These blokes were just handling the pill like it was a dry sunny day on the MCG. I knew then that these guys could play footy. It was the best footy I had seen us play all year."

The second half was, well, a write-off. Port got numbers back to minimise the damage while the Cats wasted opportunities, kicking 3.11. Still, a 56-point victory saw Geelong replace the Power in second spot on the premiership table. Harley did his best to be diplomatic and congratulate his teammates but he was a worried man. Back at the team hotel he rang his girlfriend, Felicity, and told her how much he was struggling. For a fleeting moment he started wondering if stepping down as captain was the noble thing to do. "I have to start to focus on just getting a game," he said. Felicity told him to calm down, to not think so erratically. Her advice was sound: throughout his career Harley had extracted more out of himself than many expected; he'd fought back numerous times from setbacks and he would do it again. At 28, and after 142 games, he was far from finished. "Life's full of challenges, here's another one," she said.

After finishing the phone call, Harley went for a walk and ran into Steve Hocking in the hallway. "How are you going?" Hocking asked. "Mate, I'm shithouse," came the reply. "This has actually been the toughest couple of days of my football career. People don't know how to look at me, they don't know how to talk to me." Hocking explained how the coaching panel was also doing it tough because they respected him so much. Hang in there, was the message.

A phone call from Thompson several days later provided hope. "You're in the side," the coach said. "It is a match-up thing, they (St Kilda) have got a tall forward line and we are going to use you as a tall back." Harley couldn't resist having a slight dig. "So I *should* be in the bloody side," he niggled.

"Nothing is guaranteed," Thompson replied sternly. "We pick the best side for the team we are playing against and we are playing St Kilda this week and you're in."

Hunt, who had been good against Port, was dropped in favour of the skipper. For Harley, it felt like he was playing his first game again. "I have never been more nervous going into a game of footy," he said.

In recent years, Geelong and St Kilda had developed a heated rivalry, borne out of bragging rights as much as anything.[14] Both clubs were seen as the great Victorian hope, and supporters are forever getting into arguments about which has the best list. The Wizard Cup Grand Final of 2004 saw the argument spill onto the ground. In the lead-up to the game, Thompson (and then acting captain Brenton Sanderson) went on the front foot at the press conference over Saint Aaron Hamill's attack on the man and not the ball, branding them "cheap shots".

In the opening seconds of the game, Cameron Ling was flattened by Saint Brent Guerra, who was later suspended for three weeks. St Kilda won by 22 points but Paul Chapman later added further fuel to the fire when he said: "We know we are much better than them and it will show (in round one)."

St Kilda coach Grant Thomas said he would use the "disparaging" remarks as motivation for his team. Thompson parried: "I wouldn't care what Grant Thomas said." Tit-for-tat, perhaps, but in these days of vanilla press conferences, a little extra flavour attracted its share of attention.

The Saints were again successful in round one but both clubs enjoyed break-out seasons, finishing third and fourth respectively. St Kilda lost by a kick in the preliminary final against Port Adelaide in Adelaide; Geelong by nine points to Brisbane in the other fight for a grand final berth. In 2005, the Saints again finished third, losing to Sydney in the preliminary final after the Swans, and in particular Nick Davis, had stolen the semi-final from Geelong with a miraculous goal in the dying seconds. By 2006, some believed the crest had been ridden: both clubs hit the skids, the Saints slipping to eighth and sacking Thomas after an inglorious early finals exit, and Thompson's men winning 10 games to miss the finals altogether.

Yet the rivalry survived into '07. First edition was a Sunday twilight fixture at Telstra Dome; there was a definite edge about the Cats from the opening bounce which resulted in a seven goals to four quarter. Again it

14. This was highlighted again by the Saints securing Geelong VFL Leigh Tudor as an assistant in 2009, admitting it was a decision directly aimed at gaining insight into the "Geelong way".

was Wojcinski who provided the opening play for the highlight reel. At the 13-minute mark the dashing defender received a handball from Ling near the centre … he stepped off his left foot to beat one tackler and repeated the dose to the next St Kilda would-be tackler. Two bounces later he closed on the 50m line and his straight kick earned him a nomination for goal of the year.

Star Saint forward Nick Riewoldt, who had been well held by Egan, got busy late in the second term and Harley was called in to quieten the Saints star. That didn't go well: Riewoldt had a shot to level the scores with a couple of minutes on the clock but hit the post. The Cats then scored quick goals from Ottens and Mooney to retrieve the breathing space. Five goals to two in the third quarter broke the back of the Saints, who failed to kick a goal in the last quarter as they fell by 60 points.

Bartel had by now firmed into second favourite for the Brownlow Medal. He was again best-on-ground, while Ling (three goals) destroyed the highly rated Nick Dal Santo and Gary Ablett broke clear of his shadow, Steven Baker, to light up the contest in the second half. Blake continued to improve in the ruck while Scarlett (vs Fraser Gehrig) and Egan (vs Riewoldt) took the honours. Thompson's assessment of the game might equally have been applied to the previous season. "What keeps us going is that we have been in this situation before and we have collapsed and crashed," Thompson said afterwards. "As quick as you go up, you can go down. We don't want that, which is why we just have to focus on week-to-week outcomes … quarter to quarter, to be honest."

Harley was a relieved man afterwards. "My mindset was just to get through the game, do my job and don't get any goals against me," he said. "I did that and we won. I got through, pulled up okay, didn't play great at all but didn't really think I needed to."

That wasn't how the coaches had seen it. The next day he was called in to Thompson's office where all the coaches were waiting. He was shown the side that had already been picked for the next Sunday's game against Adelaide at AAMI Stadium. "You are going to play on Ricciuto," Thompson said.

Harley told them he felt better with the first game out of the way and that he would be better for the run. Thompson's reply was typically forthright:

"Well, if you put in a performance like you did against St Kilda, you'll be out of the side."

It was a sledgehammer response, and not one he was expecting. It was being made pretty clear that he was currently considered the 22nd player picked, and was back on the brink again. "Okay, well, what do I have to do?"

"You have to do what you do best and do it to the best of your ability," Thompson said. "You mark the ball, you attack the corridor but we don't want you to chip the ball sideways anymore, which you have a habit of doing. We go through the guts now."

Harley was stunned – and fuming – when he walked out. It was getting harder for players who were under-prepared to jump back into the game these days, no matter how good you were. There were numerous examples, like Port captain Warren Tredrea, Carlton skipper Lance Whitnall and even Sydney star Barry Hall who were all struggling as a result of injury-interrupted seasons. For the past three years Harley had virtually played underdone.[15] Now, he was going to have to step up to the plate quicker than he'd ever done before.

One positive was that Ricciuto was also on the comeback trail from major injury problems. And by the time the team flew to Adelaide on the Saturday, Harley had wound himself up. "I was like, 'Stuff this, this is my last chance'," he said. "I had come up with a little motto for myself. It had nothing to do with the coaches or the club, but I just had doubters everywhere. There were a lot of people who thought he's a great bloke, really nice guy but just past it. So it became a bit about self-pride."

At the team meeting that night, Max Rooke stood up and spoke. This was an important game; Adelaide was a proven top side, a hard, big-bodied team that loved to play contested football and always beat up on the Cats at AAMI Stadium. They were also coming off a shock loss to Melbourne the week before so they would be expected to come out desperate.

"This will be our biggest test for the year," Rooke said. "We talk about coming over here and winning, it's about time we did it."

15. In truth, Harley struggled with injuries since 2005. From 2005-09, his final five season, he averaged 16 games per season, including finals, making his revered respect all the more remarkable.

The group talked about how, since the Richmond victory, it had enjoyed a lot of high-scoring victories and the new gameplan had yet to be tested under extreme pressure. "There is going to come a time in a game when we are going to be down or under the pump and that is when we are going to be tested to see how much balls we have to stay with our gameplan," Rooke said.

Pre-game predictions were on the money: the Crows were all over Geelong in the opening quarter. They gave the Cats' midfielders no space, choked up the corridor and turned the game into a slugfest. It was three goals to zip until the final 90 seconds when new father Mooney – son Jagger had been born on Thursday – kicked two in a minute to reduce the margin to eight points.

Gary Ablett came alive in the second quarter while his partner in crime, Bartel, was also thriving in the pressure and intensity of the contest. Geelong dominated the second quarter but again kicked wastefully, 2.9 for the term only good enough to go in at half-time with the scores tied.

Perhaps the most significant point of the first half was Harley. He had gone for everything in the air, taking four or five contested marks and totally dominated an admittedly out-of-sorts Ricciuto. His teammates realised the importance of having their skipper back in the swing. Scarlett, who was already close to best on ground, headed over to help pump up his mate.

An enthralling contest continued in the second half with the Crows bravely hanging on. By the final quarter their bench was down to one with key midfielder Simon Goodwin (leg injury, first quarter), defender Graham Johncock and Ricciuto all out of action.

An error from Crows youngster Jason Porplyzia decided the game. A sloppy kick from the last line of defence was brilliantly marked one-handed by Steve Johnson, who went back and drilled the match-winning goal from 40 metres. Even though there was still more than five minutes on the clock, given the way the game had been played all day and the determination of the Cats to prove a point, Adelaide wasn't about to suddenly find two goals. They didn't, and the seven-point victory set off joyous celebration in the visitor's rooms.

Thompson was pumped. "We have had some easy victories when we've got off to a big start but that doesn't test your game style, your persistence to come back and play a game like this, when there was 16 points in it all day," he said. "It was on from the start to the finish and it is what we really needed. It is great to play this sort of footy."

Sanderson agreed, thrilled: "When you can beat Adelaide in Adelaide, playing their style of footy; contested, hard, defensive accountable football. I thought that we were going to be okay, that we might be starting to build something."

To win twice in Adelaide and to thrash St Kilda told McCartney that the Cats were capable of threatening in September. "I knew then this team was capable of something very big," he said. "They (Adelaide) were coming off a bad loss, they are a proud, strong club who had a history of fighting their way out of the trenches and we held them at bay and found a way over the line. Plus, we started poorly and just ground our way back. To belt Port Adelaide there and then come back two weeks later and win again, I thought something was happening."

The win, the Cats' sixth in a row, moved them to top spot and for many players it gave them the belief that they could be capable of something special in three months' time. "We had struggled to win interstate," said Gary Ablett, who again was best-on-ground (further shortening his Brownlow Medal price). "That was a big thing for us to overcome and I have always rated Adelaide as a good, hard, mature side … to beat them over there was big. I think it gave the side more confidence and while we didn't want to get ahead of ourselves, we all now believed we had the ability to do it."

James Kelly nominated the victory as the day Geelong got their mojo back. "From the year before when we lost a lot of respect, I think that was when we gained a lot of respect back," he said. "It wasn't just 'Geelong are on a bit of a streak', it was 'Geelong are actually a good side', and that was really satisfying. You could feel it from the other teams that they thought we were a big chance."

Harley's post-match phone call to his girlfriend was a more pleasant experience this time, although one good game wasn't going to wash away the anger. He had played well, particularly in the first half, and had cut Ricciuto out of the game. "I got a lot of back slaps and stuff but I was still furious."

chapter 10
The return

"He is a truly inspiring man. I can't believe what he did today. He had four or five marks and two of them were contested in packs, it's just ridiculous."

– Leigh Tudor on Tom Lonergan's comeback match

H e had held it together all week. But as Tom Lonergan ran out for his comeback game, everything came flashing back. The collision, the pain, the doctors, the hospital … the fear. Tears welled in his eyes. "You know what to do," advised good friend, and housemate, Henry Playfair. "You've done it all before so don't worry about it. Just get out there and enjoy it."

When Lonergan emerged from the race it was to a standing ovation from senior teammates and the large crowd. Given it was 9.50am on a wet Sunday in June, it said a lot about how much the 23-year-old's inspirational comeback had touched the football world.

Almost 10 months earlier, Lonergan had nearly died on the football field. Playing just his seventh senior game against Melbourne in round 21, at Skilled Stadium, he had courageously gone back with the flight of the ball and was crashed into by Demons forward Brad Miller. The impact was sickening; club doctors immediately sensed the urgency and rushed him to hospital. Lonergan had lost litres of blood and underwent emergency surgery to remove his kidney before being placed in an induced coma.

He lost 17 kilograms after the surgery. Many, including his family and friends, believed that he would never make it back, and Lonergan himself had serious doubts. Every time he looked in the mirror he could hardly recognise a body which had withered away.

While the medical dangers were spelt out clearly, there were examples – such as former Geelong champion ruckman Sam Newman, who had played AFL football with one kidney. It was a risk, but the odds of anything happening were so slim that to him it was dismissed as a factor.

The bottom line for Lonergan was that he loved playing football and felt he hadn't got a chance to show what he was capable of in the AFL. So in December he informed the club that he wanted to give it a shot. They placed the versatile big man on the rookie list and promised that if his comeback was successful he would be elevated onto the senior list at the end of the season. At that stage, all he could do was walk. Even that had been a struggle in the first few weeks after he'd left hospital. By January he had started to put some weight back on in the gym, with every little goal achieved in his training recognised by the coaches and his teammates. "I remember in the summer when he ran half-a-lap he got a standing ovation from the players," Mark Thompson said. "It is a remarkable story."[16]

Lonergan suffered numbness around his midriff, where he sports a massive scar to forever remind him of the incident. A month from the start of the season he was back running strongly but was struck down by groin problems. Slowly he again improved and each week before a match he would do a session on the ground with fitness coach Paul Haines. For the previous six weeks he had trained with a custom-made protective guard over his kidney, completing all the physical training – including tackling and body-on-body

16. Perhaps underscoring the lack of sentiment in the game, through the end of 2009 Lonergan had played 32 games and kicked 44 goals, but there was no place for him in the 2009 premiership team – Lonergan did not play after Round 20.

work – to get the medical clearance required to resume his career. Lonergan had been forced to turn his phone off the night before his return match, such was the traffic of people text-messaging and ringing to wish him luck. His preparation had been a quiet family dinner with his parents, brothers and sisters, who presented him with a large card they'd all signed. "Mum was a bit emotional," he said. "I got some great messages. It was pretty inspiring."

As he sat on the bench waiting to be called into action against Tasmania, Lonergan adjusted the rainbow-coloured laces on his white boots, a reminder of how much his life had changed. They represented the Zaidee's Rainbow Foundation, an organisation set up in the memory of Zaidee Turner, who died, aged seven, of a burst vessel in the brain. Lonergan had become an ambassador of the foundation, which aims to raise awareness of organ donation by having sporting teams wear rainbow-coloured laces in their footwear. As a mark of respect, his senior teammates were doing the same in that afternoon's game against Brisbane.

Ten minutes into the match the call came down from Leigh Tudor in the coach's box. He was on, with a brief to run around the forward line and just enjoy it. His first touch was a handball and soon he was back in the flow. Seven kicks, three handballs and five marks was the end result, Lonergan playing about half the match.

The Cats won easily and he was swamped by his teammates and the cameras in the rooms afterwards as he belted out the theme song with gusto. "I was nervous before the game, but once I got out there everything came together," he said. "During the game it started to get easier and easier and I was able to work my way back into it. I just went for it, just instinct footy. Once you get there, the instincts take over. You just play the game and everything else goes out the window. You're running on adrenalin."

Tudor was amazed. "He is a truly inspiring man," he said. "I can't believe what he did today. He had four or five marks and two of them were contested in packs, it's just ridiculous."

There was a lot of emotion surrounding the senior game that day, with Cat veteran and unsung hero, Darren Milburn, celebrating his 200th game. All week his good mate, Matthew Scarlett, had been into his teammates about making sure they produced something special for "Dasher".

Milburn arrived at Geelong from Kilmore as an 18-year-old selection (No. 48) in the 1995 national draft. He had gone to school in Broadford with Sydney champion Barry Hall and been a top-up player with Sydney and Collingwood before ending up at Kardinia Park. Like Scarlett, he had never been one for fanfare. He rarely did media interviews and was happy to lead a fairly simple existence that centred around his two loves; playing footy on the weekends and going home to his wife, Tania, and two children, Imogen, 4, and one-year-old Jett.

His most famous early career moment came in round 22 of the 2001 season when he knocked out Carlton legend Stephen Silvagni with a vicious shirtfront in the dying moments of a match that the Blues won by 70 points. Silvagni, who was in his last year, was carried off on a stretcher. The Blues Princes Park faithful went berserk, even following and threatening Milburn in the car park afterwards. "Six years on and you still hear it (booing)," Milburn says.

While he may be quiet and mild-mannered off the field, Scarlett says it is a different story during games. "He is an animal when he plays," he said. "He's pretty quiet, but once he goes out on the field, he really inspires me the way he plays. He is so courageous and hard. Once he crosses over that line, he changes into a different guy."

Everyone at Geelong believes the versatile defender is easily the most underrated player in the AFL. "He is as good a player as we have got," Scarlett argues. "He is definitely as good a defender as we have got and he is the equal as a defender to anyone in the league at the moment. He goes under the radar a bit and is pretty underrated, but not at this club."

Milburn isn't fazed by his lack of profile. "I don't like to put myself out there, that is just the way I am," he explains. "I leave it up to other blokes. If they want to go down that path, good luck to them. But I have always grown up as a quieter person."

He certainly didn't go under the coach's radar at the toss of the coin. Given it was his milestone game, Milburn was given the honour by Harley. That was fine until Thompson watched him win it and decide to kick against the strong breeze which had started blowing down the ground. "I hadn't spoken to him about it because I thought, naturally, you kick with the wind.

Then I saw him point against the wind," Thompson said. "I couldn't believe what I'd seen."

It didn't cause any undue damage with the Lions way out of their depth in the slippery conditions. They failed to register a goal in the opening half. A lot of that was due to Matthew Egan's excellent job on Brisbane superstar Jonathan Brown, who the ball went to on every Lions' foray forward. The Cats led by 30 points at half-time but the visitors came to life in the third quarter, kicking four goals to reduce the margin to 19 at the final break. Milburn's theory of kicking with the wind in the final quarter paid off: six goals to one sealed an emphatic 50-point win.

The tackle count told the story. Remarkably, both teams laid more than 100 each, with five Lions and four Cats in double figures. Hard nuts like Mathew Stokes, Joel Selwood and Cameron Ling, who blanketed Simon Black, thrived in the conditions while Gary Ablett's class rose to the top with 37 touches (including 15 in the final quarter). Steve Johnson found a way to kick three goals. Egan, Scarlet and Harley had been impenetrable while Milburn had quietly gone about his business ... just like he had for the previous 12 years.

Brisbane coach Leigh Matthews was a legend of the AFL. A hard, tough and brilliant player with Hawthorn – he was selected in the forward pocket in the AFL Team of the Century – he coached Collingwood to its historical drought-breaking premiership in 1990 and in more recent times had won three consecutive premierships with the Lions. Now more a statesman of the game, his opinion carrying plenty of clout. After watching Geelong do a number on his men, he was moved to offer his thoughts on two particular players, Joel Selwood and Gary Ablett. Matthews described rookie Selwood as "really special", already one of the best wet weather players in the modern game. "From the first game he played he looked like he'd played 200 of them," he said. "He just knew what to do. He makes good decisions. He's been a marvellous first-year player."

As for Ablett (Matthews played with his father at Hawthorn), he was effusive. "He's a wonderful little player, isn't he?" he said. "The things good players do. They're clean ballhandlers, they keep their feet, they make good decisions with the ball in their hands and they execute well.

He does all those things. He's obviously an All-Australian player so that makes him elite."

Even his own coach had been swept up by his afternoon's work, Thompson declaring it was "close" to the best game Ablett had played. "His whole year has been outstanding – him and Jimmy Bartel, you know, their footy has gone to another level. I think (Ablett) is fitter, and we're playing him on the ball more. I think he's more determined to have more impact. I think he's maturing as a person and he wants to win and he wants to win badly. I think he generally likes helping the team win. I've always known he's had endurance, but we'd never seen him run and play a game out like that and I think that's what he's doing now."

The mid-year break did nothing to halt the Cats' momentum, although the week off didn't help Max Rooke and his troublesome body. Hamstring problems had plagued his pre-season – he hadn't played his first game in the seniors until round eight – and five minutes into the round 13 game against Sydney they struck again.

Rooke was chasing Swan Nick Malceski when he heard what he thought sounded like a massive whip crack. "It was all a bit of a blur. I was lying on the ground, and then I realised (the sound) was me," he said. "I couldn't get up. I eventually tried to jog off but I couldn't even jog. I walked off and I felt stupid because I had to walk all that way and the play was just going on around me. I went straight inside and I just couldn't move my left leg."

While Rooke was having his hamstring assessed, the Cats piled on five goals to two in the opening term as Johnson and Cameron Mooney looked dangerous. Four goals to Sydney's four points in the second quarter saw the margin blow out to 41 points.

The only concern was an expanding casualty ward. Ling had been crunched in the head by Sydney defender Leo Barry and was sitting on the bench not knowing what day it was. Bartel once again found himself in the wars, for he had also copped contact to the head and had started to lose feeling in his arm. He figured it was pins and needles so he went back onto the ground but the sensation started creeping down his other arm.

When he next came to the bench he actually missed the seat as he tried to sit down. After a few minutes of watching the game and repeatedly telling the medical staff he was okay, Bartel returned to the field. But in his first contest he was hit in the head and again dazed; he began wandering all over the ground, giving away a 50-metre penalty and ending up at the opposite end of the ground to coaches' instructions. "I went to kick the ball and I don't know how I made contact," Bartel said. "It just hit the side of my foot. The coaches could see what was happening and they brought me off. By then I was starting to get the shakes. When I was coming off I couldn't feel my right foot. I had massive pins and needles and I was banging my leg saying I couldn't feel anything.

"Then in the rooms I felt like I wanted to spew. I was having trouble breathing and then I couldn't feel my arm."

At half-time Bartel was wheeled out of the rooms, arms strapped by his sides, to a waiting ambulance. The early diagnosis was pinched nerves in the neck which had caused a major migraine. With three Cat midfielders out of action, the Swans, and in particular co-captain Brett Kirk, were inspired, kicking six unanswered goals from midway through the third quarter to reduce the margin to 11 points with nine minutes remaining.

A brilliant around-the-body Ablett snap from 45 metres steadied the ship before Johnson stepped in to kick his third, a lovely left foot effort, putting an end to any notion of an upset. Joel Corey, Paul Chapman, Andrew Mackie and Corey Enright had all stood out in what had been a typically hard and tough contest, par for the course against the Swans.

It was exactly the type of football which Thompson loved. "I thought our first half was absolutely sensational," he said. "I loved everything about it." Bartel couldn't remember much about it, although he got a chance to read all about it the next morning in what was quickly becoming familiar surrounds: a hospital bed.

chapter 11

Momentum

"This just might be the year where we do everything right and we just fly under the radar and win the whole bloody thing ... We might just scoop the pools."

– Matthew Scarlett

Stephen Wells gets hundreds of letters a year from either parents, family members, managers and even supporters tipping him off about a kid he should draft. The Cats recruiting manager has usually heard of most of them but there was something about the letter from a "John Rooke of Casterton" which captured his attention.

John was writing about his son, Jarad, who was playing senior football and was a good all-round athlete. The letter outlined how he had been runner-up in the state schools cross-country championships and was also a good 1500m runner. It also mentioned that his sister, Emily, was a promising triathlete. Wells was intrigued enough to travel up to Casterton to watch Rooke junior play. Initial thoughts were so-so; he simply marked Rooke down as one to watch.

It wasn't until the following year that Wells was convinced that Rooke had a chance of making it in the AFL. "He played at centre half-forward and was quite good, he was very competitive and very hard," Wells said. "He went into the midfield a couple of times and just made an impact which was significant for a young player playing senior country football. In the end we also found out he had a really good endurance, a 15-something on the beep test, and he was a really good kid so we wanted to give him a chance."

The Cats selected the 18-year-old in the 2000 rookie draft. Rooke stayed a rookie for two years although he was elevated late in 2002 to make his senior debut. "Once he got there, he learnt quickly and showed hardness that is so rare," Wells said.

This rare commodity was the topic of conversation at the football department meeting a couple of days following the round 13 game after Rooke's diagnosis had come through. It wasn't good. He had a seven centimetre tear in his hamstring, doctors saying it was at best eight weeks but more than likely a season-ending injury.

Thompson knew he needed Rooke for the finals. He was an X-factor, not in a Steve Johnson *kick a miraculous goal* kind of way but, in a fierce, almost suicidal, attack on the ball and the man, an invaluable trait when the heat was at its fiercest in September. "If we can get him back, even for one week ..." Thompson said. "If there is anything in the world that can get him back one week earlier then we should try it."[17]

Club doctor Chris Bradshaw had an idea. From his experience working in Europe he knew of a doctor in Germany a lot of soccer stars and Olympic athletes visited for specific treatment on soft-tissue injuries. Bradshaw jumped on the phone to his contacts overseas and finally found his man: Dr Hans-Wilhelm Muller-Wohlfarth, based in Munich. The doctor, who had treated international sporting stars Ronaldo, Maurice Greene and Daley Thompson, had become famous for using unorthodox treatments such as injecting calves' blood and honey into damaged human joints.[18]

17. Rooke has proven a durable asset since recovering from that hamstring, playing 42 games in 2008-09. Thompson's love of his hardness is underlined by Rooke averaging no less than three tackles per game – the benchmark of elite tackler – for the past five years.

18. Muller-Wohlfarth also successfully treated injury-plagued Richmond utility Mark Coghlan, who returned to the game in 2009 but was delisted by the Tigers at season's end.

He could fit in the footballer from Australia but it was going to be a costly exercise. Bradshaw estimated around $20,000 when he told Thompson and Neil Balme about his plan. "I can nearly guarantee we will probably pick up at least a couple of weeks in the recovery," he said.

Balme went to see his chief executive. "Previously I would have said, 'You have got to be kidding guys, we haven't got the money'," Brian Cook said. "But it was now something we could afford to do and it sort of fitted in with our behaviour. We had made a commitment to each other to be a touch more adventurous than we had in the past."

Thompson said sending Rooke overseas showed how far the club had come in the past six months. "Not in the eight years I had been here would that have happened," he said. It also said a lot for the development of (and respect for) Rooke, who was voted into the leadership group after just 84 games.

When he arrived at Geelong he was very much the naïve, wide-eyed country boy named Jarad. Now he was called Max and seen as a deep, spiritual thinker.

"He is very highly respected," Cameron Ling said. "As a person he is quiet but he is an obscure thinker. He is very much out there and comes up with ideas I wouldn't have thought of in a million years … and I consider myself to be pretty smart."

The name change was evidence of this. Rooke had never liked Jarad when he was growing up. In London the previous year for the exhibition game he informed everyone that he would now be called Max, his middle name (Maxwell) and the name of both of his grandfathers. Rooke arrived in Munich on the Friday with his first experience being a 210km/h hell ride in a taxi on the autobahn coming from the airport. He wandered around the city over the weekend before one of Bradshaw's colleagues from Fulham flew over to escort him to the Monday appointment with Dr Muller-Wohlfarth, who arrived dressed head-to-toe in white.

"I thought he was some sort of magician," Rooke said.

He was sent to have an ultrasound on his hamstring and X-rays of his back and pelvis. The initial diagnosis from the doctor wasn't what he'd been hoping. "Oh, this is very bad," Muller-Wohlfarth said. "I don't know, I try my best but I can't guarantee it will help." It turned out the problem was in his back, small muscles in his pelvis causing all the tension in the hamstrings. "He said it was an accident waiting to happen because my back was pretty stuffed," Rooke recalled.

He then had about 15 injections in his left hamstring and back. The first batch was an anti-inflammatory substance and it was followed by a protein mix which consisted of calves' blood and was designed to help the muscle redevelop. "That was the most painful because you could feel it spreading," Rooke said. "I was sore for about two days after the first lot of injections but it got better as the week went along."

In between the needles, Rooke also had several consultations with a chiropractor, a podiatrist and physiotherapist with his posture being a factor in his back problem. During daily visits he also got to mingle with some celebrity patients, including tennis player Martina Hingis and Italian soccer star Luca Toni.

"We were all sitting around in the waiting room and he (Toni) just walked in, with two guys running around for him, and went straight in. There was no waiting room for him," Rooke joked. "I did at least get to have lunch with the doctor one day, along with a Greek long jumper and a Jamaican 800m runner. But he knew nothing about the AFL."

When it was time to leave after five days of treatment, Rooke already felt different, and he left with some encouragement from his German magician. "You've done well, I am very confident," Muller-Wohlfarth said. He returned home with a totally different rehabilitation program. "I hadn't been happy with the process in the rehab because every time I would come back I felt like I was pushing it too early," Rooke said. "It was always the same program and it wasn't working for me. Normally what they do is, you have a few days off and then start doing straight running, basically everything you can do without pain and stuff. You start doing light weights and slowly join in the running.

"When I came back from Germany I didn't do anything on my legs, basically did no weights. I did long runs, 20-or 30-minute runs, for four or five days and then every day I ran after that I got shorter and shorter in distance and faster and faster in pace."

While Rooke was being used as a pin cushion, Bartel was up to his old tricks of making miraculous recoveries. This time it had taken a couple of attempts at the concussion tests for him to convince the medical team and coaches that he was right to bounce back from his latest hospital visit in time for Friday night football at a packed Telstra Dome against Essendon.

At half-time it looked like he may have got this one wrong. He was strangely subdued, although he wasn't the only one of the Cats not on their game early against an emotionally charged Essendon, who were celebrating Adam Ramanauskas' return from his latest cancer scare and James Hird's 250th game.

Scarlett's regular match-up with Matthew Lloyd didn't eventuate, the Bombers captain missing because of suspension, and it actually threw the defence out as Essendon defender Andrew Welsh went to his attacking goalsquare and caused problems. Welsh kicked two goals and had a hand in a couple more to keep his team within a goal at half-time.

Mooney could have won the game off his own boot in the third term but he was spraying it everywhere with four behinds from five shots to help Essendon, who by now had lost Hird to a calf injury and Alwyn Davey to a broken arm, stay in the contest. The first two goals of the final quarter by Stokes re-ignited the Cat machine and the eight-point three-quarter time lead soon blew out to 50. Chapman had been brilliant all night, kicking three goals from 34 possessions; G Ablett (31 touches) and Selwood took over the midfield. Ling slid forward to kick three goals while Mooney finished with the grand total of 3.7.

While it had been a struggle, the final 30 minutes further confirmed to Ken Hinkley what he had been thinking about a team which had now won nine games on the trot. "Every game we just seemed to be able to put the foot on the gas," he said. "Essendon were close at three-quarter time but we won the game by eight goals in a burst of 10 minutes. If we play our best for four quarters no side can go with us, that's what it felt like because we had all bases covered. We had a forward line functioning, we've always had this fantastic backline of Milburn, Scarlett and Harley. Now Egan was adding to it, Mackie and Enright. And we had this great midfield. We had Bartel, Corey, Ling, Ablett, Selwood and Chapman; it's hard to stop them all if they play well and they were all pulling in the one direction."

The one team which had a better chance against Geelong than most was Collingwood. Historically, the Magpies had always matched up well; they were very disciplined and very well coached by Mick Malthouse. And they were used to the big stage, which was exactly where Geelong found itself, with 85,497 people packing into the MCG on a wintry Saturday afternoon.

A mini-crisis had kept the Cats' executive team busy in the morning. The match was a Geelong home game, which meant the bigger the crowd, the bigger the financial windfall for the club. But a snap rail strike in Geelong was causing chaos for supporters wanting to catch the train up to the game. Cook couldn't believe it when he heard the news but he knew just the man to call. The minute Frank Costa was told, he rang Victorian Premier Steve Bracks, a Geelong supporter. Several phone calls later, the strike was over.

The contest on the ground unfolded as expected: tight, hard and physical, with bodies going everywhere and possessions earned the old-fashioned way. While the margin was only a goal at half-time, the Cats seemed to be in control but, again, wasteful kicking for goal was the problem. They kicked 2.5 in the third term, good enough to set up a comfortable 16-point victory in one of the more enjoyable games of the year.

Scarlett was the star, embarrassing Anthony Rocca with his attack from the last line. Harley, Milburn and Mackie were also good, while Ling tagged Magpie Dane Swan and snuck forward again for two goals. Mooney and Stokes were also busy while Steve Johnson again provided a priceless moment. Lining up for goal 30 metres out on a slight angle, the mercurial Cat walked in for the set shot before, at the last second, running around the man on the mark and strolling into the open goal. The move was met with a shaking of heads in the coaches' box. They had an often-used saying about Johnson: "He's going to jump the fence, you know that."

McCartney would always stir Hinkley about his favourite player. "Macca would come up and say, 'Did Stevie jump the fence today?' You knew he would just do something he shouldn't, he would get over the other side of the electric fence," Hinkley said.

"We knew there was an element of control but you had to sometimes let the reins go. At times his teammates would get angry but every time we brought him back to our side (of the fence). At least now he was acknowledging it when he did jump to the wrong side, whereas before he would say, 'Yeah … but what if I'd kicked it?'"

While Johnson had his moments, one man who had universal love was Joel Corey. Bartel, G Ablett and Selwood, who defied his age and lack of experience to thrive on the big stage, had been influential against the Magpies but it was the hardness and ball-winning ability of the man they call 'Smithy' which shone out on the MCG.

The nickname came from his teammates, who were confused when Corey and Corey Enright walked into the club at the same time back in 1999. The pair also lived together for a while so J Corey became "Smithy" and Enright became "Boris".

Ling (training) and Bartel (toughness) might be lauded for their particular strengths but Corey is a combination of both. Physically, the 2005 best and fairest winner is an awesome specimen, a 191cm midfielder who doesn't carry an ounce of fat.

"You see the Ben Cousins shots but if you see Joel Corey with his top off, tell me there is one ounce of (poor) conditioning anywhere on that body," Hinkley said. "He is amazing and he plays for keeps." Thompson likes the West Australian's ruthlessness.

"He just works on every part of his game, he is uncompromising. That probably sums him up," he said.

The sight of Corey and Scarlett dominating that MCG day had Harley daring to dream about Geelong's date with destiny at the MCG down the track. "The big stage against Collingwood, that is what footy is all about and we just loved every minute of it," the captain said. "Our big players stood up, they all played well and, the one thing we do have as a team is, our senior players all love it. They might not be outwardly emotional guys but they all love playing on the big stage. That was 10 (wins) in a row and everyone was talking about the lid and all that sort of stuff. I started thinking, 'My form is on the up, I am starting to play well. I am in the team, no question about that, so now maybe we are a chance to do it.' At the very least we are going to be amongst it, we're going to be in the top four."

It also made him think back to a conversation he had in the rooms – he could remember exactly where he was sitting – with Scarlett earlier in the year when the whole Ben Cousins controversy blew up. "This is bloody bizarre, people think we are bad eggs," Scarlett said. "They hear these stories that we are out on the piss and we're not. This just might be the year where we do everything right and we just fly under the radar and win the whole bloody thing."

"Wow, you could be right," Harley remembers saying.

Scarlett then added: "We might just scoop the pools."

chapter 12
Decision time

"The best thing about playing was going out knowing that, no matter what happens or who we played ... if we played the way we could then no team could get near us."

– Mathew Stokes

"**O**ver the last three years they are as good as I have seen, including West Coast at their best." Rodney Eade was in awe. In round one his side had shown up Geelong, winning by 20 points, but what the Western Bulldogs coach had just witnessed at Telstra Dome was frightening. In Eade's mind, they had everything: the gameplan, the structure, the talent, the discipline, the tricks. His side was undermanned, with three of its guns missing, but they were no longer in the same hemisphere as the Cats.

A frenetic eight-goal opening set the tone and by half-time it was 13 goals to four. Eade threw his side around in an attempt to find something – full-back Brian Harris went to full-forward and Brad Johnson into the middle

– but it was a waste of time. The end margin was 75 points. And the Cats didn't even have gun defender Scarlett, who was a late withdrawal because of illness. His replacement, David Johnson, slotted straight back in for his first game in a couple of months and was one of seven multiple goalkickers. He finished with two, as did Corey, the first time in his 142-game career he'd kicked more than a single.

Gary Ablett and Bartel again shared top billing while Mackie, Ling, Enright, Milburn, Selwood and Mooney (four goals) were on the next line, though you could have nominated 20 players in the best, such had been the dominance. "That reminds me of the round six game against Richmond, the way we started that," Thompson enthused. "I don't know where that came from. We talked about playing our best quarter of footy after the Collingwood game, that was a big game, and let's concentrate on the first quarter and they certainly did that. It was very impressive."

Now two games clear on top and a short-priced premiership favourite, planning for what lay ahead was very much on the agenda of Thompson and the coaching staff. There remained three or four spots in the team which were up for grabs, while youngsters like Selwood and ruckman Mark Blake would need a rest at some stage. Travis Varcoe, who had been dynamic in the forward pocket and led the league in tackles inside forward 50, had started to run out of legs and was dropped for the Bulldogs game. He was replaced by Shannon Byrnes, a nippy left-footer with a bit more experience who hadn't played since round four. A decision had to be made shortly on which one played in September, the same issue to be confronted in a number of scenarios:

Former skipper Steven King was starting to again play good football in the VFL after missing six weeks due to knee surgery. He had deserved another chance in the seniors to see whether he, or Blake, was the answer to support Brad Ottens.

Nathan Ablett or Tom Hawkins? That was another conundrum. The "Tomahawk" had gone off the boil after his early season explosion and had been cooling his heels in the reserves until being recalled three weeks earlier (with Ablett out injured). He hadn't fired against the Bulldogs, while Ablett had made his way back through the VFL.

And it was time to make a call: Josh Hunt, Kane Tenace or David Johnson? Hunt had been recalled the previous week against Collingwood after five weeks in the reserves; he replaced Tenace, who was injured. Johnson, a regular part of the backline until he too was injured in round eight, had returned and played well against the Bulldogs. Yet only one of the trio, barring injuries elsewhere, was going to play in September.[19]

Perhaps the biggest injury concern was Paul Chapman. While he had played some brilliant football in recent weeks it had been under duress and, finally, the pain in his groins had become too much after the Bulldogs game. Injury problems had started in the pre-season when he strained a hamstring which he eventually seriously tore in round six against Richmond. Chapman missed three weeks but, shortly after his return, the groin / abductor problems began. He had battled through to this point but the medical team were seriously considering putting him in for surgery, which would — hopefully – have him back by round 22. "I would wake up and go to get out of bed but when I moved my legs my groins were killing me," Chapman said. "Mentally it stuffed me more than physically. I mean my body was rooted, but mentally I couldn't do anything. I was shot, I was over it. I was hardly training, once a week if I was lucky, and when someone would say do this or do that, I was like, 'I can't do it because I'm too sore'."

Pain-killing injections were the other option but Chapman was delaying using them in the hope of a miracle. If it didn't come then he would accept injections during the finals, rather than surgery, which he was sceptical about. "Apparently it is big in England and the soccer players go and get it done and are back playing in three weeks," Chapman said. "I wasn't so sure."

The bombshell in the football world that week was the sacking of Essendon coach Kevin Sheedy, with the fall-out from this monumental decision reverberating down the highway to the Geelong chief executive's office.

Brian Cook had asked Thompson about signing a new contract a month earlier but his coach didn't want to discuss it until the end of the season.

---

19. Tenace was delisted after season 2009 after 59 games since 2004, while Johnson chose to retire with 72 games to his credit, having debuted in 2002 after being traded from Essendon. Also delisted after 2009 were Dan McKenna, Scott Simpson, Adam Donohue and Bryn Weadon.

"I don't want to be seen committing to other things, the only thing I am committed to is the premiership," Thompson told Cook.

The goalposts had just been moved. Dramatically. The club which had nurtured him, the place where he had captained a premiership – where he was a member of its Team of the Century and still retained strong links – was in the market for a senior coach, and at that minute there was none better than Thompson.

While it wasn't even August yet, the coaching merry-go-round was in top gear, with Carlton having already sacked Denis Pagan; Fremantle had just punted Chris Connolly; and clubs were lining up to convince recently retired Brisbane captain Michael Voss to turn his hand to coaching.

It was a distraction the Cats didn't need but Cook knew his coach wasn't going to budge. He sat back and watched as the rumours and speculation grew. (The most common line on talkback radio was that Thompson was still bitter about the review and he would complete a fairytale return to Windy Hill after winning the premiership at Geelong.) Appropriately, the Cats' next game, a trip to Fremantle, had a very Essendon flavour to it, with Thompson going head-to-head with his former teammate and best friend Mark Harvey. He had been installed as interim Dockers coach after they had sacked Connolly the previous week, and Harvey tasted instant success by upsetting the Crows in Adelaide.

There was to be no favours for a mate, nor the loss that many were suggesting was due. The Cats kicked six goals to one in the first quarter, including a four-goal burst in five minutes. Two came from Mooney, who had monstered Docker Antoni Grover in marking contests, while Steve Johnson and Stokes already looked to be off the leash. Harley, who kicked his 10th career goal, and Milburn were running from half-back as the Cats took control of the centre corridor on the wide expanses of Subiaco. Gary Ablett further enhanced his Brownlow Medal favouritism, James Kelly (playing his 100th game) was excellent while Ling stitched up Peter Bell and Corey thrived in front of his native home crowd.

The Cats' ongoing problems with accuracy continued; they kicked 6.14 in the second and third quarters but still led by 33 points at the final change. That radar was fixed in the final term, eight goals to two pushing the final margin to 68 points. It had been a flogging, and the story of the afternoon was the performance of Stokes, who finished with a career-high five goals.

This was fitting reward for a player who, two years earlier, had thought his AFL boat had sailed. Stokes had been a brilliant junior in Darwin and he represented Northern Territory in the national championships alongside St Kilda's Clarke brothers (Raphael and Xavier). At 16, he was named rover in the 2000 All-Australian team. An AFL career beckoned but, as he was too young to be drafted, Stokes moved to Adelaide to further his development in the SANFL with Woodville-West Torrens. If he thought success at AFL level was pre-ordained, he was wrong: he was overlooked in the next year's draft … and the one after that … and the one after that. Stokes figured the dream was over.

"I came down to Adelaide and thought it was just going to happen," he said. "My work ethic wasn't there and that's probably why I didn't get drafted. I went down to Adelaide with the belief that I'd be there for (only) a year but I just didn't work hard enough."

While one dream appeared crushed, Stokes was able to devote his time to another – his love of animals. He secured a job at the Adelaide zoo, where he became the mammal keeper, looking after the zoo's bears, giraffes, meerkats, lemurs, otters and beavers. "I thought my time was gone and I had become quite happy just working and playing in Adelaide," he said. But Stephen Wells had kept an eye on the 177cm goalsneak, who had turned himself into a polished midfielder and played well in SANFL finals. "We wanted another player who could play in the forward line but also be a "chop-out" in the midfield to give those guys a rest," Wells explained. "(Stokes) was experienced and was someone who could come in and play straight away if required. Everyone had seen him five or six years ago and he just kept playing well at senior level. We were looking at these players every year who were 17, 18 or 19 and hoping to get something, then we just realised that he was already something. He ticked all the boxes: he was tough, skilled, mature and had been a brilliant player as a junior."

The Cats also knew Stokes would appreciate the opportunity more than most, given what he had gone through. Apart from his draft heartache, Stokes had also fought back from a serious incident in Darwin when he first played senior football. An opposition player knocked him out and left him with a gash near his eye that required 12 stitches. The guilty party was later suspended for 30 weeks. "I was about 15 and this guy just came out and basically wiped me out. I can't remember a lot about it but every time I look in the mirror I'm reminded of it because I've got a scar next to my eye," he said.

Stokes, whom the Cats selected at No. 61 in the 2005 national draft, played nine games in 2006 and pushed himself over the ensuing off-season to ensure he wasn't going to be a bit player. "I didn't want to be one of those players who was here for two years and took off," he said. "I wanted to make sure I gave myself every opportunity in the pre-season to work harder and get fitter. I wanted to make sure I wasn't just a bit player who came in when there were a few injuries."

A pre-season four-week suspension didn't help his plan but it proved to be a telling fork in the road. "I remember Bomber (Thompson) said to me that if I worked hard for the next six weeks I would come straight back into the team," Stokes said. "At the time I thought it was just coach's talk to make you work hard but, when I did come straight back in, I guess I had never had that before. I never really had that much confidence in myself. For him to do that gave myself a lot of confidence, knowing that he knew he could count on me and bring me straight into the side. That was probably the turning point in my career."

The coaches liked Stokes because of his hardness. He was often told to ride shotgun with Gary Ablett to look after him and help the latter break a tag. "He is a tough little bloke," Ken Hinkley said. "He looked after Gazza a fair bit and he is an unusual mix with his hardness but he is also very, very skilful. He finds space on a footy field. I remember the Port Adelaide game in Geelong (in 2006), he ran himself ragged in a little bit of play, he was the only one putting in, and he came off the ground exhausted. The crowd loved him from then and he became a favourite of the club."

His day out at Subiaco – he thought he could have easily ended up with seven goals – not only reaffirmed his own position in the scheme of things but was another massive victory on the road. It had Stokes thinking about bigger and better times ahead. "The best thing about playing was going out knowing that, no matter what happens or who we played, or where we were playing, if we played the way we could then no team could get near us," Stokes said. "Walking out having that confidence in each other was a great feeling. Before a game you wouldn't be stressed out, you wouldn't be worried because you knew once you got in the changerooms blokes would switch on. No matter what happened out there you knew the bloke beside you was going to bust his arse just as much as you were."

It was another of the Cats' lower profile players who enjoyed his moment in the sun the following week against Richmond at Skilled Stadium. Mark Blake's pursuit of his first AFL goal had become a comical sideshow throughout the team's amazing winning streak. He'd had several very real chances, including a couple of gettable set shots, but coming into career game No. 29 he had yet to salute.

Cameron Mooney has always had a sense of theatre. At the 12-minute mark of the third quarter he recognised the moment. The Cat full-forward had the ball 15 metres out; instead of going for the easy goal he handballed over the top to Blake in the goalsquare who, while making it look quite awkward, managed to sneak it through. The fans in the outer erupted and his teammates came from everywhere to jump on the 200cm beanpole.

Not content with just one, Blake went on a goalkicking "frenzy". Early in the final quarter he grabbed the ball out of a pack and casually snapped another, this time over his shoulder.[20] It was one of those afternoons, as Steven King, who had come in for the injured Ottens, provided another bizarre highlight with a rare contested mark … over a goal umpire.

The game itself had been a fairly regulation 70-point victory. Bartel, Corey and Milburn had more than 100 touches between them, Shannon Byrnes was lively, Scarlett great and Steve Johnson kicked five goals. But all everyone wanted to talk about was Blake's goalkicking. "I loved the way he kicked his first," Thompson said.

"He has become a bit of a cult hero and it was what everyone has been waiting for."

20. Through the end of season 2009, Blake had kicked 11 goals in 79 games.

That excitement was tempered the following week when the Cats hierarchy decided to rest Blake as Ottens returned to play against Adelaide. The 21-year-old Blake, who had only played 11 games in the previous two seasons, had played in all 18 games to that point, plus the pre-season games. The coaches wanted to see if King still had what it took, so they told Blake he would be having two weeks off.

There was no tempering the Brownlow buzz around Bartel and the prolific midfielder produced yet another stellar performance. In the first quarter he had 11 disposals and kicked two goals. From his position in the Channel Seven commentary box, Dennis Cometti declared: "He's my Brownlow man!"

Bartel's understudy, Selwood, was also thriving in the cold and wet conditions, as was Corey. Five goals to one in the opening term had the Crows rattled although they re-grouped in the second and the margin was only nine points approaching half-time when Scarlett snuck forward to kick a crucial goal. Adelaide mixed things up early in the third and were suddenly taking on Geelong at its own game, playing a quick handball play-on style, but the Crows' efforts were only rewarded with four straight behinds. That was the thing about this Cats machine: if you didn't take your chances they would burn you. On cue, the switch was flicked and the home side kicked away late in the term.

The pick of the late onslaught came from a Mooney soccer of the loose ball off the ground near the boundary line, which landed in Selwood's lap 15 metres out, directly in front. The final margin was 33 points and, again, Thompson was happy about the nature of contest. "They challenged us physically and it was close for most of the day," he said. "It was the game we needed."

This was the Cats' 16th victory of the season. It meant that, with three games remaining, they could not be removed from top spot. Hawthorn, Port Adelaide, West Coast and the Kangaroos were all jostling for positions below them on 12 wins. Yet Brian Cook's joy over the achievement was reined in when he saw the back page of the *Herald Sun* the following Thursday.

"WANTED: Essendon reveals its plan to poach Williams or Thompson".

Port Adelaide coach Mark Williams, who was under contract, and Cook's own uncontracted coach had been singled out by Essendon chairman Ray Horsburgh to replace Sheedy.

A couple of weeks earlier, the Geelong CEO had a panic attack when the news that No. 1 contender Michael Voss had decided not to step into coaching immediately. He rang Thompson's manager Michael Quinlan seeking some encouragement. "He said, 'What are you worrying about, Cooky?' (But) I had to worry about the future of the footy club, not just today," Cook recalled.

Thompson had spoken to the leadership group about whether his decision not to re-sign was an issue for them. They were comfortable with how he was handling it – it fitted in with the team's ethos of not looking too far ahead. "Once Essendon got rid of Sheedy and all that, Geelong came and said, 'Do you want to re-sign?'" Thompson said.

"I said, 'No. Why change now?' I asked the players about it but it really didn't take up my time. We were on a mission."

chapter 13
Full moon

"(Thompson) said he was doing the same thing, going to bed thinking about holding up the cup at the end of the year. That was fine, as long as when you come to work you know what the process is."

– Tom Harley

"One of the best things that could have happened to the Geelong Football Club was his missus getting pregnant." Tom Harley's theory on Cameron Mooney's transformation has merit. "He just moved onto the next phase of his life," Harley added. Family man, deputy vice-captain and star forward in the best team in the land: it's been quite a change from his previous phase.

Mooney grew up on a farm outside Wagga Wagga, the youngest of three boys and, according to him, the softie of the trio. He left school when he was 16 and headed to the bright lights of Melbourne to hook up with the premiership team, North Melbourne. It had just won the 1996 flag when he walked into Arden St, taken at No. 56 in the national draft. Mooney's head was spinning from the moment he arrived but he was soon brought down to earth when he tore up his knee early in the pre-season. That ended the 1997 season before it had even started; when he finally got on the park the 195cm centre half-forward didn't get out of the reserves.

He made his long-awaited debut in round seven, 1999. Mooney was in and out of the side for the remainder of the home and away season. The Roos were again a force and Mooney played in the qualifying final victory over Port Adelaide but was dropped for the preliminary final in favour of veteran spearhead John Longmire, who had missed the 1996 premiership due to a serious knee injury.

In the dying minutes of that game, with the Roos eight goals to the better over Brisbane, defender Jason McCartney had a brain freeze. He belted one of the Lions and had his number taken; McCartney was subsequently suspended, and Mooney brought in for just his 11th senior game: an AFL Grand Final. After starting in the forward pocket, Mooney made a bad blunder and gave away a 50-metre penalty. Roos coach Denis Pagan benched him and that was where he stayed for most of the afternoon. He got on again in the last quarter – by this time North was demolishing Carlton – but made another mistake. He was again dragged and given a tongue-lashing down the phone by Pagan.

When the siren sounded, Mooney had not touched the ball once. He was the last North player up on the dais to receive a premiership medal; as he came down, Pagan grabbed him and again berated him. He was the only player the coach didn't hug after the game. A week later, Mooney was traded to Geelong to join his brother, Jason, who had started his career at Sydney before switching to the Cats in 1999. North handed Cameron over as part of a deal which landed then Geelong captain Leigh Colbert to Arden St.[21]

Mark Thompson had been Pagan's assistant in 1999 and was keen to take the promising, yet immature, Mooney with him to Skilled Stadium. He could tell there was something special but to that point Thompson felt Mooney was enjoying life off the field as an AFL footballer more than on

21. Injury deprived Colbert of the standout career many believed was ahead of him, though he still managed 209 games, playing one more game (105-104) for the Cats than North prior to retirement after season 2005.

Joel Corey stretches in the rooms. Grand Final Day, 2007.

Grand Final preparation in a dressing room prepared as close to normal as possible.

On their toes ...

A relaxed Steve Johnson, hours before
joining the elite Norm Smith Medal club.

C.LING

Cat veteran Cameron Ling played a key leadership role in the premier's season.

No more waiting as the Cats, led by Tom Harley, head up the race.

Noting Bartel's Brownlow, the Cats' Grand Final Day banner, 2007.

Sizing up the opposition ... and the anthem singer.

Bartel spins, and goals, late in the first quarter.

The Power had their moments of pressure early, but faded fast.

Quarter-time, cup still up for grabs.

Rooke's agression at the ball made him one of his team's best when it counted.

Directions from the box ...

... and out on the ground.

it. In his first four years at Geelong, Mooney floated around, going back and forth from the reserves … or getting suspended. Every year other clubs would ask about him at the trade table; every year Thompson knocked them back. Eventually, the coach had seen enough and laid it on the line – *shape up or you're out* was the message at the start of the 2004 season.

Mooney asked if he could play in defence and everything suddenly clicked. He was a revelation, an important factor in the Cats' run to the preliminary final. He backed up this breakthrough season the following year, his finest hour coming in the 2005 elimination final against Melbourne when injuries to others forced him into the ruck. He dominated the match. One of the most memorable images of the next week's heart-breaking loss to Sydney in the semi-final was Mooney openly crying on the ground shortly after the siren.

So far had he come that, in 2006, Thompson was actually talking him up as a captaincy candidate. He soon changed his tact when Mooney, who commentator Rex Hunt had dubbed "The Big Hairy Cat", started his record-breaking string of suspensions. After he gave Sydney rover Amon Buchanan a jab to the ribs in round 20, which earned him a holiday for the Cats' remaining two matches of the season, Thompson's patience had worn out. "You just have to know the rules," he said. "Ninety-nine per cent of the players adapt to it and you have got one that doesn't. Well, it's his responsibility to change."

There was talk of anger management counselling but Mooney didn't bother. The peer assessment back in December had certainly opened his eyes and from there it was simply a matter of trying to keep things in check. The fact that the team was winning every week certainly helped rein in the temper, although a bit of luck may have also gone his way.

"I didn't really change," he said. "It's just that a lot of the silly little things went out of my game."[22]

The birth of Jagger to his long-time partner, Seona, certainly had a positive impact. He now looked forward to getting back up the highway

---

22. Mooney was not suspended between his four trips to the tribunal in 2006 and Round 8, 2009 – a one-week ban for striking North Melbourne's Scott Thompson. He has faced the tribunal 13 times for a total of 14 weeks' suspension.

after training to his bayside apartment in Melbourne, rather than heading out for a few beers with the boys, which was the way he had lived for most of his football life. He also accepted the responsibility of being in charge of the forward-line and a leader in the team. At 27, Mooney had finally matured.

He cut his hair short to change his image, a point made clear to Ken Hinkley when he asked him to sign a jumper. "I said, 'You can put 'The Big Hairy Cat' on there if you want'," Hinkley said. "He just looked up at me and said, 'Nah, I think we've gone past that, haven't we?' He was pretty blunt about it, that wasn't the message he was selling anymore. He didn't want to be known as that now."

Mooney's relationship with Thompson had also been critical in the turnaround. "We have been pretty good mates since '99," Mooney said. "We've had a couple of ups and downs over the journey but, all in all, I know I get away with a lot more than most people would with him." The big now-not-so-hairy Cat was leading the charge on exacting revenge on his former team in round 20 at the Telstra Dome, kicking three goals in 13 minutes in the opening quarter. While they may have had nothing to play for – given top spot was already sewn up – the fact that the Roos were the last team to beat Geelong, back in round five, was emphasised by the senior players in the lead-up. However, despite a promising five-goal first quarter, the Kangaroos refused to go away and, at the 16-minute mark of the third quarter, the margin was only two points.

Geelong then produced one of its trademark bursts. Steve Johnson (four goals) floated in with some magic to ignite a six-goal blitz which blew the lead out to 37 points at the final break. When Mooney kicked his fifth early in the last term a blow-out was on the cards; the Roos, as their history shows, refused to die.

They clawed back to within a couple of kicks before finally relenting to give Geelong victory No.15 on the trot (by 27 points).

One Cat on a mission that afternoon was Cameron Ling. All week Hinkley had been "into him" about playing on Adam Simpson, who had racked up 42 possessions in the round five game. In an unusual move, the Kangaroos captain had agreed to wear a microphone in the game, which was akin to putting a big red cross on your forehead as far as the Cats hierarchy were concerned.

"I did the opposition stuff and all week I was cranking him up," Hinkley said. "I kept at him saying, 'Linga, he ain't getting 42' and 'Linga, don't let him get 42'. I told him I reckon 10 times during the week and by the end of the week he said, 'I know we don't want him to get the ball'."

Simpson touched it just 10 times. Corey Enright continued a brilliant season as the second tagger, keeping Brent Harvey out of the game, while Gary Ablett shrugged off Brady Rawlings' close attention to collect 31 possessions and kick two goals. Bartel and Corey were both prolific while Harley's rich vein of form continued, keeping Kangaroo dangerman Corey Jones to just five touches.

The captain had come a long way since his mid-season crisis and had even spoken to Thompson about his dreams of holding the premiership cup aloft. "We were just biding our time, treading water and I was like, 'Let's play finals now'," Harley said. "I was starting to think about winning the flag and he was the only bloke in the club who'd been in my position. I wanted to know if I should embrace it or not. He just said to enjoy it because what we were doing was so much fun. He said he was doing the same thing, going to bed thinking about holding up the cup at the end of the year. That was fine, as long as when you come to work you know what the process is and you do that well."

Jimmy Bartel couldn't understand why he felt so stiff. He was having his regular Thursday hit of golf at the Thirteenth Beach course at Barwon Heads but, for some reason, he couldn't loosen up his back during his round. That night he couldn't get comfortable in bed and it happened again when he went to the movies with his teammates the following morning. Before training, Bartel went to see the medical staff.

"I thought I must have eaten some of my own cooking, something crook," Bartel said. "They gave me some stuff but an hour or so later my guts were still a bit crook. I did the warm-up but every time I put my right foot down, all along my right hand side it felt like someone had stabbed me."

He walked off the track and was told to go and see a specialist doctor in town, who suggested appendix was the problem. He gave Bartel his card with a number to call if his condition worsened. Fortunately, Bartel was having dinner at the house of Geoff Allen, one of the club's three doctors, when he started to break out in sweats, such was the unbearable pain.

He was immediately rushed to hospital, where scans revealed his appendix was about to burst. "If it had burst I was screwed," he said. "You then miss seven or eight weeks because they have to cut you right open instead of doing just the key hole stuff."

So it was another night in hospital for the Cats star, who conceded Sunday's home game against Port Adelaide was out of the question. The coaching panel had already decided to rest Joel Selwood from the match but things got even more dramatic when Cameron Ling didn't feel right after testing a niggling hamstring on the beach at Torquay four hours before the opening bounce. All week Port coach Mark Williams had been using the media to stir the pot in an attempt to get inside the heads of the Cats for the top of the table clash. There had even been claims out of Adelaide that he had actually rung Kangaroos coach Dean Laidley for advice on how to get under the Cats' skin.

His hopes of an upset soared when he received the Geelong team sheet 45 minutes before the bounce. King had already been dropped. Now Bartel, Selwood and Ling were out. In came Blake, Byrnes, David Johnson and Henry Playfair for his first game of the season.

Everything was falling into place for Port and things got even better in the first quarter when Gary Ablett fell awkwardly. He got up clutching his knee, tried to take a few steps but had to sit down again. The stadium went silent, fearing the worst. While all eyes were on the bench to see if there was any sign of life for Ablett, Port had kicked five goals to two and looked clearly the superior team.

A six-goal second quarter by the Cats reduced the margin to five points at the long break, by which time Ablett was back on deck. But Williams had done his homework and thrown some unusual tactics at the premiership favourites in the ruck, while a midfield zone caused the slick Geelong machine to momentarily go off the rails.

The first goal of the last quarter extended Port's lead to what looked like a match-winning 25 points. Enter Steve Johnson. The Cats' freak show intercepted a sloppy Peter Burgoyne kick-in and goaled. He then nailed a set shot from the boundary line and, on the next centre break, Johnson got it again at half-forward. Instead of taking the shot, he changed his mind at the last minute and delivered an extraordinary, left-handed look away handball to Chapman, who ran in and kicked the goal.

With two minutes remaining, Ablett trumped Johnson. Brad Ottens, who was playing a lone hand in the ruck (Blake having struggled against Port's experienced pairing of Brendon Lade and Dean Brogan) found Ablett, who somehow evaded three tacklers with a series of lightning baulks to break free and nail a miraculous goal. For the first time since the opening minutes of the game, the Cats were in front.

In recent weeks the team had trained specifically to deal with a close finish. There were certain strategies which were to be employed, depending on whether the team was in front or behind. None of those scenarios had the ball in the hands of Playfair, but that was where it ended in the dying seconds, albeit only briefly, as he was swamped by Port players. The ball spilling out to Domenic Cassisi, Ablett's opponent, who threw it onto his left boot from 40 metres and kicked a goal.

Siren.

Port by five points.

The streak was over.

The crowd and players were stunned. It was like they didn't know how to behave, given it had been four months since they had experienced defeat. After getting over the initial disappointment, Thompson and many of the players started to come around to the belief that the loss may well have been a good thing.

"It gives us something to do again," the coach said. "It has given us some things to work on because clearly Port Adelaide beat us and they did some things to us that we didn't handle. It showed that we didn't know everything."

Ablett described it as a timely wake-up call. "Definitely a good time for us to lose," he said. "Finals are a whole different ball game and it kind of woke us up a bit, just showed (that) if we are not on top of our game this can happen."

James Kelly added: "It made us not think that we were indestructible."

It also showed Harley that Port Adelaide was a legitimate player in the run home. "What it did was galvanise the fact that they are a contender," Harley said. "They had been under the radar, had two streaks of six in a row and I thought, 'Hang on, they will finish top two and get a home preliminary final. Maybe we might play them in a grand final'. All the talk was about West Coast, Sydney and Geelong and then all of a sudden Port Adelaide was amongst it, too."

While the happenings in Geelong were important in the scheme of what lay ahead, another significant moment was taking place two hours away in Bendigo. Max Rooke was making a successful return in the VFL.

Matthew Egan and James Kelly were neighbours growing up in Sunbury and every day had walked together to Salesian College. By their senior year, Kelly was the football star and Egan the brilliant tennis player.

Egan had grown up an Essendon fan – his favourite player was Damien Hardwick and he had a poster of Gavin Wanganeen on his wall. But he stopped playing football after one season in the under 12s. Tennis and basketball were his main loves and he was good enough with racquet in hand to reach the satellite level.

At 18, the social lure of football drew him back and he started playing again for Oak Park in the Essendon District League, playing a role in the 2002 premiership. He loved it. Kelly, who was already playing senior football at Geelong, suggested he ditch the tennis permanently and have a crack at making the Cats' VFL side.

Kelly then asked VFL coach Ron Watt if his mate could come down for a run. Egan already had the size (196cm, 101kg) and agility, thanks to his tennis skills, but he couldn't kick. In 2003, he was in and out of the VFL side, spending time back playing with Oak Park (who won the premiership again that year) or St Joseph's in the Geelong league when he didn't get picked. The next year he quit his apprenticeship as an electrician and moved in with Tom Harley in Torquay. He started mowing lawns and working at the Rip Curl factory before Kelly urged him to have a serious crack at making the grade as a footballer.

Egan started staying behind after training, kicking hundreds of balls and working diligently on his skills. By the end of 2004 he had made the VFL team of the year. A couple of months later, Geelong selected him with pick No. 62 in the national draft. He capped off his remarkable rise to prominence by debuting in round one in 2005 as a replacement for Harley, who had actually hurt his foot landing on Egan's ankle at training. One of his first acts as a senior player was to go back with the flight of the ball and get crunched by Richmond's Matthew Richardson.

A brief stint back in the reserves occurred when Harley returned but Egan won his spot back in round 12; he hasn't been out of the side since. Geelong's final home and away game of the 2007 season against Brisbane at the Gabba was his 57th in a row.

In 2007 the 24-year-old took his game to another level. While Harley was absent with injury, Egan stepped up and became the premier centre half-back in the competition, taking on and beating the game's best key forwards including Nick Riewoldt and Matthew Pavlich.

"I have always had the mentality that I just want to do my team role," Egan said. "I am not a player that gets many kicks, I am just rapt to play and compete. I love playing on good players and I know when the games are coming up and Sando says you are playing on someone like a Riewoldt, I really look forward to the challenge."

This round 22 Brisbane visit presented the biggest and best of them all, Lions superstar Jonathan Brown. And it was all going well for Egan early. He took a couple of marks and held his ground well against Brown, yet everything changed dramatically in the final minute of the first quarter. Egan jumped up to spoil – as he had hundreds of times before – only this time his landing was awkward. He came down on the front of his foot. Initially, he didn't think anything of it and played on. At quarter-time he went to the bench, sat down and pointed out to Chris Bradshaw where he was experiencing the pain in his right foot. The doctor instantly froze. He had a fair idea what it was but held his tongue. "I didn't want to put the fear of God into anyone," Bradshaw said later. [23]

---

23. Bradshaw's instincts were correct; Egan had broken a bone in his foot. The injury did not heal correctly, and Egan – who played all 22 games to that point of season 2007 – has not played AFL football again.

Kelly came over and asked how he was. "When he described what he did I didn't want to say it to him then, as it would have shattered him, but I knew that he'd done something bad," he said.

The Cats had been on cruise control in the first half but they flicked the switch with six third quarter goals to lead by that margin at the final break. It increased early in the final quarter before Brown, perhaps enjoying Egan's absence, kicked four goals on Scarlett and Milburn to take his match tally to seven.

It was all to no avail: the Cats ended an amazing home and away season with a typically convincing 42-point victory.

Joel Selwood, whose brother Troy was one of the Lions' best, was again superb. Blake played his best game for a while, which released Ottens (four goals) forward. Mooney, who split the webbing in his left hand in the first quarter, played on and booted four goals while Steve Johnson was dynamic. He and Stokes each kicked three goals.

Enright was also among the best and had produced the highlight of the game when he had his shorts ripped off by Brisbane's Michael Rischitelli in a tackle. Much to the delight of Thompson in the coaches' box, he simply kept on playing for a couple of minutes, picking up more possessions wearing his blue Speedos. The next day the side flew back to Melbourne and Egan stayed at his girlfriend's house that night.

He was starting to panic. "I couldn't sleep, I couldn't walk," he said. "I thought, 'Something is wrong here'. I had never had an injury before … I had never been injured in my whole life."

At 9.30am on Monday, Egan hobbled into St John of God hospital for scans. When he got to the club with the results he couldn't find Bradshaw straight away so he left the X-rays on his desk. When he returned a few minutes later, he found a group of players, the physios and Bradshaw holding up his scans and looking at them. "I walked in and looked at the doc and I could tell straight away that it wasn't good," Egan said.

Bradshaw cleared the room and sat down. He pointed at the thin dark line in the middle of the X-ray: a fracture in his navicular bone. "This is probably your season (over)," he said. Tears immediately welled in Egan's eyes. "But there is a little chance of playing," Bradshaw said.

That didn't even register with Egan "I've got to get out of here," he said.

He went into the locker room, got his bag and was headed for the door when Joel Corey bumped into him. "You okay, man?" he said.

"No, it's fucked," Egan responded.

Corey, who at this stage obviously knew little of the diagnosis, tried to be encouraging. "Oh, you'll be right."

By the time Egan got to his car he was a mess. It was over. The hard work, the late night skills sessions just to make it ... now only a couple of games away from playing in a grand final, and possibly a premiership, it had been ripped away from him.

He was crying when Corey came running out. The latter had been told the news and felt terrible. For the next 15 minutes, the pair stayed in Egan's car and shed some tears together. Kelly went around to Egan's house in the afternoon after training to be with his best mate.

"I was shattered," Kelly said. "If there is anyone who deserved to play in a grand final or a premiership it was Matty Egan. He had worked his arse off from the moment he got here. He is just a great bloke and you want blokes like that to have those sorts of things.

"It was so hard sitting there seeing how upset he was. He is a very positive, happy sort of guy. All the time we have known each other, that is the first time I have actually seen him really down."

chapter 14
Something special

"He is the best young kid we've had at the club by a mile. I mean, we've had Gary Ablett, Jimmy Bartel, Cameron Ling, Joel Corey, those sorts of guys, but he is the best we have had."

– Mark Thompson on Joel Selwood

Joel Corey is hard. There are not many harder players in the competition, and he is revered at Geelong. When the ball is his object, generally nothing stops him from getting it. Until 2007. "A lot of times out on the ground, I will be running straight for the ball, this thing just goes *whack!*" Corey said. "I am only a second or two away and I'm like, 'What the hell was that?'"

That was his rookie teammate Joel Selwood.

Never before has a first-year player had such an impact on a team and the competition. Even after his first couple of months at the club, people were already declaring Selwood would be the next captain of Geelong. "When he talks to you one-on-one it is almost like you're the rookie and he is the experienced guy," Brenton Sanderson said. "He would almost be lecturing me on how to coach and how to go about my life. Seriously, that's what it felt like. This 18-year-old kid telling me how to run my life and stuff, how to coach and what we should be doing on the field. To come in and have an impact in that midfield like he did, he is a special kid."

Not does Mark Thompson hide his admiration. "He's incredible," he said. "He is the best young kid we've had at the club by a mile. I mean we've had Gary Ablett, Jimmy Bartel, Cameron Ling, Joel Corey, those sorts of guys, but he is the best we have had. He is going to be pretty special."

He is quickly becoming Ling's favourite player. "What I love most about him is that he has got talent but he is hard, he puts his head over the ball," he said.

"You see right across the AFL every year these young guys come in and they might turn it on for one game, pop out of nowhere, but they don't get immediate respect because they don't do it consistently. They don't have the respect for really putting their head over the ball, whereas Joel just keeps winning respect from all the boys. He is that old-fashioned footballer who has got the footy brain, which helps a lot, but he just works really hard on his game."

They all agree that Selwood had watched and learned from his AFL-playing brothers, Troy (Brisbane) and Adam (West Coast), and was practically pre-programmed on how to become a league player from day one. The first part of that process had started the previous year when he listened to some crucial advice when weighing up whether to play on with his troublesome knee – and therefore shore up his draft prospects – or take the risk and sit out the year.

"I had a month to think about it," Selwood said. "I went up to Brisbane for two weeks and I was deciding on whether I should keep playing throughout the year or take it easy and get the body right for draft camp and the next year. I decided to do that because I had a lot of good people saying, 'Just take it easy. You are going to get drafted so don't worry about things at the moment.'"

In May, Selwood went under the knife again. It was his fourth knee operation in two years. The initial operation to fix cartilage which had come off the bone didn't work; the screws had come out and it started to crack. "I primed my body the year before because I had the knee operations and stuff," Selwood said. "I knew I could play AFL football. I saw Marc Murphy and guys like that who went through the year before who I had played with and played against.

"I would like to see myself up with them so when I saw they were playing football and I was sitting out, I was sort of biting my nails thinking, 'What is going on here?' I always wanted to play and I wanted to play early."

Patience was rewarded. Selwood's extraordinary 2007 season was capped off on the Wednesday before the qualifying final (Geelong was to play the Kangaroos on Sunday at the MCG) when he was named the 2007 NAB Rising Star, becoming the first recipient of the Ron Evans Medal, named after former AFL Commission chairman Ron Evans, who died in March.

Selwood polled 44 of a possible 45 votes to defeat Collingwood midfielder Scott Pendlebury. He averaged 19 possessions in his 18 games for the season, ranked third in tackles (83), fourth in clearances (60), sixth in goal assists (15), seventh in hard-ball gets (46) and eighth in marks (98).

His mother, Maree, and father, Bryce, had made the trip down from Bendigo to attend the lunch. They knew the way: Troy and Adam were nominees for the award in successive weeks in 2005.

Brendan McCartney was there to enjoy the moment on behalf of the coaching panel. "We've got some terrific players down there. At times they've all made massive impacts on games (but) he just hasn't put in a bad game," McCartney said. "He's maintained his attack on the ball, fitted in with how the team's played and just wanted to win, week in and week out."

Selwood appeared much happier when the interviews and photos were done and he could get back down the highway. "I was just ready to go out and play," he said.

So were his teammates.

The wait for finals football was finally over. The mood in the playing group was about proving a point, for they were less than impressed with what they were reading and hearing from the Kangaroos' camp in the lead-up.

"We were notorious this year for giving nothing in the media," Tom Harley said. "They were on the front foot saying rankings are irrelevant now, it was all about getting in the top four and whether we are one and they are four is irrelevant. We were sort of sitting back, and without voicing it to anyone, thinking, 'You are kidding, aren't you? We were ranked number one because, look at the stats, we smashed everything. We are the best side in it'.

"They were saying, 'We don't fear Geelong'. We're like, okay, fair enough. We played them three weeks ago and they threw absolutely everything at us and, in the space of 10 minutes, we put on eight goals. We just knew we were better than North Melbourne so we were sitting back listening to them say all this stuff and we're like, 'Okay, let's just play.'"

Matthew Scarlett knew that, despite the brilliant home and away season, the sceptics were lining up waiting for a fall. "We did want to send a message," he said. "I think a lot of people were waiting for us to fall over. They kept bringing up Geelong haven't done this, haven't done that. We were a totally different side. It was Geelong 2007, it wasn't Geelong 1995 or any of that bullshit. We wanted to go out and make a stand."

Darren Milburn agreed. "We wanted to show the football world we could play."

One of the many successful initiatives introduced in '07 was the players taking charge of the final session of the week, which was always the day before the game. They determined the drills and ran the whole session as the coaches took a back seat. When McCartney walked off Skilled Stadium that Saturday morning he was a happy man.

"They were ready for a big game," he said. "Their preparation during the week was faultless. They were ready mentally and physically, they trained really well on the Wednesday and the day before (the game). They were up and about, they were ready for it. It was important for us to win our first final because it just re-affirms that you belong there."

The question of belonging was being asked about the Kangaroos in the first pre-game warm-up, 30 minutes before the start of the game. Twice they ran into Geelong's mandated space. League rules stipulate that each side has its own half of the ground for the warm-up and that under no circumstances should teams stray into the other end.

Cameron Mooney was sitting down doing a stretch when the Roos passed dangerously close the first time. He was finishing off a sprint along the square when they approached again. "They planned it, I know they did," Mooney said. "It really pissed me off and I was abusing the shit out of them."

When Kangaroos captain Adam Simpson brushed past him, Mooney lashed out. Steve Johnson was standing next to him and soon they had Roos players converging on them. "We were in there fighting them and then thought 'We'd better get out of this before they investigate something,'" Johnson said. "I had my jumper ripped off and soon I was out the back," Mooney recalled. "I couldn't believe they did it but they stuffed up. It just got us even more determined to give it to them."

Thompson was angry at the Roos' tactics and stood in the centre of the ground shaking his head and glaring at the Kangaroos officials (who were later handed a $10,000 fine). Ken Hinkley took it at as a good sign. "I saw that and thought, 'Pheewww, our boys are ready,'" he said. "I would have thought you don't do that to this team, we were as hard as any team playing, I've got no doubt about that. Basically, it just ensured that when they went out it was going to be: 'Cop this!'"

Jimmy Bartel was back in the side after missing two weeks following his appendix operation, taking the place of Travis Varcoe, who had probably had his worst two weeks for the season at the most inopportune time. Max Rooke was also making his long-awaited return after two weeks in the VFL, replacing Matthew Egan, who had had three screws inserted into his foot earlier in the week. A positive surgeon's report had him clinging onto the idea of a miracle comeback.

Given the two teams had played recently, the Cats' match committee planned a few match-up surprises. Ling, who had silenced Adam Simpson in round 20, was going to tag Brent Harvey and Corey Enright shadow Daniel Wells. James Kelly would keep an eye on Simpson this time while the plan in the forward line was for Paul Chapman to match up with Glenn Archer, who had been influential three weeks earlier across half-back, and play as a leading option out of the goalsquare ... in the process keeping him away from the Cats' main target in Mooney.

When Roos tagger Brady Rawlings went to Corey and not Gary Ablett or Bartel – and they loaded up their forward-line with talls to capitalise on Egan's absence – the Cats coaches' box was a happy place. The ball hadn't even been bounced and the plan was falling into place.

That didn't change when the ball came alive, Bartel going hard at the first contest and earning the first kick of the game for a high tackle. A minute later, Archer went back with the flight to help out Shannon Watt in a contest with Mooney, leaving Chapman free to run onto the spill and kick the opening goal of the game from 40 metres. Bartel had seven touches in the first seven minutes but the Roos showed some fight. Michael Firrito, the regular full-back who had been moved away from Mooney and onto Nathan Ablett, kicked a brilliant running goal to even the scores at the eight-minute mark. At the next centre bounce, Leigh Brown came off the wing and ran straight through Ling, knocking the stuffing out of him. He was still lying on his back in the middle of the ground when ruckman Hamish McIntosh kicked an excellent goal from the pocket to give the Kangaroos the lead.

Chapman answered immediately thanks to a one-two handball with Mooney and a quality left-foot snap and the crowd was again on its feet a minute later when the warhorse Ling returned to the field to resume hostilities with Harvey. No more goals were scored for the remaining 10 minutes, and a five-point lead read Geelong's way at the first break.

It only took 48 seconds in the second quarter for Chapman to collect his third. A brilliant Gary Ablett tackle on Roos defender Daniel Pratt was awarded holding the ball; Mathew Stokes ran on with the advantage and hit Chapman, lace out on the lead, 40 metres out. Mooney and Stokes kicked the next two of the game before the Cats produced the play of the year.

At the 18-minute mark, James Kelly found himself under pressure in the back pocket but managed to fire off a quick handball to Scarlett ... who took off and started running straight up the middle of the ground ... he sent a long handball to Selwood ... who produced a brilliant back-step baulk to evade a would-be tackler ... in the same motion he lobbed a left-handed handball into the running line of Gary Ablett. Surrounded by three Kangaroos, Ablett had time to grab it and release quickly to Ling, who gave it straight back. "This is the reason they are premiership favourites," Dennis Cometti gasped as he followed the play in the Channel 7 commentary box. Ablett ran through the centre and kicked across to Stokes on the outer forward flank. He marked, played on and shot a left-handed handball across to Mooney, who ran in from 40 metres and kicked the team goal of the season.

It had been breathtaking. Many of the 77,630 crowd were left wondering when was the last time they'd seen such a clinical, ruthless and efficient team in operation. The Kangaroos may have been thinking the same thing.

Shannon Byrnes out-marked Archer two minutes later and, while lining up, casually handballed to Bartel next to him, who unloaded a drop punt straight through the middle from 55 metres. The game was teetering on the edge for the Kangaroos.

A rare stray handball from Andrew Mackie in his defensive goalsquare gave Shannon Grant a goal against the flow. It instantly changed the demeanour in the coaches' box. "*Sloppy!*" Thompson yelled in frustration. Three minutes earlier he'd seen perfection, yet so focussed was the coach on getting the next three games right that a silly error, even when his side was six goals up and dominating, still riled him. He sent runner Duncan Kellaway out to haul Mackie from the ground.

Yet it was only a momentary glitch. Mooney earned his third for the quarter at the 25-minute mark after yet another Scarlett dash complemented expert Steve Johnson vision. Nathan Ablett joined in the party just before the siren when he accepted a pass from Bartel – his 19th possession for the half – and nailed the tough shot from deep in the forward pocket to make it a 45-point lead at half-time.

The rooms were alive. Geelong was keen to make a statement and the foot didn't come off the pedal at the resumption, with Chapman again the one who got them going in the third quarter. He kicked his fourth goal at the nine-minute mark after a beautiful Mackie pass.

A trademark David Wojcinski three-bounce dash was the highlight of the term, his long kick ending in a one-hand Steve Johnson mark in the goalsquare. Mooney kicked his fourth two minutes later before Brad Ottens joined the act to kick his first goal for the afternoon.

On the siren, Mooney kicked his fifth, a set shot from 50 metres. He was instantly jumped on by his teammates, who were now 75 points up and had the commentators reaching for the record books. Thompson urged his charges to go in for the kill yet stick to the gameplan. "I'm not interested in this final, I'm interested in playing footy," he said.

The final quarter was a procession. Seven goals to two with Enright, who had kept Wells to just 14 possessions, chiming in with two of his own. Ling had kept Harvey to just seven touches, one of those being a questionable free kick and goal 10 minutes into the last quarter. There were good players everywhere but a couple of important performances came from Nathan Ablett (three goals) and Josh Hunt, who played his best game for some time.

Fittingly, it was Chapman who finished it with a Steve Johnson handball over the top supplying his fifth goal from the goalsquare. The final margin was 106 points, the biggest margin by a Geelong team in the finals and only the fifth time in history a final had been decided by more than 100 points.

As Thompson headed down the race, he stopped to shake the hand of president Frank Costa. "It doesn't get any better than this," Costa enthused.

"Let's keep a lid on it," the coach said.

When he arrived in the rooms he was immediately disturbed with what he saw. There was a lot of people in the rooms surrounding the players. Lots of laughing and high-fiving. Thompson called over Steve Hocking and the fitness guys, Paul Haines and Dean Robinson, and told them to settle it down.

"It was just messy," he said. "There was a lot of backslapping, a lot of people around. There was this excitement that we had won a final but I was thinking it's only one final, there are still a couple of things we have to do. There were a lot of young players in there at the club, we had won our first final ... even though they didn't play in it they were excited. We had to stop all that and make sure the next time we played it was more professional."

Still, at the post-match press conference Thompson was glowing. "It was awesome," he said. "Everything we talked about during the week, it came true. For a few weeks we were waiting for this day to arrive. Sometimes it can overwhelm you, today it didn't. We've played some awesome footy, (we talked about) how important it was just to go out and enjoy what we're doing and just keep doing much of the same.

"The more you talk about it sometimes the more you worry about it. And we didn't want our boys to worry. I thought coming to the game they were quite relaxed and calm."

Asked about the importance of having a week's rest, Thompson said: "We'll take it; we don't really need it but we'll certainly take it."

He singled out Ling for praise. "I have a huge amount of respect for Cameron," Thompson said. "At the start of the year, when people were writing him off and telling him he is out of footy, I said, 'I believe in you', and I do. I just think he is one of these guys who keeps adapting because he is such a well-prepared person."

Kangaroos coach Dean Laidley was stunned. His stats sheet showed him his side had touched the ball just 274 times compared to Geelong's 407. "They just smashed us physically," Laidley said. "It was men against boys out there."

Chapman declared it the Cats' best four-quarter performance of the year. "I probably think this is the first time we have done it, the best we have played for four quarters would have been today," he said. "The guys just know our process works, and if we do that to the best of our ability then we are going to be hard to beat. Today we played the way we have wanted to all year, we did it for four quarters. We know it works and if we keep sticking to that then it is going to take a good side to get over the top of us."

The Monday review was short and sharp, and for good reason. When the coaches looked through the tape of the qualifying final they couldn't find any negatives to highlight to the players. "We debated it as coaches, because when you're giving feedback to your players, we're saying 'We were really pleased'," Thompson said.

"Obviously, everybody who follows Geelong were pleased. We said 'Aw, we'll knock them down a bit' and then we said 'Well, why?' Players get knocked down enough, clubs get knocked down enough - if you actually perform, give them the recognition they deserve. There wasn't really any part of the game that we had to improve."

Missing from the Monday activities was Mooney, who had again split the webbing in his hand and had been taken by the Cats medical staff to a plastic surgeon to have it immediately repaired. The operation would keep him out of action for a week or so because he would have to wear a brace but the doctors were confident he would be training for the final session leading into the preliminary final.

How to handle the week off for the rest of the team was a matter of great debate throughout the football department. It was obviously foreign territory and it was ultimately decided to lighten off the training rather than replicate match conditions with a hard Saturday session.

Thompson and McCartney would take that session with Sanderson, Hinkley and Bruce Cohen, a former AFL reserves player at a number of clubs who had been his assistant all year with the opposition analysis, flying to Perth to watch the Friday night semi-final between West Coast and Collingwood. The winner would play Geelong in the preliminary final the following Friday night at the MCG.

It was an intriguing match-up. The Eagles went in with the home ground advantage but without its three midfield stars. Daniel Kerr was out with a finger injury; Chris Judd had finally succumbed to groin and ankle injuries after struggling through the previous week; and Ben Cousins had torn his hamstring badly in the thrilling three-point loss to Port Adelaide at AAMI Stadium.

Meanwhile, Collingwood had easily defeated Sydney in its qualifying final on the Saturday night at the MCG and was beginning to gain momentum. They were healthy, confident and had a great record interstate under Mick Malthouse, courtesy of the disciplined way they played.

The match was a classic and it played right into the hands of Geelong. West Coast looked home late in the third quarter, leading by 22 points, but full-back Darren Glass was taken from the ground for a rest. This sparked a relative Collingwood avalanche, goals to Alan Didak and Anthony Rocca (who Glass had been beating easily) in the final two minutes reducing the margin to just four points.

After a gripping final term arm wrestle that was exhausting even to watch, the scores were tied when the siren sounded. In extra time – two five-minute quarters with a change of ends – the youth of Collingwood prevailing over the banged-up Eagles. Sanderson left Subiaco happy with the outcome. "It was an absolute slog and one of the most competitive games of footy I have seen in a long time," he said. "(Collingwood) had to fly back, apparently (at) low altitude, but then back up with a six-day break after playing extra time, playing a side with a week off. You couldn't help but think this is all set up for us."

Hinkley had noted how Malthouse had worked the interchange bench non-stop to help keep his players as fresh as possible. "Obviously Glass going off was a big factor but what I noticed about Collingwood was that they were giving everything," he said. "They were making 100 interchanges a week and they were keeping their players as fresh as they could. What it did do was made sure the whole group had an even spread of game time."

Thompson knew what human nature would be telling his players and all Cats fans. "It was a tight game, they played extra time, so you couldn't really help but think Collingwood would be tired," he said.

Harley was at a wedding that night, but he was keeping an eye on the score as best he could. "I was thinking, 'Who do I want to win?' Probably West Coast because they were stuffed," he said. "Although maybe if we played West Coast we might have taken them for granted, playing them over here in front of our crowd.

"Collingwood had to be tired but the one thing I learnt from the mid-year game against them was that you can never take them for granted. Playing them at the 'G, it's like they are playing with 19 men. If there was ever any doubt about us underestimating Collingwood, you had to get it out of your head pretty quick smart because there was going to be 100,000 people there on the big stage."

chapter 15

No second chance

*"We kept saying it is not about the result. But all of a sudden it sort of **was** all about that. Everyone, from the coaches to the players, sensed that all of a sudden it was cut throat."*

– Tom Harley

G iven that Geelong had only had one All-Australian selection in his time as coach, Mark Thompson figured four or five would be a pleasing result as he sat down surrounded by the competition's elite at the All-Australian dinner. The biggest knock on his team had been its lack of star quality. He didn't subscribe to the theory and figured the next couple of hours would prove him right.

Since Garry Hocking was selected on the interchange bench in 1996, the only Geelong player to feature in the All-Australian team had been Matthew Scarlett. Two years in a row, 2003-04, the Cats' full-back held the same position in the team of the year.

That was about to change, dramatically, as the premiership favourites provided nine players in the squad of 40. The AFL had introduced a new system. It released nominations in groups – for instance, 12 defenders were named for the six spots – to generate debate and excitement about the event.

All the players nominated had to attend the dinner and, unlike previously, they had no idea whether they were in or not. The team record for players selected was held by Brisbane in 2002, when they had six named. Essendon's dominant 2000 team could only supply four All-Australians.

The locks for Geelong looked to be Scarlett again, Gary Ablett and Jimmy Bartel. The six others – Darren Milburn, Matthew Egan, Steve Johnson, Cameron Mooney, Joel Corey and Cameron Ling – all deserved a spot, though most of them were viewing the night as more of a distraction than anything else. In truth, Ling was hoping he wasn't the odd one out, while Egan, who had made significant progress with his injured foot and was already running again, was convinced he was just there for the nice meal.

The biggest discussion around the Geelong table was how ruckman Brad Ottens had been snubbed. A week earlier he had destroyed Hamish McIntosh and the Kangaroos' big man was one of three ruckmen named in the group of nominations, along with Port Adelaide's Brendon Lade and West Coast's Dean Cox. There was also a case to say Corey Enright's name should have been in the defenders group, given the likes of Fremantle's Roger Hayden, Sydney's Nick Malceski and Brisbane's Jed Adcock had made the grade.

When host Clinton Grybas got proceedings under way, it was Scarlett who was first up on the stage after being selected in the back pocket. West Coast's Darren Glass was named at full-back. While obviously pleased to be recognised for a third time, Scarlett's excitement levels rose significantly when the other back pocket's name was read out: his best mate Milburn had finally been rewarded. The 30-year-old, who had strung together 68 consecutive matches, had enjoyed his best statistical return in 11 senior AFL seasons, averaging 21 disposals and seven marks per game, including a career-best 33 disposals against Richmond in round 18.

Adelaide star Andrew McLeod was named on the half-back flank and then came the first surprise of the evening. "The All-Australian centre half-back is ... *Matthew Egan from Geelong*". Egan heard what Grybas had just said but for a few seconds the words didn't register.

He then panicked. Egan had an understanding with media manager Kevin Diggerson that he was happy to do print interviews but never television because he got too nervous. That was all about to change as he headed up to the stage and past all the television cameras which were beaming the function live through the Fox Football channel.

"I was looking around our table and the other tables and I thought, 'I am just making up the numbers here,'" said Egan, who had conceded just 30 goals for the season. "I saw Scarlo and Dasher go up and then my name was read out. I was shocked. I was so nervous about actually having to talk up on stage because it was the first time I have ever done an interview on TV. I was shaking."

He survived, and his heartbeat was just returning to normal when Bartel joined him on the stage. The midfield star had been named in the centre with Port Adelaide's Cornes brothers, Chad and Kane, on either side of him on the wings. Bartel's numbers for the season certainly told the story. He averaged 27 possessions, was second in Geelong's tackle count and featured in the top five of every other category, including marks, inside 50s, rebound 50s, hard-ball gets and loose-ball gets.

The first time Johnson had even thought about All-Australian honours was a month earlier when his name had been thrown up in the media. He didn't take it seriously; it was crazy to think he would come under consideration given where he'd come from. "I suppose I would never, ever have thought I would be any chance of getting close to even the squad of the All-Australian at the start of the year," he said at the time. "Then a few weeks ago I started to see a few things in the media but I still didn't think about it because you would be kidding yourself to even think you could be close to that given how far away from that I was six months earlier."

Maybe the All-Australian selectors believed in fairytales. Or maybe Johnson's 41 goals from 17 games earned his position on the All-Australian half-forward flank. By this stage, chief executive Brian Cook had started to feel a little nervous. While it was a great achievement for the players and the club, he couldn't help but think about the salary cap and the All-Australian bonuses linked to most players' contracts. Not to mention what leverage an All-Australian had when negotiating new deals.[24]

At least the next Cat called up had recently agreed on a new contract, thought Cook, as he watched Mooney stride onto the stage to take his spot in the forward pocket. A career-best 55 goals during the home and away season had got him the position next to Fremantle's Matthew Pavlich, who had been named at full-forward.

For many observers, the presence on stage of Mooney and Johnson was an illustration of how far Geelong had come. The reformed hothead and the reformed drinker had turned their lives around and were now All-Australians. While Cook and Neil Balme, who was sitting across from his CEO, had reason to be slightly anxious, Thompson was admiring the fact that six out of the 12 players named so far had been his players, and Brownlow Medal favourite, Gary Ablett, was still to come.

He didn't have to wait long for that to happen. Ablett was named rover in a following division which included West Coast pair Daniel Kerr and Cox. Ablett's statistics were phenomenal: he had racked up 585 disposals in 22 rounds, second only to Kane Cornes. He had twice set a career-high of 35 touches, and had kicked 26 goals and led the AFL in inside 50s.

The interchange was next to be revealed and, after Lade and Essendon full-back Dustin Fletcher were read out, Ling was reaching for his car keys. "This sucks mate, let's go home," he said to Corey. He hadn't wanted to come in the first place but the club, via the AFL, had made it clear he had to be there. He definitely didn't need to be sitting around sipping water in a suit in Melbourne four days out from a preliminary final.

Corey was asking Diggerson if he knew the team and, like Ling, was sinking further into his seat when his name was read out. Corey's consistency had got him over the line. He had finished third in disposals – just three less than Ablett – and his 117 clearances were just one behind league leader, Sydney's Brett Kirk.

Ling's initial fears had become a reality. History showed the All-Australian selectors rarely went for taggers and, given Kane Cornes, who

24. It was to become a common problem for Cook: the Cats had nine, seven and five All-Australians from 2007-2009, with Ablett and Scarlett chosen in all three teams.

played a similar role, was already included, Ling figured he was long odds to win the final spot. But just as he was scanning the exits, it came.

There was to be no odd-one out. Ling joined his teammates in an extraordinary All-Australian feast as Geelong claimed nine of the 22 spots. Ling's ability to shut down the competition's finest midfielders had been complemented with a super efficient 27.4 goals, which had swayed the selectors in the end.

Cook was left shaking his head. He looked across at Balme, who started laughing as the pair exchanged knowing glances. "He knew exactly what I was thinking," Cook said. "I was so pleased for the guys but at the same time thinking from an organisational point of view how we are going to handle this. I was sitting in the All-Australian dinner thinking this is the best thing and the worst thing that could be happening to us. I'm couldn't help but think, '*Ka-ching, ka-ching*', in regards to how we were going to manage our contracts from here on in."

The photographers wanted the nine Cats to line up for a group shot – it was a reasonable bet that this was the first and last time a team contributed almost 50 per cent of the All-Australian line-up. Mooney was as surprised as anyone but made the point that it wouldn't mean much if the Cats didn't do the right thing on Friday night against Collingwood … who didn't even get one player in the top 40.

"It shows you we have had a pretty good year, but all we are worried about is this week," Mooney said. "It is a massive game for us. If you have nine players in the All-Australian side, it would be a bit of a let-down if you don't have a big year in the end."

Two weeks earlier, Egan had been in tears in the carpark. Now he was an All-Australian and a big chance to play again if his teammates did the right thing in the preliminary final. "I am pretty surprised how quickly it has healed," he said. "This week I am up running, training and doing skills. I don't think they would risk me this Friday, but come two weeks I'll be fine. I'm pretty much (pain-free). It gets a little bit sore after running, but you have to expect that. If I want to put myself in a situation of playing, I'm going to have to push it a little bit, but I don't want to risk my future.

"I am only 24. I'm still pretty young in footy, and the docs won't do that.

They wouldn't risk my health or anything. If I played I would be 100 per cent and I wouldn't be risking my long-term future."

Twelve hours later Egan was bouncing around Skilled Stadium. He was still on a high from the All-Australian night and was about to start his fourth running session since ridding himself of his protective boot. As he began stretching with Duncan Kellaway, the physio asked how everything was going. "I feel great," he replied.

There had been some discussion with the medical team about whether he might need orthotics inside his boot to help give the foot more support. After four stride-throughs, Egan decided to give them a shot. The next stride through felt a bit funny and, by the time he'd completed three more, he could hardly walk.

"I thought it didn't feel right and then at the end I was gone," Egan said. "The orthotics were too hard and they stuffed the foot again."

Dr Chris Bradshaw wasn't totally shocked. Even Egan, while again bitterly disappointed, wasn't surprised he'd been unable to pull off the miracle. Shortly after coming out of the surgery he'd spoken to John Quinn, Essendon's high performance manager whom he knew from his tennis days, about James Hird's troubles with the same injury.

"(Quinn) thought I was crazy attempting it," Egan said. "But I thought I had to give it a chance so I could look back and say, 'At least I gave it a crack.' But it didn't work."

He was forced back on his crutches and decided the best thing for him was to get out of Geelong. Egan headed for the sanctuary of his parents' home in Melbourne about the same time that his teammates were going through their paces in the critical main training session before the preliminary final.

While devastated for Egan, the coaches couldn't afford distraction and they were already sensing they had some troubles of their own. Training had been terrible. Balls were being dropped and there was a clear nervousness pervading the group, not just the players but the support staff as well.

Two weeks earlier, McCartney had walked off convinced the team was ready. Now he was geniunely concerned. "They didn't quite have the same spark at training," he said. "For some reason there was a lot of tension in the air."

Harley had picked up the same vibe: "It was the first time for the whole year where the result mattered," he said. "We'd gone through the whole year, the minor rounds obviously mattered but were not sudden death and we didn't have to play for top spot because we'd won that with three games to go.

"We had a second chance in the first final but now all of sudden it was like, 'Shit, if we lose we are out'. We kept saying we have got to stick to the process and it is not about the result. But all of a sudden it sort of *was* all about that. Everyone, from the coaches to the players, sensed that all of a sudden it was cut throat and we went away from what made us a good side, which was the process."

Melbourne's city centre was in gridlock two hours before the game. Traffic simply was not moving anywhere as the biggest crowd of the year converged on the MCG. There was an eerie feeling hovering over the stadium and when Mooney arrived in the rooms he had a worrying sixth sense. "I was worried we'd basically played the game 100 times during the two weeks off," he said.

It was obvious to the players that Thompson was just as nervous as they were and the pre-game meeting went a lot longer than usual, which didn't help the anxiety levels. There had been no change to the team from the qualifying final and when Steven King, who was playing in the VFL Grand Final on Sunday, made his way to his seat in the stands he was convinced that if Geelong won his hopes of playing in the AFL Grand Final rested in the hands of Mark Blake.

"I thought no matter how well I play on the Sunday, I can't play myself into a game here," King said. "Blakey can only play himself out."

Across in the executive seats, the knots in Cook's stomach were tightening. He had already been to the MCG earlier in the day, along with Thompson and president Frank Costa, to receive $14 million from Federal Treasurer Peter Costello for the stage two development of Skilled Stadium. The $28 million project was scheduled to begin after the 2008 season and expected to be completed by 2010.

Once finished, the Cats' home ground would be able to house 30,000 spectators and generate $800,000 a year in profit for the club. The State

Government was set to contribute $6 million, with the AFL having committed $2.5 million.

At the press conference that morning, Thompson had been asked about his unusual preparation for the preliminary final. "This is not a distraction at all," he said. "Today, with the way we coach, most of the work is already done. We don't have much to do with the players before tonight, to be honest."

When the Cats emerged from the tunnel, the stadium erupted. The force of a 98,002 crowd punched them in the face, for the noise was something none of them had experienced before. Shannon Byrnes was next to Steve Johnson. They had been Collingwood supporters as kids, and they both paused and looked at each other. "Can you believe this?" Byrnes asked, incredulous.

Harley won the toss and the Cats linked arms and formed a circle, just as they had before every game this season. It had been the captain's idea after watching the Australian cricket team do it earlier in the year. "Instead of the old tight huddle where everyone surrounds the captain, ours is in a ring and the 22 of us get arm-in-arm," he said. "It is just perfect for everyone to sort of talk. I'll say something and then I'll say, 'Jimmy, you got anything to say?' He'll talk about hardness and then someone else will add something."

The good news for the Cats was the late withdrawal of Collingwood's No. 1 ruckman, Josh Fraser, who again hadn't overcome a back injury. This meant Guy Richards and Chris Bryan had the task of curbing Ottens.

Ling again went to Dane Swan, who had lined up at half-forward. Next to them, Harley was on Paul Medhurst, Scarlett had taken Anthony Rocca and Milburn lined up at centre half-back on Travis Cloke. Andrew Mackie had been assigned Pies skipper Nathan Buckley while Josh Hunt was in the goalsquare sitting on the pacy Sean Rusling.

The key match-up in the middle was Irish youngster Martin Clarke running with Gary Ablett. James Clement had lined up on Steve Johnson; Harry O'Brien took Paul Chapman; Nick Maxwell on Nathan Ablett; Tyson Goldsack met Mathew Stokes; and Shane Wakelin went to full-back, on Mooney. Three of the Magpies' prime movers – Alan Didak, Dale Thomas and Shane O'Bree – had started on the bench, while the Cats had gone for youth on the pine with Blake, Byrnes and Joel Selwood alongside Rooke.

When Harley went back with the flight and spilt a mark he would have taken (as in, 99 times out of 100), it symbolised the mindset of his team. They were jumpy. A minute later he again fumbled an attempt going back across a Scarlett-Rocca contest, and there was some serious concerns in the coaches' box. At the three-minute mark Collingwood got the first goal, a Scott Burns snap from 35 metres after roving a throw-in.

Everything was slightly out of kilter. It took the most inexperienced Cat out there, Nathan Ablett, to correct the situation. He ran onto the bouncing ball at half-forward and took it with one strong grab, dished beautifully to Enright, who went long to the goalsquare where Mooney and Wakelin wrestled. Wojcinski came from nowhere to hit the contest hard; the ball spilled to Stokes at the back of the pack and he strolled in for an easy goal, his 30th of the season.

A lovely Chapman chip to Ottens, who was already dominating, set up the Cats' second goal. After 10 minutes they had finally settled and were starting to get into rhythm, although it was obvious that this was going to be a scrap. Indeed, this would be no Kangaroos-style blow-out, for the Magpies were doing what they did well: harrassing and making it a contest.

Mooney sent a scare through the camp at the 18-minute mark when he was pushed into the goalpost as he attempted a snap at goal. "I have never hit something so hard," he told the medical staff as they worked on his back. As he had been lying on the ground in agony, the ball had deflected out to Stokes at the top of the square, who turned around and kicked his second.

A controversial 50-metre penalty against Selwood for a late spoil handed O'Bree an important goal against the run of play. Shortly after, the man of moment, Stokes, struck back at the 24-minute mark, marking and converting a set shot from 30 metres for his third goal to give the Cats an 11-point lead at the first break. Before the game he had been as nervous as anyone in blue and white hoops. "I remember going into every game before Collingwood knowing there is no way they will come near us," Stokes said. "But with this one there was this unsure feeling about us, unsure about how we were going to go. I was the most nervous I'd ever been before the game so that (early goal) really put my nerves down and really set me up. I actually had five shots on goal so I probably should have kicked five for the quarter."

Such had been his impact that Collingwood coach Mick Malthouse replaced Goldsack with Clarke. It was an inspired move as the Irishman changed the course of the game early in the second quarter. His dash from defence created the first goal of the quarter to Rusling, who outmarked Hunt.

Two minutes later, Medhurst goaled from a set shot and the Pies were suddenly in front. While the gun Cat midfield trio of Bartel, Ablett and Corey were getting plenty of the ball, the forward line was breaking down. Johnson was summoned to the bench for an explanation. After cooling his heels for a couple of minutes, he returned and, in the space of two minutes, turned the game back Geelong's way.

A Gary Ablett handball sent Bartel away, and his short pass found Johnson on the lead. Keeping in character, Johnson can be erratic with set shots and sometimes barely makes the distance from 30 metres out. This shot was the best part of 45 metres but, if ever a player thrived on the big moments, it was Johnson. He duly connected with a superb drop punt that didn't deviate as it sailed through the middle and into the crowd.

Sixty seconds later, some brilliant quick-thinking between Johnson and Nathan Ablett produced a second goal for the former. The ball had been bottled up in Geelong's forward pocket and Johnson noticed that the Pies didn't have a ruckman to contest against Ablett. He instructed his centre half-forward to punch it hard towards the goals and into the space behind the pack that was forming around the bounce. Johnson then ran behind him, along the boundary, before darting inside as Ablett brilliantly thumped it into the perfect spot. Johnson simply ran in and goaled from 15 metres out.

Ottens again exerted himself on the contest – both of Collingwood's ruckmen failed to have a possession in the first quarter – at the 19-minute mark with some wonderful work from a throw-in to pinpoint Selwood, whose quick handball found Ling. A short kick across half-forward with his non-preferred right foot found Rooke, who kicked the goal from 20 metres to extend the lead to 16 points.

Remarkably, Collingwood hadn't been inside its 50 metre arc for 10 minutes. When they eventually did, it was some magic from Didak which claimed a crucial goal against the pattern. Despite having Enright on his hammer, Didak ran onto the ball at the top of the goalsquare, then somehow palmed it down with his right hand. At the same time he did a mid-air scissor kick which sent the ball over his head and through for a miraculous goal. When Rusling again marked strongly ahead of Hunt and converted from 35 metres in the final minute of the term, Geelong's control of proceedings had amounted to virtually nothing bar a half-time lead of just five points.

The Cats were frustrated, and not just with themselves. The sight of Gary Ablett throwing himself onto the ground to illustrate to field umpire Scott McLaren how Magpie Heath Shaw had just staged for a free-kick said a lot about where the Cats' heads were at.

Inside the rooms at half-time there were plenty of voices urging others to stick with the gameplan and things would open up. They had all year, so the theory dictated patience. Milburn wasn't one of those voices as he was in the medical room having an injection in his calf. He had copped a knee at the top of the calf as he attempted to lay a tackle and had since struggled to run.

With Egan out and Travis Cloke the major danger in the Magpies' forward line – Scarlett had kept Rocca to just one possession – the Cats desperately needed this particular pain-killer to kick in, and quickly.

Yet Milburn still wasn't right to go at the start of the third quarter, so Harley moved to centre half-back. The Cats came out firing but again failed to convert as Ottens missed a sitter from 30 metres out, directly in front, two minutes in. Collingwood's first inside 50 for the quarter at the four-minute mark turned to gold again. Leon Davis capitalised on a Ling fumble to snap truly on his left from 35 metres to put the Pies back in front. Six minutes later, James Kelly received a handball from Ottens and nailed the shot from 35 metres on the run to regain the lead but it was short-lived: Medhurst seized on a Mackie kicking error to find Cloke, and the big left-footer iced the shot from 45 metres.

While the Pies couldn't miss, the Cats were blowing chances. By midway through the term they had kicked just five behinds for the quarter. Since quarter-time they'd had 25 inside 50s to nine yet led by only three points.

That soon changed when Medhurst put Collingwood back in front with a clever snap at the 17-minute mark. It could have been more a minute later if it wasn't for the heroics of Corey, who produced the play of the night. Bryan had managed to find space at half-forward and, after marking, the big ruckman played on immediately. He was about to unload from 40 metres when Corey dove across his boot to execute the perfect smother. He not only stopped the shot for goal but came up with the ball, which had somehow stayed in his arms.

The next 10 minutes were an arm wrestle, though the good news was Geelong's due to the return of Milburn. It wasn't until the final 30 seconds that the Cats found their second goal for the term when Clement was pinged for a deliberate out-of-bounds play right next to the point post. Mooney was awarded the free kick; he expertly took a couple of steps in from the boundary line and snapped truly, although a lapse in concentration from the Pies defenders helped his cause. His kick had kept surprising low and could have been touched if anyone had been standing on the goal line.

Mark Thompson was calm as he addressed his team at three-quarter time. While he was concerned his side didn't have its usual run and confidence, he was sure they would find a way. Plus, the fatigue factor for the Magpies after extra-time in Perth the previous week would surely be a factor. Right?

Harley took control of the discussion when the players linked up arms for the final time for the evening. "Okay fellas, we're putting our foot down now," the captain urged. "There is no tomorrow, there is absolutely no tomorrow. This is it, this is the big stage and if we are going to be any good then let's just hone in on the next 10 minutes and go hell for leather."

Another Cloke bomb on the run from 45 metres after just 50 seconds hadn't been part of Harley's plan. But a minute later some Johnson magic – an intercept and nice pass to the leading Mooney – kick-started the Cat machine. Johnson himself got his third goal of the night two minutes later when Gary Ablett sent a 55-metre kick from the wing which he read well and marked.

Paul Chapman had been having a quiet night. Yet his impact was timely, presenting at the nine-minute mark to take a diving mark from a Corey pass. As usual he executed perfectly from 35 metres. Harley's wish had become a reality, the Cats on a roll and leading by 17 points. Thirty seconds later, the moment of the game arrived. The Cats had cleared the ball brilliantly from defence and Gary Ablett, who along with Bartel and Corey was approaching 30 touches, kicked long to a one-on-one contest between Mooney and Wakelin. When the big Cat pulled down the mark, up in the box something disturbing caught Thompson's eye. Scarlett and a few of the defenders were celebrating, running up to each other and exchanging high-fives.

"It was too early," Thompson said. "It is a great lesson in footy matches, you should never start to celebrate until you know you are in a position where you can't lose."

Mooney blew the shot for goal and Paul Haines, the fitness coach who doubled as runner on match days, was immediately by Scarlett's side relaying the coach's thoughts. "We weren't celebrating that we won the game, we were just trying to gee each other up," Scarlett said later in his defence. "We'd just done a great passage of play and it was like, 'C'mon, let's keep playing', but it certainly got us into trouble."

Trouble was heading their way in the form of Cloke, the breakout star who some weeks later won Collingwood's Copeland Trophy for the club's best and fairest.

He marked strongly in front of Milburn to kick his third goal at the 14-minute mark and claimed another golden opportunity from the next centre bounce when Wojcinski slipped over at a crucial time. This allowed Swan to surge forward and hit Cloke on the lead 35 metres from goal. The youngster missed, but the Cats' lead was down to 11 points with just under 10 minutes remaining.

While Johnson may have been the Cats' man for the big moments, the Pies had one of their own in Didak. Ironically, he had also had a controversial season marred by off-field dramas but all was forgiven when, at the 17-minute mark, he swooped on a ball which had gone over the top of the pack. Despite Enright again being on his hammer, he dribbled through the goal to make it a five-point ball game.

Enter Gary Ablett.

The ball had gone over the boundary line at half-forward for Geelong. G Ablett sensed for about the first time all evening that some space had opened up around the contest and he quickly indicated to Ottens where he wanted it. "We have worked hard over the years for us to get less numbers in the forward line and I was surprised because, at that particular contest, there weren't many around the ball," Ablett said. "So I whispered to Otto, 'Tap it into space and I'll see if I can get onto it.'"

Ablett pushed off Maxwell, who was trying to hold him, and ran to the designated spot just behind the ruck contest. The ball was delivered on a platter by Ottens and his teammate easily shrugged off an attempted Richards tackle, sprinted towards centre half-forward and kicked an extraordinary over-the-shoulder snap from 40 metres out. "I have practised them since I was a little kid," Ablett said. "I would have rather snapped it than been running into an open goal with a drop punt."

The crowd erupted as the helicopter kick spun the right side of the post. Dennis Cometti in the Channel 7 commentary box rose for the occasion: "Cometh the moment, cometh the man." Eleven points to the better, and with just under eight minutes left on the clock. The extreme intensity was starting to take its toll on both sides. Harley looked around him and saw a couple of his mates suffering, as he was.

"It had got to the stage where you were spent," he said. "Most players don't play for more than 80 per cent of a game. I am one of those, but I hadn't gone off for the whole game. I was cramping and then I was looking at Mackie and he was doing the same. Dasher was hurt so we had some players down and it was just so cut throat."

Josh Hunt was feeling sick and had actually taken medicine to settle his stomach down at half-time, while Johnson had joined the ranks after his shoulder was crunched, driven into the ground by Bryan. He had tried to side-step the Magpie ruckman but got pinned for holding the ball. Johnson immediately went to the bench and was in a lot of pain as the clock counted down the final three minutes.

From that moment nearly every play contained a seemingly heroic act. Ottens, Milburn, Bartel, Corey and Ablett seemingly either had the ball or were in the close vicinity. The Cats started to chip it around to kill some time but, so switched on were the Magpies, they let few players get loose. Something had to give. It did, in the form of a Marty Clarke run. O'Bree had off-loaded a quick handball to the Irishman, who skipped through the middle of the ground and kicked long to a one-on-one contest between Scarlett and Rocca.

Harley was 20 metres away and started sprinting to the contest. "I knew there was only a few minutes left and I thought, 'I have to go (to the contest),'" he said. With his eyes fixed firmly on the ball in flight, the Cats skipper arrived in time and floated across to execute the spoil. Unfortunately, he also made contact, albeit minimal, to Rocca and it was enough for umpire Shane McInerney to blow his whistle.

Scarlett couldn't believe it. "That wasn't a great free kick," he said later. Replays seemed to back up his case and, to add to the drama, Rocca managed to injure his leg when he fell to the ground. When he hobbled off, Medhurst took the shot at goal from 30 metres ... with 80 seconds on the clock. The formerly much-maligned Fremantle Docker, who the Magpies had taken in preference to Steve Johnson during the previous year's trade period, showed ice ran through his veins. He kicked his third goal for the night, and Collingwood was within five points.

Coaches can do little in these scenarios. They had set structures in place and trained for this moment throughout the year. Plus, they figured the experience of the 2005 Sydney finals heartbreak, when Swans forward Nick Davis stunningly ended their season, must help them over the final minute.

Hinkley knew if the Cats forced a stoppage from the bounce then they would be difficult to beat. "We felt if we forced a stoppage it would be a shitfight in there," he said. "Joel Corey, Cameron Ling, Jimmy Bartel, they don't step backwards when the ball is there to be won."

McCartney could already see the players getting themselves organised. "You could see them on the ground actually talking to each other, communicating what they wanted," he said. "The last two minutes of any game, if there is less than a goal in it, a lot of it is in the lap of the gods. We just rolled the dice with our best players around the ball. Some great players just have a way of knowing their way around a footy ground, knowing where the ball was going and they do what is needed."

Bartel is one such player. He had spoken to McCartney throughout the year about such a scenario. "He said, 'If you ever feel in a game for a minute or two that we need someone to go and sit down in the hole, just go down and do it,'" Bartel said. "I thought in those last couple of minutes I would go down there."

From the centre bounce the ball was pushed out towards the wing. A good Mackie tackle on O'Bree caused it to spill to Wojcinski, who found some space along the boundary line with a nice baulk and then tried to find Stokes with a long handball. But Stokes was tackled immediately, and the ball dribbled across the line for a throw-in with 29 seconds remaining.

From the throw-in, a quick kick by Collingwood defender Tarkyn Lockyer sent the ball back towards the wing. Enright looked in best position to mark but he was spoiled by Bartel, who followed up and bundled Didak, ball and all over the boundary line. Ling was screaming at his teammates to set up for the throw-in – possibly the last of the year – but realised they were all on the same page.

"We'd clearly learnt from that Sydney game a couple of years ago," he said. "That Sydney game they had just walked us all away and created this space for the stoppage and Davis kicked the goal. Joel Corey, Jimmy and I were calling blokes in saying, 'Pack the stoppage, don't let them walk away.'"

Geelong's season was riding on this next play.

At the other end of the ground, Mooney had only just realised how dire the situation was. "I looked up at the scoreboard and there was, like, a minute to go. It struck me that we were only five points up," he said. "I honestly thought we were three goals up and I couldn't believe what was happening."

On the bench, Selwood was about to land one on his teammate Blake who was making him even more nervous. "How long have we got left?" Blake kept asking. "How long?" Upstairs, Neil Balme sat in the second row of the coaches' box and was happy to see No. 3 in between the throw-in and the Collingwood goals. "The only thing I saw was that Jimmy Bartel was somewhere between the ball and their goals and I felt a bit more relaxed," he said. "I thought, 'He is not going to let this go.'"

But the events of the final 10 minutes had frazzled some nerves. Hunt had swapped opponents with Milburn a few minutes earlier and was suddenly a lot more on edge. Rusling had been taken off, so his more experienced teammate called a change.

"Who have you got?" Hunt asked.

"Leon Davis, and he's sitting back there near the goals," Milburn responded.

There are two players who could pull off the incredible for the Magpies. They were Davis and Didak. Two years earlier, Hunt had been the one on Sydney's Davis. "Are you sure you're right with that?" he asked Milburn but the veteran smiled and jogged off.

It was actually Didak who managed to get a quick kick away from the boundary throw-in towards half-forward, where Swan and Rooke were locking arms. The ball just eluded Rooke's outstretched arm and bounced high in the air towards Bartel. In that split second he made an important decision on how he was going to handle it.

"It sat up and I knew there were people around me," Bartel said. "If I pretended that I was going to get rid of it or take a step then the umpire could have paid prior opportunity, so I took it and just fell to the ground. I knew that was no prior opportunity because everyone just jumped on me. I knew there was not that much time left so I held it and fell to the ground."

Corey looked around as the players were climbing off Bartel, readying themselves for the bounce. He instantly felt in control. "We were all set up," he said. "We weren't all right behind the ball, we were an even spread and that moment was probably the strongest for me because I knew then as a team we were better."

Ottens was a lot more worried. "I just kept saying to myself, don't give away a free kick," he said. "I mean, if you trip over and nudge him in the back then he's having a shot at goal." Likewise Enright, who was trying to keep Didak in check. "My heart rate was well and truly up," he said. Just as Ottens and Bryan stepped into each other and the ball headed skyward, the siren sounded. Geelong by five points.[25]

---

25. This result was, in many operational respects, even more relevant to the club than the Grand Final outcome. CEO Brian Cook admits the club might have unraveled had the Pies won that night. "I wouldn't be here anymore, and neither would Frank (Costa)," he says.

Enright grabbed Ottens and tried to pick him up but couldn't lift him. Players came from everywhere as pandemonium broke out around the MCG.

Balme broke the momentary silence in the box: "We'll have to fucking play better than this next week if we are going to win."

McCartney was keen to savour the moment before looking ahead. "Let us have five minutes would you," he barked back.

Hinkley felt the same. "Because of the amount of work we had done right through the whole year, it was just amazing. You just wanted to have some sort of a moment," he said.

While the others were heading down onto the ground, Thompson went straight to the rooms. "I wasn't happy and I wasn't sad," he said. "I was excited about being in the grand final. I thought we probably deserved to be there based on our year, not on our performance on the night."

Hunt was feeling worse and worse as the players lingered on the ground to soak up the incredible atmosphere. Then Blake walked past and gave him a little friendly jab in the stomach. "Well done," he said. Hunt curled over in agony, let fly with a punch and then vomited on Blake's boots. "It was just black, so I knew something was wrong," Hunt said.

Corey, who had played his 150th game, led the team in after being chaired from the ground by Ling and Wojcinski. He'd been one of the many heroes, collecting 31 touches (including 13 contested possessions, five clearances and eight tackles). Ablett had virtually the same stats (31 possessions, 11 clearances and eight inside 50s).

Bartel had 30 touches and Ottens, who played the greatest game of his life, compiled 23 touches, nine marks, 15 contested possessions and 24 hit-outs.

At the other end of the spectrum, Blake had just one kick, three handballs and 12 hit-outs. King was already on his way out of the MCG. He thought the Cats had been lucky to scrape through and felt his stocks were rising by the minute. "I thought if I had played that game I would have been able to contribute so I thought I was in with a big chance," he said.

Thompson was pacing the changerooms, waiting. The players arrived and were still celebrating when he directed them straight into the meeting room. He firstly congratulated them on making the grand final and then let rip. "You are kidding yourselves if you are happy with the way you played tonight," he said. "You are kidding yourselves. If you are going to play like that next week then you are going to be embarrassed. You'll get beaten by 10 goals."

His rant did the job, ensuring that when the players went back out to warm-down, conduct their media commitments and catch up with family and friends they had already turned their focus to next week. Ling and Chapman certainly had. "At least I get a chance to redeem myself," Ling said after having a rare off night – Swan had slipped his clutches to be the Magpies' leading possession winner.

If Chapman's groins were really hurting, so was his pride. He'd had minimal influence, just 15 touches and one goal, but already he was convinced things would be different in the grand final. "I was disgraceful, I was stuck in the goalsquare and I couldn't run, I was rooted," he said. "But I knew that meant I would play well in the grand final. I think one of my attributes has been that if I play bad one week, I am going to step up the next week. I just knew."

Thompson's first media commitment was an interview on Channel 7 with his former Essendon teammate, Tim Watson. "It wasn't probably the night we were really looking for," he said.

Fortunately for Blake he was doing stretches 10 metres away and didn't hear his coach's next comment, for his fragile confidence would have taken a hit if he'd heard Thompson's assessment of Ottens' Herculean performance. "I wish he could play 100 per cent of the game but we have to take him off for a spell," Thompson said. "Every time he was on the ground we had momentum and when he went off we let Collingwood back into the game."

Watson ended the interview by saying it must be a great feeling to be in the grand final. Thompson simply shook his head. "I wish I was happier."

McCartney was more positive. He knew the team wouldn't play that poorly again and was heartened by how the brilliance of individuals down the stretch had got them through.

"Probably for the first time in a while we had to rely on some great individual efforts to get through," he said. "There were some remarkable individual performances at the death. Guys like Joel Corey, Gazza, Ottens and Bartel, they were just awesome."

Hidden in the medical room was Hunt. Two rubdown tables had been pushed together so he could lie down with a blanket covering him up.

"They gave me lollies and stuff to try and settle it down," he said. "I lay there for ages and when I started to feel a little better. Then I stood up to have a shower and spewed up again."

Eventually, he managed to get dressed but he couldn't drive. His father and brother took him home. "We were in my car so that made me determined not to spew in there," he said.

While he was desperately trying to keep himself together on the way down the highway, Cook was breaking his regular post-game routine. Normally he would head straight home; instead he called into the Albert Park Hotel for a few drinks.

"I don't normally do that but it was just such a relief," he said. "It was as though something had lifted off the body, these chains that had been wrapped around me had gone."

Back in Geelong, Hunt's condition had deteriorated. At 2am he rang Haines, who had told him to call if he needed anyone. Five minutes later, the fitness coach picked him up. "I felt bad because it's two in the morning and we both should be so pumped about the grand final. Instead I'm in the back of his car looking like death warmed up. And we're on our way to hospital."

chapter 16

Brownlow boy

"Do you think you have got the premiership attitude? Have you boys got it, got the premiership attitude? Because what we've seen so far certainly isn't that."

– Mark Thompson

During the 2006 VFL finals series, a jumper with No.13 on its back would hang next to the door of the changerooms. Before each match, the entire team touched it as they ran out. It was a mark of respect for Tom Lonergan, their mate who was fighting for his life in hospital.

Two days before the grand final, Lonergan had finally been released from hospital and made the effort to get to the game. The sight of him making his way into the rooms after the Cats had lost to Sandringham made a lasting impression on many. "To see Tom come down that day, to see one of your mates who has just lost 17 kilos," VFL coach Leigh Tudor said. "There was a lot of emotion about it."

Fast forward 12 months and there is no jumper at the door. No.13 has lined up in defence on Coburg's young gun forward, Richmond listed player

Jack Riewoldt. Lonergan's mother, Tricia, had already shed a few tears when the Cats ran onto the ground because she remembered exactly what shape her boy was in the last time they'd been at Princes Park.

Geelong was a hot favourite thanks to the number of senior players who were running around. In particular, Henry Playfair, Charlie Gardiner and Tim Callan had been brilliant throughout the whole season but, because of the strength and injury-free run of the senior team, they hadn't got a look-in. Not once had they complained; for people like Mark Thompson and Neil Balme, that said a lot.

"They weren't whinging," Thompson said. "We gave them a lot of respect, we recognised their performances and the fact they were playing great footy and weren't getting back in. We gave them a lot of encouragement, we included them, it was the club. The two teams were one."

Balme believed the way the VFL team had conducted itself throughout the year had a major bearing on the success of the AFL team. "Every time they played they were outstanding, between them that trio got three games but never, ever was their a whimper saying, 'What about me?'" he said.

"They all had a good case but they didn't play, yet they knew they were part of the act. They were treated fairly in that they were always considered but it just didn't quite work out."

It was certainly working now for Playfair who was marking everything in the opening half at centre half-back. Scott Thompson, a top-up player who was a spitting image of Matthew Scarlett, was dominating from full-back while King and the likes of Brent Prismall, Jason Davenport and captain James Bryne – who a couple of weeks earlier had won the J.J. Liston Trophy for the VFL competition best and fairest – were seeing plenty of the ball.

While they had controlled the contest, bad kicking (2.8 in the second quarter) meant the lead was just 14 points when Tudor looked at his match-ups board at half-time. He needed a spark and Lonergan was his man. The previous week he'd moved forward in the preliminary final against North Ballarat and kicked three goals. So far he'd dominated Riewoldt; the teenager had just one touch, a smothered kick, in the first two quarters.

The next 25 minutes belonged to Lonergan. He kicked five goals as the Cats piled on 7.6 to a solitary point to blow Coburg away. A brilliant trap, twist and snap from 40 metres started the avalanche with a contested mark near the point post and a banana kick for another. "It was out of control," Tudor said of Lonergan's blitz. "He marked everything, he kicked banana goals, he kicked them on the run, from snap shots and from set shots."

His performance sent a buzz through the senior team, which had gathered as a group in a special area of the stand, cordoned off from the public. Thompson was also enjoying the day a lot more than the last time he had been to the ground. He had spent the '06 VFL Grand Final in a corporate box being grilled by the media about the review and his meeting with the board that morning ... where it had been decided he would continue as coach.

This time the topic of conversation was the Port Adelaide-Kangaroos preliminary final which the coaching panel had flown over to watch at AAMI Stadium the previous day.

Port had obliterated the Roos, winning by 87 points. The game was over even before half-time thanks to Port's running power through the likes of David Rodan, Shaun Burgoyne, Danyle Pearce and Domenic Cassisi. Brett Ebert and Daniel Motlop had been dangerous in the forward line, while Troy Chaplin continued his career-best form in defence. The only home team downside of the day was a serious achilles injury to veteran defender Michael Wilson.

However, it didn't come without controversy. The celebratory antics of captain Warren Tredrea and Chad Cornes following goals in the third quarter had been labelled by many as an insult to the Roos. Tredrea arrogantly bowed to the crowd after kicking his third goal in 10 minutes, while Cornes produced an outrageous goose-step.

McCartney and Hinkley both came away thinking that if Geelong played to its strength then they would very much be in the game the following Saturday. "We saw a couple of things that we thought we can't let them do," McCartney said. "They'd been a very well coached club, a very well organised club and they did some things to us down here (in round 21) which they were able to do to the Kangaroos. We didn't want that to happen again.

"Our best chance was to make it a really physical, contested game, which is us. That experienced group in the midfield have been brought up on it, they relish it and they actually like to play that way."

Slowing them down and cutting their space was the key, according to Hinkley. "The Kangaroos couldn't slow them down and as everyone knows if Port gets a share of the footy and get plenty of space then they have some great players," he said. "But I came away thinking if we play them at contested footy I think we'll be okay.

"They other thing was they were quite young. While they had 10 premiership players, they also had 10 very young players whereas we had a very experienced team. While we hadn't played in a grand final, we'd played in a preliminary final and just lost in the semi-finals so for three or four years we'd been right there, apart from that one year where what could go wrong, should go wrong, did go wrong."

The other major topic of conversation was the ruck. Brendon Lade and Dean Brogan had been dominant again. Their strength and experience stood out. Mark Blake had been average in the preliminary final and poor against the Power four weeks earlier. In front of them, Steven King had just been instrumental in the Cats' stunning second half which had just won a premiership. He had 19 disposals, nine marks and 34 hit-outs in the 74-point victory and, while he was big news, Lonergan, who finished with six goals, was even bigger; his remarkable year was capped off by being awarded the Norm Goss Medal for best player on the ground. "This is one of the best days of my life," said Lonergan, his voice wavering, as he accepted the medal.

He was quickly swamped by his family and the people who had been through the journey with him. Trish was again in tears while his father Bernard, brother Marc and girlfriend Elise O'Neil were close to it. They rang his other siblings, sister Kate, who lived in London but had flown out last year when he got hurt, and another brother, Terry, who had just played in a premiership in Queensland. "It's been such a big year," Longergan said. "It is only 12 months ago that I was sitting over there in the (coach's) box thinking about the future. I then walked across the ground and I was that sick, I weighed 70 kilos or whatever. I came in the rooms and the boys were flat, they'd just lost. It's been such a big year, to turn around and win the flag, kick a few and contribute was just amazing. This is the best finish I could have asked for. I was hoping for it for so long."

As Hinkley got to his car, he couldn't help but acknowledge what all the signs were saying. "I started to think, 'Hang on, how much can keeping going our way?'," he said. "This is just meant to be."

David Wojcinski didn't get to enjoy the VFL Grand Final victory as much as others. Half-way through the game, he started to feel cold. Given it was a nice sunny September day, it induced some concern.

Then he started shaking. He managed to see out the match but by the time he got home and collapsed on the couch he was feeling terrible.

Hoping it was just a 24-hour bug, Wojcinski went to training the following morning and explained his symptons to the medical staff. Go home and rest was the message. He hadn't been the only one seeking the doctor's advice, as several Cats were feeling the pinch from the preliminary final.

While Steve Johnson could hardly move his right arm and hadn't got much sleep over the weekend, he was a lot happier than he'd been on Saturday morning when he drove to hospital to gets scans on his shoulder. "I kept thinking, 'Please don't show anything'," he said. It came up positive, with no major structural damage, but he would require a cortisone injection to numb the pain for the grand final. A quick trial was done, putting Johnson's mind at peace. "They gave me a short-lasting jab to see if it was going to work for the grand final and they said if it numbs it then you'll be right," he said. "Thankfully, it did and felt alright, so from then on I wasn't really worried about it."

Josh Hunt had spent the night and half of Saturday in hospital. The doctors had placed a camera down his throat and found that his severe vomiting had split the lining of his stomach. "That was why it was black," he explained. "Apparently I also had little stomach ulcers in there as well, and that didn't react well with the blood, which was what was making me spew."

Hunt was loaded up with tablets. While his throat was still sore, he was sure he'd be back at full capacity in time for Wednesday's main training session. Darren Milburn wasn't so sure he'd be out there then, but nothing was going to stop him running out on Saturday. His calf was still sore, however a pain-killing injection pre-game would again do the trick.

Max Rooke and Tom Harley were both feeling fine when they walked into the coach's office for the normal Monday briefing. That was about to change. Each week a couple of the leadership group meet with the coaching staff to give feedback on the previous week and any other issues. Thompson was waiting. He was still annoyed with how the team had trained and then performed in the preliminary final. He needed them to understand the opportunity they had and he also knew Rooke and Harley were resilient characters who would take up the challenge. "Do you think we have got the premiership attitude?" he asked Harley. "Have you boys got it, got the premiership attitude? Because what we've seen so far certainly isn't that."

The skipper was taken aback, as was Rooke. They started to question where Thompson was coming from when Hinkley intervened. "Tom, you trained like shit," he said. "If you thought you trained well you are fooling yourself. It was just terrible."

Thompson continued: "Don't be happy to be here, we've still got to win this thing. Forget about that stuff about enjoying the week, we are here to win a game of footy."

When they left the office, Rooke was fuming. "To me and Harls it was like he (Thompson) doesn't think we can do it. It fired me up and when I told a few of the other blokes it fired them up."

"Bomber was a bit testy," Harley said. "He couldn't understand how we could get the break on Collingwood like we did, then let them get back within five points, and we were a bit the same. Really, everyone was still a bit testy about it."

On the drive up to Crown Casino for the Brownlow Medal count, Joel Corey's girlfriend, Natalie, asked him for his tip. "I reckon Jimmy will win it," he said. While Gary Ablett was the overwhelming favourite, Corey had seen from close quarters the impact Bartel had on games and he was regularly surprised when he looked up the paper the next day and Bartel wasn't in the best players.

Bartel wasn't thinking about winning, he was just worried about not looking silly on the red carpet. This was the first time he had been invited to the count because, while he had polled well previously, he'd always been ineligible because of suspension. He figured because his partner was teammate Tim Callan – his girlfriend Pernille had recently returned home to Denmark – he would escape having to get his photo taken. "I thought if I take Tim they are not going to want to take a photo so I snuck around and I was giving Lingy the finger while he was posing," Bartel said. "Then they asked me and I said, 'No way, I'm not having a photo with him.'"

By contrast, Ablett and his girlfriend, Lauren, were the stars of the show. They were stopped almost every step of the way for photos and interviews. While the hype was buzzing around him, Ablett was pretty sure he wouldn't be the one getting up at the end of the night to do a speech. "It was exciting to be classed as a favourite because of everything I had put in for the year and the pre-season," he said. "But at the same time I didn't expect too much. I have known from previous years the umpires haven't given me a lot of votes so I didn't expect too much." Bartel felt the same and had a $50 bet with Steve Johnson before the dinner started that he would not poll more than 10 votes. He was drifting with the bookmakers, starting at $10, with Ablett a firm favourite at $2.10.

The AFL decides who is invited from each club. Geelong was represented by Harley (every captain gets an automatic invite), Ling, Corey, Johnson and the stars of the show, Bartel and Ablett, who were seated next to each other, a major bonus for Channel 7, who had a permanent camera on them. Joel Selwood was also there, as the NAB Rising Star was always on the guest list, but the best bit for Corey was looking around the room at all the other players getting into the beers.

"They had blokes on the screen all drinking beer and it felt good to be on the waters because we had to play," he said. "I reckon it made us tighter, made our table that bit tighter."

It wasn't until round three against Melbourne that AFL CEO Andrew Demetriou first read out 'Three votes, Geelong, J Bartel' . He had another one before Ablett started his run with a best-on-ground against Richmond in round six and then got two behind Bartel the following week against West Coast. That was the beginning of an extraordinary run for Bartel, who polled in five consecutive games, including three best-on-grounds, to be the joint leader on 17 votes at the end of round 11. Ablett was on 11 votes.

"They were making you as nervous as possible because the whole night they had shown past winners on the big screen," Bartel said. "They had a big tribute to Len Thompson and he was saying he got a bit giddy when he had been here with the likes Chris Judd and Michael Voss. I'm watching him say that and then Mark Ricciuto was up there, all these great players."

Ablett was regularly comparing notes with his mate, with whom he had played alongside since Geelong Falcons days. "We were chatting all night because it was quite surprising," Ablett said. "There were games where he didn't think he was even close to getting any and he got some. Then there were games where I didn't think I was going to get votes and I did."

The whole table was getting involved, predicting before Demetriou read out the vote-getters who it could be. A four-game drought allowed Bartel to momentarily relax before another three votes (Ablett got two) against the Western Bulldogs in round 16 lifted him back in contention.

"Are you going to win it?" Harley asked.

"Nah, I can't win. I didn't play the last two rounds because of the appendix," Bartel said.

Privately, he didn't want to "vote" again. "I didn't want to be close enough for someone to come over the top in the last two rounds," he said. "Then it would have been like, 'What if I hadn't had the appendix?'. I didn't want to be close enough to get pinched on the line."

But in round 18, when he got the three votes for 32 disposals against Richmond, Bartel found himself leading the Brownlow Medal. The sweat was well and truly forming on his brow when he got another three votes the following week against Adelaide.

He now had 26 votes but only one game to go. Bartel has collected 36 disposals against the Kangaroos in round 20, so he was definitely in the mix. Corey remembered the game distinctly. "I remember running around next to him that day thinking, 'Jimmy is killing it today,'" he said. "But again that was one of the games when I looked up the paper and he wasn't in the best."

Everyone at the table was doing their own calculations. "If you get two here the worst case is someone can tie you," he was told. Bartel figured he was a good chance to get one or two votes. Demetriou sensed the occasion and took his time. "One vote, Geelong, G Ablett". Bartel's teammate now had 20 votes but was out of the race. The dangers to Bartel were Kangaroos rover Brent Harvey and Brisbane star Simon Black.

"*Two votes, Geelong, J…*" – Demetriou lingered for dramatic affect – "*Corey.*" Bartel's mind was spinning. He was trying to do his own sums but was struggling. All he kept hearing was someone next to him saying: "If you get three here, they can't get you."

"*Three votes, Geelong J…*" – again the long pause – "*Bartel*".

He froze. "You've won it," screamed his teammates.

"Nah, these blokes have got two more rounds," Bartel said nonchalantly.

"You are seven up! They can't get you!! "

The photographers had swarmed around the Geelong table and host Bruce McAvaney then declared: "Jimmy, you've won." Bartel had polled in just 11 games with eight best-on-grounds elevating him to 29 votes, seven clear of Harvey, Black and West Coast's Daniel Kerr (who was ineligible due to suspension).[26]

He was still in shock when he got up onto the stage and shook hands with last year's winner, Adam Goodes, who placed what is known as 'Charlie' around his neck. "I'm trying not to shake," Bartel told McAvaney. "I would like to thank my teammates because without them you are nothing. And you never forget where you come from, Bell Park. And always, my family."

Forever the stats man, McAvaney informed Bartel and everyone else that he had polled the most votes ever by a Geelong player – surpassing Alistair Lord's 28 in 1962 – and that it was the fifth Brownlow in the club's history, but the first since Paul Couch in 1989.

Yet the stat Bartel liked the most was the fact that his votes combined with Ablett (20) and Corey (12) totalled 61, the most by any three players from the one club in the history of the 3-2-1 Brownlow Medal system.

Thompson was a proud man as he watched the humble 23-year-old talk with such sincerity on the stage. "He is very modest. He is just a man's man and I love the way he goes about his footy," he said. "We knew he would go well. I do the coaches' award every week and had him and Gary just getting votes every week, so you knew they would be up there. You knew they were under the umpire's eye, which is great, and he now has a Brownlow Medal. And the good thing is I don't think it will affect him one bit."

---

26. Two years later, Ablett would go one better, securing the 2009 Brownlow Medal with 30 votes. Ablett, Joel (16) Selwood and Bartel (13) combined for 59 votes, two short of the 2007 mark.

Judd, who the previous week had announced he was leaving West Coast and coming home to Victoria, summed up the feeling in the room. "It was a great result," Judd said. "He had a great year and, the thing is, he is the sort of player who is really respected by most players in the competition. He is a really deserving winner."

Bartel was whisked away to a press conference, where he admitted he was still coming to terms with what had just happened. "I still can't believe it has actually happened," he said. "Like everyone here, you watch great players win. It's hard to think about how much it means right now, but it's something someone can't ever take from you. I am definitely embarrassed by it at the moment. It is a pretty humbling experience to get your name read out at the Brownlow, let alone win one."

The victory had people all across Geelong jumping in their loungerooms, none more than Bartel's mother, Dianne, a teacher who had single-handedly raised him and his two older sisters, Olivia and Emma, since he was a toddler. She had worked two jobs but every night she would be there to take the kids to whatever training or games were on. Still, she didn't let her only son start playing football until he was 10. And she made him wear a helmet which he sported right through to the Geelong Falcons, until he was convinced to ditch it.

It had been obvious during his early days with the Bell Park Dragons, then at school footy with St Joseph's, that football was his calling. At 16 he won the club's under 18s best and fairest by more than 100 votes and, during one game in the juniors, he was clapped off the ground by the opposition, such was his dominance.

After being a star at the Falcons and an early first-round draft pick, Bartel struggled at the start of his career. Thompson deliberately made him earn his stripes. "He turned into an awesome player. A few people around here always thought he would, but I wasn't always one of them," he said. "I gave him a hard time, which I do to a few boys. That is part of coaching."

McCartney was actually a relieved man when Bartel's name was read out as the winner; he thought he may ruined Bartel's chances by taking him off early in the round 20 Kangaroos game. "I thought, 'I've cost him the

Brownlow', because he was on fire early and then he was the first one off to have a break. The problem was we then couldn't get him back on for six or seven minutes," he said. "The ball was over the other side and the guy we were trying to take off got caught up in play."

The midfield coach would regularly have to talk to Bartel in the huddle while the doctors stitched up or bandaged the latter. "There were at least three games during the year when you'd talk to Jimmy in the huddle and he'd have stitches over his eye, under his eye, on the other eye," McCartney said.

"They were things from going back with the flight or putting his head over the ball. But it didn't matter to him, he'd just look straight back at you. He's not hard to love and I think the football world acknowledged that a real warrior had won the award."

After a brief celebration in a private room just off the main ballroom with some of the Geelong officials, Bartel and Callan hit the highway. His teammates were already nearly home and one in particular was a relieved man. "It was good to get it out of the way," Ablett said. "Leading into it as the favourite, and in the past you've seen a lot of favourites that never win, so it was good that it was now over and I could just concentrate on the weekend."

Bartel was thinking the same thing when he arrived home to find people had already been leaving notes of congratulations on his doorstep. When they kept appearing at 2am and knocking on the door, he decided he had to do a runner if he wanted to get a good night's sleep. He crept out a side door and went to Callan's house in Barwon Heads.

Before his head hit the pillow he placed "Charlie" on the bedside table next to him. Six hours later he woke up. First thing he did was check to see if it was still there.

"I wanted to make sure I wasn't dreaming it all," he said.

It was the players' day off but, when Bartel arrived at the club to do more media committments, he found all his teammates there waiting to congratulate him. They all tried on the medal and many, like Bartel, could still not believe he'd won it. "It was very weird," Kelly said. "It was like, I don't know if I can talk to him, I mean he's a *Brownlow Medallist*, and I was asking him if we could still be mates."

The angle of the media conference focussed on the Brownlow Medal curse and how three of the past four winners had failed to add the premiership medallion later in the week. "I don't believe in curses, mate," Bartel stated. "It sort of frustrates me a bit that what happens in the past everyone thinks is going to happen again. I don't see how that is going to affect our game this weekend."

He said he was ready to now focus on Saturday. "I don't think it will be too big of a distraction. I have got some pretty good teammates here to keep me down to earth."

As he was speaking, they were doing just that with a practical joke on the club's honour board. Already the new Brownlow Medallist's name had been painted on but his teammates had added their own touch to it. If there was one thing Bartel hated, it was having his name mis-spelt. So there it was on the board, freshly painted: "Jimmy Bartels".

chapter 17

Seven days

*"Don't think about **being** premiership players; train and play **like** premiership players. Do that first."*

– Mark Thompson addresses the playing group
in Grand Final week

Mark Blake had felt anxious ever since he was rested for those two weeks late in the season; like he was continually looking over his shoulder. His confidence had taken a hit and Blake had struggled to get it back.

This was never more evident than in the preliminary final. During the first quarter he made a meal of a marking attempt. He knew it didn't look good but he was praying the coaches would adopt the attitude of staying with a winning combination. The 22-year-old had made great strides in 2007, playing in 22 games (compared to eight the previous year). He just hoped he had enough credits in the bank.

The ruck debate had become the main talking point of Grand Final week. One man dragged into the debate was his father, Rod, who played

176 games in the ruck for Geelong between 1971-83 and now lived on the northern NSW coast; many other former ruckmen were also getting asked for their thoughts. Blake survived to Wednesday without hearing anything and arrived at the main training session a bundle of nerves.

Steve Hocking had arranged for a gate around the other side of the ground to be open so the players could park inside Skilled Stadium, instead of the normal carpark, where the media was camped out. It was a "closed" session, yet there were photographers climbing trees to get their pictures and news helicopters circling.

The football management team had started planning for Grand Final week almost two months earlier. They needed a strategy if the season continued as it had promised and, to this point, everything had gone according to plan. Keeping it as normal as possible was the Thompson goal. While everyone understood that it was anything but a normal week, with events like the Brownlow Medal and Grand Final Parade on the agenda, internally it needed to be business as usual.

Part of that involved the media strategy. Normally the Grand Final teams have an open day early in the week where up to a dozen players, sometimes even more, are made available for interview. That wasn't happening at Geelong, simply because it went away from their stated aim of keeping everything the same. It wasn't a popular decision but media manager Kevin Diggerson maintained it was the right one for the players.

The day after the preliminary final victory, Mooney was made available, then Harley did an interview before the VFL Grand Final. On the Monday, James Kelly and Bartel had been part of a press conference with Premier John Brumby, when he announced the state government's contribution to the new ground redevelopment. The following day it had again been Bartel in front of the cameras, this time as the Brownlow Medallist. By Wednesday, the players were deemed a no-go zone. The traditional open training session for the supporters was to take place the following morning, with only a very light wor-out on the agenda.

The other major decision involved Grand Final eve, and it gave players the option of staying in Melbourne. Every year the AFL booked out two city hotels in the chance of the Grand Final hosting interstate teams. Neil

Balme had asked the league to hold onto the booking, then took the idea to the leadership group.

A Friday afternoon training session was scheduled at the MCG following the Grand Final Parade. The thought of not having to battle the traffic one more time appealed to the players, who gave it a thumbs up. Partners and families were also allowed to stay, which would help sustain some normality about the preparation. The most important part of the preparation wasn't far from starting when Harley called together the senior players and discussed what the coaches had said on Monday. "We've done nothing really," he said. "We've got to jump back on the horse and it all starts on the track."

Thompson had a message of his own before the session started. "Don't think about *being* premiership players; train and play like premiership players," he said. "Do that first." In the space of two hours the vibe around the Geelong Football Club changed completely. Not a ball was dropped during the session, which had gone like clockwork. The reserves players had held off their premiership celebrations to take part in the main training session, as they usually would, and their presence had a significant impact on the senior players and coaches. "The VFL boys had won the flag and they had every right to go out and celebrate," Brenton Sanderson said. "But they all came in and trained with the senior group and everyone trained really well. You could sense that they were ready to play. They weren't nervous at all and looked really sharp."

Thompson had picked up on the calmness of the team. "They trained exceptionally well," he said. "They were very calm and that was one of the messages from all the coaches. It was all about being professional, really well planned and relaxed."

One player who couldn't wipe the smile from his face for the whole session was Shannon Byrnes. The previous day he had been called into the coach's office and told the news: he was playing in the Grand Final.

"I was in the media as a chance to be dropped, I think there was four of us named," Byrnes said. "Bomber took me into the office on Tuesday and said, 'Don't listen to it at all because we are picking you'. It was good to know I was in but I wasn't allowed to tell anyone until Friday." While the strike rate of rookies making the grade is on the improve every year, not a lot is usually expected of them … especially when you're the last selection of the club, and at No. 40. "I remember Bomber and John Peake both said, 'We should just get the speediest player we can get,'" recruiting manager Stephen Wells said. "That was Shannon, he had super speed and a good footy brain."

The 175cm rover from Shepparton quickly earned respect, playing 19 games in 2005 but, like many, he struggled the following year. The emergence of Travis Varcoe had forced him to cool his heels in the VFL but Byrnes had come good at the right time – he impressed with 19 possessions in the preliminary final – while Varcoe tired badly late in the season. At the end of the session, Hinkley made a beeline for Harley as the team was walking off. "That's the sort of training we want, Tom," he said. The captain smiled. He knew exactly what Hinkley meant.

One person who wasn't smiling was Blake, who had a quick shower and left. There still hadn't been an indication of what was happening but he felt so claustrophobic at the club that he bolted for home. An hour later his mobile phone rang. It was Thompson, who said he wanted to come around and see him. "I knew then I was in a fair bit of strife," Blake said. Fifteen minutes earlier, King and Scarlett had been called into the coach's office. Thompson knew how much what he was about to say meant to Scarlett, plus his presence – given they couldn't locate Blake – might not make the events in that the room so obvious.

King's heart was racing. "You can either make me or break me here," he thought, as he watched his coach of eight years sit down across from him. Thompson didn't beat around the bush. "You're in," he said.

"Thanks, mate," was all King could muster.

"Don't thank me. You're in because you are in our best 22 this week."

The former captain could feel the adrenalin racing through his body. "I won't let you down. I will do whatever you want me to do." Keeping quiet was his first instruction because Thompson didn't want anyone else to know before they got to Blake.

There had been many times during the previous six months when King, who had made his debut way back in 1996, thought this moment would never come. "It was a very lonely sort of year," King said. "You find yourself in a position where no one really wants to look you in the eye and help you out. When you have been around for a while, a former captain of the club, it is always hard for people to tell you that you're not playing."

He almost gave up hope after he wasn't recalled following the round 21 loss to Port Adelaide, when Blake had struggled. "I thought I might have been a chance to get in the side after the Port Adelaide game which we dropped down at home," King said. "After that week I probably thought the worst. I thought, 'I'll just do the right thing and make sure I win a flag in the VFL, just control what I can and see what happens.'"

Thompson, Hocking and Brendan McCartney headed to Mark Blake's house. The coaching panel had spent a lengthy session going through every possible scenario at the match committee meeting. "We don't normally have long match committees, we're normally done in an hour, but we spent more than that on this," Thompson said. "In the end we just had a responsibility to pick a team that was going to win one game of footy. Everyone had been waiting 44 years to win one and we all knew Blakey would be really, really angry. We knew it would affect him and he might want to leave.

"But in the end we had to make a tough call and play the player that we thought was going to win us this one game of footy. We had to put our best team out there for that one game and that is something you don't do every week of the year.

"You give a lot of players games during the year to give them experience. But for this one game, the fact (that) King was experienced, he had played reasonable finals footy and the fact he had played so much continuous footy building up to that game gave us more confidence in his body."

As the trio approached Blake's house McCartney thought about how police and doctors every day of their lives delivered shocking news.

While he may have sensed it was coming, when Blake heard the words he was crushed. His mother, Maureen, was devastated and the tears flowed. While he knew Thompson had done the right thing by telling him face-to-face, he didn't want to hear about how this would make him a stronger person and player in the future. He had supported Geelong his whole life. His dad had been a great player, a best and fairest winner at the club, and

Blake had sat in the crowd as a young kid and watched the 1992-94-95 Grand Final losses. He loved the club, yet the chance to play in the team which could break the 44-year-old premiership drought had just been taken away from him.

To escape, he went and played tennis. He was taking his anger out on the court when his mobile phone started going berserk. "I thought, 'What the hell has gone down now?'" he said. Back at the club, Neil Balme was about to dial the Blake family's number. "I was going to ring Mark's mum as a squaring off, just checking in," he said. "Just before I did I said to the guys, 'We need to consider that this will get out you know'."

That second Balme's phone rang. It was someone from SEN declaring they'd been told Blake was out and wanted confirmation. There was another call and it was a producer from 3AW. "Jesus, I think it's out," he said.

An emotional Maureen Blake had rung her best friend to talk through the news of her son's axing. *She* had told her daughter, who passed it onto her boyfriend. *He* then text messaged radio station SEN. By the middle of the afternoon it was all over the airwaves. Initially, Balme was angry about the leak. He rang to find out what happened but at that time the Blake's also had no idea how it had got out. Maureen was still very upset and his questioning didn't help things. When Mark was told what had happened, he rang Balme to have a go at him.

"Mum was doing it pretty tough at the time," he said. "I rang up Balmey and had a crack at him because by that stage I didn't care what I said. I had nothing to lose."

The toughest part for Blake was fronting up the next morning for training; to make matters worse, it was the open session with 10,000 fans and dozens of cameras all looking at him. The first person he saw when he arrived was King. "Mate, I don't know what to say," King said. "I'm feeling for you."

There was only one person in the room who had any idea about what he was feeling and that was Sanderson. In 1995, Geelong coach Gary Ayres had dropped the then 20-year-old defender for the Grand Final in favour of Grant Tanner. "I probably didn't really deserve to play, whereas Blakey had a genuine case to play," Sanderson reflected. "But the scars are still there, forever. I am still very bitter about being dropped for the Grand Final.

I said to Blakey you carry those scars for ever but no one likes anyone who complains, whinges and whines about the whole thing."

It wasn't the players who were making the news during the light session. They came out in small groups at different intervals for only brief periods. Rather, Diggerson had a run in with camera crews and reporters who ignored his edict to keep off the ground. "Leave the grass," Diggerson said. "You're kidding yourself, guys. This is no negotiation. I look forward to seeing myself look like a fool on the TV tonight, but please leave the grass."

His prediction was right. The media man erupting was spun into the Cats showing signs of cracking, which made everyone in the inner sanctum chuckle because they were feeling the complete opposite. It was chalk and cheese compared to the previous week. After making his point on Monday, Thompson had flicked a switch and was a different man. He was relaxed, and that flowed through to his players, who were excited about just going out and playing with freedom instead of the anxiety they had experienced against Collingwood.

Balme, who had been through two Grand Final appearances with the Magpies in recent years, marvelled at how the build-up had been handled. "The coach and the coaches were outstanding," he said. "It was probably as relaxed a week of coaching as I have ever seen. They were very positive, very calm and it was a fantastic exercise of handing over to the players. They virtually let the players say, 'This is what we are going to do', and they helped them with that. It was a wonderful example of how to really coach."

Aside from Blake, there was another player who was doing it tough, albeit for totally different reasons. Wojcinski had made it out onto the training track for the first time that morning but he had struggled. He had a quick shower, spoke again to the doctors – informing them that he felt like he was getting worse, not better – and headed home. When he got there he collapsed on the coach and fell asleep. After three hours he woke up with the worst headache of his life. He started to panic. "I seriously thought, 'I'm not going to be able to play,'" Wojcinski said. "I was literally on my death bed I thought, and every hour or so I would start shaking for 20 minutes. I was going to bed with two pairs of pants on and a jumper, socks; just trying to keep warm even though it wasn't a cold night."

He was too out of it to see *The Footy Show* on Channel 9 on Thursday night, when Port Adelaide coach Mark Williams arrogantly declared a spot for the 2007 premiership photo was already picked out at the Power's home base at Alberton. He was talking up his club's premiership winning culture, highlighting Geelong's history of losing five Grand Finals since 1963. "There are a lot of people coming over from Adelaide that are really looking forward to the game and we just want to do what Port Adelaide does, win premierships," Williams said.

McCartney had seen enough. He switched off his TV and went to bed a contented man. The one thing you don't do against this Geelong team was talk it up. Many teams had tried and failed throughout the season and he was now more confident than ever that the exact same thing would happen on Saturday.

If he'd kept watching, he would have seen the segment on the new Essendon coach Matthew Knights. Brian Cook certainly saw it. He was happy that distraction had now taken care of itself but he hadn't been aware that the Bombers had, unbelievably, still been asking the question of his coach only a couple of days earlier – Thompson had received a text message from an Essendon official while his manager Michael Quinlan had been called to find out about his status.

Cook's contentment was short-lived. His phone started ringing at 6am with an unexpected problem. Defender David Johnson had been arrested and charged with drunkenness and resisting arrest outside a Geelong nightclub. Police had been forced to use capsicum spray to subdue the 25-year-old, who had played in the VFL Grand Final victory. It was out of character for Johnson, one of the most liked players in the group.

It wasn't the start to Grand Final eve Balme had been expecting, either, as he set about talking to the police and finding out as many details as possible. The Johnson incident was certainly the topic of conversation when the players met at Skilled Stadium to catch a bus up to Melbourne, where they would drop off their gear at the MCG and continue on to St Kilda Road, where the parade started.

The mood for the trip was very relaxed. Diggerson's antics on the TV news got a going over but soon the focus became the parade. It was a pretty ugly day, which was expected to have an impact on the crowd, but it became obvious a few clouds weren't going to keep premiership-starved Cats fans away. The city streets were packed with more than 60,000 people to watch the procession of cars make its way to the steps of the Old Treasury Building in Spring St.

The good news for the day was the presence of Wojcinski and his little boy, Alfie, in the parade. "I woke up not too bad," he said. "I was a lot better than I had been but still nowhere near 100 per cent. I rugged myself up for the parade because it was raining and freezing cold, which wasn't exactly ideal."

Byrnes and James Kelly weren't fazed by the weather as they shared a car and had the video camera out filming their journey along Swanston St. "I didn't expect there to be so many people," Byrnes said. "We were taking pictures of the crowd and saying into the video, 'This is ridiculous, getting paraded through Melbourne. When will this ever happen again in your life?'"

Jimmy Bartel was also a bit stunned. "It was amazing," he said. "I knew we had a bit of support but didn't realise we had that much. It was phenomenal just seeing it all."

After the formalities of being presented to the crowd and both captains holding up the premiership cup for the cameras, Thompson and Harley went inside for a press conference alongside Williams and Port captain Warren Tredrea.

Both coaches and captains went back a long way. Williams and Thompson were mates from the Essendon days while Tredrea and Harley had played on each other many times in junior football in Adelaide. Both were part of Port Adelaide's inaugural squad when the club came into the AFL competition in 1997.

Harley, who had made the All-Australian under 18 team, played just one game for Port in 1998 … against Geelong. He didn't get onto the ground until the final minute of the game, and his sole possession was a kick off the ground for a goal. And his previous Grand Final experience had not been a good one. Harley's SANFL club, Norwood, had been coached by Peter Rohde, the former Melbourne player who was now Port Adelaide's football manager. In 1997, the Adelaide Crows won the premiership and, because the SANFL Grand Final was a week after the AFL, several of the Crows players became available. This resulted in Harley being dropped for the Grand Final, which Norwood won.

After his brief appearance in the seniors, Harley wanted out from Port, and Sydney and Geelong were the clubs showing the most interest. After flying to Sydney and looking around, he was sold on the harbour city, but a deal couldn't be swung. Instead, he ended up at Geelong in exchange for pick No.37.

Harley and Tredrea had started playing on each other when they were eight years old, but they had followed dramatically different paths to this moment, where in 24 hours they would oppose each other as captains in an AFL Grand Final. Tredrea was a three-time best and fairest winner and three time runner-up. He had been the All-Australian centre half-forward four years in a row, from 2001-04, and Port's leading goalkicker six times. He also captained the 2004 premiership team in the absence of regular skipper Matthew Primus.

Under player honours for Harley in the 2007 AFL guide it reads: *captain since 2007*. That's it. He was regarded as a reliable, honest defender, and his appointment 12 months earlier was questioned by many, who still held the belief that the team's best player, or close to it, should be captain.

There was never any doubt at Skilled Stadium he was the right man for the job, although no-one expected him to be such a stunning success. Harley saw the role as being captain of the club, not just the team. He took it upon himself to know everything that was happening at the club; he would attend management seminars with the rest of the staff and worked closely with the communications and marketing departments about how best to spread the club's message.

"Tom Harley is a terrific captain," Cameron Ling, his vice-captain, said. "He has allowed a lot of the communication lines to open up between players and coaches, players and administration, players and the board. That whole thing Harls has really been a great driver and it was a good choice to appoint him if you look at where our club needed. He has that ability, that real strength to open up communication.

"And now that he is back playing great footy, taking those big strong marks, his on-field leadership is really up and going. He really is a very, very good captain."

Matthew Scarlett believes Harley is responsible for the complete makeover of the playing group. "Tommy has definitely got us as a closer group," he said. "He has had a tremendous year and played a massive part in the success we've had so far."

Thompson admires the 29-year-old. "I have a lot of respect for Tom, I always have for players that have stood up for a long, long time," he said. "I know he is not one of the most talented footballers going around but there is more to being captain than that and he is a great captain."

Harley and Thompson had spoken earlier in the week about how to handle the pressure of being captain on Grand Final day. The coach's advice had been simple – share the load. "On Grand Final day you are going to have to let people help you because from my experience it is very hard, almost impossible to be a great leader and great player on the same day," Thompson said. "You can be a great leader and forget about your performance and not play well or be a great player and not lead. Just encompass everyone, get everyone to come along for the ride."

Harley was thinking about that conversation as he was listening to Thompson beautifully manage the press conference. Williams was again trying to stir the pot, focussing on the selection of King. "It's a huge responsibility for Steven King. He's old school Geelong," Williams said. "To bring him back now, there's going to be a huge amount of pressure on him. A lot of the Geelong people would be looking at it thinking, 'Blake's done a great job all year.'"

Thompson shook his head and looked down at the table, where his fist was clenched. He was desperately try to keep himself under control. "He is actually a great bloke but inside I just wanted to punch him to shut him up," he said. "I wanted to say, 'Mark, stop it'. But I knew I couldn't stop it because Mark was being smart and it was hard not to say anything. I didn't want to because it's not about the two coaches yapping. We had been pretty quiet all year and I just wanted the players to put on the show."

When asked for his response to the "old school" tag, Thompson simply replied: "Mark might've meant old school as being very experienced, an All-Australian player and best-and-fairest player." Harley smiled at his coach's response. He had been sick of all the talk from Port Adelaide, particularly the emphasis on how they had a significant edge because they'd played been there and done that three years earlier. "I was sick of hearing about experience," he said. "Fair enough, if you had been there and lost it like West Coast had done against Sydney, that's experience and you learn from that. I was talking to Scarlo about how they were talking about big-game experience and stuff and we were like, 'Whatever'.

"They played in 2004 when the stadium was half full so the biggest crowd they had played in was, say, 70,000 against Brisbane. We had played Collingwood during the year and there was nearly 90,000, the Kangaroos final there was 80,000 and then Collingwood in the preliminary final was nearly 100,000.

"Sure, they may have won a flag but they didn't have big-game experience. What do they get at Football Park, maybe 28,000? The whole big-game mentality was just rubbish. We knew we were going to have 90 per cent of the support on Saturday so we'd show them what big-game experience is about."

When Harley was asked at the press conference about the perceived advantage to Port, with 10 premiership players in its side, he gave a toned-down version of his thoughts. "I'm not sure about the Grand Final experience side of things," he said. "We have played in some big games, last week was a pretty big game in a pressure cooker environment, so time will tell. You have got to start your Grand Final experience somewhere. Port started theirs in 2004. We start ours tomorrow."

The training session at the MCG lasted just 30 minutes with the whole team, including the emergencies Blake, Varcoe and Brent Prismall, having a very leisurely kick-to-kick on the hallowed turf. Harley spent most of the time stretching, as did Paul Chapman, while Milburn dispelled any rumours that he wasn't right by cruising through comfortably.

In the team meeting which followed, Thompson took the floor. The tradition throughout the year had seen the assistant coaches do a lot of the presentations and interaction early in the week with the senior coach taking over closer to the game.

He ran through the match-ups again. Ling was to lock down on Shaun Burgoyne; Corey Enright to run with Danyle Pearce. Mathew Stokes would have the big job of keeping Peter Burgoyne's run from defence in check, while the Cats were expecting Domenic Cassisi to go to Gary Ablett and Kane Cornes to Bartel. The main match-ups in defence would be Josh Hunt on Brett Ebert, Harley would take Daniel Motlop with Scarlett and Milburn rotating off Tredrea and youngster Justin Westhoff, who was to be targetted. The plan was for whoever was on the teenager to run forward at any opportunity.

But, again, the focus of the meeting was more about how Geelong was going to play, rather than the opposition. They needed to play hard, contested football and get back to the confident, play-on style which had been so successful throughout the season. There was confidence in the air as the group parted, the players left to their own devices until they again came together the next day to complete their mission. The majority headed to the Holiday Inn in Spencer St, where they would spend the night. Chapman drove to his parents' home in Fawkner, Josh Hunt to the home of his girlfriend's parents in Essendon, while Mooney headed to his apartment in Port Melbourne.

The only three making the trek back to Geelong were Milburn, Andrew Mackie and Brad Ottens. They would stick to their routine of travelling to and from games together and, when Ottens finally got home, he crashed onto the couch. "When we were training at the 'G' I was trying to enjoy it because it was the last training session of the year and you're on the 'G', all that sort of stuff ... but all I could think about was I just wanted to get home," Ottens said. "I was so drained."

He'd felt that way since the preliminary final, which he described as "the most intense game I have ever played". His performance finally put an end to the criticism which had plagued his career ever since he was named All-Australian in 2001. Ottens was pegged for stardom from the moment he was taken at No.2 by Richmond in the 1997 national draft. He had been an All-Australian under 18 player and was the son of South Australian football star, Dean Ottens, who had been a member of Sturt's famous team which won numerous SANFL premierships through the 1960s-70s.

Ottens delivered on the expectation in the Tigers' push to the preliminary final in 2001, when he kicked 46 goals alternating forward and ruck. Yet a back injury which required surgery to remove part of a vertebrae changed everything. After a long time on the sidelines he struggled when he returned, appearing to have lost some mobility and losing his way. After three more disappointing seasons, the 202cm and 108kg giant had fallen out of love with Richmond; Tiger fans reciprocated the feelings and at the end of 2004 he decided he needed a change of scenery.

The Cats and Sydney were the frontrunners as the country lifestyle of Geelong appealed to Ottens. He had never settled in the city, having grown up in the bush – he spent his first 12 years living on a cattle station outside Katherine in the Northern Territory. Geelong unleashed its big guns in Frank Costa, Brian Cook and Thompson to convince him to make the move. "We talked a lot about why Geelong would be a good place for him," Wells said. "We wheeled out everybody and there were two aspects to it. One, Geelong the football club we thought were a chance to win a premiership in the next few years. The other part we hoped appealed was Geelong the town. Being a country boy we thought Geelong would be a good place for him."

To make the deal happen, Richmond was demanding two first-round draft picks. Geelong already had No.16 but they had to find another one. Enter Melbourne, who told Wells they would do a deal for their first pick, No.12, for a quality midfielder; Brent Moloney was the man they wanted. Moloney had just had a breakthrough season.

A pre-season draft selection in 2003, the powerfully built kid from Warrnambool was one of the coach's favourites with his hardness and long kicking. "It was a very sad day for Bomber because he had a great affiliation with Brent," Wells said. "He was very upset he was leaving but it was a decision that had to be made."

The Cats drafted Ottens more as a forward than a ruckman. Over the previous decade they'd tried desperately to find a gun forward with some spectacular flops along the way, such as West Coast pair Brett Spinks and

Mitchell White. Sydney's Jason Mooney hadn't worked out either, while they'd also had a major move at Hawthorn's Jade Rawlings the previous year. Rawlings changed his mind at the last minute and ended up at the Western Bulldogs.

Coming off a preliminary final appearance in 2004 and with the addition of Ottens, Cats fans were licking their lips. However, by mid-season the jury was well and truly out about the star recruit and mounting criticism triggered an extraordinary response from Thompson in a post-game press conference. "For some silly reason you people (media) wanted to assassinate him – that is just rubbish," Thompson said. "You people, all of you. *All of you*! It's just rubbish … leave him alone."

While his body improved the next year – he managed 22 games in 2006 – his 26.20 goals wasn't the return the Cats were expecting. After his first full pre-season in five years, Ottens had finally found his feet at Geelong as the No.1 ruckman in 2007, the stepping up of Mooney and Nathan Ablett in the key forward posts allowing that to happen. "I wasn't performing very consistently up forward and the better footy I was playing was in the ruck," Ottens said. "The more that happened, the more I played there. It was never a distinct decision, it was just something that happened but being fit makes playing in the ruck a lot easier."

While he was having his regular Friday night Japanese dinner before hitting the sack early, his best mate Mackie had just finished off a pasta cooked by his girlfriend and headed out to the movies. The comedy *Superbad* did exactly what he wanted – gave him a few laughs and took his mind off football.

In Melbourne, his teammates were doing all sorts of different things to try and do the same thing. Stokes was in his sister's hotel room playing with his nephews; Joel Selwood had been over to Southbank to have dinner with his family and then had an ice bath and massage in the trainer's room; the Ablett brothers were watching a DVD together.

Bartel was recovering after getting over-excited with the buffet dinner. "I had 10 kilos of mashed potato, a few steaks and about two litres of ice cream," he said. "It was a classic case of overeating when it is all there in front of you in a buffet."

King had seen Williams' crack at him on the news and was amused. "If I was Chocco (Williams) I would have been doing the same thing," he said. "It was probably pretty smart by him and if you had any doubts in yourself they would come out. But I knew I was going to play well. I just needed to be given the opportunity." He had settled into his room for the evening with girlfriend, Danielle, watching a couple of in-house movies with a sleeping tablet ready to ensure he enjoyed a good night's sleep.

Max Rooke had been for a walk around the streets, had a coffee and then spent some time surfing the net on the hotel's computer with Enright. (The pair had found footage of Diggerson's blow-up on YouTube and were in hysterics, watching it repeatedly).

Both teams had been assigned security guards, who went with the players when they went for a stroll around the streets. Ling got talking to one of them as he headed to 7-Eleven to get some snacks and was happy to hear about the guard's assessment of his team. "He said he couldn't believe how relaxed and what good blokes we were," Ling said. "Apparently it was a lot different at the other hotel. As I said to him, 'There is no point getting stressed out now, mate.'"

Steve Johnson met some mates for coffee. As they parted one of them said: "Just bring back Norm Smith with you when you see us next."

Johnson laughed.

"Yeah, no worries boys."

chapter 18
No more waiting

"I'm not worried about this game. This is my stage, this is where I do it, a full MCG on Grand Final day. Why do you think they put air in my lungs for?"

– Steve Johnson to Ken Hinkley, Grand Final day, 2007

Tom Harley sat bolt upright in his bed. It was 1am. He was in a cold sweat. Three hours earlier he had taken a sleeping tablet, just as he normally did before a game, to make sure he got the rest required. Instead, he was having the most bizarre thoughts.

"What if we don't win?" was the question on high rotation in his head.

"If we don't win, what is going to happen? What are they going to make of me? What do they make of the team? What do they make of everything?"

His girlfriend, Felicity, was sound asleep next to him. For the next hour-and-a-half he stared at the ceiling as his mind raced with doubts he had never thought … until now. Eventually, he fell back to sleep but by 6.30am he was again wide awake. Now, he was nervous about going into the game with not enough sleep.

Neil Balme was up early as usual and was taking the dog for its morning walk when he started to feel crook; he wasn't the only staff member to wake up feeling sick on the club's biggest day.

Thankfully, there were no such problems at the Holiday Inn. One of the first down to breakfast was Joel Selwood, who read the newspaper while a few of the girlfriends chatted. Soon more teammates started to float in, with the caricatures on the front pages of both daily newspapers quickly becoming a talking point. In particular, Gary Ablett's cartoon in *The Age* had them in stitches.

Across town, Paul Chapman had woken up and immediately thought about his brother, Glenn. He had been a talented football umpire and it had been their dream to one day be on the AFL stage together, Glenn umpiring and Paul playing. That dream was shattered for ever when, in 1998, Glenn was killed, run over in Strathmore by the recycling truck on which he was working. Paul can still vividly recall his name being called over the school PA to come to the office. He then waited outside and knew something was terribly wrong when he saw the family's car being driven up by a lady he didn't know. His mum sat in the passenger's seat, crying.

Chapman still shudders when he thinks about that day, the shaking with shock and the instant nosebleed. Every time he looks in the mirror he is reminded of Glenn, for his older brother's face is tattooed on his right shoulder blade. On the biggest day of his career, Paul was sure his number one fan would be looking down on him.

In Essendon, his best mate Josh Hunt was sticking to his routine. Even though his girlfriend was away, working in Dubai, he had rung her parents and asked if he could stay the night, just as he had throughout the season. Hunt was renowned for getting very nervous before games and doing bizarre things to try and keep his mind off football. This week he'd decided to paint the feature wall in his bedroom.

"I used to be a serial nervous person," he said. "But it was weird because when I woke up (on Grand Final day) I didn't feel nervous. I was alert from the minute I got out of bed."

Steve Johnson was one of the late risers. He'd had the best sleep-in of his life. The previous night he'd almost polished off a block of chocolate and there were two bars left; he made short work of them as he flicked on the TV. Johnson started watching a panel show as the guests were giving out tips for the Norm Smith Medal. Former Kangaroos superstar Wayne Carey was next up. "Steve Johnson," Carey said.

"Oh, shit," Johnson thought.

The enormity of what lay ahead hit, and hard. "That's when I thought to myself, 'Shit, this is pretty big now, this is Grand Final day'. You are really involved in it now."

While most of his teammates were in their rooms listening to iPods or watching DVDs, Cameron Ling was still sound asleep. At 11.15 he stirred. The team bus was due to leave the hotel in 45 minutes. "I slept well but I still had enough time to grab a bit of brekky and then off we went," he said, a surprisingly laconic approach to the biggest stage in the game.

By this time the "Geelong crew" were almost at the MCG. They had been told to leave earlier than usual and, with Andrew Mackie behind the wheel, they hit the road at 10.30. "(The club) said, 'Make sure you leave early because there is going to be traffic,'" Brad Ottens said. "There wasn't. It was probably the least traffic we'd had all year and we were there almost an hour early." Darren Milburn wasn't happy, although at least he got to watch his former team, the Calder Cannons, play in the TAC Cup Grand Final. "I don't like getting there too early because you seem to want to think about the game a bit more," he said. "I try to arrive just when you are supposed to so, we just sat in the stand and watched the game, which Calder won."

Cam Mooney had spent the morning playing with his son, Jagger, and had hooked up with the team at the hotel so he could ride with them on the bus to the ground. From the moment he walked into the changerooms he had a good feeling about things. He wasn't the only one.

Mark Thompson was more nervous than he realised. On the drive up from Geelong his partner, Jana, asked if he wanted her to drive because he just wasn't focussed on the road. The Thompson mind, naturally, was elsewhere, running through scenarios which could play out that afternoon in the game which would make or break him as a coach. But once he was in the changerooms, he felt in control.

There were no streamers or banners up on the walls; no 'Eye of the Tiger' motivational songs being played. "It was pretty similar to a normal, regular sort of a game," Thompson said. "We tried not to let too many people in. If we sensed someone, the support staff was not doing their job or was in the way, we'd get them out. We just wanted every person that was in the rooms to have a particular job and to just do it. The players' job is to prepare for a game; their job is to help players prepare for a game."

Hinkley had been in this situation as a player three times and knew more than most what the day meant. "Unfortunately, this game might be the undoing or the absolute making of a footy club," he said. "I arrived nice and early and everything felt relaxed, the players were really okay.

"There were blokes taking 48 minutes to get their rubdown. Tommy Harley was doing his thing, making sure every part of his body was right. There were other blokes just doing what they do, having a chat and a laugh and I had a bit of fun with Stevey."

He was used to Johnson's confidence and arrogance in their normal muck-around conversations but even Hinkley was left shaking his head after their pre-game chat. When Hinkley asked his half-forward how he was feeling, Johnson replied: "I'm not worried about this game. This is my stage, this is where I do it, a full MCG on Grand Final day. Why do you think they put air in my lungs for?"

Hinkley couldn't top that. "I have got confidence and sarcasm, arrogance, all those things … but he eats me," he said of Johnson. "Some people think he's kind of quiet but he's anything but shy when you know him."

It is no surprise to learn that Johnson's football hero was Peter Daicos. He had been a mad Magpies fan and spent hours out the front of the family home, opposite a golf course in Wangaratta, practising 'Daicos-isms' with his brother, David. Two light poles 40 metres apart were the targets. Each time they hit one, a point was scored. Every kick was taken from where it landed.

Despite his freakish skills being obvious from a young age, Johnson almost didn't make the grade. He tried out for the Murray Bushrangers under 15 side and failed. He was injured before a trial game for the under 16 squad and was again rejected. The following year he wasn't even invited to try out for the under 17s.

He figured the crux of the problem was his ungainly running style. He shuffled, Cliff Young-style, and to many he looked slow. In reality he had an above-average aerobic capacity and covered the ground as well as anyone. Johnson then implored two local running coaches to improve his technique. It worked and, as they say in the classics, the rest is history.

As he mucked around in the changerooms having shots at bins, Johnson was enjoying a sense of belonging. Before his suspension earlier in the year he had never felt that connection with his teammates. "I feel like I am part of the team now," he said. "I can see that my teammates like having me out there. That has probably been the most enjoyable thing – knowing that when you run out with your teammates, they like having you out there.

"I have had my differences in the past with a few of those guys (in the leadership group). I can see why – I haven't been serious enough about my footy. Now that I look back and see where I was, I can understand why they were all like that with me. Now there is a mutual respect amongst myself and them and pretty much the whole group. That is probably the most pleasing part."

As usual, Scarlett was the first player dressed. He liked to get into his full kit straight away and then wander the rooms. Every player had their own little routines. Harley and Johnson lived on the massage table, having their bodies checked and double-checked by the training staff. Hunt sat in the corner in his own world, iPod loud enough that everyone around him could hear what was playing, while Shannon Byrnes also became very edgy.

Gary Ablett and Jimmy Bartel kicked 'bananas' at each other and had little games about who could hit the mark on the wall, or the door, while Ling stood around and chatted to anyone in the vicinity. He led the laid-back types, along with Joel Corey, Mackie, Ottens and Milburn.

Harley and Corey Enright, who was surprisingly vocal given his quiet nature off the field, were the ones who fired everyone up, as did fitness coach and runner Paul Haines, who provided non-stop encouragement.

Nathan Ablett was keeping to himself, as usual, but he had received a quick visit from his famous father, who called into the rooms to wish his two sons good luck. Other pre-game rituals included James Kelly ensuring he was the last to get strapped, and Mooney refusing to touch the banner when he ran out. Chapman, who always had a cold shower before he went out, was making sure he got around to the younger players. "I thought if Port Adelaide were smart they would go around and attack the young blokes and try to get them early," he said. "So I went up to Stokesy and said, 'How are you feeling?' He looked straight back at me and said: 'I feeling fine, I am just ready to go, ready to do my job'.

"He said it so sincerely that you could tell he was just ready to play, he didn't want to be best on ground, he just wanted to go out and do his bit. From then on, as soon as I saw him, I thought we are going to be hard to beat today. I knew I was feeling good and I was ready and — just the look on his face — he was ready to go."

Chapman had been the first in queue in the medical room for a pain-killing injection. He had one in his troublesome groin; Milburn required one for his calf; Johnson had a couple jabbed into his shoulder. Mooney was getting attention on his hand while Wojcinski was downing Panadol and Panadeine Forte to ward off yet another headache. He was doing as little as possible in the warm-up to conserve his energy; predictably, he was feeling a bit flat.

A room to the side of the main area had been set up with a television showing highlights of the season. People could sit in there and read the *Football Record*, or just hang out away from the players. Travis Varcoe was in there when Thompson walked in. It was half-an-hour until the bounce but the coach was already thinking of next year.

"You ran out of steam this year," Thompson said to Varcoe. "You had a really good year and you have got to build on it because next year we want you in the team." Varcoe knew his coach spoke the truth. "You're right," he said, as he watched himself on the television produce one of his trademark steals.

Harley was stretching his back and hamstrings for the 20th time in the past hour when board member Campbell Neal came up to him. "Tom, I just love what you say to the guys, you are just a natural orator," Neal said. "I am going to make a point of listening to what you say to the guys ... I'm going to take notes."

The skipper nodded his head and started to worry. At that point he had no idea what words of wisdom or inspiration he would produce. But

Thompson already knew what he was going to say; when the team was called into the meeting room for the final time his message was simple and short.

"You guys know what you have got to do. If you guys do what you have done all year and play our way, we win the game. Port Adelaide are the ones that have got to do something special, play above themselves.

We are the best team in the competition, we play to our game we win the game. We don't need to play above ourselves. We don't need Gary Ablett to be the superstar, we don't need players to play the greatest game of their lives.

"If every bloke plays their role, plays our way, then we win. There is no question."

Then it was time.

The players huddled at the doorway of the changerooms before moving into the corridor which took them to the race. Harley quickly brought them together for a quick word and then continued on towards the race. A Channel 10 producer stopped the skipper and asked if they could wait a minute or so because Port Adelaide were late coming out. "No, I don't think so," Harley replied. "We are going out when we want to go out."

As he approached the top of the race, the noise started to infiltrate the senses, he stopped again. "Guys, this is it," he said. "This is what it's all about." He could see smiles all round from his teammates. They were ready.

The moment was bigger … larger … more overwhelming … than any of them could have imagined. The roar of the crowd and a sea and blue and white shook them for a few seconds while they got their bearings. "You just felt invincible," Harley said.

An official team photo immediately after the players burst through the banner was organised. Thompson sat next to Harley and Ling. The coach then scampered off and headed for the box, where already his team was set up. Sanderson sat next to Thompson with his board man, Alan Carter, on the other side. He had to keep up with the match-ups and player movement on the ground so that at any point Thompson, who had met Carter during his brief stint at the Kangaroos, could know exactly who was where.

Hinkley sat next to Sanderson; McCartney was at the opposite end, next to Carter. All had headphones on and could talk at any time to Ronnie Watt or the two runners, Haines and Duncan Kellaway, down on the bench. Computer screens in front of each coach showed up to the minute statistics.

In the second row sat Balme, who was feeling so unwell he wasn't sure he'd see out the game; Steve Hocking, whose role was to monitor the interchange bench rotations; and VFL coach Leigh Tudor. There was also a special addition for the Grand Final – Matthew Egan was seated at the rear. While Mark Blake sat in the stands hiding his emotions behind a large pair of black sunglasses, Egan had wanted to be a part of the big day. He had told Thompson and Sanderson earlier in the week to include him in everything.

"I came back after my time away and said to them, 'I know I am not going to play but I want to be a part of it. I want to feel like I am still in the team,'" he said. "So I went to every meeting, I was in the meeting before the game just with the 22 players and then obviously in the box." He had also addressed the defensive unit during the week, with not a dry eye in the room. "He wished them all the best and said he wished he was out there with them," Sanderson said. "There were guys with tears in their eyes because they loved playing with him. It was pretty awe-inspiring."

When the teams lined up for the national anthem, Mooney took the opportunity to cast his eye over the opposition. He liked what he saw. "(Port) had so many young blokes," he said. "I knew you could pressure them, especially their young forwards. We had Scarlo, Dasher and Harls down there and they are just ruthless. They were always going to bash the shit out of them."

Kelly and Chapman weren't interested in Port. They were casting an eye over the national anthem singer, Natalie Bassingthwaighte. "I was pretty uptight and nervous and it was funny because when she was singing the national anthem I looked at her because I've always had a bit of a crush on her," Kelly said. "I'm looking at her thinking, 'She's hotter than she is on

TV'. I elbowed Lingy next to me and he said, 'Yeah, she's hot'. That sort of relaxed me, broke the ice a bit and then I was okay, I'm ready to play now. It's funny how something like that can do that.

"Then to see all the past players on the ground, and the premiership cups lined up behind (Bassingthwaighte), that also gave me a bit of a buzz – just thinking about the legends there and how amazing it would be if we could be in the same boat as those guys with a premiership cup."

The only time Chapman hadn't thought about football for the whole day was when he looked at the Rogue Traders singer and former *Neighbours* star. "The national anthem sent shivers up my spine and I was looking at her thinking, 'Gee, she is looking hot today,'" he said. "Then I looked back and I was instantly locked in. That was the only time I didn't think of footy and from then I was on. I was ready to play."

Harley won the toss, then the team came together in its ring. The captain spoke first, then Max Rooke, the luckiest man out there given he thought his season was over a couple of months earlier. He was like a timebomb; the previous week Thompson had warned him to hold back because he didn't want a report on his hands.

"It was good knowing there was no tomorrow," Rooke said. "It's your last game and you can just go for it. I wasn't worried about getting reported and it is the best feeling. In the preliminary final you are worried about going hard because you might accidentally hit someone and go out for a week. It is an awesome feeling playing and not worrying about anything."

He lined up on the wing for the opening bounce. As Ottens and Dean Brogan contested, Rooke came flying through the middle of the pack and crashed into Port midfielder David Rodan. While the execution hadn't been the best, his actions sent a message. "He came off the wing in the first seconds and bounced off four guys," Sanderson said. "It almost summed up why the club spent all that money sending him to Germany because he was such a crucial part for us. He really set the tone."

After Bartel got the first touch of the game, a quick handball, the ball spilled out to the wing where Corey, Chapman, Kelly and then Rooke all chased after lone Port player Danyle Pearce. "When I saw four of our players chasing one bloke I thought, 'Shit, these boys are on. Port are going to be in a bit of trouble,'" said Milburn, who had lined up on Justin Westhoff in the back pocket.

All the match-ups had gone to plan. Ling and Shaun Burgoyne were running around the middle of the ground; Enright was on Pearce on the outer wing; Kane Cornes went with Bartel and Domenic Cassisi next to Gary Ablett. The Cats had started Wojcinski, Selwood, King and Brynes on the bench while the biggest surprise from Port was Brendon Lade starting on interchange.

The Cats' first foray forward came after a free kick was reversed. Cassisi decked Ablett off the ball. Chapman took the free kick and went long to Mooney, who produced a big leap but couldn't take the mark, and split the webbing in his left hand again. Given the baggage he carried into the game from his performance in his first Grand Final, it wasn't the start Mooney was looking for. "I dropped the mark and thought, 'It's going to be one of those days. I am going to have a shit day,'" he said.

Port ran it out of defence through Pearce, who had five bounces before he was brought down by a brilliant tackle from Harley. Already the signs were good for the Cats, with their intensity at the man and the ball standing out, as were their tactics; Milburn sprinted off Westhoff at the three-minute mark for a shot for goal from 50 metres which was punched through for a behind.

A rushed behind gave Port its first score and Hunt his first kick for the game … and his first blunder. He tried to thread it to Enright 35 metres away but instead landed it in the arms of his opponent, Ebert, who ran in and luckily missed the shot at goal. Hunt re-loaded again and, instead of being gunshy, he again went with a pinpoint pass that hit Ling, laces out, on the 50-metre line.

"I just didn't kick it hard enough," Hunt said of the first one. "I took a bit off it and tried to sit it between five of them and (Ebert) ended up being the front one and it just landed in his arms. The next one I didn't really think about it too much, which is something I would have done in the past. I just saw Lingy and thought I can get it there. The first one had at least spun all right so I let rip on the second one which got there. We were away."

The Cats again moved the ball through the centre corridor, Mackie sending it long towards Stokes, who attempted a "hanger" on Peter Burgoyne but landed awkwardly, hyper-extending his right knee. A groan rang out across the MCG as Dr Chris Bradshaw sprinted from the bench to Stokes, who lay motionless clutching at his knee.

"I thought it was over," Stokes said of his afternoon, and possibly the entire 2008 season. "I don't know what I was doing because I have never gone for a speccie before but I think I just got hit in the wrong spot and spun around. I felt the pain straight away. I didn't even remember we were in the grand final because I just thought, 'This is 12 months out'. Blokes say they can hear a 'pop' when they do recos and I had heard something go bad."

Stokes was the type of person who never liked showing he was hurt – he saw that as a weakness – so he tried to get up but couldn't move. "I tried to put the knee down and it just wouldn't stand up," he said. "I knew I was in a bit of trouble. I am one of those guys who doesn't want to be stretchered off and when I saw it coming out, I made sure I got helped up and then carried off."

He was taken straight down to the rooms for what Stokes described as "the most frightening 10 minutes of my life". He couldn't walk or feel his leg but, after a couple of minutes, Bradshaw provided some good news. His examination had revealed no structural damage and he would give him a pain-killing injection to see if it responded.

Stokes had been replaced by Byrnes, who could only think of one thing as he ran onto the ground: doughnuts. "I had been to 10 grand finals throughout my life," he said. "I just remember seeing blokes in the paper with doughnuts (0 kicks, 0 marks, 0 handballs) next to their name for the granny. "I just wanted one touch. I sprinted across the ground and Stevie Johnson saw me and I was just lucky to get a kick straight away. I'd got one in the first 20 seconds and thought, 'Well, if nothing else happens, there are no doughnuts.'"

His first touch was important as he found an open Chapman, who went long from 50 metres for what looked to be a goal until Mooney marked it right on the line. "It was my first kick in two Grand Finals and I thought, 'You fucking beauty, I can't miss this,'" Mooney said.

Chapman was initially annoyed with his full-forward until he thought about what it meant. "Moons probably should have shepherded it over the line but I realised that him getting his hands on it early was better for the team than me just kicking the goal," he said.

It had taken seven minutes for the first goal; the second came just a handful of minutes later with a wonderul tap-on by Kelly, who lay on the ground in the centre with Port defender Michael Pettigrew sliding in with his knees. It dribbled to Chapman, whose pass hit a diving Mooney at half-forward. He shaped to have a shot but short-passed to Johnson, who marked, took two steps and nailed the shot from 45 metres. As Corey ran back to the middle he already had a good feeling about this game. "There was nothing I saw in the first 10 minutes that worried me," he said. "It was just a matter of time for us. You can't be up by 10 goals in the first few minutes but we were playing in a way that could make it happen (eventually)."

When he got to centre he was met by King, who was on for his first run and had steam coming out of his ears. "I knew if I got a chance I was playing as if it was going to be my last game ever," King said. His mates, especially Mooney and Scarlett, had fired him up about throwing his weight around. That's exactly what he did at the bounce, charging at Cassisi, who had received the ball, and smacking him around the head. While he gave away a free-kick, the Port midfielder was forced off with a blood nose and the football world knew Steven King was back in the big time. "It was just perfect how it played out, although I guess I would have loved to have 'stuck' the tackle," King said. "But getting him off with the blood rule was a good result and it made me feel like I knew what I was there for."

The exposure of Westhoff continued, this time with Scarlett running off the youngster to have a set shot from 35 metres, which missed. While the full-back had been lining up, Wojcinski ran on for his first appearance, and the next few minutes summed up his week. "I was still a bit flat and I tried to get myself up as much as I could. That's why I went a bit overboard early on and gave away three free kicks in the first five minutes," he said.

A late spoil on Darryl Wakelin was the first, followed by a reckless dive into the back of youngster Travis Boak, but it was the third infringement – when he carried Tredrea forward in a tackle and got into his back – which proved the most costly. The Port captain dusted himself off and kicked the goal from 20 metres to get his side on the board after 17 minutes.

It was Johnson's turn to be in the bad books on the next play. After brilliantly intercepting an attempted handball from Jacob Surjan, he attempted a banana kick from 30 metres out instead of dishing off to Mooney, who was five metres in front of him, and in the clear. The flashback to the bad old days wasn't missed in the coach's box with Hinkley knowing that his man had just "jumped the fence" again.

All was quickly forgiven because Gary Ablett immediately came up with his own brilliant interception. Troy Chaplin tried to centre the ball from the back pocket to Cassisi. The kick hung in the air and Ablett easily got there to punch it ahead, gather and nail the shot from 20 metres to provoke the biggest roar of the day from the 97,302 crowd.

Shaun Burgoyne got the quick reply a couple of minutes later. A brilliant tap by Lade at a boundary throw-in set him free to run into an easy goal. Yet the reply came quickly again, this time a great team goal set up by a dashing run by Hunt along the boundary line on the wing. He then centred the ball (as demanded by the team's gameplan) to a contest which Ottens crashed, forcing the ball over the back to Chapman, who casually chipped over the top to Johnson ... who somehow had again found space. He strolled in and kicked his second from 20 metres.

On the boundary line, a Lazarus-like resurrection was taking place: Stokes was doing run-throughs. Five minutes later he was back on and immediately into the play being awarded a free-kick. "I remember thinking, 'I have got to make someone pay,'" Stokes said. "I saw a pack and just jumped into it and got a free-kick. That calmed me down a bit as I could still feel my knee and couldn't hit top speed or change direction very well. But I was out there. I don't know who invented local anaesthetics but they are great things."

There are many great moments in Grand Finals that can define the game. It wasn't obvious that this year's might be about to arrive when Pettigrew marked in the back pocket and started to casually run forward with a bounce. Chasing him was Ottens, but that didn't faze the Port defender, who had another bounce and, when he saw the Geelong ruckman still coming, went for a third bounce. Finding an option to kick to was on

Pettigrew's mind, not his lumbering pursuer. So when he was suddenly pinned from behind by the outstretched arms of a diving Ottens, he was as surprised as everyone at the ground. Ottens had willed every ounce of determination out of his body and made the tackle. The coach's box immediately erupted, particularly Sanderson.

"For me as the defensive coach that was the moment," he said. "The slowest player on the ground chasing down Pettigrew, who has got speed, for me that was when I thought, 'We're really in this'. I just loved it."

The Brownlow Medallist's moment came two minutes later. A series of quick handballs went from Gary Ablett to Kelly to Selwood, who produced yet another jaw-dropping act which defied his inexperience: he sold the dummy to a Port defender, then fired off a handball to Bartel, who took two steps and drilled a left-foot helicopter goal from 45 metres.

His fist-pumping celebration was well under way before the ball had floated through.

"The whole build-up was just pressure, pressure, pressure," Bartel said. "The way (the ball) got to me, it had been bouncing all over the place and then, 'Boom!' I just hit it sweet, like a golf swing. You know when you feel like you don't think you've swung hard but it just goes? That's what happened with that kick."

A Kelly miss from a set shot after the siren – his seventh possession for the term – made the margin 23 points. It could easily have been more, with the Cats leading the inside 50 entries 17-8. Johnson was the leading possession winner (eight), with Chapman and Milburn also seeing plenty of it with (seven), while King had made an immediate impression with five disposals, three marks and four hit-outs.

Earlier that week, Harley had asked Thompson what it looked like when the team was on song. "I'll tell you exactly what we look like," the coach had said. "At some stage in the game, whether it's the first quarter or whatever, this is when I know we are on: the ball will be in the centre of the ground and Port will kick it into our defensive 50. You will mark it and you will handball it off to Scarlett. He will shimmy and kick it to Milburn, who is at centre half-back. Milburn will handball it to Mackie, who hits up

Mooney, who is leading up from centre half-forward. He will give it off to Chapman, who will kick it long to Nathan Ablett. He will make a contest and it will result in a front-and-square goal to Gary Ablett or Stokes."

The description had made a lasting impression on Harley and he thought of it as he watched Geelong kick the opening goal of the second quarter. While the names changed, the principle had been the same. He'd actually started with the ball in the back pocket and handballed it to Hunt who, under pressure, handballed to Corey. He quickly gave it back to the running Hunt, whose pass hit Rooke on the wing.

He chipped it to Enright in the middle of the ground, who played on, ran through the centre and kicked to Stokes on the lead at half-forward. A handball across to Johnson set up his third goal as he was being pushed to the ground.

The Cats were on song. In the next eight minutes they would produce some of the best football for the year. A free kick to King at the next centre bounce saw him chip it wide to the run of Mackie, who then squeezed a short kick to the leading Stokes. He handballed to Ling, who bounced off three Port players and somehow got a handball across to Rooke, who took two steps and nailed the goal from 50 metres.

Three minutes later it was again set up from the last line through the run of Scarlett and Enright. Stokes got involved, getting it to the running Scarlett, whose short pass found Chapman but did not travel the required distance. No matter: a sloppy Peter Burgoyne tackle around the neck gave away the free kick to Chapman, who had no problems icing the shot from 50 metres. After seven minutes in the second quarter, the margin was 41 points.

In the stands, Frank Costa had seen all he needed. He turned to his wife and said: "Shirley, will you stop being nervous and silly. You have got an opportunity to really enjoy a winning grand final by Geelong. Just sit back, laugh and enjoy it."

She refused to. Brian Cook was the same. He got very nervous watching games but his president wanted him to know that the 44-year drought was over. "Cooky, will you stop being a worry wart," Costa said. "We are absolutely killing them and we have got this game."

Cook couldn't believe Costa had gone the 'early crow' and turned away. "Cooky, you have to look at the facts," Costa continued. "They are beaten in every facet of this game; their rucks, which had been a big worry, we are killing them. There is no way they can come back."

Two minutes later, courtesy of a player very close to the president's heart, Costa's declaration looked to be on the money. Nathan Ablett hadn't been sighted in the opening term, and there had been concerns in the coaching ranks about him on the big stage. "I was as nervous as anyone leading into the finals, thinking 'Which Nathan Ablett is going to turn up?'" Sanderson confessed.

Well, Ablett announced himself on the Grand Final stage at the tail end of the play of the day. While lying on the ground in Port's goalsquare, Enright managed to get a handball to Bartel, who was instantly tackled but still moved the ball onto Wojcinski. His left foot pass hit Rooke on the wing. He passed to Mooney, leading up the centre corridor, who played on and handballed wide to Selwood ... who kicked long to the youngest Ablett. Port defender Toby Thurstans found himself caught out of position and pushed back hard, knocking over Ablett to give away the free kick and goal.

From the next centre bounce, Gary Ablett roved the tapout but was tackled immediately. The ball spilled to Selwood, who ran on and kicked long to Nathan Ablett, who took a brilliant one-handed mark just 15 metres out from goal. He then casually played on to snap the goal over his shoulder.

Brisbane champion Michael Voss, seated in the Channel 10 commentary box, was stunned. "It's been absolutely awesome watching this team," he said. "They are winning in every facet of the game and doing it with such power and precision. They look unstoppable."

Geelong had kicked seven unanswered goals; it had been 25 minutes since Port Adelaide had actually scored. Chad Cornes stopped the procession at the 13-minute mark when he marked strongly and goaled. The game's frenetic pace slowed momentarily, with bad misses by Rooke and Ottens putting the brakes on. Chapman's second goal of the term, at the 26-minute mark, was his side's first for 15 minutes. When the siren sounded, the Geelong players received a standing ovation. The lead was 52 points, the third highest half-time margin in Grand Final history.

In 1970, Gareth Andrews' flatmate was Terry Waters, the captain of Collingwood. That year the Magpies were leading Carlton by 44 points at half-time of the Grand Final and, famously, lost. Ted Hopkins came off the bench for the Blues and kicked four second half goals to snatch the premiership. As those around him started to celebrate a Geelong premiership, the vice-president was still nervous.

"With Terry Waters being my flatmate, I lived through the whole 1970 experience," Andrews said. "And Teddy Hopkins is still one of my best mates so I would not let go about the whole 1970 thing. Plus, I remember a game against Hawthorn in 1989 when Geelong were 56 points up late in the second quarter and got beaten. Then, of course, last year against West Coast. I don't trust football."

Mooney shared the paranoia as he walked into the rooms. "I still had that mentality of a year ago, where we can just completely pack up and lose games," he said. "I'd had that mentality all year."

Ottens remained dirty on himself for missing the easy goal. "I thought the door is still a little bit open for them because if we'd kicked those goals it would have been all over," he said. "There was still a lot to be done."

Those concerns were quickly allayed by the atmosphere in the rooms. "It was intense," King said. "Blokes were screaming at each other not to let up, not to go kick-chasing or get forward and be hogs. You knew that third quarter was going to be intense."

Rooke was confident the situation was under control. "The only way we were going to lose was if we dropped off, and I knew we weren't going to," he said. "Maybe a year or two before some guys may have got ahead of themselves but I knew that wasn't going to happen. It is such a good feeling when you know everyone is on the same page, everyone is thinking the same thing."

After the first 30 seconds of the third quarter, there were a few more coming around to Rooke's view, including the coach. It had been the rugged midfielder who cleared the ball from the opening bounce, sending it to centre half-forward, where Kane Cornes found possession. Another brutal Corey tackle knocked the ball loose, and Stokes ran onto it, hitting Mooney on the lead. He went back and slotted his second goal of the game from 45 metres tucked up against the boundary line. "I was really pleased that within 30 seconds Moons was having a shot for goal and it was brought about by good attack on the ball and good ball movement, plus he kicked the goal," Thompson said.

Chapman, who'd had another pain-killing injection at half-time, knew it was Geelong's day as he watched the Mooney kick. "It was a great kick. Probably his best kick all year from a set shot," he said. "That's when I thought, 'This is us.'"

During half-time, Hinkley had given Johnson a gentle reminder about not jumping the fence again. Twice in the first half, including just before the siren, he'd had a shot instead of passing. Mooney was in better positions on both occasions.

Perhaps it previously would have gone 'in one ear and out the other'. But, at the five-minute mark, the new Johnson put it into practice. He took a pass from Mooney and was 40 metres out, deep in the forward pocket next to the boundary line. While the umpire tried to line him up, Johnson wasn't looking at the goals – he was looking at Bartel, who was running towards the goalsquare from the other flank. A wonderfully placed, low and penetrating kick gave Bartel the perfect jump at it to take the mark 15 metres out, directly in front. "Having known him since we played junior footy together, I knew exactly what he was thinking and he knew what I was doing," Bartel said.

A rare Rodan possession a couple of minutes later resulted in a behind for Port. The former Richmond player, who had enjoyed a superb season, had just three possessions to half-time, the same number as Ebert and Westhoff, with Motlop one worse.

Milburn took the kick-in and played on before going long towards Chapman, Harley and Tredrea near the wing. "We were all sort of together and they ran past me and I thought, "Gee, I'm slow,'" Chapman said. "Then all of a sudden (they) sort of stopped on the spot and I thought, 'This is going to work for me here'. So I just leapt and it came off." Chapman revived memories of Alex Jesaulenko's screamer in the 1970 grand final, putting his knees into the back of Tredrea to pull down the mark of the day. "You dream of taking a massive hanger on the big day so I was pretty happy about it," he said.

Everything was going Geelong's way. Thompson enjoyed the view as his players largely did as they pleased. Even Ottens managed to take four bounces down the members wing. When Cassisi, the man who had kicked the goal to stop the winning streak in round 21, had a shot on the run from 30 metres directly in front and kicked out on the full, Thompson knew he was going to be a premiership coach.

For a few minutes he kept the feeling to himself. But after watching the play which set up a Shannon Byrnes goal at the 15-minute mark, there was no longer any need to hold back. The passage of play had started at half-back, where Wojcinski took two bounces and handballed to Stokes - who had been brilliant since he returned from his knee scare – on the wing. He baulked an opponent, took a bounce of his own and went long to Ottens on the lead. The ball was punched away, but there was Johnson, front and square. Reinforcing his new calling in life, he again passed off, this time with a short screw kick to Nathan Ablett. An unselfish handball over the top to Byrnes in the goalsquare, and the lead was 70 points … and the grand final was over.

"In the three Grand Finals I played in there was a point where you would just look at each other on the ground," Thompson said. "You just make eye contact and there is a little bit of wetness in the eye, it's like 'Yep, we're premiers'. That happened for the coaches, too. We just sensed that the way we were talking to one another we knew we had done this. We could sit back for a quarter-and-a-half. How many coaching groups get to sit back for that long?"

He cracked a gag, which prompted Sanderson to have a look at the scoreboard. "I looked up at it and thought, 'Shit, this might be over,'" he said. "No one actually said it in as many words but Bomber made a joke. You could sense everyone just relaxed."

Hinkley didn't know what to do. "It was almost like a game throughout the year, where we had the game well won and all we were worried about was making sure we rotated the players and kept them fresh," he said. "But this was the Grand Final, we don't have to do that because next week they're not playing. So I was thinking, 'What are we going to do?' Give me a Coke or something."

On the field, Harley found himself getting emotional. After the goal had been scored, Mackie high-fived him and said: "Man, you are a premiership captain." Immediately, tears welled in Harley's eyes. He quickly re-grouped and said to his teammate: "Ruthless. C'mon Mack, pass the word around, let's be relentless."

Nearby, Gary Ablett, who had been carrying a broken toe after being stomped on late in the first quarter, was also doing some scoreboard calculations. "Surely, they can't come back from this," he thought to himself.

A Tredrea goal from a Motlop tap-on a minute later brought the focus back and inspired a four-goal blitz in the final 10 minutes of the term. King, who was going from strength to strength, took another contested mark from a kick-in at the 20-minute mark and short-passed to Johnson. Instead of blazing away, he set it up to the goalsquare, where Ottens ran onto it and marked inches from the goal line.

At the next centre bounce it was again King who beat Lade. "I was rapt to be contributing, not only be given a game and be seen as a charity case," King said. "I wanted people to say, 'Gee, that is why he played'. To get that respect back from my teammates was important as well."

King grabbed the ball out of the next ruck contest and handballed to Ling, whose quick kick forward saw Nathan Ablett make a contest; the ball spilled to Corey, who had run forward out of the middle. A quick handball to Chapman secured his third goal. Nathan Ablett then kicked his third, four minutes later from a free-kick, before another textbook Geelong transition play fell into place to take Mooney to the same tally.

Three-quarter time margin: an AFL grand final record 90 points.

In the stand, Cook approached Costa. "I think you might be right," he said.

As the coaches made their way to the ground, it was agreed what the message had to be. "Let's just play this the right way, don't lairise," McCartney said to the midfield group, before pointedly noting that the Power had done precisely that against the Kangaroos in the preliminary final. "Don't do the things the club we're playing had done the week before. Be humble and treat the game with respect."

Sanderson was stressing the importance of the next 30 minutes for the image of the club to his defenders. "You are going to win a Grand Final but you are going to lose a lot of respect if we lose the last quarter by five goals by carrying on and showboating," he said. "I have just been in awe of everything you have done this year as a team, you have just been amazing … so play this last quarter like you have done all year."

Hinkley was urging the forwards to play the right way but Johnson was missing from the group. "Stevie, Stevie. Come here I want to talk to you about something."

Johnson turned around and looked at his coach. "Kenny, don't call me Stevie," he said with a smile. "*Call me Normie.*"

Hinkley was gobsmacked. It was a classic Steve Johnson thing to say. "There were a number of players in the running (for the Norm Smith Medal), like Chapman and Scarlett, but him being him thought, 'I've got this in the bag.'"

Thompson then addressed the entire group. "We've done everything right and you'll get a lot of respect if you just keep playing the way you are playing," he said. "Let's send a pretty strong message to the whole footy world that the Cats are the real deal."

He then paused and looked around into their eyes. "Let's bury them."

"How do they measure in history as a team?" Michael Voss threw the question out there just after he'd watched Geelong kick its third goal of the final quarter at the eight-minute mark. The margin was now 108 points. The previous highest winning margin in a Grand Final was 96 points (Hawthorn over Melbourne, 1988).

Voss provided his own answer. "You would have to say one of the best ever."

Thompson's urging had hit the right spot, and the accelerator was well and truly down. Scarlett to Chapman, who had three bounces through the middle, and long to Mooney, who was infringed by Wakelin. The first goal of the last quarter came after four minutes.

Chapman going long three minutes later resulted in Ottens punching down into the lap of Ling, whose right foot snap put the margin into three figures. After setting two up, Chapman got his fourth for the day a minute later when he outmarked Pettigrew one-on-one following an Enright cruise through the middle and long bomb to the square.

And so on it went. At the 11-minute mark, a one-two between Scarlett and Mackie sent the full-back running again, with one bounce before going long. This time Johnson marked strongly going back with the flight. Instead of going back and taking the easy shot, he typically did something different; he kept going with his momentum and, as he was falling to the ground he managed to dribble through his fourth goal.

The Geelong party officially started at the 15-minute mark. Once again the build-up to the 23rd goal of the afternoon was superb, with Bartel handballing to Gary Ablett, who found Johnson on his own at the 50-metre arc. His shot drifted across the face, where Mooney marked in front of Nathan Ablett. For the second week in a row, he then cannoned into the point post. After shaking himself off, the Cats full-forward took one step in from the boundary and snapped truly.

Mooney now had five goals. Amazingly, in a season of domination that figure equalled the highest kicked by a Geelong player for the entire year. Mini celebrations started breaking out all over the ground and, of course, in the stands. As the ball was coming back to the middle, for the first time Ling sensed himself relaxing. He started looking around the crowd, at the sea of blue and white. Ablett jogged past and snapped him out of his daydream. "Hey mate, we're premiership players," he said and started laughing.

Cook and Costa rose from their seats and embraced. The crowd around them erupted, with the television cameras catching the poignant moment between the two architects of the premiership victory. "Let's go downstairs, mate," Cook said. They took Alex Popescu, the club benefactor, with them. The 91-year-old timber merchant had played a critical part in keeping the club alive in the bad old days – often he would take care of the payroll when times were tough – with his donations to the football club believed to have run into the millions over the decades.

A few rows away, Stephen Wells was crying. This was only the third live game the recruiting manager had seen for the year and he was overcome with emotion. "It just justified everything," Wells said. "We could have gone through a long time and not won anything. People said we had been there too long and that it was too long to win a premiership. In my time at the club we'd had five grand finals, two preliminary finals and five night grand finals, so I reckon we have always given ourselves a chance to be okay. To actually win it is unbelievable. Everything I could possibly hope for."

Down in the race, the VFL players and a number of former club champions were assembling, including Billy Brownless, who was also in tears. On the ground it was Mackie's turn to get in on the act, kicking his first goal for the day courtesy of a 50-metre penalty from Chad Cornes.

Stokes was walking up to half-forward when he saw Haines coming towards him. He immediately knew what the runner wanted. He was about to get dragged and would end the game on the bench. "Just a quick break," Haines said.

"I'm not that dumb, Hainesy," Stokes said.

The ball started coming towards them and Stokes tried to plead his case again. "Are you sure Hainesy?"

"Yeah, just a quick break."

As soon as Stokes got to the bench he knew he'd been set up. Already sitting down were Nathan Ablett, Selwood and Byrnes. He shook his head, sat down and then looked at all of them and with a big smile said two words: "Premiership players."

In the coaches' box, Sanderson suggested to Thompson that it was time to get down on the boundary line. "You might as well head down, mate, and enjoy this," he said. "We'll be right up here."

"I'm not going unless you come," Thompson said.

"All right, I'll come with you."

Then McCartney joined in. "If you guys are going, I'm coming."

With five minutes to go, the entire Geelong coaches' box was empty. When Thompson got down onto the ground the tears came. He hugged everyone on the bench: the players, coaches, doctors and trainers. On the field, the players had started organising their celebrations.

Johnson had changed his tune on the medal. He walked up to Chapman and said: "How are you going, Norm?"

"Don't call me Norm, you'll be Norm," Chapman said, and both of them cracked up laughing.

Ling was trying to find Bartel. They wanted to be close to each other on the siren, but he momentarily forgot about that as he watched Shaun Burgoyne run in and kick a goal. A couple of minutes earlier he had been taken off him. "They wanted me to relax and go forward but I didn't want to and told them, 'I want to finish the job on Burgoyne,'" Ling said. "But they told me to relax and put Rookey on him. Then when he kicked his second goal I just stared at the bench. Then I thought, 'You can probably relax now and stop stressing.'"

At the centre bounce, Ling realised he was a long way from Bartel, who was up on the wing, so he started jogging around to the other side. The Cats hadn't scored for the last eight-and-a-half minutes but no-one cared, particularly Scarlett, who was focussed on trying to engineer it so Harley ended up with the ball on the siren.

The pair played a bit of kick-to-kick as the clock ticked past 30 minutes. Eventually, the chain was broken, the ball sent long to the wing, where Ottens took yet another contested mark. Scarlett started screaming at his ruckman, who duly obliged and kicked it 40 metres backwards to him. Just as the ball left his boot, it came.

For 44 years a town and a football club had been waiting to hear that siren. When the ball landed in his arms, Harley, who had been oblivious to Scarlett's plan, threw it immediately to the heavens and screamed.

Bartel and Ling jumped on each other and fell to the ground in a bear hug. Gary Ablett sunk to his knees with two arms raised to the sky. Mooney pumped his fist then immediately went to Wakelin, who had announced his retirement in the lead-up, to shake his hand.

Spot fires of Geelong players jumping on each other broke out. Fittingly, the old stagers of Milburn, Scarlett and Harley locked arms. Behind them, Hunt was running to the ball bin behind the goals. At the opposite end, Chapman was doing the same. The week before the pair had planned it and Chapman had yelled out to Hunt five minutes earlier to not forget the ball. "When I ran in and scooped up a ball, one of the kids who was holding them said, 'I don't think you can do that.'" Chapman said. "I just took it and put it up my jumper and then we met each other in the centre."

As Thompson strode out to meet his players, the television cameras swooped. "It's very emotional," he said. "It's just amazing. We've put a lot of work into this football club to get it to this state, it's been a long time since we won previously. It's just amazing to see the people who have waited so long, to actually see the look in their eyes."

Gary Ablett could hardly speak when he was asked about what this would mean to his father. "I'm speechless and emotional," he said. "Put is this way, I will cut the medal in half and give him half." Scarlett was spent. "I'm bloody tired," he said. "It has taken too long to win one … we've won this for everyone, all the ex-players, everyone."

Harley was overwhelmed. "It has been a perfect year. We swept the pools." And Bartel was relieved to be adding to his medal collection. "I loved the Brownlow but all I wanted was a premiership medal."

As the players gathered for the presentations, Mark Williams made sure he shook the hand of every Geelong player. He had a brief conversation with Thompson, where he admitted his pre-game tactics had been necessary because he knew it was the only card he had to play.

Egan and Blake were there; mixed emotions were consoled by jubilant teammates. Diggerson sought out Thompson and Harley to prepare them for the speeches, making sure they didn't forget to thank both the Geelong and AFL sponsors.

Sarah Birch, the media and communications assistant manager, was busy handing out Geelong premiership caps to players, not to wear, but to give to the Auskick children who would be presenting the premiership medallions. The idea had been her brainchild earlier in the week and had taken some arm-twisting with the AFL to get the go-ahead. Birch had watched how, in previous years, the children had all but been ignored once the players, understandably caught up in the moment, got their medallions.

After last year's NAB Cup victory, Byrnes had been so excited that he had forgotten to shake hands with the little boy who'd given him his medallion. For the next week, the communications department had received dozens of emails and calls about the incident. This had stuck in Birch's mind, yet her initial idea to give each child a showbag full of goodies was rejected by the AFL. After some heated debate, the two parties agreed on a cap.

The first presentation was for the Norm Smith Medal. The consensus at the ground had it down to three, and all had excellent cases. Johnson had finished with 23 disposals, nine marks, six inside 50s and 4.2 goals; fellow half-forward Chapman collected 21 touches, seven marks (including the best of the day), eight inside 50s and four goals; Scarlett had an incredible 29 possessions from full-back, plus eight marks, four inside 50s and two behinds.

Former Carlton strongman David Rhys-Jones, who won the medal in 1987, had the job of presenting. Given he'd had many *colourful* moments in his career, it was fitting he read out: "Steve Johnson."

Immediately his teammates pounced. Water squirted from every direction as Johnson made his way through the pack and onto the stage. It had been a bizarre day in many respects and this capped it off. "I felt like I was running on thin air all day," he said. "I never fatigued at all, I'd never run like that, it was hard to explain."

When he got to the stage, Johnson thanked Port Adelaide, then Cats supporters. "You bloody deserved this," he said. "This one is for you and, to the boys, bloody great effort." Then he paused for emphasis. "Premiers."

Each player was then called up in number order, starting with No.1 King and finishing with favourite son Ling at No.45. The caps were a massive hit. "It forced interaction," Diggerson explained.

Harley, despite being No.2, was made to wait until last. Tommy Hafey, a four-time premiership coach at Richmond, presented Thompson with his medal before it was the captain's turn to step to the microphone. He didn't forget his lines, thanking Port and the league's sponsors, which included Toyota (he didn't mention them specifically, then plugged Ford, the Geelong sponsor for 82 years … which drew laughter from the crowd).

"To our boys, it has been an amazing ride, what a turnaround from last year," he said. "I love you all. It has been a long ride and we played with spirit and *WE ARE GEELONG!*"

Harley's scream rocked the stadium, such that Thompson had to wait a few seconds for it to die down before saying a few words. When Port had won the flag in 2004, Williams had played up to the crowd with his tie, in a choking gesture. On stage, he had made a point of having a go at Allan Scott, the trucking magnate and major sponsor, who had come out during the year and said Williams was no longer the right man for the job.

If ever anyone had reason to stick it up a few people on the dais, it was Thompson. But that's not his style, nor his football club's. He thanked the Power and everyone who worked at Geelong before singling out Popescu and Costa. "He is very, very special man for Geelong," he said of his president. "Thank you for hanging around and supporting the Cats and being so patient," Thompson told the fans. "It has been a long time but we got there. Well done."

Fred Wooller, captain of Geelong's 1963 premiership team, climbed onto stage to present Harley and Thompson with the 2007 premiership cup. "He was just as proud as punch and he was like, 'Here you are boys, take this off my bloody hands,'" Harley said.

They lifted the cup above their shoulders, a moment Harley and Thompson had been talking about for months. The rest of the players quickly swarmed on as the confetti started to spray around them and the photographers got busy with the classic team photos. The lap that followed was one of the longest in recent memory. "For eight years I have thought, 'What I am going to do?'" Mooney said. "I said to the boys, 'Just walk the whole lap because you might not ever do it again.'"

The players stopped to talk, hug and kiss almost every Geelong fan. They took turns hanging onto the cup while Mooney, Wojcinski and Milburn all had their children with them at some stage. Some players threw their boots into the crowd; most just walked around in a daze of happiness. "That was the most fun I have ever had in my life," Ling said.

For Costa, the victory lap was his highlight of the day. "Just watching the players, who took such a long time to go around," he said. "They gave the crowd absolutely everything, they hugged them, kissed them, they jumped on the fence and at one stage the whole fence collapsed. Just the joy and happiness on the faces of all of our fans was something to behold. No-one had left the ground, it was the happiest thing I had ever seen."

Harley actually injured his knee in the fence collapse. "I saw my older brother Sam, he was about three deep and I leaned over to him and the fence collapsed," he said. "I almost did my knee, it was a disaster and it was actually pretty sore for a while."

Mooney climbed up and stood on the fence with the cup raised to the heavens (in what he knew would make a great photograph). "I made sure I got some really good shots for the wall," he said.

The Ablett brothers walked together with thoughts of their dad, who had won the Norm Smith Medal in the losing 1989 Grand Final. "Obviously it's something Dad wanted," Nathan said. "But this is for everyone around the club." Gary Jnr was just grateful he got to share the moment with his younger brother. "It meant a lot to me," he said. "It has been tough for him and I don't think people realise. He has come straight out of local footy. I went through the TAC Cup, a big learning curve but it helped me out a lot with my footy when I first came down to the club. Whereas he came straight out of local footy and to be a bloke like he was, his body wasn't fully matured, he had a lot of people saying during the year, 'He doesn't look like he is trying and this and that'. I think it was just more he was learning the game, his body was still maturing.

"No-one can take it away from us now. We have done the ultimate together. It has been a dream to play AFL footy as a kid and we have won a premiership together. He kicked three goals and I was more stoked about him kicking goals than I was about me kicking a goal. I honestly was, because it just meant a lot."

With darkness descending on the stadium, the team gathered in a large circle with the premiership cup in the middle and belted out the theme song. For Milburn, this was his moment. "It's the moment you will always cherish, just the 22 players in the huddle singing the song," he said. "It changes your life, really."

By the time they filed down the race, the rooms were packed with family, friends and media. Mooney led the way with the cup and the players were ushered straight into the coach's room. Thompson wanted them to enjoy it together for a few more minutes; he knew from experience the rest of the night would be mayhem and mostly a blur.

They again sung the theme song with even more gusto, then the coach gave them one very important tip. "Enjoy it, but I have won three flags and the first two were write-offs. I couldn't remember anything," Thompson said. "I was drunk by 9pm so if I can give you any advice, just pace yourself."

For a few moments they just talked about the game amongst themselves. "There was no bullshit or blokes coming up sucking up your arse like we knew was going to happen outside," Stokes said. "It was just the boys and the coaches, sitting around for 10 minutes just talking. I really enjoyed that time and it was probably the moment I will take out of the whole premiership."

The Crown Lagers were cracked and, for many of the players, that was the first beer they'd had for months. While there had never been an official rule put in place, it had been agreed around mid-year that drinking in public was not a good idea. Over the past six weeks, alcohol had been cut out all together.

Mooney took the cup outside, looking for champagne, while others went in search of more beer, in particular Johnson, who was enjoying his first alcoholic drink for the year. His joy was interrupted as he was required at the press conference with Thompson. "I always knew this group was good enough to be a premiership side," Johnson told the assembled media. "But you never dream of playing in a grand final and winning a premiership when you're at where I was. I was pretty much out the door. It's just a fairytale."

Mark Thompson was glad the monkey was off the back of the club he had learned to love. Notably, it was the first time in the game's history that a coach had won his first flag after spending seven seasons at the one club without ultimate success. "The changes we made around the club last year have been fantastic," he said. "Everything we have done seemed to have worked. Our players and our club has been on an absolute mission this year and we let nothing stand in our way. Everything was focussed towards winning a premiership."

He'd again been reduced to tears in the changerooms when he embraced his brother, Steven, and his good friend Garry Harrison. He had been his board man on the interchange bench until a tragic accident in 2004 left him paralysed and in a wheelchair.

Hinkley was exhausted. "I thought I might have been a bit more emotional, having been through the losses, but there was a part of me saying, 'Thank

God it's over,'" he said. "We couldn't have worked any harder this year."

Sanderson was feeling the same rush as the players. "I'm so happy, obviously I would have loved to have been playing but the next best thing is to be coaching," he said. "When you talk about a premiership and you hear people say how great it is, well, it is even better. Everything I dreamed it would be like, it was even better and I didn't even play."

McCartney was proud about what this would mean for the people of Geelong. "This will bring pride and confidence to the city, which I think is a wonderful thing," he said. "I'm so happy for our supporters because now they had something to be really proud of as a club. They could go to the football with confidence and a lot of self-esteem that Geelong is a pretty good club to support and be a part of.

"And there is satisfaction that our style of play had stood up. The boys we drafted had stood up; the longer you stay in this game the more understanding you have that it takes a fair amount of time before they play anywhere near their best and a little bit more time to play their best. You get a small window with them, maybe two, three or four years with them at their very best. It is not unlike raising kids, just that they're older, as you go through the tough times with them, teach them the straight and narrow, give them what they need and want. It is a great day."

All through the changerooms, players were sharing the euphoria with loved ones. Selwood was getting his picture taken with his three brothers; Stokes was with his mum and dad and sister and also on the phone to his aunty's house in Darwin, where the rest of the family had gathered. The Abletts were hidden in a back room with father and sons enjoying a quiet moment together.

The players wanted to stay at the MCG for ever but an attempt to take the cup out into the middle again (now that the crowd had disappeared) was scuttled. The team was required at Federation Square, where they were to be presented to thousands of fans.

Cook and former board member, Greg Giles, decided they'd walk to the reception. The CEO had not had one drink for the day and, as they walked up Wellington Parade, they came across a party happening in one of the terrace houses.

Giles called out to the people. "Hey, how about giving Cooky a beer, he's the CEO of Geelong."

"Bullshit," came the response from partygoers. Cook pulled out a business card and did a deal. "I'll give you tickets during the year if you give me a beer." They continued walking and, by the time they got to Federation Square, the team had just arrived. Cook suggested to Giles that they keep walking the rest of the way to Crown Casino, where the official function was being held. "We'll do a few pubs along the way," he said.

They hadn't gone far when they heard the magical words.

"We are Geelong, the greatest team of all …"

It was coming out of Young and Jackson. When they opened the door they found Geelong people everywhere, singing the theme song. Cook quickly grabbed a beer and, when a few of the fans recognised who they had in their company, they jumped up on a table and started singing too. He did the same and soon the entire pub was singing the Cats anthem.

Then the table collapsed.

"Mate, we'd better get out of here," Cook said to Giles.

The irony of that incident – something he wouldn't have done since he was 21 – was that Cook's theory on the success of the club centred around people growing up. "I think we have all grown up this year," he said. "Everyone has grown up, the boys in the VFL, the Gary Abletts of this world, the Brian Cooks of this world, the board. We certainly grew up last year, too, but to actually go through what we have done, and to achieve what we have eventually achieved, is a reinforcement of what we know can work and can't work with people's behaviours, and how we managed difficult situations.

"It is a great growing exercise, what has happened over the past couple of years. I don't think supporters quite understand the intensity inside football clubs, especially if you are on a mission like our boys were. Not that I have been there but, to me, it was like SAS stuff.

"We changed our ways a bit, we became more protective of our people, more protective of our information, had more closed sessions and did things that people don't normally do in Geelong. We became a bit of an elite army outfit."

chapter 19
Mission Accomplished

"We thought there would be 5000 or maybe 10,000 outside so when we walked out on stage and saw 35,000-plus we were blown away. It was the most amazing thing I have ever seen."

– Cameron Ling at the "day after"

Joel Corey and Tom Harley were like little kids mucking around in the back of the car. They were exhausted, but couldn't stop laughing about what they were doing at that very moment. It was 5am. Driving the car was a girl they'd only met a couple of hours ago. She had worked at the Truffel Duck restaurant, where the club had arranged a private function for the team once they got back to Geelong.

She also lived in Torquay and said she'd give them a lift home, as well as the third passenger: the premiership cup. Sarah Birch had been in charge of it for the entire evening but when she saw Harley, who was in pretty good shape, was heading home she gave him a proposition he couldn't refuse. "Can you look after the cup?" she asked.

The cup was now sitting in the front seat with its seat belt on. After posing for a photo with their driver, Harley bid farewell to Corey and took the cup inside his house. Suddenly, he started to worry. What if he lost it? What if someone broke in and stole it? He figured the best place for it was to lock it in the bathroom.

When his girlfriend, Felicity, stirred three hours later, Harley said: "How are you going? Oh, the cup is in the shower."

They then took a series of photos with the cup all over the house before going out for breakfast. This time Harley hid it in the laundry basket under a heap of clothes. At 1pm they drove back into Geelong for the family day at Skilled Stadium with an anxious Birch on the phone wanting to know where the cup was. "You've still got it?" she kept asking. "Where is it?"

"Don't worry, we're on our way," Harley said, looking down at his prized new possession next to him.

Around the same time that Corey and Harley were getting their lift home, Frank Costa had received a phone call. After the function he had stayed the night in Melbourne and had only been in bed for a couple of hours when the phone rang. It was his son-in-law, Peter Reivers. When Costa heard his voice he thought something must have been happened to one of the children. "What is wrong, Peter?"

"You've got trouble," Reivers said.

"What trouble?"

"The police are after you."

Costa's office in Myers Street, Geelong, was a converted church. With a bell tower. He had always said that if the Cats won the premiership he would have the bells going to the tune of the club's theme song, and play them all night. As the finals approached, the president had employed electricians to install new speakers and prepare things should he get to make the call.

Just after the siren, Costa had made that call, and the bells had been ringing ever since. The problem was, it was driving the neighbours crazy and keeping everyone in surrounding Newtown awake. They had called the police, who had tracked down Reivers. Costa immediately rang his assistant and had the bells stopped, although he planned to personally turn them back on when he got down there in a few hours.

The centre of Geelong had been cordoned off by police since the final siren had sounded at 5.13pm, as Cats fans spilled into the streets to celebrate. Cars did laps, tooting horns, as people hung from every building waving flags and singing the theme song. There were few arrests as the community partied in style.

After Truffel Duck, which hadn't turned out to be the amazing party everyone had expected, the players slipped away in different groups. Most went to Corey Enright's house, which was just a couple of blocks from Skilled Stadium, where the partying was set to go up a notch in the afternoon.

The gates had opened at 11am. By 1pm Brian Cook had a problem, as the police and city council were already worried about the size of the crowd and had shut the gates. And the players were still two hours from appearing on stage.

"It was unbelievable," Cook said. "We only had regulations for 28,000 people, we reached that at 1pm and they weren't arriving until 3pm. The police were understandably worried and they shut the gates, so we got the mayor involved and got the gates opened again. We ended up with 35,000, which is just unheard of. If we had come back the night before, which we got criticised about (not doing), it would have been a disaster fitting 35,000 in there in the dark, as we have no lights."

When he stepped onto stage, the CEO was briefly lost for words. "I can't believe what I'm seeing out there," he told the crowd. "People are asking me about a dynasty ... let's not worry about that. Enjoy what you have now because it doesn't happen very often."

After the applause for his opening statement died down, Cook continued. "Someone asked me straight after the game, 'What is next?' I said, 'Party for three months.'"

Costa's entrance was met with more hysteria. "I couldn't see a blade of green grass, the oval was completely full of people and every stand was full," he said. When he finally got to speak, Costa declared: "I think this is the single biggest happening in Geelong's history."

The coach was next. He had been stunned the night before about the impact the victory had on the people of Geelong. Now he was blown away. "We are happy that you're happy," he said. When asked by compare Billy

Brownless whether he would coach the Cats the next year, Thompson replied: "Bloody oath."

By the time Brownless and his assistant, former captain Andrew Bews, started introducing the premiership players, the scene was reminiscent of a rock concert at Wembley Stadium. There were people as far as the eye could see and the players were genuinely shocked. "We wanted to have a few beers in the rooms of the footy club because that is where it all started," Ling said. "We thought there would be 5000 or maybe 10,000 outside so when we walked out on stage and saw 35,000-plus we were blown away. It was the most amazing thing I have ever seen."

The players looked in various states of dishevelment, although they managed to don some form of club attire. Rooke still had his suit on from the previous night's function. Ling was sporting his suit trousers but had found a new club polo to put on.

Instead of VB cans in their hands, most carried Powerade cups in which the beer had been poured. That had been another directive from the hierarchy, in keeping with their desire to ensure everything about the victory was handled in a dignified way. Their entrances had been spectacular in several cases. Enright, sporting bright red vintage sunglasses, had produced a forward roll onto stage, while Scarlett struck a bizarre pose which had a little bit of WWF about it. Chapman re-enacted his speccy and continually took hold of the microphone to rev up the fans.

By 4pm it was all over. Within half-an-hour the crowd had gone, the rain had arrived and the players had retreated to the changerooms. "This is what I dreamt about when you win a grand final," Kelly said. "Just the boys sitting around in the rooms, it's my best moment."

For the youngest member of the team, the family day had rammed home what he'd achieved. "This was one of the best days of my life," Selwood said. "Seeing old blokes in the carpark just crying and cuddling, I guess that is when it sunk in the most to me. I had been a Geelong fan all my life but I didn't actually know how much it meant to them until then."

At the other end of the spectrum, Harley was starting to put into context what his team had just done. "Let's be honest, this will go down as one of the greatest seasons ever," he said. "The hype and aura around that 1963 side has been amazing and the legend has grown and grown. To be a part of a side that has won a premiership for Geelong, for the community, I don't know what to say. I could retire a very happy person right now."

Eventually the party moved on to the yacht club, where the club's staff had gathered, then to local nightclub institution, Lamby's, where the current day heroes shared the glory with a lot of ex-teammates and legends of previous Geelong sides.

Mad Monday began bright and early at the Lord of the Isles Hotel, opposite Skilled Stadium. Breakfast was bacon and eggs. And beer. Everyone called in for a few pots throughout the day, including Cook and the coaches, with the highlight for many coming at 3pm when a replay of the grand final was put up on the big screen.

After watching just a couple of minutes of the pre-game segment, Harley found himself choking up. By the time the ball was bounced, he was bawling and quickly went outside to regroup. He rang his girlfriend, looking for some clarity. "I'm a mess," he said.

When he went back inside a few minutes later and sat back down, Milburn took one look at him and asked: "Are you alright?"

Harley looked around at his teammates smiling, laughing, drinking and having the best times of their lives. "Yeah," he said, nodding his head.

He was thinking about the bond he now had with the 21 other players with whom he'd run onto the MCG two days earlier. "We have now got a special bond which is unbreakable," Harley said. "It sounds corny but it's true. We will go down as the team that broke the drought. And whatever we do from here, whether we win another one or whatever, this side in 2007 will forever go down in history. You can't replicate a journey like that."

He had shed many tears on the day and night itself, but as Mark Thompson sat in the Ford Falcon ute with the premiership cup and looked around him at the 20,000 fans lining Malop Street for the parade through Geelong, he found himself melting again. He had been a premiership coach for four days now, but he was still coming to terms with it.

People were hanging out of windows. Workmen were downing tools and cheering their heroes as the convoy of vehicles moved slowly by. "It all suddenly got to me," Thompson said. "I'm okay with a lot of things but to be held in that regard, it is just uncomfortable."

Cook was in a ute behind him and understood what his coach was feeling. "I am sure everyone at the football club has broken down at some stage," he said. "Just through the emotion of the whole thing, one way or another."

McCartney was also overwhelmed. "It was a pretty humbling experience," he said. "Some of the people in our club have achieved great things in football, most of us are pretty down to earth, working stock people so it is pretty humbling to have people applauding you for winning a game of footy."

The future of King was the focus of the media's attention. "Being 28, and with my history over the last couple of years, I will definitely be realistic about where I am at. Hopefully we can come to something that looks after both parties," King said. "The last thing I want to do (is get in a dispute). I would definitely take one year so I could stay with this group."

The only player missing from the parade was Nathan Ablett, not a great shock to anyone given his reluctance for the spotlight. The parade ended at City Hall, where the mayor, Bruce Harwood, presented Ling with the official mayoral robes. The vice-captain had been dubbed the 'Mayor of Geelong' in an article in the *Herald Sun* during the finals and it had gathered legs to the point where the city made him honorary mayor for a day.

"Nobody will ever pay rates in Geelong again," Ling declared to the crowd, which had gathered in Johnstone Park. "And you've all got the rest of the week off to come celebrate with us."

For many of his teammates, Wednesday afternoon signalled a time for rest. Most had hit a big wall, virtually losing their voices. An ailing Scarlett already had spent a day in bed. The plan was to regroup and be ready to fire the following evening at the best and fairest count, which was being held back at their favourite haunt, the Crown Palladium Ballroom.

More than 1500 supporters attended the function, which began with every player on the list being introduced to the crowd. They walked out onto the stage, past the two premiership cups which sat at either end of the stage, down the steps at the front and to their seats amongst the faithful.

It was a wonderful touch, and illustrated again how Geelong had done things all year. Everything was about the team, not the individual. Everyone in the room had played their part in creating history, none more than Frank Costa, who was first up to the microphone.

Many times over the past few days he'd thought about what he had said at this night 12 months earlier, when his club was in turmoil and he had been forced to make an impassioned plea.

Tonight his message was a simple one. After gesturing to the crowd to settle – following prolonged applause – Costa scanned the full circumference of the room. "Twelve months ago when we gathered in this room I asked all of you for just one thing," he said. "That when we met again this year we could do so with pride in what we had achieved in 2007."

He then bent down slightly to get closer to the microphone: *"MISSION ACCOMPLISHED."*

Epilogue, 2007

"Frank Costa and I sat down and we were getting ready to start reviewing the year when Cooky reached down and just put the premiership cup on the table. It was a lovely touch and basically finished the review then and there."

– GFC vice-president Gareth Andrews

A week after sitting in the motorcade going through the streets of Geelong, Steven King found himself sitting in St Kilda coach Ross Lyon's office at Moorabbin. Twenty-four hours earlier, the one-year deal he thought was going to materialise with Geelong had been taken off the table. The club where he had spent a third of his life was suggesting he should hang up his boots.

After a week of soul-searching, and weighing up some offers from other clubs, spurned Grand Final ruckman Mark Blake had informed the Cats that he wanted to stay. This was the catalyst for the position King now found himself. Lyon had liked what he saw on Grand Final day and was willing to grant the 28-year-old his wish to play on.

"If I hadn't pulled my weight in that Grand Final side there is no way I would be continuing to play," King said. "I guess to go up against an All-Australian (Brendon Lade) and what people say is the best ruck combination going around, to get on top and win your position, it gave me a lot of confidence after the game to think, 'Yeah, I can still play this game.'

"Geelong wanted me to retire and I had some calls from people saying, 'Are you sure you want to go to another club?'. But the way I felt in that game, on that day, with my performance, it doesn't get any more intense than that. And knowing I didn't have to have any operations and the body was starting to feel good, I thought, 'Let's have a fresh start, get out of my comfort zone and take on another challenge.'

"You see some players go to other clubs and it is the best thing they have done. I guess at the back of my mind I know I have got an AFL premiership now. If it all goes pear-shaped then so be it. I've probably done everything I wanted to do in football at Geelong."

Geelong made it clear it would do anything in its power to help any player who wanted to have a shot somewhere else. When the draft deadline arrived at 2pm on the Friday, King became a Saint. He was joined at the last minute by Charlie Gardiner, who that morning hadn't even been in the picture until his manager pushed him up to the Saints in a charity deal for a sixth round draft pick (which the Cats were never going to use).

Henry Playfair went home to Sydney for pick No.44, while Tim Callan went to the Bulldogs in exchange for No.60 in the November draft. Geelong later used this to get yet another father-son-selection, Adam Donohue, the son of former full-forward, Larry.

"We ended up getting nothing for three players and I think Geelong, as a club, should be applauded," Mark Thompson said. "That is the way the system should work because we wanted to help them to play." The club followed through on its promise to return Tom Lonergan to the senior list, also elevating Jason Davenport – a housemate of Gary Ablett's – off the rookie list. The pacy midfielder took over King's No.1 jumper.

After more than six weeks off, which saw players spread to different parts of the globe (including a footy trip for a dozen or so to Bali, and another reunion of sorts at Matthew Scarlett's wedding in Hamilton Island), it was back to business at the end of November. Many had interesting stories about their new-found fame as premiership players. Joel Corey was at his mother's house back in Perth when he had his moment. "This pest control bloke came around to my mum's house and they weren't home so I had to open the shed for him," he said. "He saw mum's name and said, 'You're not the premiership player Joel Corey are you?' He didn't say 'Joel Corey, who plays for Geelong'. He said, 'Joel Corey the premiership player'. I liked the sound of it and I said, 'Yeah mate, that's me.'"

Jimmy Bartel was at Rome airport when he experienced his memorable moment. "There were 30 people deep in this line and I had a Geelong thing on my bag," he said. "Then I heard this deep Australian voice from the back of the line say, 'Why the hell would you barrack for Geelong?' "I turned around and said, 'Who do you barrack for?' He said, 'Essendon', and then I said, 'Didn't we win this year?' He nodded and said, 'Yeah, fair point', and then walked off."

Most players came back refreshed and eager to go again, with one major exception: Nathan Ablett. After just a few days back at the club, Ablett told Thompson and the leadership group that he was struggling for motivation and wanted to quit. They convinced him to take some time away from training and think things over during the Christmas break, but on Monday January 7, the 22-year-old, who played 32 games and kicked 46 goals in three seasons, walked away from the game. In a prepared statement which he wrote himself, the youngest of the Ablett clan fronted the media: "I have decided to take a break from AFL football for the time being. I feel as if I don't have the passion and commitment to continue playing at the highest level. To do so therefore would be unfair to the club and the players. I am planning on getting away from football for now, however, I may look to continue on playing at the VFL level.

"Being involved in a winning grand final is something that doesn't happen to a lot of players and I feel privileged and honoured to be part of the 2007 premiership team."

Ablett will remain on the club's list in 2008, and Thompson holds out hope of a return. "We are hoping that one day he comes back and that one day is pretty soon. There has always been something about Nathan that we were a little bit unsure about," he said. "He is not really like a lot of other young men who were so passionate about the game and would do almost anything to play. In saying that, he has got enormous ability and we haven't given up hope that he will play for Geelong again."

Gary Ablett, who defeated Bartel to win his first Carji Greeves Medal back in October, had tried to convince his brother not to walk away from AFL football. Yet he understood it was the right decision. "I think it's taken a lot of guts what he's done," Ablett said.

A new year wouldn't be complete at Skilled Stadium if it didn't start with Steve Johnson getting himself into trouble. A week after the Nathan Ablett bombshell, the Cats' hierarchy had to deal with the Norm Smith Medallist being caught driving at 128km/h in a 50km/h zone.

Police pulled over Johnson and Shannon Byrnes as they were driving through East Geelong on their way to Eastern Gardens golf course. They immediately impounded the car under "hoon" laws. The first two people Johnson rang were Thompson and Tom Harley.

Johnson lost his licence for 12 months and was fined more than $1000. After meeting the leadership group it was decided that he would also do 50 hours of community service through the Transport Accident Commission, where he would meet the victims of recent traffic accidents.

"It was a brain fade, I was on the way to a golf course and at the corner I just took off," Johnson said. "Three hundred metres down the road I was, basically, pulled over and my car was taken. Probably within 20 minutes I had notified three or four people from the footy club about what I had done. There was no reason for travelling at that speed. I have no excuse for it. It was a silly thing to do."

Brian Cook said a suspension was never considered, while a large fine wasn't seen as an effective penalty. "We knew (people would call us soft) but we are true to what we believe in. We very seldom fine people ... because we just don't believe it necessarily changes behaviour. We are of the belief a significant community input has a better chance of changing Steve's behaviour and that's why we haven't gone down the path of a fine."

The other disappointing news on the player front was another setback for Matthew Egan. He had further surgery on his foot in February and was expected to miss at least the opening half of the 2008 season.

On a happier note, love was in the air for two premiership players. Harley and his girlfriend, Felicity, were engaged; Mooney and his long-time partner, Seona, followed suit.

For Cook, who was awarded AFL life membership in February, dealing with the Ablett and Johnson situations reined in the premiership celebrations, which for the first couple of months had been exhausting as the cup travelled all around the state. The CEO took it to one important meeting, when he met president Frank Costa and vice-president Gareth Andrews for his annual review.

"Frank and I sat down and we were organising our papers getting ready to start reviewing the year when Cooky reached down and just put the premiership cup on the table," Andrews said. "It was a lovely touch and basically finished the review then and there."

Almost every player, coach and staff member had at some point taken the cup with them to a function. Ken Hinkley took it home to Camperdown; Andrew Mackie visited a nursing home with it to honour a promise made to two-time premiership captain Fred Flanagan; the cup did a tour of the Ford factory, and Costa took it with him when he made a speech at Geelong Grammar, where hundreds of kids and their parents queued up to have their photo taken next to it.

"Wherever that cup has gone, it has made such an impact on people," Costa said.

Costa and a number of board members took it to visit John Button, the chairman of the club's foundation, who was in hospital suffering from cancer. "Helene Bender presented him with a miniature cup and he was just over the moon," he said. "To see John Button and the thrill he got from that, as well as his wife and son, who was out from England and a passionate Geelong supporter as well, they were just overcome by it."

One of Costa's favourite stories centres around the final score in the grand final: 24.19 (163) to 6.8 (44). The two players who played all year but missed the Grand Final were Mark Blake (No.24) and Egan (No.19).

The last time the Cats won the flag was 1963 (the final score was 163) and Port's score of 44 was exactly the amount of years since then. Plus, on the Thursday before the game, Costa had received an email from finance manager Rob Threlfell about the Cats Sports Foundation, which had just launched a bequest program.

"We'd had four bequests come in and they added up to $163,000," Costa said. "I just reckon it was in the stars." The triumvirate again shook hands on a new agreement, with Thompson committing for another two years. In doing so, the coach made a telling revelation. "I'm certainly much more a Geelong person than I am Essendon person now," he said.

Three weeks after the premiership victory, Cook – who later would be voted the 2007 Australian Sports Executive of the Year by the Confederation of Australian Sport (the same organisation named Geelong "Team of the Year") – took out all the interview notes from the review which he had kept in his safe and burnt them. All that remains now is one single 70-page copy of the report, which he keeps under lock and key in the safe.

In December, he sent a staff memo around thanking them for the year and outlining the extra financial bonus they would be receiving. In it, he outlined the achievements of the club in 2007:

- Winning the AFL Premiership
- Winning the VFL Premiership
- Jimmy Bartel winning the Brownlow Medal
- Steve Johnson winning the Norm Smith Medal
- Joel Selwood winning the NAB Rising Star Award
- Mark Thompson winning the AFLPA Coach of the Year Award
- Gary Ablett winning the AFLPA Player of the Year Award
- James Byrne winning the Liston Trophy for the VFL
- Tom Lonergan winning the Norm Goss Medal
- Selection of nine All-Australian players
- Exceeding 30,000 members
- Approx. $2 million profit
- Net Asset growth from $6m to $8m

- 19.9 million viewers watched us on TV
- Over 900 player appearances in our communities
- Attraction of $26m of the $28m required for stage two Skilled Stadium redevelopment
- Business operations profit up $2.0m on 2006
- Over $1.5m merchandise sales from our Cats shop
- Approval of 80 gaming machines for our proposed Pt Cook entertainment complex
- The development of our brand identity (Club values and visual identity)
- Completed a $1m Club Cats refurbishment
- Record satisfaction rates for sponsors, members and players.

Cook finished the memo: "Thank you for playing your part in these achievements and being part of what is arguably the greatest year of any club in the VFL / AFL history."

chapter 20
May, 2008, and business as usual

"A lot of people out there are probably unfairly on our backs at the moment. Their expectations are obviously really high. Top of the ladder, eight wins and the best percentage in the comp – it's not a bad position to be."

– Tom Harley

May, 2008. The first two months of Geelong's premiership defence smacked of business as usual. Eight games, eight wins. And there was no indication that things were going to change in the lead-up to the biggest game of the season, a Friday night blockbuster against Collingwood. More than 78,000 people packed into the MCG that night, hoping to see something similar to the previous year's memorable preliminary final epic, in which the Cats had scraped through by a kick.

That had been the expectation in the Geelong coaches' box but, as early as the opening five minutes, eyebrows were being raised. The Magpies looked "on". They were hunting in packs and tackling fiercely, with the pressure causing uncharacteristic turnovers from Cats players who were clearly rattled. At quarter-time they were down by 26 points; by half-time the margin had blown out to 51 and the game was effectively gone. The winning streak – and arguably the aura of invincibility – was shattered.

Assistant coach Ken Hinkley was as stunned as anyone who attended that night. "In footy today, if you have a day or a night where nothing goes right for you and everything goes right for your opposition, once you get into a bit of a rut it's hard to stop it," he said. "We'd won eight games in a row and everything was going well, and we hadn't been anywhere near that position for a long, long time. When it turned that night, it turned ugly."

The final margin was a humiliating 86 points, 20.14 (134) to 7.6 (48). Collingwood unleashed an extraordinary 85 tackles, 36 more than Geelong and way, way above the AFL average of 52.

"You almost have to say, 'It was a bad night, let's move on' and put it out of the way as quick as we can," Mark Thompson said in his post-match media conference. "We just had a bad night. A really bad night, right from the start, right to the very end. (The players) are not happy, nobody is happy. It's been a long time since we have lost a game, and it's been a long time since we lost one by 86 points, but it gives us a chance to work on a few things."

Here was the first chink in what had otherwise been an exemplary display by a football club in first reining in, then moving on, from the euphoria of the drought-breaking premiership victory. Any fears of a hangover had been clinically erased with the tone for the new season set by the senior coach. When the players had gathered for the start of pre-season training, Thompson drew a line in the sand. The 2007 Grand Final would not be discussed. It would only be used as a "coaching tool" from that point on.

The message certainly got through.

A trip to Football Park on a Thursday night for the Grand Final re-match opened the new season, and the champs rolled out a brilliant first half. Geelong led by 31 points at the main break, laying the foundations for a nine-point victory. Only 17 of the premiership-winning 22 made the trip, with Brad Ottens (foot), David Wojcinski (finger), Max Rooke (calf), Nathan Ablett (retired) and Steven King (traded to St Kilda) the absentees. In their place were debutant ruckman Trent West, second-gamer Ryan Gamble, Mark Blake, Tom Hawkins and Kane Tenace.

While the Blake-West ruck combination didn't quite have the same impact as Ottens-King had eight months earlier against Power big men Brendon Lade and Dean Brogan – they lost the hit-outs 46 to 14 at AAMI Stadium that evening – there were familiar names in the best players. Paul Chapman and Mathew Stokes each kicked three goals, Gary Ablett was dynamic, and Cameron Ling, Joel Corey and James Kelly were everywhere. Still, the second half fade-out didn't impress the coach.

"You get a bit angry because we haven't seen some of the players make mistakes like that for a long while," Thompson noted later. "I suppose you've just got to get used to it and accept that it is Round 1 and you never know what to expect."

There was little to raise the coach's ire the following week, with a 99-point defeat of Essendon coming on the back of 462 possessions – the second-highest total in AFL history. A week later, the Geelong faithful enjoyed the opportunity to relive some of the great memories of the previous September when the premiership flag was unfurled before the Round 3 game against Melbourne at Skilled Stadium. On a cold and windy Sunday afternoon, the flag was delivered by parachute into the middle of the ground with much fanfare, although the drawn-out ceremony wasn't a hit with everyone. "It didn't help our preparation standing around waiting for the skydivers to come in," was Chapman's brutally honest assessment of the historic event.

The players took longer than expected to warm up against the lowly Demons, who had a new coach in Dean Bailey, a former Essendon teammate of Thompson. An improved second half, thanks mainly to five goals from the impressive Hawkins, secured a lacklustre 30-point win.

Next came St Kilda. Much of the build-up centred around the King-Blake battle, and Cameron Mooney best summed up the feelings of the Cat faithful watching their former captain run around in Saints' colours. "I hated it," Mooney said.

"It was weird, it was horrible. He's a great mate, he gave 12 years of his life to the footy club and we played in a premiership together. It was tough, even just looking at him. But that's the way footy goes, I guess."

Blake, who had bulked up over the summer, more than held his own against his former teammate and claimed bragging rights as the Cats cruised home on the back of a seven-goal third quarter to win by 42 points. From the big picture perspective, overshadowing the result or the margin was the fact that the club had unearthed a "good'un". Harry Taylor, the Cats' surprise first round selection in the 2007 national draft, that day announced himself in the big time. The 21-year-old from East Fremantle was moved onto Nick Riewoldt, who had torched skipper Tom Harley in the early going. Taylor dramatically reduced the superstar's output in the second half.

"If the umpires don't give him three (Brownlow) votes today, they all should be sacked."

Mark Thompson was in awe, just like everyone else at Skilled Stadium that afternoon. Gary Ablett's 35-possession display against Sydney in Round 5 was simply remarkable, even by Ablett's incredibly high standards. The Swans climbed within three points early in the last quarter before No.29 took over, kicking three goals to inspire an eight-goal final term.

For the record, the umpires saved their jobs – Ablett did earn the three votes that day.

Same story, different name the following week against Fremantle at Subiaco. After Dockers giant Aaron Sandilands had put on a clinic – Ottens remained absent, and Blake was no match – to lift his team to the brink of the upset of the season, Joel Selwood stepped in to ensure the reigning premiers prevailed. Ablett and Jimmy Bartel were being tagged out of the contest, so Selwood, the youngest member of the midfield machine, produced a 14-possession last quarter which brought the Cats back from a 25-point deficit at the final change to win by a solitary point.

The ladder told one tale, that of the defending champions picking up where they left off. This appeared to be a young, motivated team with youth and talent on its side and a level-headed coach at the helm. It was arguably even more dangerous with a premiership now under its belt and the burden of history removed. Yet the games themselves told another tale; indeed, a pattern was appearing with the Cats. They were simply flicking the switch when required in matches, seemingly day-dreaming their way through a contest until they had to get busy. Against an undermanned Brisbane at home in Round 7, scores were level early in the last quarter, yet Geelong won by 27. The next week against Richmond, they were a goal down at half-time and responded with a seven-goal third term to put the match to bed. True, good sides can quickly change gears ... but it is no guarantee to happen every week.

And certainly not when it counts.

While it may have been making some in the outer restless, the coach and captain weren't losing any sleep. "People are expecting us to win by massive amounts. Well, it's probably not going to happen all year, so get used to it," Thompson argued.

Harley agreed: "A lot of people out there are probably unfairly on our backs at the moment. Their expectations are obviously really high. I don't really understand it. I am not sure what people want. Top of the ladder, eight wins and the best percentage in the comp – it's not a bad position to be," he said.

The Collingwood debacle moved the goalposts considerably, yet it was not the Magpies who had Geelong fans most concerned, despite the fact that Mick Malthouse's men seemed to hold the combination to the Cats' safe full of secrets. Rather, an equally traditional and respected rival was making waves across town.

Hawthorn had emerged as the primary threat, its new "rolling" defensive zone proving confusing and strangling the effectiveness out of opposition teams. After nine rounds, the Hawks were undefeated, taking over top spot from Geelong and looking equally as intimidating – and appreciably more dangerous in attack – than the Cats. Not surprisingly, the spotlight of the football world was already shining on Round 17, the only time those two teams were scheduled to clash for the season.

In the meantime, an old-fashioned, physical mid-week training session was the trigger to get Geelong players' minds back on the job. It worked. They took out their anger on Carlton – after a close first half, the Cats did a "Collingwood" on the Blues, laying 29 tackles to nine in the third quarter as they kicked 6.8 to one point. The end result was a 56-point win driven by a convincing 81-46 tackle count. Brad Ottens played his first game for the season, having finally recovered from a torn plantar fascia ligament in his foot, while Steve Johnson kicked five goals. Yet most excitement for the night was reserved for someone else in the forward line.

Tom Lonergan had come into the team as a late replacement for Cameron Mooney. It would be Lonergan's first senior game since he suffered the horrendous, life-threatening injury in Round 21, 2006. He lined up in the goalsquare and was clearly nervous, kicking three points in the first quarter, but the fact that he was getting his hands on the ball was encouraging. Seven kicks, three marks and a goal was his overall return in a performance which had his coach declaring his long road back had been more than worth it.

"He was fantastic," Thompson said of the 24-year-old. "To make his way back into the team ... I know for a while there he was just motivating the whole footy club. Tom is that sort of special person around the club."

The Collingwood defeat now seemed like a jolt, but no more than that – defeating an arch-rival such as Carlton can quickly put the spring back into a club's step. There was, however, another distraction to consider as the premiership defence unfolded. A headline in the following day's paper took the gloss off the victory and instigated some anxious phone calls between club officials: *"Gold Coast set to sizzle with Cook?"*

The AFL's 17th franchise wanted Brian Cook as its chief executive. The Cats' biggest concern? Cook admitted he was very interested, and it would continue to be a low-lying but simmering storyline for some weeks.

Gary Ablett was again in the headlines in Round 11 as he firmed into Brownlow Medal favouritism by collecting a career-high 39 disposals against North Melbourne, which included 12 inside-50s, two clearances, five tackles and two goals. "He's in the form of his life," Thompson said afterwards. Mooney returned after a week out and booted seven goals in the 13-point win but the downside was a hamstring injury to full-back Matthew Scarlett.

Not that he was missed over the next two weeks, with a 59-point win over Port Adelaide – which had mistakenly tried to rough up Ablett and Selwood (the pair responded by sharing 62 possessions for the day) – followed by a 135-point smashing of West Coast, the biggest loss in the Eagles' history on its home track of Subiaco. Ablett was best again, churning out his fourth 30-plus possession game as the quality of his football elevated to a new, inspired level, while Mooney and Chapman each kicked five.

In many respects, the Cats were biding their time until they got the chance to face off with their two main challengers, the Western Bulldogs and Hawthorn. Those matches were scheduled back-to-back in Rounds 16 and 17 and fans has circled that fortnight as the litmus test for a season which looked to have hauled itself back on track after that pounding in Round 9. In fact, the Collingwood affair was by now all but forgotten.

An 11-goal win against Adelaide and a 12-goal drubbing of Fremantle were useful support bouts for the main events, though they came at a cost. Cameron Ling had his cheekbone broken by crude contact from Docker Dean Solomon, who was suspended for eight weeks. More importantly, Ablett hurt his ankle in the same match and was expected to miss the best part of three games.

Countering this concern was the news that Cook was staying. There was a collective sigh of relief in the corridors of Skilled Stadium on the eve of the Bulldogs game as Cook announced he had knocked back the AFL's lucrative Gold Coast offer. "I was going to the Gold Coast at one stage, I had one foot on the plane," he later conceded. "I was very serious about that. It was very inviting, it was a very good offer and in many respects I think I had the opportunity of a lifetime.

"The chance to put all my skills into a pot and my experience and be allowed to demonstrate them, that was really exciting. To start the whole thing from nothing was very attractive as I'd done it in WA with a couple of things, and now I have a lot more experience and wisdom.

"What got me staying was my kids. I couldn't leave them. I've got three children, albeit all adults now, and I've got one grandchild and a second on the way. I just couldn't pack the bags and go because in a way my career doesn't matter that much; I am just not that ambitious any more. I used to be really ambitious but, while I do care about my job, I don't care about the future. I think it will look after itself."

For the first time, Cook advanced the relationship with club president Frank Costa to more than just a handshake. This time it was all down on paper as the two men added their signatures to a three-year contract. "That was the first time I have signed an agreement with the club," Cook said. "The way I looked at it, I knew Frank was thinking about leaving (at the end of 2010). I had no problem with a handshake with Frank but at that stage I didn't know what future lay ahead in terms of who the new president was going to be."

Costa, who had been overseas when the Gold Coast had pursued his CEO, was appreciative that Cook delayed making a decision until he returned to state his case. "I was able to explain how we still have an enormous challenge here in Geelong," Costa said.

And so to the main event, a two-week journey that would say much for the Cats' seemingly impervious position at the head seat of the game's table. As expected, the Bulldogs proved to be a significant hurdle. Scores were level at half-time and the Dogs were still only 14 points in arrears at the last change before the Geelong machine put the foot down – much to the delight of a capacity home crowd. Eight goals to one in the final term saw the margin blow out to 61 points.

Quite a statement, and so was this: "Our last quarter was extraordinary," was Thompson's assessment.

The defence had been magnificent, with Tom Harley inspirational and Darren Milburn – *who had 19 touches in the first quarter* – and Matthew Scarlett the joint-leading possession winners on the ground (32). Joel Corey and Jimmy Bartel controlled the midfield while Ryan Gamble kicked four goals and Johnson and Mooney three each.

From a fans' perspective it was the perfect build-up for the Friday night MCG meeting against the Hawks. Hype had shifted into overdrive all week and the size of the crowd, 86,179, said plenty – particularly given it was the middle of winter – about how excited the football world was for a match-up it had craved for months.

The champions faced a legitimate contender, a team riding on the back of a remarkable breakout season from Lance "Buddy" Franklin. In truth, it is difficult to recall a player with such a dazzling bag of tricks since Gary Ablett Snr. Franklin had used the 2007 finals series as his coming out parade. As good as his home-and-away season had been, his efforts in the first elimination final against Adelaide, when the last of his seven goals won a thriller with just seconds on the clock, stamped not just potential greatness. A new force had arrived.

He was showing no signs of slowing down, either, although the Hawks had lost three times to that point of the season, including the previous week against mid-table St Kilda. Still, it took little of the gloss off this showdown Nor did the Cats' preparation, which hadn't gone precisely to plan. Eldest statesman Milburn withdrew from the game due to a virus which had forced him into hospital the previous night to have three litres of fluid pumped into his body – he was replaced by David Johnson for his first game of the season. Ablett and Ling were absent, while another premiership ingredient, David Wojcinski, was missing with an Achilles problem. If the absences left the Cats' slightly undermanned, they barely eroded the pre-match excitement as minutes ticked down to the first bounce.

Perhaps highlighting the significance of the clash, there were some initial surprises from the coaches' box, the sort of surprise moves often reserved for September. Andrew Mackie lined up on Franklin, Thompson looking to create a run-off mismatch. Plus, regular Hawk defender Campbell Brown started forward. Both moves worked in Hawthorn's favour, with Scarlett forced to replace Mackie after 10 minutes and Brown engineering a couple of goals. Despite this, the Cats were cleaner through the midfield and, with Johnson and Chapman alight, they had kicked six goals to three at quarter-time.

The match took a potentially defining twist late in the second quarter when Chapman's suspect hamstrings again let him down; he had clearly been best afield to that point, having collected 16 possessions and two goals, and his departure seemed to deflate the champs. With Franklin heating up, the Hawks surged in the third quarter and, 35 seconds into the final term, they edged ahead courtesy of a Mark Williams goal.

For the first time in some weeks the Cats were seriously under pressure and in search of that "extra gear". In the box, however, Thompson was excited about the prospect of what lay immediately ahead. Undermanned against a worthy challenger that was on a roll, the coach suspected he would learn a lot about his side in the half-hour ahead. Thompson would therefore have been thrilled at what unfolded: a Bartel goal quickly reclaimed the lead, and the Cats were not headed again. Bartel, the reigning Brownlow Medallist, was superb in gathering 36 disposals, while others to step up included Corey Enright, Joel Corey and Selwood. The end result was a gutsy, hard-fought 11-point victory which had the coach beaming as the Cats improved to 16-1, with a percentage of 151.

"We didn't have everything go right for us and we played a pretty good team," Thompson said. "We lost momentum a few times, and then regained it, and in the end our will to win was better than the opposition's, especially by some of our midfielders.

"What they (the players) said to us, and the footy world, was that they didn't want to lose this game of footy. They went over and above the call of duty, some of them, to help this team get over the line."

The 2008 season then resumed normal programming in the next couple of weeks. Scarlett's 200th game was celebrated with a 63-point win over Richmond, while Ablett's return was the highlight of a 116-point mauling of Melbourne. The next challenge came not in the form of a team, but in the state of the ANZ Stadium playing surface for the Round 20 clash against Sydney. There was much debate in the lead-up about the condition of the ground as the Cats' hierarchy was understandably seeking to avoid risks so close to the finals. Hence, it was decided that Chapman would miss a third game due to his hamstring ailments and he was joined in the stands by Milburn (groin) and Scarlett (back).

It mattered not. A seven-goal burst in the opening quarter and a six-goal blitz in 12 minutes of the third term set up a comfortable 39-point victory. A significant gap was opening up between the Cats and the rest of the competition; they now sat four wins clear on top of the ladder and a whopping 34 per cent clear of their two main challengers, Hawthorn and the Western Bulldogs, who both suffered shock losses in that round.

Aside from the Collingwood hiccup, the season was fast becoming – to borrow a Magpie expression – a cakewalk. As far as Sydney coach Paul Roos was concerned, Geelong already had both hands on the premiership cup. "I think if they play their best there is no one who will beat them," Roos said. "They're the benchmark. I think there's no question they're a cut

Unbridled joy after 44 years of waiting.

Despite the agony of split webbing, it was elation and redemption for Mooney ...

... and a time to finally savour for the coach.

CEO Brian Cook enjoys the moment
with club benefactor Alex Popescu.

The family club.

In the captain's eyes, all is forgiven for Norm Smith Medal winner Steve Johnson

A thrilled Fred Wooller hands over the silverware.

Cameron and Jagger Mooney take in the feeling.

Memorable: Cameron Ling with the game's holy grail.

For president Frank Costa and CEO Brian Cook, the moment was reward for faith in a football team.

Tom Harley shares the spoils with elated Cats fans.

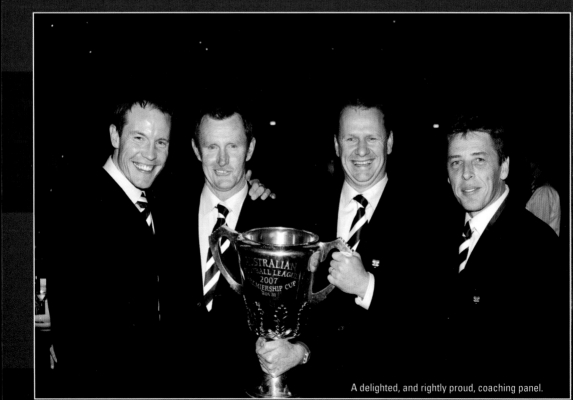

A delighted, and rightly proud, coaching panel.

above every team in the competition by a fair margin."

In the Geelong rooms, Thompson had his issues. The high level of traffic in and out of the medical room had him thinking his concerns about the ground had been justified. A couple of days later those fears became reality. Mathew Stokes had pulled up sore in the groin and looked to be showing signs of the dreaded osteitis pubis, while James Kelly had sustained a quad injury. There were others who took longer than normal to recover from the game, not ideal so late in the season and, on reflection, it would prove to be a highly significant 120 minutes in the Cats' premiership defence.

"It was a really hard surface, a really moving surface," Ken Hinkley explained. "We felt we didn't recover coming out of it and it seemed from that game on we had some issues."

There were concerns with the much-lauded defensive structure the following week, when North Melbourne's David Hale exposed the Cat backline by kicking eight goals (four on Taylor and four on Scarlett). Being dominated by a tall forward wasn't ideal, particularly with Hawthorn still looming as the biggest threat and given the Hawks had two of the best power forwards in the business, Franklin and Jarryd Roughead. If Hale's heroics weren't enough to get his side close – the Cats won comfortably by 33 points – they gave observers something to think about.

Several selection conundrums were now presenting themselves, too. Tom Lonergan had held his spot since his comeback in Round 10, forcing Tom Hawkins out. Hawkins had then suffered a foot injury but was back playing in the VFL. Wojcinski had returned in the reserves while another 2007 premiership player, Shannon Byrnes, who had laboured through an indifferent season to the point such that Travis Varcoe was strongly contending for his spot, had played the last three weeks in the seniors. Impressive young midfielder Brent Prismall had also held his ground since Round 16 and deserved to remain, while Ryan Gamble stayed in the mix.

Of course, pressure on selection is a positive by any measure. But none of the Cats' fringe players were demanding selection as much as teasing the match committee.

The final game of the home-and-away season was a non-event. West Coast had only won four games for the year; its cue was well and truly in the rack. The Eagles travelled to Skilled Stadium and, while scores were level at quarter-time, it was a 20-goal to six Cats' landslide in the 90-minute tune-up that followed. Steve Johnson bagged six and Lonergan four. Yet the revolving selection door continued, with Max Rooke missing because of a one-game suspension and Andrew Mackie (back) a late withdrawal.

It capped a remarkable home-and-away season. Geelong went 21-1 and the thrashing of the Eagles lifted its end-of-season percentage to 161.84 – ironically, the highest single-season mark since West Coast posted 162.2 per cent in 1991.

After sailing through the season with scarcely a blip on the radar, there were genuine concerns about the health of the team as it reached the September dawn. The high player rotation was unsettling; many insiders thought it had even impacted on the standard of training. The world was far from caving in – Geelong had just completed one of the game's most commanding home-and-away seasons in history – but, for the first time, some internal alarm bells were sounding.

Oh, and that dominant Eagles' team of 1991? It lost to Hawthorn in the Grand Final.

chapter 21

Preparing for back-to-back

"There was probably more euphoria last year but we are just as motivated, we are just as driven and we are thankful for the experience of last year. But it doesn't actually do that much for you in the end."

– Mark Thompson

It was more a hunch than anything tangible. There was no specific moment that shook Stephen Wells' world when it came to Harry Taylor, more a cumulation of interest which led the Geelong recruiting manager to the opinion that Taylor was, to use a detective term, "a person of interest". "You wouldn't say he was a stand-out at all," Wells said. "He wasn't even setting the world on fire the year we drafted him but he looked like someone who might be useful."

Taylor hadn't followed the traditional path of prospective AFL draftees. He had grown up on a farm in Northampton, 475km north of Perth, then attended boarding school in Geraldton. After finishing Year 12, instead of moving to the big smoke to pursue a football career, he spent a year in the real world. "I was never anything outstanding as a junior," Taylor admitted. "When your typical blokes are 17 and 18, getting into development squads and all that, I was still growing. I hadn't really matured enough physically and mentally. I wasn't as tall and I was probably 70kg with gumboots on.

"So I worked for a year, mainly labouring work, and tried to bulk up. I learnt to basically cook and clean, do all those things that you need to do to live independently and prepare myself for life beyond uni."

Taylor moved to Perth to begin his physiotheraphy course and to start playing football with East Fremantle. That the concept of playing in the national league was an abstract one would be understating it – he didn't even entertain the prospect of playing AFL until his second year of senior football at the Sharks, when his teammates (who included former Melbourne Brownlow Medallist Shane Woewodin) convinced him he hadn't missed the boat.

Wells only spoke to him for two minutes at a WA screening test for prospective draftees. This was brevity by design – he didn't want to let other clubs know he was interested in the 193cm Taylor, as he had already done his research and knew Taylor had a fantastic professional attitude. "I was pretty confident he was a mature person who would do whatever he could to play good AFL footy," Wells said.

Yet, as is typical of every draft, Wells had a dilemma. There was another player competing for the Cats' first selection, and a significant family connection was adding to the temptation. Joel Selwood's younger brother, Bendigo Pioneers prospect Scott Selwood, had shown he possessed many of the traits that had so endeared Joel to the Cats coaching staff. "We were a bit torn – we would have loved to have had Scott but we just went for a different type of player," Wells explained. "In the end it came down to a more specific need. Tall defenders are a bit harder to find."

The selection of the 21-year-old Taylor at No.17 (Selwood went to West Coast at No.22) sent a murmur around the draft room. The consensus among many was that the Cats had gone early on the tall left-footer, for while he existed on many of their drafts boards, Taylor was projected as a late second-round option, if not later.

Once again, however, a Wells hunch proved to be on the money.

It didn't take his teammates long to work out Taylor wasn't your regulation draftee. Apart from the fact he lived and breathed football, the country boy was fascinated by World War II; he drank cognac, wore zinc cream in every game he played and had never been out of WA before he climbed onto a plane to cross the country to his new home.

But probably the biggest and most impressive eye-opener was the diligence with which Taylor went about his work, compiling dossiers on each of his opponents. It was a portfolio which grew faster than any could have expected – indeed, Taylor was required to make multiple early entries in his debut season following the continuing streak of bad luck for teammate Matthew Egan, who required further surgery on his troublesome foot.

Throughout his 18 games during the home-and-away season, Taylor had played on many of the game's biggest names, such that his dossier was brimming with opposition talent. Mark Thompson had another challenge for him in the qualifying final: St Kilda captain Nick Riewoldt. The coach liked what he saw back in Round 4 and was again prepared to roll the dice with his first-year defender.

It was soon obvious that Taylor's job would be slightly easier than expected, as the ball was down the other end of the ground for much of the opening term. A rampant Bartel was continuing his brilliant form with 12 first-quarter possessions and it was only due to the Cats' wasteful kicking (3.7) that the game remained alive. A largely positive 30 minutes, although there was one major blow: a season-ending injury to Brent Prismall, whose knee buckled as he simply went to pivot on the half-forward flank. Sadly, it would be his last act as a Geelong player.

By half-time, the game was effectively over, in no small part due to the fact that Taylor had kept Riewoldt to just four possessions. The rookie had received some valuable help from old boys Scarlett, Harley and Milburn, and it continued in the third term – six goals to two as the Cats blew out their lead to 73 points. Still, the margin was tempered by injury, and not just Prismall. The sight of Paul Chapman gingerly jogging off late in the quarter triggered a series of expletives in the coaches' box. The word coming back from the bench was that he had "copped a corkie", but it was complicated by the fact that he felt tightness in the hamstring.

The rest of the Geelong players spent most of the final term ensuring they didn't go down the same track as Prismall and Chapman, as the game petered out. Taylor wasn't happy when Riewoldt scored his one and only goal, but the end result, a 17.17 (119) to 8.13 (61) triumph, illustrated the gulf which had opened up between the top couple of teams and the rest. Just about every Cat had been involved; Bartel finished with two goals and 34 disposals, while Ablett, Corey and Milburn were all in 30-plus territory. Mooney and Ottens kicked three each and Lonergan bagged two in the second half.

Taylor, who had openly been labelled the weak link in the Cats' defence in the pre-match assessments, was brilliant, collecting 22 possessions (including 10 marks) and keeping Riewoldt to just nine. "I know that he has been open and he has had a little bit of personal criticism, some people see that as a weakness in Geelong but we have been really supportive of him," Thompson said. "He played a terrific game individually and I thought he got amazing help from his teammates."

The Chapman news was initially positive. Club doctors didn't believe he had torn his hamstring and a planned scan was labelled as "precautionary". The week off earned by victory would assist his situation and also ensure James Kelly, who'd missed three games, would be available. David Wojcinski was the other obvious inclusion.

A heavier workload was seen as the answer to making sure there was no repeat of the previous year's preliminary final fright. As the Cats spent their weekend off planning for a return to the final four, the semi-finals had gone according to script – the top four teams at the end of the home-and-away season would be playing off in the preliminary finals. The Western Bulldogs were Geelong's opponent. Hawthorn would take on St Kilda.

Paul Roos' earlier observation that the Cats had both hands on the cup was then underscored at the All-Australian dinner. Seven Cats were selected, two for the first time. Captain Tom Harley's career-best season was rewarded with a spot in the back pocket next to his good mate Matthew Scarlett. Jimmy Bartel was on the wing, Joel Corey in the middle, Gary Ablett the obvious selection as rover and Steve Johnson filled a half-forward flank. The previously underrated Corey Enright finally received some recognition, selected on the interchange bench in the team of the year. "It's mind-blowing, really," said Harley, who was named vice-captain, "because I think a lot of the guys have got in this position, myself included, by playing a role within the side. To get individual recognition for something that really is just a team job is a really satisfying feeling. The coaches must be super proud of what the guys have been able to achieve over the past 18 months and hopefully it keeps going.

"It's an amazing run and it probably doesn't mean much unless we win (this year's Grand Final), but we can't think about that at the moment. One thing that's made our club really strong, I reckon, has been the week-by-week mentality."

The status on Chapman remained upbeat. There was no hamstring tear, and he had been able to train on the "off week" Sunday, running and kicking at top speed. However, by Wednesday the wheel of caution had turned – he was ruled out, Cats officials deciding not to flaunt with his injury history. By now, Thompson was recognising the downside of having the week off. The coach could sense that his team was ready to play and could feel the weight of expectation increasing by the day.

"It's a long time, even as a coach, you are just sitting around," he reflected. "I could have played it on Wednesday but we just had to wait another couple of days and I knew they would be the longest two days. It had been a pressurised year, it really had. The longer it had gone the more pressure that people were putting on us with the expectation to win."

The Western Bulldogs' intentions were obvious. All of their ball going forward was going to be directed through Shaun Higgins, the highly talented youngster who was Darren Milburn's opponent. The theory was driven by the fact that Milburn liked to play "off" his man and help out others in the defence, hence he could be exposed if you had the right match-up. Higgins was exactly that, a classy, highly skilled and mobile forward. And in the opening quarter of the preliminary final, he was lighting up the MCG.

For the second year in a row in the penultimate game of the season, Geelong's home-and-away season freedom appeared to be restricted by big stage nerves. The Bulldogs jumped out of the gates and it seemed to take the best slice of 20 minutes before the Cats could restore order. A six-point lead – they kicked three goals in time-on through Wojcinski, Rooke and Lonergan – was a stunning advantage at quarter-time given their clearly nervous start. Bartel, Stokes, Corey and Ablett, who had started the game with Jason Akermanis as his opponent, then "got busy" in the second term, and the favourites extended the margin to 21 points at the main break.

When Travis Varcoe, one of the best in the opening half, goaled at the two-minute mark of the third quarter, the expectation of the 70,000 present was that the best team in the land was about to hit the accelerator. Instead, it was the complete opposite as the Bulldogs threw their own switch, taking control for the next 40 minutes. Many of the Geelong players were strangely subdued, a disturbing sign for the hierarchy.

"We went in with the (pre-match) expectation that there was no doubt Geelong would be playing in the Grand Final," Ken Hinkey said of that preliminary final test. "In fact, many were saying there was no doubt Geelong were going to win the Grand Final. The thing is, you play that well all year, you just have to get into the Grand Final. It was almost like a huge burden to get through and it seemed to be weighing them down in the game."

Two goals in three minutes by young Bulldog Jarrod Harbrow midway through the third quarter ignited the game. The Dogs could have been closer had they not squandered several easy chances in front of goal, and a Varcoe pass to Mooney set up a much-needed goal to push the lead back out to 18 points at the final change.

The Bulldogs' tactics of slowing the play and maintaining possession were stifling Geelong's ability to open up the contest with its normal run and overlap. Once again it was all the opposition early in the last term but, much to the relief of the defending premiers, the Dogs kept missing. It took a typically courageous act from Max Rooke to finally break them.

The ball was kicked high towards the goalsquare and Dogs captain Brad Johnson was clearly in best position to take a saving chest mark. Rooke thought otherwise. With his eyes on the ball, he charged back with the flight and cannoned into Johnson front on, jolting the ball free. The Bulldogs were convinced it was a free kick to their skipper – it seemed a reasonable claim

– but no whistle was blown. Rooke pounced on the loose ball to snap the match-winner. Thus ended a tough night at the office, such that the mood in the rooms after the contest was nothing except businesslike. The song was sung but it was far from a boisterous rendition. "We can't get carried away," noted James Kelly, who'd gathered 18 possessions in his return. "We've still got a job to do. There's still one more game to go and we just focus on recovering our bodies and getting ready."

Ruckman Brad Ottens agreed, summing up the mood of the group when he said, "I think everyone knows there's still work to do. It was a bit of an unknown last year and not many guys had even played finals footy, so to come through that and know what's coming is definitely a bit of an advantage for us."

Thompson admitted to a sense of deja vu after watching his team again struggle through a preliminary final, though he noted that the post-match attitude should not be misconstrued – or overvalued. "There was probably more euphoria last year but we are just as motivated, we are just as driven and we are thankful for the experience of last year. But it doesn't actually do that much for you in the end," he said.

Thompson declared Paul Chapman a 90 per cent chance of playing in the Grand Final and he took the unusual step of guaranteeing Varcoe his spot in the team. In fact, he was quite open about a number of selection issues, not a common trait as coaches prepare for the final game of the year.

"Travis won't go out, this was probably the best game he has played and I was really happy with him," the Cats coach said. "Wojcinski did enough, he kicked a goal and won enough of the ball to say he will probably stay in. And it was good to have Kelly back. I'm glad he got that run in, which he and Wojcinski needed before the Grand Final."

The Cats had won 42 of their past 44 matches. Yet as Hinkley left the MCG 24 hours later, having watched Hawthorn destroy St Kilda by 54 points, he had an uneasy feeling. "The Hawks got through in smashing style," he recalled thinking. "I just knew momentum can play a part at that stage of the year."

chapter 22

An afternoon to forget

"I can't believe you have chosen this day to be selfish. I can't believe, of all the days, this is one you decide to do it."

– Mark Thompson, half-time of the 2008 Grand Final

Mathew Stokes was in trouble. He had pulled up sore in the groin after the preliminary final and was hoping it would improve as the week went on, which had basically been the way he had existed the previous month – just surviving, and hoping his groin would recover each week in time for the following game. Club doctors were aware of the issue but, after Stokes passed all the relevant testing, the decision was basically left in his hands.

Which, when it comes to a Grand Final, is rarely an ideal scenario.

"I'll be right," was Stokes's message to his coach. He figured he had played out the previous year's Grand Final with a bung knee, so a little groin pain shouldn't be a problem.

The same thoughts were going through Travis Varcoe's mind. He, too, had emerged from the preliminary final with a concern, a sore right ankle following the game of his life. Given Varcoe had missed out playing in the '07 premiership, there was no way a nagging ankle would stop him from running out on Saturday afternoon.

Paul Chapman was a relieved man. He had run at 100 per cent on the Monday of Grand Final week and had pulled up well the following day. In his mind, it meant he was ready to go, although the coaches (and his teammates, for that matter) wanted to see him get through the main group session on the Wednesday. Chapman navigated that hurdle comfortably. He was seen by many as invaluable, and he was ready.

David Wojcinski was a nervous man. Despite a solid outing in the preliminary final, he believed the odds were stacked against him because of the Achilles injury which had cost him most of the latter half of the season. "I knew I hadn't played much footy in the second half of the year and it was always in the back of my mind," he said. When the tap on the shoulder and the bad news came, Wojcinski was gutted but understanding. From the coaching staff's perspective, once Stokes, Varcoe and Chapman all declared themselves fit, Wojcinski was always going to be the unlucky one due to his interrupted season.

"Fit and in good form, he's in our best 22, no doubt," coach Thompson declared at the Grand Final eve press conference following the city parade. "Everybody in the room and everybody who knows Geelong would know that." Maybe so, but it was not convincing enough for Wojcinski's hopes to stay alive.

Much of the questioning in the lead-up had centred around whether it would be a physical Grand Final given the Hawk reputation for "unsociable" football. There was also intrigue over the fitness of Hawks star Luke Hodge, who had injured his ribs in the preliminary final. Thompson wasn't buying into it, nor was he prepared to consider targeting any perceived chink in Hodge's armour. "Do I look like that sort of coach?" Thompson responded when asked whether his men would zero in on the Hawks' vice-captain. "I think we're going to try and play the best football we can play. We don't know whether Hodge has got sore ribs or not and it's almost irrelevant. We should just concentrate on playing the best football we are capable of playing and make sure we start that way and finish that way."

Hodge's name was very much on Stokes's mind as the latter went through the warm-up. While many had thought Max Rooke would start on the Hawthorn playmaker, the Cats had decided to first go with Stokes, given his ability to get himself in dangerous positions and kick goals. The thinking was obvious: force Hodge to be more accountable.

The other key match-ups included Cameron Ling taking responsibility for dynamic Hawks captain Sam Mitchell, while Gary Ablett was going to start forward before moving into the midfield, where the Cats figured Chance Bateman would be his minder.

Matthew Scarlett had the job on Franklin, who had kicked 102 goals in the home-and-away season to secure the Coleman Medal. Harry Taylor had kept Jarryd Roughead in check in Round 17 and would get him again. Tom Harley was to take Campbell Brown; Josh Hunt would stand Mark Williams (who had kicked five goals in the preliminary final). Veteran Darren Milburn and Rooke started on the bench, alongside Grand Final debutants Mark Blake and Varcoe.

After a playful tap at Hodge's ribs just as the ball was bounced to start the match, Stokes locked in for the biggest job of his career. 120 seconds later, he was already in trouble. The Cats' first foray forward through Jimmy Bartel had ended up in a marking contest which Hodge read better, clearing with ease. Thirty seconds later, Ling broke through the centre and went towards the pair but the kick was short and fell perfectly into the hands of the Hawk. "C'mon Stokesy," was the frustrated call from Thompson in the coaches' box.

Thankfully, the ball soon re-entered attack and one of the feelgood stories of the season got his chance to shine. Another Bartel entry had been marked by a diving Tom Lonergan. This was the stuff of movie scripts and fairytales – the favourite son who fought back from a near-death experience to kick the opening goal of the Grand Final. Lonergan clearly read the script, for he went back and calmly drilled the goal from 40 metres.

The euphoria was short lived, for the next 10 minutes belonged to Hawthorn's run and carry, which sliced apart its opponents. Bateman goaled on the run from 50 metres, then three Cyril Rioli bounces down the wing set up a Xavier Ellis goal. When Roughead dribbled one through after being fed a Williams handball, the margin was 13 points. More importantly, Geelong was clearly rattled.

Consecutive 50-metre penalties to Ablett stopped the run but Brown slotted a beautiful goal from 50 metres in the pocket to make it four goals from eight entries for the Hawks. Rooke was summoned off the bench, and his brilliant tackle on Hodge earned a holding-the-ball decision and generated a goal. A minute later, Cameron Mooney snapped brilliantly from the pocket before Paul Chapman had his first meaningful touch of the game – a set shot from 40 metres which he missed.

With two minutes remaining in the first term, Mooney again produced something special. Trapped against the boundary line on the half-forward flank, he repeatedly looked inside for better options but there were none, so he chanced his boot … the kick skimmed through perfectly at the feet of the goal umpire. In the space of five minutes, the Cats had reclaimed the ascendancy but a Williams goal (after Rooke had given away a 50-metre penalty) reduced that margin to one point.

Thompson was the first coach onto the ground and he went directly to Stokes. He had trusted his goalsneak to make the right call about his fitness and, right now, the coach wasn't seeing the Mathew Stokes he knew. Hodge had done exactly what the Cats feared – he had helped out Hawthorn's other defenders while finding plenty of the ball himself.

After the restart, a Chapman goal from a free kick in the opening minute helped momentarily ease Thompson's tension but Rioli created the reply shortly after.

Then it started.

Chapman ignored an open Steve Johnson and instead took a snap for goal. It missed. A few minutes later, ruckman Brad Ottens also had a brain fade. Gathering the ball in the forward pocket, Ottens ignored two teammates, including Lonergan, who was alone at the top of the goalsquare with no Hawthorn players in the vicinity. Ottens took the shot for goal, and he too missed.

Both acts were "un-Geelong-like", and there were plenty of other signs indicating things weren't as they should be. Two quick Hawthorn goals pushed the Hawks ahead and then, to cap off what had been a frustrating first hour, Harley was knocked out after being crunched in a marking contest. The worst was yet to come. In the final play of the half, Mooney marked a long ball from Johnson just five metres out, near the left-hand goalpost. Figuring his side needed a rev up, he hatched a plan in his head as he walked in to take the easy shot. "I thought I'd kick this high and as soon as I kick it I'll run through the man on the mark and start a bit of a half-time biff," Mooney explained.

The "biff" didn't eventuate for a simple reason – Mooney badly shanked the kick. Instead of taking on a couple of Hawthorn defenders, the Cats centre half-forward put his head down and jogged off, embarrassed and not a little stunned at what he'd just done.

In the rooms, Harley was lying on a bench, concussed. He had no idea where he was; perhaps he was the lucky one when his coach stormed in. Thompson knew the statistics sheet in his hand indicated that Geelong should be well ahead, yet it had managed only one goal and nine behinds in the second quarter and found itself three points down. Equally disturbing was that much of it was its own doing. The Cats had entered 50 no less than 33 times for 6.12 and had numerous players with big numbers – Steve Johnson led everyone with 19 possessions – which gave more weight to the coach's perspective that too many players were chasing kicks or trying to be the goalkicking heroes.

What he couldn't understand was why his players were going away from the team ethos which had served them so well for the best part of two seasons. "I can't believe you have chosen this day to be selfish," Thompson said as he surveyed his players in the meeting room. "I can't believe, of all the days, this is one you decide to do it."

As he went back with the ball in his hands just 90 seconds into the third quarter, Cameron Mooney wasn't sure whether it was a good or bad thing that he had an immediate opportunity to make up for his humiliating miss on the half-time siren. A fine juggling mark had set up a shot from 35 metres out, directly in front. From the second it hit his boot, Mooney knew he'd blown it again, having tried to guide the ball through. It hit the post.

Three minutes later it was Lonergan's turn. He marked deep in the pocket but his banana kick also found the post, which meant the Cats had kicked 11 behinds in a row.

"We would want to start taking some of these chances or we're going to get in trouble," Hinkley said to his fellow coaches up in the stand, airing the thought which had clearly gripped the ground and his players. Hinkley knew Hawthorn was going to get a "run on" at some stage – the Hawks were too good not to and, if Geelong didn't have the score on the board when it happened, the Cats were in dangerous territory.

Once again it was Ablett who provided the salve, ending the goal drought by kicking a brilliant running goal from 30 metres to regain the advantage, however narrow. And several other signs suggested things were starting to turn their way.

For while the Cats were down a man, with Harley yet to re-emerge, their opponent now had two absentees. Key defender Trent Croad had limped off during the second quarter with what was later found to be a badly broken foot. In the opening minutes of the third term, midfielder Clinton Young, to that point one of the best on the ground, severely rolled his ankle and had to be helped off the ground. In modern football, a two-man bench is customarily a death sentence. But every time Geelong seemed set to gain momentum, Hawthorn would answer with a goal. This time it was Franklin, who opened his account for the day with a 50-metre bomb from the pocket. The Hawks were proving more than an annoyance. They were taking their opportunities and – crucially – it was evident that the Hawthorn camp, and its support base, was beginning to believe an unbelievable upset was possible.

Mooney's nightmare continued at the 10-minute mark when he sprayed another set shot from 40 metres. It levelled the scores, yet the frustration at the inability to impact on the scoreboard was beginning to boil over. Hawthorn's next goal said a lot about where the Cats were at. Michael Osborne had won a free kick for a high tackle from Josh Hunt and, instead of taking the shot from 50 metres, he simply handballed to Hodge, who had ambled up next to him. It was the oldest trick in the book yet the Cats fell for it and the Hawks star had no trouble steering it through off one step. One stitch at a time, the defending premiers were coming apart at the seams.

Ten minutes later, Hinkley's voiced fears became a reality, and it came in the form of an entirely unexpected force. Stuart Dew, the Port Adelaide premiership player Hawks coach Alastair Clarkson had lured out of retirement that offseason, changed the face of the Grand Final.

Dew had been a surprise third-round choice of the Hawks. After a year out of football, few thought he had much to offer following 180 games with the Power. But players like Dew don't lose their self-belief or ability, and his challenge was to get fit enough to perform consistently. The early signs were disturbing – he missed 10 home-and-away games with hamstring problems. But his big-game experience would vindicate Clarkson's use of a third-round pick on the 2004 premiership player.

Moved to the forward line, the prodigious left-footer set up a crumbing Rioli goal with five minutes remaining in the term. He then seized on a Harry Taylor turnover and, off one step, kicked the goal from 55 metres. Less than 60 seconds later, Dew was tackled by three Cats, yet he managed to squeeze a handball out to Mark Williams, who dribbled through another. And he was not done yet – with two minutes remaining, Dew received a handball from Franklin and casually snapped truly to send the spirited Hawks 30 points up.

The seams were well and truly split, and the stuffing knocked out of Geelong. At the other end of the ground, Mooney simply shook his head. Like most of his teammates, he was in shock.

"We're done here," he conceded to himself as he peered up at the MCG scoreboard. "We've lost it."

There was a pulse, however soft. Steve Johnson understood the immediacy of the situation, sending forward a 60-metre torpedo which floated over the back of the pack and into the arms of defender Darren Milburn. For once, a Cat didn't miss. Then, just as Hawthorn captain Sam Mitchell stripped Ablett of the ball, a downfield free kick was paid to Johnson, who finished the job. Two goals in less than a minute had the margin down to 17 points at the final break and breathed life back in to the contest.

When he reached the huddle, Thompson made a beeline for his forwards. Nothing had clicked in attack and, although they desperately needed to find a system that would produce – it was too late to reinvent the wheel. Thus

Thompson simply reverted to a consistent Geelong theme: don't give in and convert your chances.

Hope was nearly extinguished in the opening minute by that man Dew, who again wheeled onto his left boot but this time missed from 55 metres. Jordan Lewis then missed a set shot before Geelong finally got its first opportunity – it was again Mooney, who found himself in space at centre half-forward. Ahead, he had Johnson alone to his right and Rooke running back towards goal. Mooney picked the wrong option, targetting Rooke, and by the time the ball arrived so had Campbell Brown.

Thirty seconds later it was Ablett's chance. Bursting onto the ball at half-forward, he set sail for home but it drifted to the wrong side of post. The Cats again seemed to have the run of play but could make little inroads on the scoreboard. That extra gear was lurking, and there was enough time, but those wasted opportunities in the second quarter seemed to have doomed them.

Harley returned at the eight-minute mark, seeking to inspire his team, but another fluffed chance by Varcoe turned the ball over and Hawthorn did what it had done all day: nailed its chance. This one was a classic Franklin left-foot monster as he roared around to his left from the half-forward flank. Mitchell – brilliantly held by Ling all day – then kicked another goal just 60 seconds later.

Game over.

Silence filled the coaches' box. The Cats had lost what many had thought was the unlosable Grand Final. In front of them, the players were going through the motions before it ended the way it had started, Lonergan kicking a goal from a set shot to leave the scoreboard reading: Hawthorn 18.7 (115), Geelong 11.23.(89).

As the Hawks celebrated, Geelong players dropped to the ground, grief-stricken. Ablett, who five days earlier had been forced to deal with the disappointment of again being pipped for the Brownlow Medal, was in tears. He had easily been his team's best player, such that he was a reasonable candidate for the Norm Smith Medal, a rare honour on a losing Grand Final team (and, ironically, won by his father 20 years ago to the day, in a Grand Final failure against Hawthorn). As Thompson observed later,

"I was thinking about (Gary winning) it, to be honest. I thought Gary would be up there in the voting. His performance was sensational. He looked like he just wanted to win so much.

"I wish he had a few friends."

The honour for the best player on the ground went to Hodge. Thus ended a horror day for his original opponent, Mathew Stokes, though he wasn't the only one to struggle. Chapman hadn't been his destructive self, Varcoe had arguably been overawed and Kelly had suffered from second-up blues. Mooney was also distraught, the horror of his missed shots set to haunt him in the months ahead.

Thompson's statistics sheets were both damning and barely believable. Somehow the Cats had lost despite entering the 50-metre arc 62 times compared to Hawthorn's 43, an extraordinary disparity. The Cats dominated most of the key statistical indicators, including clearances (41-27) and rebound 50s (51-24). It is almost – but obviously not – impossible to lose a game of football with such a statistical superiority.

Three hours later, the players and coaching staff arrived at the club's post-match function at Melbourne Park. What had been expected to be a glorious coronation instead had the feeling of a memorial service for something departed. That thing was the Cats' apparent invincibility.

The events of the afternoon had yet to fully sink in for some. Chief executive Brian Cook and president Frank Costa addressed the gathering. "We will take adversity and use it as a lever for next year," Cook said. "The last thing we want to see is any 'scapegoating', any player blamed for not playing as good as they could have today."

It was then Thompson's turn to take to the stage and speak on behalf of his men. "We are a sorry, sore bunch of men who just want to go home, but we can't. We have to face the music," he said. "But I've got no doubt the core of what we are about as a club is ripe. This side has been the best side all year but on the one day it matters we lost.

"We should not blame each other. If you are going to win well, and we were applauded for how we won last year, then we should lose well as well."

chapter 23

A time
to reflect

"Unless we took the next step in a lot of areas we were going to remain a good club but we were never going to enter the territory of greatness."

– Geelong CEO Brian Cook

The report in Brian Cook's hands was revealing. A substantial document, it was destined to never leave Cook's office safe. Leading Teams, the corporate leadership company which had played such a strong role in guiding the club's 2007 fortunes, had conducted a review of the 2008 Grand Final. Be it players or coaches, nothing – and no one – was spared. "From my point of view it was a bad day," Cook said. "It wasn't a bad year, it was a bad day. The players and coaches did their own review, which was kept internal and has never seen the light outside the walls of the Geelong Football Club.

"It would be safe for me to say that the key theme was about selflessness and on that one particular day, for some reason, the players did not jell or work as a dynamic like they normally did during the year. There were some selfish acts early (in the Grand Final) which set the scene for the whole game. That was probably I think the key theme for the Grand Final. And basically that became the key thing for '09."

Even months afterwards, many at the club were still coming to terms with what had gone wrong on the final Saturday in September.

"We weren't playing great at the most important part of (the season)," Matthew Scarlett said. "We had players injured who shouldn't have played. We didn't play well as a team on the day, there were a lot of things that happened, which is why we didn't win. It's a lesson we have to learn."

Jimmy Bartel also felt like the team had limped to the line. "We were the best team all year but we weren't the best team in September," he reflected. "It was a weird day, a bitter feeling, something you experience and go, 'I don't want this again'."

Vice-captain Cameron Ling thought too much emphasis had been placed on the club's remarkable winning streak. "During the whole year we felt we had to win every game and we had to win by 100 points," Ling said. "We probably did peak a little bit too early. I mean, we played amazing footy throughout the year. It was more important to win every single game of footy and through that we took in (to games) guys who were sore. We were probably running out of legs a little bit.

"The other thing is, we thought it was just going to happen even when we were missing our opportunities in the second quarter (of the Grand Final). We still thought, 'That is okay, we will still run away with it.' Hawthorn were too good, they are a quality side and you can't have that sort of attitude against them. They played terrific footy and stuck to their guns. We were obviously kidding ourselves."

Cameron Mooney agreed.

"Everyone had the mentality that it would just happen," he said. "We were good enough just to win even if we played poorly (during the season). We would turn it on for a quarter and the game would be finished. I think that was always the mentality of everyone."

Steve Johnson, the joint-highest possession winner in the Grand Final with 34 touches, believed the problem ran even deeper. While difficult to pinpoint, Johnson had the feeling that the Cats, as a team, had started to lose trust in each other. "When we are at our best, we go into a game where you know that every single player will just play their role to help the team win," he said. "It's not about who plays the best, who kicks the goals, it's not about that. In 2007, we were the best *team*, we were a unit. Every player who took the field, it didn't matter who, they knew their role and they were expected to play it. If they didn't they would be told about it.

"It felt like we had been doing it for so long and right at the end it did feel like we were questioning each other a little bit, we were maybe wondering whether each player was going to play their role each week."

And so to the coach.

Mark Thompson, who had a DVD of the Grand Final at home for two-and-a-half months before he sat down to watch it – even then, he switched it off half-way through the last quarter – knew mistakes had been made in a lot of areas. He also knew that the relatively easy ride the Cats had enjoyed through a memorable home-and-away season was less than ideal when it came to preparing for the finals.

"We didn't do enough right," he said, "in match committee, in training, with how we attacked the game. We'd hardly played any close games, we hadn't been in that level of stress in a game. There were a lot of things that we just didn't do."

Paul Chapman was aware of the heavy criticism in the fall-out of the loss but he had no regrets about putting his hand up to play. "I wouldn't have played if I didn't think I was right, that is not what I am about," he said. "Obviously I wasn't at my best, I would have thought I'd be more competitive. The result didn't go our way but it wasn't because Stokesy didn't do something or I didn't do something. It was a day where nothing went right for us. We didn't take our opportunities so I'm not wearing that if I hadn't played we would have won, or anything like that. We put ourselves in a good opportunity, we were the best team in it, but just on the big day we didn't do it."

It had been a tough year for Chapman. His behaviour and professionalism had been questioned several times during the season, to the point where it was agreed he should leave the leadership group midway through the season. Chapman had always done things differently but the club and coaches felt it was time he fell into line with the rest of the playing group. At his post-season review, the star forward was told as much by management. "It would be fair to say every player went through a 360 (after the Grand Final loss) and Chappy probably had more challenges than a lot of others," Cook said.

A positive note for the hierarchy was that Chapman had already decided on embracing some lifestyle changes. "Injuries drag you down mentally as well as physically," he said. "That is what I found and I was in a bad place for a while. Nothing seemed to be going right." So while most of his teammates were putting their feet up or lying on various beaches around the world during the break, Chapman started training by himself. "Obviously something wasn't working," he explained. "It was more about getting my body ticking over, rather than having six weeks off and then coming back and training hard. I stopped for four weeks, although I made sure I still did a lot of walking in that time, and then after that I started running again."

Chapman wasn't the only player to confront football's hard reality at his post-season review, for young forward Tom Hawkins was also told a few home truths. There was a feeling that the 20-year-old hadn't worked hard enough to get himself fit and available for the finals campaign. Given the way the forward structure had struggled in the Grand Final, his presence may have made a difference.

"Hawk got a really direct message about what is expected and the requirements to be an elite player at AFL level," Ken Hinkley explained. "It doesn't just happen because you were a great junior school player or you'd dominated an U/18 carnival. Once you make the step up there was an attitude needed. You want to be ruthless about what you are trying to achieve.

"(Joel) Selwood shows that, he has that incredible balance of hard work and being a competitor as well as having the ability to enjoy a good time when the time is right. Hawk hadn't quite figured out everything that he was required to do. He didn't have any real footy disciplines in his day-to-day life so he received a reminder of what was required."

The players weren't the only section of the club forced to stare hard at the mirror following the defeat: Cook and his management team also took a collective breath. "I think we probably had to look at ourselves a bit and understand that unless we took the next step in a lot of areas of the club then we were going to remain a good club, a nice club, but we were never going to enter the territory of greatness," the CEO said.

On November 14, 2008, a planned workshop included the executive team and the board. Thus started the process of developing a plan to achieve Cook's vision of greatness. Over the four months that followed, different stakeholders were introduced into the discussion – including players, coaches, middle management and sponsors – with a list of objectives for the period 2009-13 agreed.

They were outlined in a 15-page document titled "*Good to Great – By 2013*". Also included was a list of the club's values:

Respect – for our club, partners, communities and each other.

Precision – in every action and activity.

Adventurous – in mind and spirit.

Conviction – in our purpose and potential.

Unity – through inclusion.

Commercial but considered.

One of the primary key performance indicators listed was to "play in the AFL finals each year and win at least one AFL premiership between 2009 and 2013."

There also was a vision of what the GFC would look like in 2020, when it had become a great club: "It is 2020 and we have won more premierships than any other club over the past 15 years and we are the most admired football operator in Australia.

"We have become the benchmark for others to emulate, running smoothly and professionally with ample resources, international and internal experts and world-class facilities. Our players are considered role models for the code, displaying a conviction to winning and performance that is akin to a religion. Our superb coaching and training practices set the style of play and we dominate on-field."

Ironically, some of the club's new values and objectives were expected to be ignored in the first competition of the new season. Dominating on the field in the NAB Cup simply wasn't on the agenda.

In fact, a first or second-round exit was the forecast, but a first round departure was avoided thanks mainly to that man Ablett. Again. He simply picked up where he had left off four months earlier, dominating the game by kicking four goals from 23 possessions to secure a 35-point victory over Adelaide at Etihad Stadium. Ryan Gamble also kicked four, while some new faces in midfielder Simon Hogan, Jeremy Laidler and Dan McKenna earned a taste of senior football.

There were a couple of new faces in the coaches' box, too, with Brisbane's triple-premiership player, Nigel Lappin – who had been forced into retirement by an ankle injury at the end of 2008 – joining the panel. So too did Geelong Football League premiership-winning coach Dale Amos, who became the new VFL coach. His appointment came after St Kilda tempted Leigh Tudor with an offer he couldn't refuse, Saints coach Ross Lyon making it clear he wanted insight into some of Geelong's intelligence.

The biggest change in the playing ranks was the loss of Brent Prismall, who sought a trade to Essendon in search for more opportunities. At one stage the Cats were trying to introduce the Bombers' troubled speedster, Andrew Lovett, but it was ultimately done for pick No.39. Stephen Wells used that slot to snare Steven Motlop, younger brother of Port Adelaide's freakish forward, Daniel.

A new-look leadership group had also been crafted over the summer, a move many saw as the start of the search for the leader of Geelong's next generation. The "ins" were significant: Gary Ablett, Jimmy Bartel, Joel Selwood and Corey Enright. The inclusion of 20-year-old Selwood after just two years on the list was notable (and some actually believed he was already capable of doing the top job). There also was a sense that 2009 could be Tom Harley's final campaign so his successor (if it wasn't going to be vice-captain Cameron Ling) needed to be groomed. In the shake-up, Joel Corey was promoted to deputy vice-captain after Cameron Mooney and Max Rooke indicated they wanted to stand down from the group. Chapman, of course, had already left midway through the previous season.

Mooney figured the changing of the guard was crucial for the development of the team. "If we are going to go anywhere, the younger blokes are going to have to take control a bit more," he said. "It needs a new, fresh look."

There was certainly a different look about the team which boarded the plane for the Round 2 NAB Cup fixture against Port Adelaide. The trip had been met with a lukewarm response from the match committee, which had spent a lot of time discussing how to rest players throughout the year and various means of structuring the season so there would be no repeat of the 2008 struggles.

From as early as February, 2009, everything would be designed to have players peaking mentally and physically for September. Research was conducted by Ken Hinkley and fitness coach Dean Robinson, who looked into how elite soccer teams in the English Premier League – clubs which typically also carry substantial European commitments – rotated and rested players. "They (EPL) play so many games over there. It is a bit different to ours but we looked at everything," Hinkley explained. "We came up with a plan (identifying) players that, if you had a perfect world scenario, you would give a rest in Round 12 to Round 16 to get them ready (for finals).

"We wanted to not have the position like late last year where we went into the finals underprepared physically. It wasn't that we didn't want to win every game but if we were to lose a couple because we haven't got our best people available, well, that's okay."

More than a third of the Grand Final team stayed at home for the Port Adelaide trip, with six new faces earning a chance at senior level. "We took a team over there not that we thought can't win but the reality was they shouldn't have won," Hinkley admitted.

Problem was, win they did. Mathew Stokes kicked three of his four goals in the final term en route to an 18-point win. One senior Cat present was Chapman who, for the first time in years, had completed a pre-season without a glitch. He looked like a different man. New faces to impress included Nathan Djerrkura, a pacy forward pocket in the Stokes mode, and tall forward Scott Simpson.

The rotation of senior players continued for the semi-final against Carlton, with names like Bartel, Mackie, Blake, Selwood, Enright and Stokes enjoying a spell. But the Blues, who had played near full-strength line-ups in the opening two matches, took a similar philosophy into the match, resting big guns including Chris Judd and Brendan Fevola. It virtually handed Geelong the game by default. The 17-point win secured a showdown with Collingwood in the NAB Cup Grand Final. While not everyone was reintroduced for the final – no player had played in all three preliminary matches – the attitude changed slightly with Thompson seeking to field a team which resembled the one he would be using in the season-opening Grand Final re-match against Hawthorn. The injured Harley was the only one missing from the defensive line although, late in the first quarter of the NAB Cup final, another vital cog was struck down.

What looked like a simple chase and bump ended Josh Hunt's season. His left knee buckled following an innocuous collision with Magpie Paul Medhurst. It was a cruel blow for Hunt, who was turning 27 the next day; he was coming off his best season, having played 23 games and established himself as a vital link between defence and attack for the Cats.

The sight of him being carried from the ground clicked his teammates into action. Scores were level at quarter-time but it then deteriorated into a rout, Geelong kicking 15.14 to 4.4 in the final three quarters to win by 76 points. Selwood pipped Ablett for the Michael Tuck Medal for best afield, and later admitted the Grand Final loss to Hawthorn had been in the players' minds in the lead-up. "Any premiership you play for you want to win and Matty Scarlett made that pretty clear at the start of the game. Cameron Ling did, too," Selwood said.

Apart from the loss of Hunt, Thompson couldn't find any negatives. "We couldn't have played any better," he said. "I think we made our intent known pretty early in the week that we didn't want to get to another grand final and lose it. We put a fair bit of work in training into the tactical side of it and the players sent a pretty strong message that they were here to play."

For the CEO it was an unexpected boost to the bank balance, although the players requested that $50,000 of the $180,000 winner's cheque be donated to the Victorian Bushfires Appeal. "It was a surprise because really we hadn't focussed on it at all yet we ended up winning the thing," Cook said. "The coaches experimented, they played young players but they were hungry. It was as though they hadn't had a meal for a while."

Truth be known, it was simply a promising appetiser.

chapter 24
The son rises

"I have never really seen him have this commitment and appetite to get the ball as often as he did. You almost knew that when he was going for the ball it was going to him."

– Mark Thompson marvels about Gary Ablett

Tom Harley had known for months he was in serious trouble. He had tried to remain optimistic, and the medical experts had told him his knee would start to improve. Problem was, they'd told him that at the start of December. It was now the end of March, the eve of Round 1 of the 2009 season, and the knee felt exactly the same: damaged.

Harley had a history of knee problems since arriving at Geelong a decade earlier with knee soreness. He had become accustomed to managing the issue well, to the point he had soldiered on manfully to be one of only six Cats to play every game in 2008. "I just threw everything at '08 as I thought we were on a good thing here," he said. "I had done a whole pre-season and I felt good. In the end I played 25 games but I really struggled towards the end of the year.

"I knew I was in a bit of strife with the knee so I had the surgery. I thought I was going in basically to have a 'scope, which means eight weeks off then a modified program up until December. Then I would get really stuck into the pre-season from January on and be right to go for the whole year."

That was all good in theory. Yet the first signs of trouble occurred when he tried to get back to light running before Christmas. "It was literally babystep running," he said. "I would run for 50 metres and then walk for two laps. When I was really struggling with that I said to the doctors it was no good."

The message was persistence. Club officials gave him another training program to take with him on his New Year break to Lake Conjola on the NSW south coast. "I remember trying to run laps on this little oval up in NSW and thinking to myself, 'This is not going to get any better at all'," Harley said. "It was just not making any progress so when I came back to Geelong in January I knew in my heart of hearts I was going to struggle to get up for the start of the season. And it turned out I wasn't even remotely close to playing in the NAB Cup."

Further examination of the knee revealed he had significant bone damage, in three different spots, which not only complicated the healing process but slowed it dramatically. Round 1 was out of the question. "That was quite depressing," the captain said of being in the stands for the Grand Final re-match against Hawthorn.

Next to him sat Josh Hunt, who had flirted with the idea of radical synthetic graft surgery on his knee, and actually spoken to Sydney's Nick Malceski (who had come back in three months following the procedure) before deciding to have a traditional knee reconstruction.

Hunt's season was over.

They were the only two missing from the '08 Grand Final team, replaced by David Wojcinski and Ryan Gamble, while the Hawks had several big names on the sidelines.

One who *was* present in the brown and gold that day was Luke Hodge; the mere mention of his name caused Mathew Stokes to shudder. The Cats' goalsneak had spent the off-season questioning himself about whether he should have played in the Grand Final. It had been his worst game of the season by far – three kicks, one mark, four handballs, one behind and one tackle – and left him devastated.

"All that was going through my head was, 'Should I have played?'" Stokes said. "It was doing my head in so I just tried to accept it, that I made the decision to play and Bomber (Thompson) stood by me. "He had asked me if my groins were fine, I said I thought they were. The worst part was coming off the ground and not being able to look my teammates in the eye, knowing you let them down. I'd definitely say a few of the boys thought I played with an injury."

Straight after the Grand Final, Stokes fled town with his girlfriend, Jess, heading to Fiji and then to Darwin to be with his parents. "I probably didn't deal with it that well," he said. "It took me a long time to get over it. It was pretty hard to accept as a player that you stumbled in the biggest game of the year. I went to Darwin and it was pretty hard because everyone had questions and I didn't really have any answers.

"When I came back I didn't know what I wanted from footy and Bomber put it to me that I had to have something to aim for. I hadn't really thought about it until then and my goal is never to let the team down again. I feel like I did that in the Grand Final and I never want to be in that situation again."

Thompson was confident Stokes and the rest of his Cats had moved on from the 2008 debacle. He declared them "mentally and physically" ready for the Round 1 re-match, referring to the previous year's pre-season as being out of kilter. "It's definitely a shock when you play into September for the first time. We were sort of a little bit under-prepared at the start last year."

The Grand Final loss might not have been playing on Geelong minds – so they claim – but the football world had undergone a major shift on the strength of that 2008 upset.

Many believed the Hawks had claimed a premiership before their time was due – the extension of that argument is they were still improving, and with only veteran Shane Crawford departed, there was every reason to believe the Hawks were the favoured team in 2009. Even their president, outspoken former Victorian Premier Jeff Kennett, had weighed into the season build-up, claiming Geelong lacked the "psychological drive" of his club.

It set the stage for a fierce Round 1 battle which got more than willing on several occasions, particularly after Hawthorn ruckman Simon Taylor was reported for dropping a knee into the head of Joel Selwood. The Cat youngster was forced from the ground under duress.

Yet Thompson had other issues, most notably a disturbing sense of "here we go again" with his team's goalkicking. In the first half, Geelong kicked 8.16 to 8.4, a disappointing result given Gary Ablett's dominance of the game (23 possessions to half-time). Still, the Cats kicked the last three goals of the second quarter and broke open the match with the first four after the long break. Early in the last term the lead was out to 43 points before a late onslaught from Lance Franklin and Jarryd Roughead. The Hawks kicked six straight – their twin towers bagging three each in the final 15 minutes – before Thompson sent Matthew Scarlett, who'd suffered an ankle injury, back onto the ground to steady the ship.

"It's a good wake-up call for us," noted Steve Johnson, one of the best with 27 possessions and two goals.

The coach was frustrated that he again was talking about bad goalkicking against the Hawks. "We missed a lot of shots again, which is disappointing, especially set shots," he said. "It just goes in runs like that and it will correct itself, it's not as if we can't kick goals from set shots, we have proven we can. It's just a little thing we are going through."

Cameron Mooney, in his first game of the season, again missed a couple while Johnson had three behinds to his name. Another to miss three times was Brad Ottens, yet coach Thompson would have been delighted nonetheless – Ottens dominated on the back of his first uninterrupted pre-season in recent memory, and shaped as a key factor in the club's bid to restore order to its world.

Not that Mark Thompson needed reminding, but it's funny how quickly things turn in football.

From the coaches' box, it looked like an ordinary centre square ruck contest. The problem was that Brad Ottens had crashed to the turf after contact. Thompson watched the ball get cleared before his eyes diverted back to his ruckman, who still hadn't moved. Thompson's heart sunk.

A trainer and the club's doctor, Chris Bradshaw, were now helping the 202cm giant to his feet but he was unable to put any weight on his right knee. The replay on the television above the coach showed it had been a classic case of the ruckman's curse, Ottens and Richmond's Troy Simmonds clashing knees in the contest.

It wasn't even quarter-time in the second game of the season. The Cats had already lost Josh Hunt for the year and also promising young forward Mitchell Brown – their first-round pick, at No.15, in the 2008 National Draft – who had broken his leg in the VFL earlier that day. Now, as Ottens limped off, a major piece of the puzzle was being threatened. Indeed, a typical result of that clash was posterior cruciate ligament damage, and Thompson knew it. "You get worried when they can't get up," was his read of the situation.

An assessment could wait, but at least the coach didn't have too many other concerns at half-time, the Cats 29 points up and seemingly cruising. That changed in the next 30 minutes, however, with the Tigers (who had been humiliated in the opening game of the season against Carlton) kicking eight goals to remarkably take the lead at three-quarter time. Skilled Stadium was silent. Enter Steve Johnson. Reaching into his bag of magic tricks, the All-Australian half-forward kicked three goals in the final term to avert the scare, with the Cats winning by 20 points.

"We were tired from the Hawthorn game," the coach noted afterwards, although he wasn't just relieved about the win but also the updated prognosis on Ottens, which indicated the ruckman suffered only a medial ligament strain. Historically, that meant for only a 4-6 week recovery period. Or so they thought.

A five-day break had fitness and recovery staff working overtime to get players up and running for an Easter Thursday night showdown with Collingwood at the MCG. The short turnover appeared to have thrown the Cats out in the opening term, as the Pies kicked five goals to two to lead by 20 at the first change. Their response was emphatic. Paul Chapman, Jimmy Bartel and Matthew Scarlett turned the game with an eight-goal second-quarter blitz but, as had been the case in the opening two games of the season, the Cats again lost momentum, allowing Collingwood to creep within 14 points at three-quarter time.

Thompson, who had been criticised for being too laidback at times, was extremely animated in the huddle as he demanded his team get back to playing "the Geelong way". His outburst worked, inspiring a soccer goal from Steve Johnson and a clever snap from Shannon Byrnes in the opening minutes of the final term, reclaiming the momentum and driving a 27-point victory. Gary Ablett, who had had been restricted to just four possessions in the first quarter, had 27 in the second half for a game-high 37, though he played second fiddle to Chapman, who kicked four goals from 35 touches.

"I was very happy for half of it and very angry for the other half," was Thompson's take on his team's third win of the season, although he did produce a smile when quizzed about Chapman.

"He has had a fantastic summer."

"We can't do much more than what we tried to," a frustrated Adelaide coach Neil Craig said. "You'd come a long way to watch those sorts of players."

That's exactly what Craig's players had done – watched – as they weren't able to lay a finger on or do anything to stop Gary Ablett celebrating his 150th game milestone with arguably the best game of his career. It was a performance that left 40,000 fans at AAMI Stadium (plus his own coaches, and even teammates) shaking their heads. Ablett's stats read: 46 disposals – 13 kicks, 33 handballs, seven marks, three tackles, 14 contested possessions and 3.1.

There was actually some disappointment in the coaches' box as they'd rested the champion late in the game – the Cats kicked seven goals to two in the last quarter to win by 48 points – which may have cost him the chance to break the magical 50. "That game was probably a new level," assistant coach Brendan McCartney said.

Thompson couldn't believe how every time Ablett went near the ball it literally ended up in his hands. "I think that is probably his best (career game)," he said. "I have never really seen him have this commitment and appetite to get the ball as often as he did. It didn't matter if there was one player or two players on him. You almost knew that when he was going in for the ball, it was going to him because every time he would just get his hands on it."

It was much of the same the following week against Brisbane, with again the most interest surrounding Ablett and whether he could get 50 touches. After 27 in the first half, he had to settle for 42, one of which was a candidate for goal of the year. The degree of difficulty was extreme on that late April afternoon, with 30kp/h winds and hail slicing across Skilled Stadium. Adding to the problems was that construction work had started on the new stand on the western side of the ground – there was a big gap where the Ross Drew Stand and Past Players' Stand had been. This created a wind tunnel effect, making it almost impossible to score goals from that pocket.

Of course, the word "impossible" is clearly not in Ablett's vocabulary. In the last quarter, with the game well and truly over (the Cats led by 12 goals at three-quarter time) the superstar ran straight into the teeth of the wind tunnel and, from next to the boundary line, somehow guided the ball through from 45 metres. It had to be seen to be believed.

"Has anyone kicked a goal from that pocket the way he did today when the wind was blowing in that south-westerly direction?" was the question Thompson posed afterwards. Needless to say, everyone present knew the answer.

Ablett aside, there were several other significant performances that day. On a difficult afternoon for tall forwards, Geelong fans got a glimpse of the attacking structure they'd been waiting to admire for a couple of years. The combination of Tom Hawkins and Cameron Mooney clicked brilliantly; the pair both accumulated 20-plus possessions and three goals. Hawkins, in particular, was generating excitement for his second efforts and tackling pressure, not traits that had marked his earlier appearances.

"I thought it was clearly the best game he has played," Thompson stated. "I know he has kicked more goals and everything else in some games but just the way he was involved in the game. He looked like he was confidently running around and he knew what he was doing, he was having some influence. You can ask people to be relaxed, to be comfortable. You can ask them to do so much but until they actually get it ... today it looked like he got it."

While the coach's spray at the end of the previous season had been timely, it had already clicked in Hawkins' head that things had to change drastically.

The events of the past two Septembers were his motivation. After watching Joel Selwood taste premiership success in their first season of 2007, he was again envious the following year when his close friend, Melbourne Grammar schoolmate and Hawthorn midfielder Xavier Ellis, did the same.

"In my first year our team won. Last year the Hawks won and 'Zave' is a good mate of mine. I saw in those two years how big premierships are and what they mean," Hawkins said. "It made me decide that's what I want to do, made me more determined. In my first two years I just wasted the opportunities. I suppose I didn't commit myself to football as much as I should have."

Over the summer, Hawkins finally got the "respect" he hadn't previously earned from his teammates. Despite being confined to the rehab group because the club didn't want to take any risks with his foot injury, he worked overtime under the watchful eye of Harley and Mooney. The results came in the form of a streamlined body shape, a new-found work ethic and the chance to make the goalsquare his own.

But while things were finally working out for one big Cat, an even bigger one was having problems. Brad Ottens' comeback from his knee injury had hit not just one snag, but several. An arthroscope had revealed a medial ligament strain and a badly damaged patella tendon. A week after the operation he suffered a bleed in the knee, followed by a serious infection. Just like that, Ottens' expected return date had been pushed out to mid-season.

In his absence, Mark Blake had been receiving some more than handy support from rookie-listed ruckman Shane Mumford, a 200cm,105kg giant from Bunyip, whose appetite for the contest was impressing the Cats' hierarchy. Some wonderful ruckwork at the opening bounce of the Round 6 game against Melbourne provided one of the highlights of the season. And surprise, surprise, it involved G. Ablett.

The superstar rover ran onto the tap in the middle of the ground, took one bounce and drilled the goal from 55 metres. All in just nine seconds! It certainly sparked some debate in the coaches' box. "I've never seen a quicker goal in league football," Thompson said. "Has there ever been one?"

This was a day of firsts at the MCG, with the Cats breaking their own all-time possessions record (set the week before against Brisbane) by collecting 498 disposals in a 43-point win over the hapless Demons. Chapman and Bartel were the stars with 41 each but the story of the game was the groin injury to Ablett midway through the last quarter. It forced him out the following week against Sydney, although a couple of big names returned in vice-captain Cameron Ling, who'd missed two weeks with an Achilles injury, and a very relieved captain Tom Harley.

A trip to Sydney to see leading knee expert, Jenny McConnell, had been the turning point for the skipper. McConnell specialised in the treatment of patellofemoral pain syndrome and used unique taping and training techniques to get her patients up and going again when most traditional methods had failed.

"For a while there I almost thought it was curtains but then I went up to see Jenny and she devised a bit of a different plan and worked on different exercises," Harley said.

"The beauty about seeing someone external was that they were not driven by player deadlines and getting up for games and all those sorts of things. She was really pragmatic about it ... after seeing her it really started to turn the corner and I was able to get on the park. Bomber was adamant that I come straight back into the ones, which was an awesome show of faith, and to be honest I probably wasn't ready."

Harley got through comfortably enough and was part of a defence that strangled Swans star Barry Hall who, matched against Matthew Scarlett, didn't touch the ball in the second half. It was a strange game, however, and – in stark contrast to the previous week – the Cats took 25 minutes to kick their first goal. That came courtesy of Steve Johnson, who exploded in the second quarter, kick-starting a seven-goal term in which he contributed 4.4 goals from 17 possessions, forcing Sydney coach Paul Roos to shift away All-Australian defender Craig Bolton.

Sydney showed its customary fight, kicking three of the first four goals of the third quarter before Geelong steadied. Joel Corey and Joel Selwood were everywhere, both finishing with 34 touches to set up a 51-point win. While that was win No.7 on the trot, Geelong found itself second on the ladder behind a St Kilda team setting all kinds of defensive records. Indeed, its pressure football was the major talking point of the competition.

As part of AFL experimenting with the draw, the Saints played their Round 7 game against Collingwood on a Monday night at Etihad Stadium. It gave Thompson and his coaching staff the chance to have a first-hand look at the club which loomed as its main challenger, given the Hawks' slow start to the season. The Cats coach came away after watching St Kilda destroy Collingwood to the tune of 88 points, thinking of one person – his former assistant Leigh Tudor.

"One thing I can't believe is that no one has spoken about Leigh Tudor leaving Geelong and being at St Kilda," Thompson said at his weekly press conference. "They seem to be playing like Geelong."

chapter 25

Absorbing the lessons

"We walked off the MCG last year as losers. We're not going to walk off losers this year."

– Joel Corey presents the mid-season training program to the playing group

The criticism hit home. While it wasn't acknowledged as the reason for the 2008 Grand Final loss, the Geelong coaching panel conceded it needed to be more flexible and reactive to different scenarios within games.

Exhibit A was the destructive eight-minute path cut by Stuart Dew on that cruel September day. Perhaps little could have been done; even the Hawks later conceded they had not exactly planned Dew's game-turning move to the forward line – the former Port premiership player instigated the switch himself. But the truth was the Cats' box did little to counter Dew's influence, such that the momentum – and a premiership – was gone.

Subsequently, a lot of the pre-season focus had been on tinkering with game styles, structures and players' roles. There would be less predictability and more versatility. "We wanted more Plan As, Plan Bs and Plan Cs and to look at the evolution of the game, pick the trends and stay in front of them," Mark Thompson explained.

The guinea pigs were mainly the midfielders. In a throwback to his father's days, Gary Ablett would play more out of the goalsquare while the likes of Paul Chapman, Steve Johnson, Mathew Stokes and Travis Varcoe would enjoy increased minutes in the midfield rotation. At the other end of the ground, roles changed through necessity: no Josh Hunt for the season and no Tom Harley for the first couple of months had forced star midfielders Joel Corey, Jimmy Bartel and James Kelly to learn the ropes as defenders. In Kelly's case, he was pegged as Hunt's replacement in unusual circumstances.

"Bomber, Sando (assistant coach Brendan Sanderson) and I were the coaches for the Victorian game the previous year and because of the amazing midfield talent in that side we played Kel at half-back," Ken Hinkley explained. "We came out of that game thinking Kel can play at half-back, he looked really strong in one-on-ones there, really comfortable. So when Josh went down it wasn't, 'Who is going to go back?' it was, 'Kel is going to go back'.

"We'd seen him do it at the higher level, at state level, and while that game was a bit of a free for all, it stuck in our minds how good he'd looked down there."

The deal was closed in Round 1 when Kelly, who spent all summer training in the midfield group, started on a wing before floating down back. "At quarter-time, in one of the huddles, they said that I might be needed down there," Kelly said. "Bomber and Sando then spoke to me during the week and said, 'You are a defender'. I said, 'No worries at all'. Personally, I've enjoyed the challenge. The way I see it, if the team needs me to play there, I will fit in with wherever they want me."

In Round 8 against North Melbourne, Kelly was asked to revert to type and return to the middle of the ground due to the absence of Ablett and Chapman. The result was a career-high 37 possessions as the Cats kicked seven unanswered goals in the second quarter to lead by 54 points at the main break. That stretched out to 70 points by the final siren, although a relapse by Cameron Mooney saw him reported for striking former teammate Scott Thompson.

A short jab to the stomach of the North full-back ended up costing Mooney a week – the ninth suspension of his career – and he incurred the wrath of his coach. "It was just a silly thing," Thompson said. "He'd been good for two years and it was a little lapse. You could sort of see it was going to happen. Unfortunately, it doesn't matter what you say to him."

Mooney's absence became a major problem the following week as the Cats found themselves under siege in the final term against the Western Bulldogs in Friday night football at Etihad Stadium. With Ryan Gamble in hospital by half-time, badly concussed, and Chapman suffering a compound dislocation of his finger in the last quarter, Thompson was desperately shuffling the deck against a highly skilled opponent which was running all over them.

The game should have been sealed much earlier as the Cats led by six goals midway through the third quarter, thanks again to Ablett and Selwood's dominance and Johnson's five goals. But with Jason Akermanis allowed off the leash, the Dogs charged, kicking six goals to three in the last term to have an unlikely chance at victory after the siren. Dogs captain Brad Johnson's shot for goal from 10m out on a very tight angle missed.

After going "crazy" in the box for the first time in a long while, by the time Thompson got down to the rooms to address the players he was excited about the benefits this hard night at the office would have down the track. This was exactly the type of game they hadn't experienced enough of in 2008, and it ultimately cost them when it mattered most. "There was good pressure on the players, good pressure on all the staff, good pressure in the coaches' box," Thompson said.

"It doesn't really matter who you play. If you play a close game, it's always a good thing. Sometimes you lose them, sometimes you win them. But it's that moment that you're living in the last quarter when every little thing you do is so important. Those matches you remember for a while because they're pretty significant."

An improving Essendon, which had spouted its potential to expose the Cats for pace, was next. And as had been evidenced numerous times over the previous two seasons, the tactic of talking it up pre-game against Geelong was a recipe for disaster. A six-goal first quarter became 12 goals to three at half-time. By three-quarter time, the Cats' lead was 82 points and the Bombers had gone inside 50m just 21 times. Cameron Ling blanketed their playmaker, Jobe Watson, Corey Enright had kept Andrew Lovett in check and the flexibility of Andrew Mackie was on show as he shut down the lightning-fast Alwyn Davey.

But the story of the day was the clinic that Steve Johnson put on for 48,852 people at Etihad Stadium. He kicked four goals in the third term alone, taking his personal game tally to 6.2 – more than Essendon (5.3) scored for the first three quarters.

"He bordered on unstoppable today at times," Essendon coach Matthew Knights remarked afterwards. "I thought it was pretty close to a 10-out-of-10 game."

Johnson's freakish afternoon had the Geelong coaches' box bubbling, with Thompson revealing Neil Balme had been unable to control himself. "Balmey just giggles in the box watching him," he said. "Stevie has probably never been in better form and has never been happier with who he is, what he does and how he lives. His path and how mad he was off the field, how he's curbed all that and how professional he's become ... it's been an amazing turnaround."

While they had reason to celebrate, the 64-point win (exactly the average winning margin of the previous three games against Essendon) came at a cost. Harley broke down again with a hamstring strain late in the first quarter. The injury to the captain was particularly concerning for a number of reasons, including that of a milestone: he had come into a season that many expected to be his last needing to play 16 games to reach 200. Harley had managed only four matches by Round 10 and was staring at a possible month on the sidelines.

Another injury concern was Joel Corey, a late withdrawal against the Bombers. Corey had been battling a plantar fascia problem in his foot all season, and it had reached the point where he was struggling to run.

Tom Hawkins was also struggling but it wasn't his body letting him down, rather his form. After kicking no goals against the Bulldogs when he'd been the focus of the attack in the absence of Mooney, Hawkins again failed to get on the scoreboard against Essendon. His credits from earlier in the season were being erased by the match, though he earned a reprieve for the trip to Perth to play the West Coast Eagles and responded with three goals on a strange afternoon at Subiaco. The Cats kicked the first five goals of the game but, rather than impressing the coach, it set off alarm bells. "I don't like the way we've started," he remarked to his fellow coaches. "It's a bit easy."

The early assessment was accurate. Thompson's team reverted to playing what he called "relaxed" football – he suspected it was already looking forward to the following week's mid-season break – to allow the Eagles back within three points in the third quarter. The highlight of the term was young Eagle Jamie McNamara running onto the ball on the wing and kicking the wrong way, into the Cats' forward 50, where Shannon Byrnes pounced to kick a much-needed goal. The final margin was 22 points, with Ablett again best on ground courtesy of 43 disposals and two goals, while Chapman kicked three in his return game.

Though it went largely unnoted at the time, the most significant thing to emerge from the game was a niggling pain in Johnson's hip. "I had actually felt pretty tight in the week leading up to the game," Johnson said. "On our captain's run on the Friday I was bending over thinking, 'Shit, it feels pretty sore'. I didn't know what was going on because the week before when we played Essendon I felt physically the best I have ever felt. I had heaps of physio before the game but I wasn't in peak physical condition. I did okay but thought with the two weeks' rest I'd be sweet, that it would just come good."

While Johnson played a few rounds of golf and many of his teammates went bush or interstate to catch up with family and friends, an important gathering of the football staff took place at Skilled Stadium. Every member of Geelong's fitness, medical and coaching staff had been summoned to a mid-year summit to devise a strategy for the rest of the season. Looming over the meeting was the mistakes of 12 months earlier – leading to the broad physical deterioration of the playing list – and all were determined to learn from that experience.

"From a conditioning perspective last year we were going down," team doctor Chris Bradshaw said. "We learnt a fair bit from last year."

For instance, rehabilitation manager Dean Robinson felt the focus on the winning streak in 2008 had impaired crucial decisions in the fitness and rehabilitation areas. "Last year we went out and tried to win every game, or put our best effort on the field every week," he said. "But the season is so long and, being premiers from the year before, everyone is coming after you and it takes so much out of you. By Grand Final day last year the edge was off us, the bodies were a bit fatigued and there were a few injured guys.

"We didn't kick well. That is not blaming anyone, but I think fatigue last year obviously affected the kicking. We knew we had to change this year."

A plan was devised to hit the players with a tough six-week training block coming out of the bye which would possibly cost them a couple of games along the way but the fitness and conditioning gains would be significant for September.

The leadership group was then introduced into the discussion, and it was decided that Joel Corey would present the new training program to the players. After running through what was required, Corey finished his speech with a simple message to his teammates: "We walked off the MCG last year as losers. We're not going to walk off losers this year."

It hit the spot with everyone in the room.

chapter 26

Winning when you lose

"It was probably the most intense game of footy I have ever played in. The build-up, two teams at the height of their powers ... as a spectacle it was probably as good a game of footy that has ever been played."

– Tom Harley on the Round 14 clash with St Kilda

"I don't really know what is going on with Cam's head at all." A frustrated Mark Thompson channelled all Cats' fans when he aired his concerns about the state of his spearhead, Cameron Mooney, after watching more goalkicking yips against Fremantle in Round 12. Mooney's return in the Cats' 19-point win had been just two behinds – the first a missed set shot from 30 metres and his second a blown chance from the top of the goalsquare after he had decided to quickly play on ... yet still butchered the kick.

What Thompson didn't realise – and precious few knew about – was the extent of the personal demons Mooney was battling.

Frankly, his well-documented misses in the 2008 Grand Final were haunting him to the point where he felt it was affecting his life. "I carried it with me everywhere," Mooney recalled. "Just driving up and down the highway every day (from Sanctuary Lakes to Geelong), it would always be going through my head. Even when I stopped thinking about it, 30 seconds later it would just pop back into my head again.

"It was just wearing me out, I was exhausted. It was just annoying as it would never leave my head. That's why I lost interest during the start of the year a bit, I wasn't working hard and I got fat."

Mooney hadn't played a game in the pre-season and, while he had worked nicely into the home-and-away rounds, once the season settled into its grind he was in trouble. Those frustrations boiled over in Round 8, when he was suspended for a silly incident which dipped him into trouble with his teammates and coach.

Thompson had sensed there were still issues in the lead-up to Round 1 and even tried to snap Mooney out of it on the eve of the game. "Mate, stop. It's not worth it," the Cats coach said. "No one blames you, so move on."

But Mooney couldn't.

"Mentally I wasn't there at all," he said, adding that lifestyle issues were also tinkering with his mindset. "I put on weight because (Mooney's partner) Seona was pregnant again so my weight went up as well. The skinfolds were no good and the goalkicking was probably at the all-time low."

Since joining the League in 1999, Mooney has compiled a respectable 59 per cent career conversion rate in front of goal. In his two breakout seasons as a forward, 2007-08, he booted 119 goals, a remarkable feat so late in his career given he had never bettered 28 in a single season before. In those two years he converted at a 62 per cent clip, marginally better than his career rate and perhaps bordering on respectable. It was more the manner and timing of his misses, especially on that doomed Saturday in September 2008, that had stripped bare his confidence.

Yet he was clearly putting more pressure on himself than any external forces could apply – that Fremantle game was his first goalless outing of the year. Thompson was as aware of that as anyone – he sent a text message of apology the day after his post-Dockers game comments became back-page news. It wasn't a problem for Mooney, who'd always enjoyed a healthy relationship with his coach; he suggested it must have been "a slow news day".

Even before the Thompson comment, Mooney had decided to make changes, beginning with an overhaul of his goalkicking routine with Geelong's skills expert David Wheadon. More importantly, he had also decided to talk to someone other than himself – an expert – about what was going on inside his head.

Shannon Byrnes' take on his role in the scheme of things at Geelong says a lot about the speedster who has played as many games in the VFL as the AFL over his six years at the club. "I've got no doubt I'm going to look back at the end of my career and be that proud to say I've played with some of the greats of all time at this club," he said. "I could name probably 10 of them who'll be regarded as Geelong greats."

Byrnes knows his place in the pecking order and is aware that, if he plays his role every week, he will continue to run out next to his champion teammates. After five goals from 26 possessions against Fremantle, his coach was moved to admit leaving him out of the previous year's Grand Final had been a mistake.

"It was probably his best game, absolutely, for the club, to kick five goals," Thompson said.

"Without his contribution we probably wouldn't have won. He missed out on last year's Grand Final and probably, if we had our time again, we probably should have played him."

The biggest sign of just how far Byrnes had come – apart from the fact that he was keeping Mathew Stokes out of the side – came the following week against Port Adelaide where he was again the Cats' leading goalkicker with four goals in a 34-point win which was sewn up after a seven-goal-to-one first quarter.

Captain Tom Harley that week impressed in his return and admitted the players, like everyone in the football world, had already been looking ahead to the much-anticipated St Kilda clash in seven days' time. "We have been watching them in awe, to be honest, so we will see how we go," he said. "The whole footy world is talking about the game. The build-up is going to be awesome. You don't often get the opportunity mid-year to have this sort of game."

One Geelong player not as excited as most was Steve Johnson, who wore a confused and somewhat disturbed demeanour as he sat in the medical room.

"After that game was the time I thought, 'Shit, I am nowhere near where I should be'," he said. "Because I could still sort of run at that stage I didn't want to be seen to be complaining about a niggly sort of thing. I figured it was something footy players play with all the time, but after the game I realised I was in a bit of trouble."

Johnson tried to "get up" to play against St Kilda but several days into recovery he could still barely jog, so he was booked in to see a specialist. "It was hard to pinpoint where my pain was. I kept saying I don't know where it is but it was in my groin and my abductor was also really tight," Johnson said.

It took just two minutes of examination for Johnson to be told the news he and the club did not want to hear. "I can tell you 100 per cent that you need an operation," the specialist declared.

Johnson immediately did the sums in his head, for he knew an operation meant at least a six-week recovery, which at that stage of the season was paramount to a footballing death sentence. "I can't have an operation at this stage," he responded. "What can I do without having an operation? Is there exercises I can do to get me through?"

The doctor relented, providing him with a list of strengthening exercises which would help. But Johnson was still looking at a month in the stands. Best case.

The biggest game of the season was only five days away but, as Mark Thompson sat down in front of the club's board, his focus was elsewhere. The coach had been asked to present the football department's plan for the coming months; he was keen to emphasise the point that his focus was on September, not what happened in Round 14 against St Kilda.

"The challenge this year is to make sure that when we reach September our guys are in the best possible condition, physically and mentally," he said. "You have to understand that if we lose two or three games on the way through that is not of a real consequence. I think we will finish top two anyway and we are no better off if we finish first or second.

"Therefore there is no way we will be risking players between now and September. The whole focus will be on getting this team right for the bigger battles down the track."

President Frank Costa liked what he heard. "It made a lot of sense," he said. "Last year we got to the finals and we weren't as sharp as what we had been during the year. Listening to Mark, we all felt that the football department was on the right track. They had a plan and they were going to stick to it."

There had certainly been lots of talk about plans in the lead-up. All the meetings during the week had focused on the Saints' defensive pressure and how they liked to dictate the way their opposition played. In fact, St Kilda's defence had conceded 200 points less than Geelong, which sat second in the rankings. It was also prolific at scoring goals from stoppages, while its numbers in denying teams inside-50 entries were off the charts.

The coaches had discussed whether to hold anything back tactically for later in the year. The decision was made to put everything on the table. "We have got to know if we can beat St Kilda and we are going to try and do it," Thompson declared.

The atmosphere and crowd inside Etihad Stadium, which hosted a record attendance of 54,444, did justice to the build-up. Never before had two undefeated teams come together in Round 14 and the AFL had delayed the start of the game by an hour to accommodate Channel 7 to go live with its broadcast. Everything was in readiness ... except the Geelong players.

They were stunned by St Kilda's onslaught from the opening bounce. The Cats were like rabbits in a spotlight, melting under the extraordinary pressure which all week they'd heard so much about and seen highlighted on video. It took the most attacking side in the recent history of the game 25 minutes to kick its first goal; by that stage, the Saints had five on the board.

"They came out and they were ready to play, they were on fire," Jimmy Bartel later noted. "I think we had watched so much of them and seen how well they'd been playing that I think we were waiting for it to happen. It took us a little while to realise, 'C'mon, let's stop watching the game and let's start attacking it'."

For Tom Harley, the onslaught confirmed just how good St Kilda had become. "In '07 and '08 we were the best defensive unit but they were miles ahead of what we were doing," he said. "To actually read about what they did and I think, as players, we probably didn't realise how good they were until we saw them first-hand. It was like 20 minutes into the game and we hadn't kicked a goal and it was like, 'Gee, you know what, they are a pretty bloody good'."

Cameron Mooney had a perfect view of what was happening – it was something he hadn't seen in a long time. "Their frontal pressure was huge," he said. "I was watching from centre half-forward and the boys usually flick it around and then bang it down in your forward 50. But we just couldn't get it out. The amount of times I was watching and it would be handball, handball, tackle and then it was, 'Oh shit, it's not coming down again'. That was the biggest thing at the time which probably surprised us or made us realise how well they were going."

Two late goals made it a little bit more respectable at quarter-time and Thompson was sensing that the shock was starting to wear off. "They jumped us and just played footy, whereas we were very conscious of what they were doing," he said. "We probably looked at them too much, we were quite nervous with the ball and they just capitalised on our mistakes."

The most critical move of the match was made at the first break with Max Rooke shifted on to Sam Fisher, who had done what he pleased across half-back for 12 possessions in the opening 30 minutes. Most of the other match-ups came as predicted. In the midfield Clinton Jones was running with Gary Ablett; Cameron Ling was on Nick Dal Santo; Corey Enright had Leigh Montagna on a wing and Joel Selwood was going head-to-head with Lenny Hayes.

Harry Taylor was again on Nick Riewoldt, while Matthew Scarlett had Justin Koschitzke and James Kelly had been assigned dangerous goalsneak Stephen Milne. At the other end, the inexperienced Zac Dawson was manning Mooney for the Saints, with Jason Blake deep in the square pitted against Tom Hawkins.

Three goals each in the second quarter stabilised the game for the Cats, who were starting to find some rhythm, although a relapse by Mooney had been met with a collective groan in the coaches' box. The troubled spearhead had earned a set shot from 30 metres out on a slight angle. Instead of taking it, he passed backwards to Bartel on the 50-metre arc. Bartel missed.

Despite being swamped early, the Cats had stuck to their gameplan and were throwing the ball around by hand. In the third term they started to find a way through the wall, creating a 15-8 inside-50 entries advantage. Three goals to two (one being a long bomb from outside 50 by Mooney) closed the margin to 10 points at the final change. Game on.

Two St Kilda goals inside the opening eight minutes of the last quarter re-established what many thought was, given the closeness of the game, a match-winning lead. But the Cats weren't finished as Bartel, Paul Chapman and Joel Selwood played inspired football. Three consecutive Geelong goals, including another from an impressive Mooney set shot, reignited the contest. When Mathew Stokes got on the end of a polished Mooney effort, scores were level with the clock well into time-on. The Cats had been enormous, fighting back from five goals down. When Joel Corey received a free kick about 45 metres out, they suddenly appeared to have a chance to snatch it with just over 120 ticks of the clock remaining.

That disappeared in the split second it took umpire Ray Chamberlain to utter the words "*Advantage, play on!*" which ended up being a disadvantage to the Cats. The mistake allowed St Kilda to clear along the wing, where Luke Ball found some space. Knowing there was little time remaining, he went long to the top of the square. It was a smart play – the right play – but from Thompson's vantage point in the grandstand it seemed the Cats had enough numbers back to handle the situation. What he hadn't seen was Michael Gardiner running in from the opposite side.

The Saints big man, brilliant all day against Mark Blake and Shane Mumford, launched himself at a pack which parted like the Red Sea. His 199cm, 100kg frame soared above his captain, Riewoldt, who was wrestling with Taylor, and the ball stuck in his hands.

Even putting aside the remarkable circumstances, it was close to the mark of the season. And it came with just 90 seconds on the clock in the game of the year. Blake, who had been a couple of steps behind Gardiner but had pulled out of the marking contest, was looking for a place to hide. That said, he was feeling better than Taylor, who was lying on the turf, out cold.

Taylor copped the full force of the incoming Gardiner, wearing the contact across his jaw and head. For several minutes the Geelong medical team kept him still on the ground, ensuring there were no spinal issues to concern them, before carrying the youngster off the field on a stretcher. The wait didn't deter the former Eagle ruckman, who had easily played the best game of his brief St Kilda career – he had no problems putting through his fourth goal of the day to put the Saints six points clear. This was a worthy finish to an epic encounter.

For a team which had suffered just its fourth defeat in its past 59 matches, there was a surprising sense of relief in the rooms. Thompson spoke to his players about how they needed to feel the hurt of the loss. He also understood that, given the run of success they had enjoyed to that point of the season, tasting defeat would be good for them in the long run, as would any experience in a close game.

The consensus take?

A lot of good could be taken from the Sunday afternoon showdown. The Cats had fought back from five goals down in the first quarter and done it without two of their big names in Steve Johnson, a late withdrawal who was never a realistic chance to play, and ruckman Brad Ottens, who was still struggling with his knee. Yes, Ottens may have made a difference against Gardiner, but the question was academic at best. The question answered, however, was that the Saints were legitimate contenders.

"The winner of that game was destined to have bragging rights," Thompson said. "A lot of the spotlight would go on them and the other was just going to fade away and become the underdog instantly at that point. We had been that team (under the spotlight) and if we won we would have remained that team. In some ways it was a perfect result because we showed we could play against them and at the same time sneak back under the radar. We hadn't done that for a long time."

Scarlett was also all about the positives. "I was far from devastated," he said. "From a players' perspective we weren't that disappointed losing that game. It got the monkey off the back and we weren't going to go through every game trying to win it after that. All the pressure and all the talk of going through undefeated, all that stuff, was going onto another club."

There were benefits to be drawn from the actual game style, too. Brendan McCartney saw a lot he liked in the way the Cats operated strategically in the second half. "They jumped us with their defensive pressure and we struggled to move the ball but there were enough signs later in the game that told us if we were to be brave with the footy and take the game on we could find a way through, which we did late," he said.

Mooney sensed that it would be a different result the next time the teams played. "In a way it was a huge relief not to win the game in the end," he said. "To be five goals down and to only lose by a kick when we didn't have Otto and Johnno … the next time around we weren't going to give them a start, we'd have those guys back and Gardiner wasn't going to kick four against us. There were things there where I thought if we play them again in a tight game, I reckon we'll be right."

Harley was particularly taken by the enormity of the event. "It was probably the most intense game of footy I have ever played in," he said. "The build-up, two teams at the height of their powers, also the fact it was indoors and all those sorts of things made it an intense game of footy. As a spectacle it was probably as good a game of footy that has ever been played."

Little did he know that, in just under three months' time, he would be re-assessing that statement.

chapter 27
Nursing bodies

"I told them that when your coach says anything can happen in a game of footy you can now believe it ... The players will know what it means (beating all odds) for the rest of their lives."

– Mark Thompson after the Round 17 comeback defeat of Hawthorn.

It wasn't going to be a tough session. The short break – and the fact a number of players had pulled up sore from the game of the season – saw to that. In fact, there already looked like being a number of changes for the trip to Brisbane: Cameron Ling had hurt his knee during the St Kilda match but managed to play out the game, while Darren Milburn had rolled his ankle and, annoyingly, Matthew Scarlett's back had seized up.

Ken Hinkley was watching a couple of young defenders, Tom Gillies and Jeremy Laidler, who had impressed in the VFL and were in the mix for a senior promotion, particularly with Scarlett and Milburn out. Out of the corner of his eye he noticed James Kelly in conversation with one of the doctors. Kelly was pointing at his hamstring and, as he gingerly made his way off the track, the assistant coach figured he needed to start looking for another replacement.

By Friday, as the Cats assembled at the airport, Ling, Milburn, Scarlett and Kelly had been joined by Gary Ablett (calf) and Travis Varcoe (shoulder) on the absentee list. Andrew Mackie was coming to Brisbane but he was carrying a corked thigh which required further assessment the following afternoon before the game. "Early in the week there were a couple who were touch and go but later in the week there were blokes coming from everywhere who we thought would be okay but weren't," Hinkley said.

The mass omissions caused a furore. Betting on the game was suspended a number of times but those inside the club cared little for this apparent inconvenience, for this was the new way at Geelong. Anyone with any sort of a niggle in July would not be risked as every decision on player fitness looking ahead to the bigger picture.

"They were legitimate injures," Ling said. "I have always said that the hardest part of the season is from Round 13-14 through to Round 18. It is the dead of winter, it is always the hardest part and there were a lot of guys who were carrying injuries for four or five weeks. It probably came to a head. Blokes probably pushed through a few niggles because they wanted to play in that St Kilda game and it caught up with them."

Despite Mackie declaring he was confident he would get through, he was pulled out at the last minute as part of the "no-risk" policy, gifting Laidler his first game. Gillies had already been selected as Scarlett's replacement, with the other "ins" being Tom Lonergan, David Wojcinski, Ryan Gamble, Nathan Djerrkura and forgotten midfielder Kane Tenace.

An even first quarter gave hope that, despite the seven changes, Geelong might be able to snare a win against the odds. A seven-goal second quarter from Brisbane put an end to that theory with Geelong's half-time score of 6.5.(41) being its lowest since Round 20, 2006. Brisbane superstar Jonathan Brown was too physically strong for Lonergan, while rising star Daniel Rich was dominating through the middle of the ground. Things didn't improve in the second half with more injuries to Djerrkura (thigh) and Bartel (hip), who crashed into a goal post. The Lions had outplayed Geelong in all areas, collecting 71 more possessions and 50 more marks, with Brown finishing with 15 marks and four goals. The final margin was 43 points but it wasn't the loss which was the concern ... more the way the Cats rolled over.

"I felt like I was coaching about six years ago," Mark Thompson said. "It was a terrible game and it was so un-Geelong like. Considering the way we'd played six days before, we hadn't played a game like that for a long time. It just wasn't Geelong."

Brian Cook was also having flashbacks to a much darker time. "It took us back to the days of 2001," he said. "It was certainly different and something we weren't used to."

Paul Chapman, who had a game-high 35 disposals, had been the Cats' best player and was angry with his teammates. "Even though we had blokes out I just thought we would have given more than we did," he said. "We looked really easy to beat and that was really disappointing."

Bartel believed it was a culmination of things, echoing his coach's thoughts that the flavor of the match was a poor reflection on the standards the club had set for itself. "We didn't play like Geelong," he said. "I think with so many blokes out a lot of the guys copped their lot a little bit, which is un-Geelong like. We want to fight out every game no matter who is there but I think the guys were just tired."

Yet lingering over the loss was the psychological drain from the previous week against the Saints, plus the physical toll that game had taken. Tom Harley thought the mental letdown from the St Kilda game had been a factor. "That game took a huge toll physically but I reckon looking back there was probably a bit of a mental toll as well," he said. "We'd been up for so long, everyone had built up the game, it had been spoken about since Round 6 onwards so we got up for it. What can sometimes happen is you mentally switch off a little bit (after that game). It is like you reach the climax, you mentally switch off and without actually knowing it you physically switch off as well. I reckon that might have happened to a few of the guys."

For Joel Selwood it was certainly foreign territory – for the first time in his career he'd lost a game interstate. Incredibly, the road victory over Fremantle earlier in the season had been the Cats' 12th consecutive interstate win, a League record which came to a screeching halt at the Gabba.

At 19, Shane Mumford was pushing 130kg. The 200cm giant from Bunyip spent most weekends drinking beer and eating junk food; he was legendary for his ability to consume between 12 to 16 sausages in a sitting at the local football club's barbeque.

Mumford worked as a boilermaker and played footy on Saturdays with his mates just for a bit of fun. But in 2006, something changed. He rediscovered his love of the game and capped that season by taking 28 marks in the local Grand Final, which Bunyip somehow lost despite being five goals up at half-time.

Mumford was encouraged by one of his mates, another local Jason Davenport, to come down to Geelong and try out for the VFL team. Davenport, who lived with Gary Ablett, was on the club's rookie list and he had got in the door at Skilled Stadium through a mate of his, Josh O'Brien … who just happened to be Ablett's cousin. The big man decided to pursue the dream, and achieved mixed success in his first stint, playing six matches as a top-up player and the rest back at Bunyip. "I was still a bigger sort of a bloke and I was beating some AFL-listed ruckmen in the VFL," Mumford said. "That gave me a bit of a kick along because I thought if I got myself in good shape, what could I be able to do here?"

From the moment the 2007 season finished, Mumford didn't touch alcohol or junk food and for the first time started eating vegetables. He also hit the streets of his home town, running up to 8km every second night. The fat was falling off him. When he turned up at Geelong for the start of pre-season training, Cats officials were stunned by his transformation and recruiting manager Stephen Wells was asked to come down and cast his eyes over Mumford, who had lost almost 20kg in eight weeks.

"He was a different bloke," Wells said. "It was like 20 per cent of his body weight (shed) and that gave us an indication that the penny had dropped."

With the rookie draft only a week away, it was agreed that "The Mummy" would be worth a punt. "We all knew he had some ability in the ruck," Wells said. "If you are going to be a rookie you have to have a bit of talent but you normally have to have some extra bit of drive, that something extra to fall back on. That (weight loss) showed he was willing to do something a bit extra to give himself a chance to get on an AFL list."

Less than six months later, in Round 6, 2008, Mumford made his AFL debut against Fremantle giant Aaron Sandilands at Subiaco Oval. He played the next two games before making way for Brad Ottens, who returned from injury. In 2009, he had again been elevated off the rookie list to cover for Ottens and he had played every game from Round 4 onwards. "I just love his follow-up and that is the reason why he's in the team," coach Thompson said. "He tackles and he joins in the game."

Another chapter in Mumford's fairytale story was written in Round 16 when he was handed the No.1 job. Mark Blake was dropped to the VFL after several weeks of poor form despite Ottens, who had suffered numerous setbacks, being still unavailable. The surprise move to enter the game with one ruckman was as much about the coaching staff's desire to experiment with different scenarios throughout the season. Mumford's back-up against the Demons were youngsters Tom Hawkins and Harry Taylor. "The thinking behind it is, if we've only got one ruckman in form, what do we do?" Thompson said. "Are we prepared to play one ruckman like a lot of other clubs to provide an extra midfield type player on the bench?"

The coach had been happy with what he saw in the 46-point win over the Demons, even though Melbourne's combination of Mark Jamar and Stefan Martin easily won the hit-outs, 49-25. "It's not an experiment you do for one week," Thompson said. "We'll probably have to have another look at it but we were pleased with what we saw today."

The Demons were no match for a Geelong team which had enjoyed the return of a handful of stars, with Ablett collecting 40 touches, Scarlett 30 and Cameron Ling restricting Melbourne's playmaker, Brock McLean, to just seven possessions. Still, as ever there seemed to be a downside: the Cats lost Harley and Bartel to injuries.

A seven-goal to zip first quarter set up the victory, which ushered in more tinkering from the coaches' box. Joel Corey spent time at centre half-back on the Demons' most dangerous forward, Matthew Bate, while Mackie moved up to the wing and Tenace and youngster Simon Hogan spent a lot more time in the midfield.

Meanwhile, the hysteria around Ablett and the Brownlow Medal continued to grow. It had gotten to the point where Thompson pleaded for calm, for the coach was concerned the continual fascination was an unnecessary burden on his champion. Once again it had hijacked the lead-up to the second Grand Final re-match of the season against Hawthorn.

Betting was suspended on the Brownlow when rumours of Ablett aggravating his calf injury at training spread through the football world. There was nothing wrong with him, although the club suspected the fact they could no longer fully close training sessions was the reason for the misinformation. The construction of the new stand meant their once private sessions were now witnessed by dozens of building workers. The mail about an injury at training had actually been right but it was a case of mistaken identity. It had been James Kelly who'd suffered a setback, re-injuring his hamstring.

Ablett was in the thick of things at the start of the game the bookmakers were convinced he wouldn't be playing. Geelong kicked the opening three goals against their Grand Final nemesis. The Hawks had struggled for most of the season but, by smashing Collingwood the previous week, they were showing signs of getting their groove back. It was obvious to Thompson that the Hawks had it back by half-time – Lance Franklin kicked three in a row in the second quarter and Hawthorn led by 14 points. "You looked like you couldn't defend against an under 9s team," an angry Thompson bellowed to his players, opening what he would later describe as one of his best bakes for a long time. "That second quarter was disgusting."

He fingered veteran Darren Milburn for being too casual and saved some wrath for Joel Corey, who had made some terrible turnovers in the first two quarters. To add to his frustration, both of his key defenders, Matthew Scarlett and Harry Taylor, were gone for the day due to groin strains.

The Thompson "spray" worked to a degree. The Cats improved after the long break but Franklin was heating up and had five goals to three-quarter time. On the Channel 10 telecast, boundary rider Andrew Maher summed up the state of play when he said: "Scarlett and Taylor are out, Geelong are tired and Hawthorn have got the wind. It's going to be a smashing."

When Brent Guerra added another Hawthorn goal at the two-minute mark of the final term, Maher's assessment seemed to be on the money as the lead blew out to 28 points. Even up in the Geelong coaches' box the frustration had turned to resignation.

Within minutes the mood had altered drastically as the Cats suggested they had not yet flown the white flag of surrender. Corey responded to his coach's urge to lift, Selwood was in everything, Ling was keeping Luke Hodge at bay while Mackie looked to have Franklin finally under control. And when the exuberance of youth in the form of Simon Hogan and Travis Varcoe engineered three quick goals, the game was back on. Two more followed soon after. When Bartel hit the post with three minutes remaining the scores were level.

It was Hawthorn who had first chance to ice the game, young midfielder Josh Kennedy running onto the ball at half-forward. Instead of taking the shot he opted to handball to Franklin, who was screaming for it alongside him. If ever a player was equipped for match-winning heroics it was Buddy, but Mackie had other ideas and a magnificently executed lunging tackle turned the ball over.

The Cats managed to break across the outer wing but it was halted. When Hawthorn engineered a stoppage, a draw looked to be the likely outcome. Somehow, though, Corey managed to extract his 12th possession of the quarter, sending the ball high off his boot about 20m towards the forward pocket. A brilliant if unheralded block from Stokes allowed Bartel to mark on his chest. Seconds later, the siren sounded.

Bartel had never kicked a goal to win a game in his life, not even in his junior days. As he lined up the shot from a tough angle in the pocket – with the scores level – he wasn't thinking goal. He just wanted to score. "I just wanted to kick it over the man on the mark and make sure we scored," he said. "I wasn't really caring about a goal, it was just don't kick it out on the full. It was pretty windy out there and I just wanted to make sure that I got a score."

He did exactly that, guiding the ball through for a behind which ignited an outpouring of emotion from the Geelong players. They had kicked 5.3 in the final term against the reigning premier to snatch a memorable victory, 15.9 (99) to 14.14 (98). A shell-shocked Maher managed to extricate Bartel from the celebrations. "That is a pretty special win when you consider how poorly we played in the second quarter," the champion midfielder said.

Inside the rooms, the song was sung with a gusto not seen in a long time.

"A ruthless, competitive team. That's what they are because they were not supposed to win that game," was Hinkley's assessment.

Not for the first time in his coaching career in Geelong, Thompson was in awe. "I told them that when your coach says anything can happen in a game of footy you can now believe it because you have been part of it," he said. "It was an extraordinary effort. The players will know what it means (beating all odds) for the rest of their lives."

He singled out Selwood, who had a career-high 42 possessions including 10 marks, 11 tackles and a goal. "He was outstanding. He was an amazing player today, clearly the best on the ground. He never lets you down and you cannot say enough about him as a person or a player."

The result was noteworthy in many respects moreso than the four premiership points. Having staved off the Hawks for the second time that season, they had managed to halt a potentially pivotal fortnight for the defending premiers, who were showing signs of stirring. The defeat meant that Hawthorn remained a chance to miss the final altogether, a stunning turn of events for a club which had been deemed to have won a flag even before its genuine "premiership window" had opened.

After the nightmare of the previous September, the Cats could only hope.

The meeting was tense, for everyone in the room shared the frustrated about the topic under discussion: Brad Ottens. Time was on the wing, and while medical staff were angling to give the No.1 ruckman another week of training, Thompson wanted to roll the dice and play him in the VFL.

"Let's just play him in the VFL and at least let him run around," the coach said. "If he's going to train, he might as well play half a game in the reserves. We just need to see him out there, we need to see if he's still a chance."

Were it not for the serious consequences of his absence, the plight of Ottens had almost reached comical proportions as he had been listed as "2-3 weeks" on the club's injury list for the previous three months. Even at board level eyebrows were being raised, particularly when Neil Balme made his monthly appearance.

"Balmey would get asked at every meeting by Frank (Costa) or one of the directors about Ottens," CEO Brian Cook said. "He would honestly say every time that he was expected back in two weeks, he said it for the whole year. That was what honestly the football department thought but in the end no-one believed us. It even got to the stage where the board where asking, 'Is Balmely fair dinkum or is he having us on?'"

The biggest concern revolved around the fact Ottens still had not been able to run, which had caused significant shrinkage of his quadricep. It then took time to get the muscle working again as he battled continued soreness. So while Thompson's wish was granted, there was a distinctive hobble about the All-Australian ruckman as he made his way to full-forward in the VFL game against Casey, which was being played as a curtain-raiser to Geelong's Round 18 home game against Adelaide. For the next hour or so he crashed a few bodies in the wet conditions – the GPS monitor calculated him running 4km – gathering four possessions which included three marks and a shot for goal which hit the post.

"It was great to just get out there and be part of a team again," Ottens said. "Just to have a run around, get some contact and get to a few contests was really good."

His was not the only significant return that week. In the main game against the Crows, Steve Johnson had his first outing for a month and certainly hit the ground running, setting up the first goal of game to Stokes and looking to be back to his old self in the first half as the Cats ran out to a three-goal lead.

"I was flying in the first quarter, I was up and down the ground and felt awesome," Johnson said. "But then my fitness went. The previous four weeks I wasn't allowed to do barely anything, I wasn't even allowed to swim because they didn't want me to kick my legs, so it was to be expected."

Alongside him, Paul Chapman had felt something he hadn't experienced all year. Late in the second quarter, he had felt that all too familiar pinching sensation in his left hamstring. "I was really happy with body and form going into Round 18 and then for it to happen, I was like, 'Shit, why now, a month out from finals?'" he said. "During the week I'd been crook and I couldn't get to the main training session so they wanted me to do it the next day, get some run into me. I think I might have trained a little bit too hard but they needed to get run into me if I was going to play on the weekend. I ran and I did feel it a little bit that day but I didn't think anything of it."

Given his history with the injury, he knew it wasn't a bad one and told the coaches and medical staff that he would be able to see out the game. They agreed but requested he just play deep forward and limit his amount of movement. The Cats managed to get the advantage out to a comfortable 27 points early in the third term before Adelaide piled on four straight goals. A late Ablett goal got the edge back out to eight points at the last change but the tough Crows outfit were looming large. With no Scarlett, Taylor or Tom Lonergan (a late withdrawal) and Tom Harley struggling after a knock to the head, the Cat defence was under siege in the final term as the Crows kicked quick goals. Brett Burton and Kurt Tippett had four each as veteran Darren Milburn's 250-game celebrations not going according to plan.

Approaching time-on, Adelaide's lead was 10 points before a one-legged Chapman imposed himself on the game. He had already managed to boot four for the afternoon; that quickly became six with back-to-back bombs from outside 50 metres pulling his team out of the fire. Crows ruckman Ivan Maric had a shot from the same range with 20 seconds on the clock but it fell short. Geelong had escaped again, 14.9. (93) to 13.13 (91).

Thompson sensed the players had found something special to honour their favourite warrior. "I think the guys really played for Darren Milburn today," he said. "There are only six other people in the history of our club who have played more games than him. He's joined a very elite club and it was pretty important we helped him celebrate this wonderful milestone."

Another favourite, Jimmy Bartel, had also celebrated a milestone, his 150th game, and he'd done it in style, collecting 34 touches to push for best-on-ground honours with Chapman. "He was enormous," was Thompson's assessment of Bartel. Yet what was pleasing the coach even more was the fact his team was getting exposed to tight finishes, something which had not happened the previous year and had ultimately come back to bite.

"We have had three (close ones) in five weeks and it is a great experience because we showed a lot of character to get up and win today," Thompson said. "There have been times when we haven't had to perform under pressure but the last month it has been outstanding. We have really enjoyed it. Not that we have done everything perfect, it's just a good dress rehearsal for what's going to come."

How true those words would come to be.

"Has anyone else got anything to say?" Mark Thompson was pacing the meeting room in the bowels of the MCG. He had just watched his side put up one of its worst performances for some time. The Cats hadn't given a yelp in the final quarter against Carlton, allowing the Blues to stroll home by 35 points.

"If it was easy, anyone can do it." Joel Corey's statement hung in the air.

"Where did you learn that from?" Thompson asked his deputy vice-captain.

"You."

The coach smiled and ripples of laughter rang out through the playing group. Corey had broken the ice, at least momentarily, and relieved a tension which was becoming suffocating. It had been a horror Friday night and not exactly good timing by actor Guy Pearce, a long-time passionate Geelong fan, who was a guest in the coaches' box for the first time.

After kicking the opening two goals of the game it had been all downhill as Carlton kicked seven of the next 10, and it could have been more had Blues star full-forward Brendan Fevola kicked straight. With Matthew Scarlett and Harry Taylor still absent, Tom Lonergan had again drawn the short straw but he had struggled from the opening bounce.

Fevola finished with 4.6 from 18 kicks and 11 marks. He was the match-winner as the Blues kicked four goals in the final term to Geelong's three behinds. Carlton captain Chris Judd was easily the most influential midfielder on the ground, while Joel Selwood and Corey Enright had been the best of a bad lot for the Cats.

Perhaps the most embarrassing performance had been that of Steve Johnson, who had only been cleared to play half-an-hour before the opening bounce. In hindsight, it was a seriously flawed decision, one his coach later classified as "a disaster".

"I was really sore and played probably the worst game of my life," Johnson said. "I just felt like I had no power at all."

If Johnson lacked power, Cameron Mooney had no faculties, having been concussed in the second half. "(My daughter) Billie had been born on the Thursday and I was in the rooms not knowing what day it was," he said. "I had to ask a few of the boys if she'd been born yet. When they said she had been born I was like, 'Get me out of here, I have to go to the hospital'. I don't remember much about the game. Although I gathered pretty quickly that everyone thought it was a big deal and everyone thought we were gone."

Tom Harley knew the knives were out. "We know there will be talk about the end of an era and all that sort of stuff, well, go ahead and write if you want," he instructed the media at a press conference immediately following the game. "We would like to think we have got more resolve than to just be blown down by some headlines in the newspaper. Sometimes I reckon when you have your backs against the wall you find out the real character of the club and individuals. I am really confident we have got the personnel within the club to bounce back.

"When you come from that sort of place it is more rewarding than winning them all on the trot. Losing games in these past six weeks is something we haven't done for a long time but it happens in footy. We are 16-3 and there are 14 other sides who would like to have a record like that. It is not all doom and gloom by a stretch."

Brian Cook was puzzled. He knew how good the people and the organisation were but, as he left the MCG that night, he was feeling uneasy. "I just thought, 'This is going to be very hard. This is going to be very tough'. It was going to be an extraordinary outcome for us to win (the premiership) given where we are right now," he said.

"I felt we were really going to be up against it this year. We had been up for such a long time and I thought the boys might be getting tired. I had to check that with the balancing note that the boys had gone through a very hard training period during that time. You had to try and have faith but there were times where I didn't think we could make it. I had faith in everyone's willingness to train hard (and) willingness to stick to the plan but was the plan going to work? The best laid plans don't always work."

Twelve months of planning had gone into the biggest event in the club's history, a massive party for Geelong's 150th year celebrations which was scheduled for the following evening. A purpose-built marquee, which held 1500 people, had been created on the Geelong waterfront for the extravaganza.

"We could have had it at Crown Casino and made an extra $250,000 profit, rather than go down to the waterfront, and that was a big decision to make," Cook explained. "We decided, as a board and an executive group, to stay in Geelong. The event cost $600,000 to put on and it was at best a break-even situation for us but it was so important – it did a lot to integrate the club.

"There were a lot of past players and officials who came back. We had 300 past players there, which is about half the number of those living players who have worn a Geelong jumper in its history – they had come from all over Australia and all parts of the world."

The focus in the event build-up had been as much about who wasn't coming, in particular the Cats' two greatest players, Graham "Polly" Farmer and Gary Ablett Snr. Cook and a contingent of officials had visited Farmer in Perth when the side played over there mid-season but, unfortunately, Farmer wasn't well enough to make the trip for the birthday party. As for Ablett, the CEO had spoken to him a number of times but had no idea what his movements were until he received a phonecall at 4pm on the Saturday afternoon. The great man was coming.

Ablett's attendance meant for some last-minute shuffling of seats. When he arrived, more than an hour after the rest of the crowd, the placecards at the table hadn't been re-arranged. David Johnson and David Wojcinski were listed to sit alongside Gary Jnr and Nathan, who had made the trip down from the Gold Coast. New seats were quickly found for Johnson and Wojcinski as the club's reclusive superstar made a low-key entrance – with personal security guard in tow – to be with his sons.

The evening was a stunning success, including current players making presentations to premiership heroes of previous eras. Many club greats were interviewed on stage, including the current premiership coach who unwittingly used the forum to send a message to his team. "We're in a position now where we've won a premiership two years ago, we were there last year and we lost a game that was really important to us," Thompson said when asked about legacy he wanted this generation to leave. "Are our boys going to find something and win two premierships and win the respect we've deserved and searched for?

He paused before adding: "Or are we just going to just fade out?"

It was a statement both intense and compelling, and it had the entire the room hanging on his every word. A few of the crowd started cheering in response to a coach's challenge which had been delivered in the most powerful fashion. It certainly hit home for Harley. "I just sat back and listened to it, I don't know what his motives were and whether it was a bit of theatre or whether it was a direct crack at us or it was a crack at the supporters or the media or whatever," the captain said.

"I think he just spoke from the heart. I saw it as a bit of challenge in that if you guys dig deep, stick to the plan and all those things then the rewards will be there."

Thompson later regretted his inspirational speech, hinting it may have been the result of too many celebratory drinks. "I don't like what I said. I have never used that as a vehicle to relate to players and that's what I was disappointed in myself about," he said. "It was just the way I was feeling and I probably shouldn't have ... I regret what I said. I have got too much respect for the playing group to try and intrinsically sort of motivate them through public. I don't do that."

The speech was certainly a topic of conversation when the leadership group met on Monday. They had become increasingly concerned with the frustration of the playing group. The team had been getting away from its core values. The ruthlessness, intensity and hunger for every contest had dropped away, as well the accountability. All these issues were then raised in front of the entire playing group with the major point being the time had come, with three weeks left in the home-and-away season, to get things back on track.

"It had been a bad few weeks which had dragged on a bit," Scarlett recalled. "I guess we were pretty dirty with each other. The Carlton game was probably the lowest point and while I don't think you lose trust, the boys weren't real happy with each other for a couple of weeks."

The coaches could sense the friction in the group but their position was that it had been driven by the inability to play a settled line-up. "Some of our players were frustrated, as much as anything with their own form, and they were frustrated with how the team was going and that is pretty natural," Brendan McCartney said.

"I don't think you are going to find any organisations where you don't have those periods. It can't be a honeymoon where everything is perfect all the time. There were enough people in the club who realised we were still missing key players, we were finding our way through a really tough, arduous season where at that stage everyone thought the premiership could be won by any of four or five clubs.

"We were just meandering through and that caused frustration but to the players credit they sat down as a group and said, 'This is the opportunity we have, we should take it otherwise we are going to look back with a lot of regret'."

There was certainly a sense among the playing group that people had written them off. Comparisons were being made to the great Essendon team of 2000, a combination which only won a single premiership during its three-year window at the top. "It was kind of good for us in a way because a lot of people were saying, 'Maybe they are not as good as what they were two years ago'," Gary Ablett said. "People dropped off us but it had been a tough time because we had a lot of different players coming in and out. While it was good for the future, it was just very different as in the previous years we had not had too many injuries and the team was quite settled."

Johnson had also noticed a difference in how the players were being received compared to previous years. "Suddenly people were jumping off us," he said. "Instead of walking down the street and people being right behind you and saying, 'You're going to win it', people were saying, 'Are you going to win?' That sort of thing takes its toll and you do start to question things a little bit, even though you know you are capable. I'm sure some of our players were questioning whether we were good enough. The loss against Carlton was really, bad as we had a pretty good side in and they just took to us."

Harley figured reality had kicked in for some players. "I think there was a realisation that we weren't bulletproof at all," he said. "That we suddenly weren't the best."

Tim Watson's extraordinary criticism of Gary Ablett caught many off guard at Geelong.

"I reckon he has become obsessed with the whole idea of being the best player and going out there and being the best player," Watson said. "There have been a number of occasions this year when I've been watching Geelong play, where he has done the individual thing and not the team thing, and gone for goal when there's been players that have been in better positions.

"I reckon he has been overwhelmed by this desire to actually win a Brownlow Medal and maybe he just needs to temper that a little bit as well."

A premiership teammate of Thompson, Watson used his morning breakfast radio show on SEN to launch the stinging assessment. There was no doubt Ablett was going through a patch of form, much like that of the side, that wasn't his very best. Yet he was still better than most players in the competition.

Ken Hinkley had sensed something wasn't right. When he heard about Watson's public attack he summoned Ablett into his office. "I'm close to Gaz and I think it hurt him," Hinkley said. "I think there were other things going on that were affecting him as much as Tim's comments. I called him into my office and said, 'Mate, what is going on? This is not you. What I am watching is not you'. He was pretty honest and from there on we talked about what made him such the good player he was and it was always based around winning contested ball and hard-ball gets.

"I remember early days when Gaz first went into the midfield, we would look every week at his hard-ball gets and contested ball to make sure he was winning his own footy. The goal from then on for him was to be in the top two. He always looked at that because Chris Judd is always there.

"Whether he would admit it or not, he wants to be as good as Chris Judd, actually wants to be better than Chris Judd. He measures himself by the best and he wants to be better than them."

They both agreed that playing Sydney in the coming game was ideal given that the Swans make you play that hard, contested style of football. By the time Ablett left the office, Hinkley knew Sydney was going to regret that Watson had opened his mouth. "We often talked about how to handle all the Gary Ablett pressure and people saying things about you," he said. "His comments have always been that when people say things about me it makes me go harder because I want to prove them wrong. He is that competitive, he will do whatever it takes. While he says he doesn't care what they say but it does spur him on, it does get him going as he is a proud animal."

The Ablett response was predictable: stunningly emphatic. Despite the close attention of talented young Sydney tagger Kieren Jack, he produced one of his best ever outings, collecting 44 possessions (18 kicks, 26 handballs) which included eight clearances, four tackles and one goal. He almost single-handedly carried his side to victory, the Cats hanging on in a thrilling final quarter to prevail by five points.

"He was out to prove a point," Thompson said. "I think anyone would have been hurt by what was said because Gary is very much a team, team, team player. I suppose the best thing he did was go out and play fantastic footy. He has overcome a lot of challenges, Gazza, in his life, and his teammates were so pleased for him. There was a lot of admiration for him."

Cameron Ling felt the insinuation Ablett wasn't a team player was way off base. "You could tell that one got to him a bit and I thought he handled it well, as he let his footy do the talking," he said.

"He just got on with trying to help the team win. In Gary's mind, from day one of the pre-season it has been about winning the premiership this year and making up a little bit for last year. He's a champion player, an absolute superstar but he is such a nice bloke. He doesn't carry on like he is 'the man', it has never been about him.

"He just really wants to win, just really wants to be a part of a successful team and successful club. Everybody has got different roles and Gary's role at certain times is to break the game open because he is so good. But it is not just all one way, he plays accountable footy. He tackles hard, blocks for teammates, he helps me with my man and will chase after him a lot for me if I am out of position.

"His leadership continues to develop, his attitude is always first rate and he continually delivers on the field as part of the team."

While the game had been close – the Swans kicked the final two goals – there had been a number of good signs, including Mark Blake's impressive return after four weeks in the VFL. Corey, who finally felt like he had his running back after battling foot problems all year, was brilliant with 38 possessions while Mooney looked revitalised, kicking 3.3.

On the flipside, more injuries. Travis Varcoe hurt his shoulder while Johnson's woes continued when he felt a rip in his problem hip, abductor and groin area when he lunged to spoil a ball in the second quarter.

Johnson managed to play out the game but in the back of his mind knew he couldn't keep going like this. Something had to give, and he already had a feeling it was going to be his season.

chapter 28

Let the
hair down

"It was good looking around the rooms before the game and there were a lot of familiar faces, a lot of experience. That gave everyone confidence."

– Matthew Scarlett surveys the Geelong rooms before Round 22

"I'm doing a lot of talking but there's not much happening." It was becoming an all too familiar post-match feeling for Mark Thompson. His side had again served up some of its best and worst in the space of a quarter, with the end result a 14-point Round 21 loss to rival premiership contender the Western Bulldogs.

"It's been difficult," the Cats coach said of a two-month period in which his team had lost four of eight games. "I don't think we could have ever seen it coming, that we would struggle as much as we have in games in such a short time. The second quarter was horrible to watch and to be involved with. We played better in the third quarter, but to play that poorly in the second and much better in the third shows there's something wrong, and that's my concern."

An even bigger concern was the fact Paul Chapman, in his first game back after missing two weeks, had again felt "awareness" in his hamstring during the second quarter. The doctors cleared him to return but a debate in the coaches' box had determined it wasn't worth the risk.

Five goals down early in the third quarter, the Cats erased the deficit in 20 minutes on the back of Gary Ablett, Cameron Ling in his 200th game, Cameron Mooney (four goals) and Tom Hawkins (three goals). They edged three points ahead at three-quarter time and were still in front midway through the final term before the petrol tank ran dry, clearing the way for the Bulldogs to secure a top-four spot for the finals.

At the end of the game the Geelong players gathered in a huddle in the middle of the ground. Matthew Scarlett spoke. He had already conferred with Ling and captain Tom Harley during the week about his plan for an old-fashioned bonding session for the players at his Torquay property the following day. The timing was perfect – Geelong had an eight-day break until the final home-and-away game of the season against Fremantle at Skilled Stadium. More importantly, the senior group felt the playing group needed to be around each other in a relaxed environment.

"I thought it would be good to get the boys together and have a good day at my house, just have a bit of fun, basically," Scarlett said. "It was a bit of a grind there for a few weeks so I just wanted to enjoy each other's company, get that closeness back and realise that we were still in a good position. We were going to finish second and had a great opportunity to win another flag."

Harley, who hadn't played against the Bulldogs because of knee issues, appreciated where his good mate was coming from. "(Scarlett) said to us he knew the idea was basically everything we are against, as we like to be very professional and we don't endorse bonding sessions, but when things aren't necessarily working you have got to try something different," the skipper said. "I can say easily that Scarlo is the most influential player on the list and the fact it was his suggestion carried a lot of weight. I said to him and to the group, 'Just get out of the day what you need to get out of the day'. From my point of view, because I didn't play against the Bulldogs I had to look after myself. I didn't have a drop of alcohol but if you needed to have a blow-out or you needed to have a deep and meaningful with one of your teammates then that's what the day was about. Let's be mates and get out of the day what you want."

The location was perfect. Scarlett's five-acre "ranch", which includes his own *Field of Dreams* baseball field mowed into the front paddock – he is a devotee of American sports. Understandably, that got a big workout, as did the garage-turned-bar with TV screens showing races from around the country.

The players' chef, Adrian, had been seconded for the day to prepare a feast. The session went all day and there was still a handful hanging out into the early hours of the morning. "It had been a hard year, not an enjoyable year, because we had never done anything socially together," Ling said. "It was just business, business, business all the time. It wasn't about going and having a drinking session, it was about the boys getting together and hanging out. Playing a game of baseball, having a punt and spending time together just to realise that we are actually all good blokes and all good mates."

Jimmy Bartel was in no doubt the day would have a positive effect on the group. "We get into a mode where we are not allowed to do anything," he said. "It is just football, football, football and you don't get a chance to spend any time in relaxed mode really with any of the whole group. As much as it is frowned upon, we needed to have a beer and just sit there and act like 20- to 30-year-old blokes and just forget about footy (and) enjoy each other's company."

One player who missed it was Brad Ottens.

D-Day – actually, *D-Night* – had arrived for the ruckman. All roads led to Chirnside Park in Werribee for the VFL team's Saturday night fixture. There had been considerable debate the previous week about picking Ottens for the seniors but more evidence was required to show he had turned the corner. Hence, the entire football department, plus the CEO, made the short trip up the highway. It took Thompson just 25 minutes to declare his No. 1 ruckman was back in town and would be playing the next week.

"I saw him for a quarter of footy and I thought he is just running and jumping, he is competing and following up," Thompson said. "That's all I needed as I knew then we were going to play him the following week and that he was a chance to help get us to where we want to go. Three weeks earlier I didn't think he was a chance at all. The doctors did keep saying that these things can turn the corner really quickly if you keep working, even when it is sore, just keep working and sometimes the soreness just goes away. They ended up being right and it was a pretty awesome feeling driving home from Werribee."

"If you can't play this week, we're not going to be able to play you in the finals." It wasn't what Steve Johnson wanted to hear from his coach, though he'd been expecting it. Johnson was sitting in Thompson's office after once again having sat out the main Wednesday training session. "Your fitness is not going to be there and we have no guarantees that your body is going to get through a game," Thompson said. "Yeah, I know," Johnson conceded before throwing up the only card he had left in the pack. "Well, maybe I need to go in and see that surgeon, find out what is going on."

This was far from the ideal scenario but Thompson was at least heartened by the fact the medical team had indicated surgery didn't necessarily mean the All-Australian's season was over. It all depended on what was found during the operation.

"The doctors and physios were saying that is the only way that I was going to get close to 100 per cent," Johnson said. "At that point they figured I was playing at about 60-70 per cent, tops, and while it (surgery) was risky in itself, they weren't going to be able to play me in a final at that percentage."

The next day, Johnson flew to Hobart, where surgery under Dr Michael Pritchard was booked in for the following morning. Pritchard, who used advanced arthroscopic techniques to help diagnose and treat disorders of the hip, was the man credited with saving Lleyton Hewitt's tennis career. Before going into the theatre, Johnson made it clear to his surgeon he would do *almost* anything to be a part of the Cats' finals campaign.

"If it is f...ked, and that's how it feels, then just fix it as I can't do anything about it," Johnson said. "But if there is a minimal thing you can do which can possibly give me a chance of getting back, then do it and I'll come back for more surgery later if needed."

Back in Geelong, Ken Hinkley, who had gone through the selection process for the Richmond senior coaching position and reached the final two, was staring at his whiteboard contemplating life without his biggest asset. "I thought the season was over for Stevie," Hinkley said. "It was a big thing for us to hear, that he'd gone in for surgery, because while Geelong has never been given credit for its forward line I knew the importance of Steve Johnson. He was as important as Buddy Franklin or Fevola or Jonathan Brown. He was Nick Riewoldt, that's what Steve Johnson was for the Geelong forward line."

When Johnson woke from the operation, he immediately felt stronger. It turned out he had a torn ligament sitting inside his joint that hadn't been allowing the muscles to work properly. "I've taken the ligament out and you should feel a lot better for it," Dr Pritchard said. "And it might be something you can come back from a bit quicker. Normally an operation means it takes six weeks to reach your full potential but if you really push it, which is risky, you might be a chance." Music to Johnson's ears.

A physiotherapist then did some testing on his hip – the exact same exercises he had done the previous day when he'd first arrived – and the results showed he was already 20 per cent stronger. He was able to walk to the bathroom and sense the actual hip was a lot freer in its movement. Johnson was immediately on the phone to Hinkley. "It feels stronger," he declared. By the next day, he was already on the exercise bike.

"Guys, just take some time to look around and have a look at your teammates," Tom Harley said in his Round 22 pre-match address. "If we are going to do anything this year, this is the group. This is it."

For the first time since Round 2, Brad Ottens was playing. Next to him, James Kelly was making his first appearance for seven weeks. Harley was also back after a week out and the team was starting to get its old feel back. In particular, the defence.

"It was good looking around the rooms before the game and there were a lot of familiar faces, a lot of experience. That gives everyone confidence," Matthew Scarlett said. "We got our backline back at the right time of the year and Kelly was very important to that. Everyone was talking about Otto and Stevie Johnson but Kelly was underrated. He was crucial."

Kelly picked up from where he had left off. Sweeping around the Skilled Stadium backline with his poise and skill on full display, Kelly certainly didn't look like someone who hadn't played for a couple of months. Indeed, there seemed to be more energy and risk-taking about the entire Cats' list and they dominated the opening term, collecting 142 possessions (the highest count recorded in a first quarter) to Fremantle's 55. Four players had already reached double figures, with Darren Milburn the leader of the pack with 15. By half-time, the lead was 43 points and the contest was over. Ottens, who had replaced Shane Mumford in the side, came on at the six-minute mark of the first quarter and immediately delivered two pinpoint taps down the throat of Gary Ablett. A contested mark sliding on his knees also set up a goal for youngster Simon Hogan. By game's end he had played 60 per cent of game time and had 13 disposals, eight hit-outs, seven tackles, four marks and six contested possessions.

"He was fantastic," Thompson enthused while also admitting there had been some excitement for the first time in a while in the coaches' box about the look of the side. "There weren't too many blokes in the medical room and there was a sense that it was time to get going."

Cameron Mooney, who combined with Tom Hawkins for 15 marks and five goals, felt the ruthlessness returned against the Dockers in the final tune-up for September. "We were our ruthless, hard selves," he said. "It was just a really good hard game where we kind of bashed them up a bit. You could tell we were back then."

Jimmy Bartel thought the balance of the side was finally right. "Blokes were moving a bit more towards home, towards their positions and all the experience was back," he said. "Everyone was just settled and comfortable in their surrounds. And it was also the way we played. We played the real Geelong way, real brutal and ruthless footy. It was pretty tough conditions, about five degrees, it was windy and rainy but the boys were focused and just ruthless."

Hinkley sensed an acute momentum shift. "The momentum started to build in the positive whereas it had been all going downhill for everyone," he said. "All of a sudden Ottens is back, Kelly is back and Stevie Johnson reckons he's going to play, so maybe there was still life in the old dog yet."

chapter 29

A definitive statement

"We were really keen that, if we did get the ascendancy at any stage of the game, we wanted to make not only a statement to Collingwood but make a statement to St Kilda, who was sitting back watching."

– Tom Harley after the preliminary final

"**B**emused" would be the best way to describe the Geelong players' take on the excitement associated with the fight for third on the ladder. The result of the last game of the home-and-away season between the Western Bulldogs and Collingwood would decide who would play Geelong in the qualifying final.

The Bulldogs managed to kick clear in the final term and claim a 24-point win that elevated them 0.3 per cent above the Magpies to set up another meeting with the Cats, just a fortnight after beating them in Round 21. Broad observation of the match focused on the loser having the harder finals assignment against St Kilda, which had lost only twice all season.

"We found it amusing that everyone wanted to play us in the finals, everybody was calling us out," Jimmy Bartel said. "The Bulldogs and

Collingwood played Round 22 and the winner was saying 'we get to play Geelong and that is the best result'. The boys saw that as a bit of a shock."

Shock was what the Bulldogs experienced in the opening 30 minutes of the final. The Geelong of old, led superbly by Matthew Scarlett, stamped its authority on the 2009 finals series. The defence was in tune, with Corey Enright collecting 17 possessions in the first term and Darren Milburn, who had been targeted by the Dogs 12 months earlier, also finding the ball at will.

As ever, the Cats had some player management issues to deal with: Paul Chapman, who had been recalled along with Travis Varcoe, was having his time on the ground carefully monitored in his comeback. Geelong had already lost Max Rooke to a quadriceps injury before the start of play; he was replaced by Simon Hogan.

It scarcely dented the confidence or structure of a team that had rediscovered its mojo. Although the Bulldogs kicked the first goal of the game through ruckman Ben Hudson (who, surprisingly, started in the goalsquare), Geelong booted seven of the next eight goals. "I think it was a bit of a surprise for the Bulldogs, to be honest," Mark Thompson said. "We'd played in Round 21 but they were playing a different team in the final. That is something you learn from experience, the players wouldn't have done it two or three years ago. I think they understand the game, the demands and they know that it was time to get serious."

Scarlett was pleased the switch had been flicked.

"Something clicked and we just went 'bang'," he said. "The difference to the previous couple of years was that a few more sides emerged that were a chance to win the premiership. We thought we'd better be at the top of our game if we wanted to win."

The Bulldogs regained some composure in the second quarter, clawing the margin back to 20 points by half-time, yet Geelong control was restored by goals to Chapman and Bartel in the final two minutes of the third term, ensuring a commanding 35-point lead at the last change.

All of Thompson's experienced big-time performers had been at their best – names such as Ablett, Ling, Enright, Mooney and Scarlett – which said a lot.

The Bulldogs' own big-time performer, Jason Akermanis, helped spark an unexpected revival in the final quarter. The Dogs suddenly had more run although they were wasting too many chances to make a significant impact on the scoreboard.

Still, when Shaun Higgins converted brilliantly from the pocket with five minutes remaining, his team had closed within 13 points.

Thankfully, cooler heads prevailed in the final minutes. The Cats managed to hold possession and wind down the clock to book a spot in their third consecutive preliminary final, 14.12 (96) to 12.10 (82).

The backline had been outstanding. Scarlett (30), Enright (35) and Milburn (31) combined for 96 touches and 34 marks. Ablett was the best midfielder on the ground, gathering a typically classy 31 possessions, while Bartel led the goalkickers with three, Chapman kicked two and David Wojcinski showed a welcome return to form. Tom Harley, who described the opening quarter as outstanding, said the familiarity of the team and the way it played put its rivals on notice.

"We had a really familiar look about us. Apart from our own form and mindset, other teams would have looked at the line-up and thought, 'Gee, they have started getting their stuff together at the right end of the year'," he said. "It felt to us that, with all the planning that had gone in, all the pieces to the puzzle were starting to fit together."

Yet Thompson remained confused by his side's performance. "There were elements of us playing really good footy and there were elements that were just horrible, too," he said.

The week off was going to be handled a lot differently than in previous years, according to the Cats coach. "We have had two cracks at it now where we haven't handled the week off that well," he said. "We are just going to train them for two weeks, just keep it very normal and footy-focused, basically."

The victory was ideal timing for Rooke's recovery and also for Chapman, Ottens and Kelly, who had only recently returned from nagging injury concerns. Most of all, it fell perfectly into the hands of Steve Johnson, who had started running the day before the qualifying final and was already planning on training fully with his teammates the following week.

The message from the coaching panel was clear: play your role. Thompson had been ramming it home over the weeks leading into the finals and the players did not have to look any further than the midfield coach to find out the value of doing just that.

Earlier in the decade, Nigel Lappin played in three consecutive premierships with Brisbane. In the final two years of that amazing run, the Lions had similar preparations to what Geelong had experienced in '09. After initially struggling to deal with a retirement forced by his body's betrayal, the former midfield star had found his feet as a mentor and coach, becoming an invaluable font of information for players like Cameron Ling.

"I would ask him about what Brisbane in their second and third premiership years had been like and he said they were never the best team throughout the home-and-away season," Ling explained. "But come finals time every bloke knew that they just had to play their role as best they possibly could for the team. And they backed in that the way they played footy was the right way to play footy. They just had this inner confidence that if everyone played their role they were good enough to win big, tight games of footy.

"Nigel spoke about gaining confidence from working for each other and together rather than trying to gain confidence out of trying to get a kick as an individual. That was what we were trying to lock into and Bomber drove that message all the time. It wasn't about our individual superstars; it was about playing as a team for each other."

Much debate in the football department had centred on the best way to approach the week off. In 2007, the Cats lightened off and almost lost to Collingwood. Twelve months later, they had probably trained too hard and again looked vulnerable against the Western Bulldogs. This time it was to be full-on footy.

After the normal review and recovery from the qualifying final, Ken Hinkley did a presentation on the teams who were playing off to be their next opponent, Adelaide and Collingwood. He strategically elected to do the Pies last because they were his tip to get through to the final four.

"We trained, played, we prepared and we talked footy for the whole two weeks," Hinkley explained. "We did an opposition analysis on both teams that were playing on the weekend so that when they were watching Collingwood play they should be looking for this or that. Adelaide was the same."

Hinkley was on the money. The Magpies set up a repeat of the 2007 preliminary final by coming from four goals down at half-time to win by five points. Even before the game, Pies coach Mick Malthouse had started the mind games with Geelong. In his weekly newspaper column in *The Australian* he had written that the pressure on Thompson and his team was "excruciating".

"The Cats are feeling the heat of being expected to deliver a little more from three great years of football. Coaches and players are well aware of this and there's perspiration showing," Malthouse wrote. "It's hot on that tin roof. The weight Geelong is carrying is excruciating. Geelong will be just another good team if it doesn't win this year. That's a massive pressure to take into a final. If I am reading it right, I think Bomber Thompson is showing that pressure ... I think he knows as most people do that this is the year the Cats really have to strike."

The extraordinary attack was laughed off by the Cats. Frank Costa sensibly didn't get involved and when Thompson was quizzed about it at his mandatory weekly press conference he straight-batted it beautifully. "He's (Malthouse) a knowledgeable man. He has a lot of experience, he knows the caper so he is just playing the game," Thompson said. "But if he thinks that we are under more pressure than anyone else, any of the other three teams, well, he's fooling himself because we're not. We are all under the same pressure."

The reality was the Cats only had minor apprehensions playing Malthouse's team. Others seemed to be living off that close final two years earlier, but those at Skilled Stadium were more confident these days. "We beat them in the NAB Cup Grand Final and we beat them in Round 3. We had built great confidence about playing Collingwood," Hinkley said. "In the NAB Cup we did some really good stuff and got some great results. The message to the players for the game against Collingwood was: if we did the things that had brought us this far, we should have an edge."

Gary Ablett already had that mindset. "It felt like a couple of weeks leading into the finals, and then in the finals, we switched on and trained the way we wanted to train," he said. "There was just a feeling in the club, the guys really had belief, they were really confident, which I think is a big thing in AFL footy. You see a lot of talented sides over the years and they never achieve what maybe they should with the talent they've got.

"I think a lot of that comes back to playing as a team and the confidence within you. We knew we had the team to win it and that when we play well as a team we think we are about impossible to beat."

Once again, the Cats' dominance was illustrated in the All-Australian team, with five players selected, the same number as St Kilda. Ablett, Matthew Scarlett, Corey Enright, Joel Selwood and Paul Chapman were all honoured. It was the fifth time Scarlett had been selected in the team of the year and it moved him to second on the club's list, albeit a fair way behind Gary Ablett Snr's eight All-Australian selections. Scarlett's reaction underscored the shadow that Ablett Snr still casts at Geelong.

"Any time you're mentioned with the great man it's a great honour," he said. "I'm not sure I'm going to catch his eight but I'm very honoured to get in the side again, it's awesome."

Ablett Jnr was named as rover for the third year running while the previously underrated Enright made it two in a row. Selwood, in just his third year, was named on the wing and the hard work of Chapman paid off with a spot on the half-forward flank alongside St Kilda captain Nick Riewoldt.

"I think (it's been my best year), injuries had killed me a little bit (last year) and have a little bit this year, but I have been able to string a few more together and I'm honoured to finally be an All-Australian," Chapman said.

Incredibly, the night's results took the number of All-Australians running out for Geelong in the preliminary final to 13. Included in that list was Johnson who, according to the coach, had been "explosive" in his first main session. While Johnson had breezed through the two main sessions of the second week of the preparation, the same couldn't be said for Mathew Stokes, who was facing a major dilemma.

Stokes had again pulled up sore in the groin following the first final. It presented him with a disturbing case of déjà vu, having faced a similar scenario prior to the 2008 Grand Final. Stokes then performed one of the most courageous acts of his career; he walked into Thompson's office and withdrew his availability for the preliminary final. While he felt he could have survived the rigours of the game, the memories of the previous year and Luke Hodge still haunted him.

Stokes knew he had taken a massive risk. Should the Cats play well, he knew he was no automatic recall for the Grand Final. Thompson was stunned by the decision, as were Stokes' teammates. "He wasn't feeling quite 100 per cent so he pulled himself out," the Cats coach said. "He could have played but what he did was the really selfless thing for the team."

Stokes and youngster Simon Hogan were the two omissions for the preliminary final. Johnson and Rooke returned. In a change from the previous two years, the Cats were playing in the second preliminary final, with St Kilda taking on the Western Bulldogs on the Friday night. That turned out to be a thriller, which interrupted some of the Geelong players' preparations – the delayed telecast was too late for Bartel, who went to bed, while Harley watched the first half on television, a delayed telecast, before looking up the internet to see who had won before his head hit the pillow.

The coaching staff attended the game and agreed that St Kilda had been lucky to get through with a seven-point win, which brought back memories of their own escape in 2007. "We obviously scout matches every week and normally you try to duck out and beat the traffic to get home. This time I stayed right until the end," Brendan McCartney said. "It was an amazing game and both sides could have won."

And so to Saturday night.

A lot of the preliminary final talk centred on the meeting of two years earlier between the two sides on this stage. But much had happened in 24 months. The Cats had won and lost a Grand Final, in the process building one of the most impressive win-loss records in the history of the game.

As noted, however, they had seemed to gain a psychological edge over a team that had routinely pushed or beaten them. You would not have known it from the early phases of the game, however – after six minutes, when defender Harry O'Brien goaled on the run from 50 metres, Collingwood led 2.2 to no score. The Cats had scarcely touched the ball.

Fittingly, Brad Ottens showed exactly why he was so important to the mix. After starting on the bench, the big man came on after eight minutes and crept forward, marking on the lead from a Selwood pass. He then calmly went back from 45 metres and slotted the goal. Several minutes later, Shannon Byrnes converted a clever banana shot from the boundary. And when a lively Tom Hawkins then tapped beautifully down to Chapman at the 16-minute mark for one of his traditional snap-around-the-shoulder goals, the Cats had the lead.

As expected, Magpies midfielder Scott Pendlebury's miraculous "recovery" from a broken leg was a Malthouse smokescreen; he didn't take his place, which meant Ling took the job of negating prolific Magpies midfielder Dane Swan. Enright was running with the dangerous Alan Didak, Andrew Mackie was minding Leon Davis, Harry Taylor had Travis Cloke and Scarlett took John Anthony.

Inside the opening 20 seconds of the second quarter, Chapman had his second goal, again as a result of a clever tap-on from Hawkins, who was already having the better of the experienced Simon Prestigiacomo. "Hawk" then got reward for his efforts with a goal of his own, a monster 55-metre kick from the boundary line that extended the lead to 20 points.

A Leigh Brown goal against the play, courtesy of a Milburn 50-metre penalty, got the Magpies back on track before this season's tactic of frequently playing Ablett out of the goalsquare paid off at the 10-minute mark. O'Brien was penalised for a hold, and Ablett converted.

Hawkins kicked his second goal at the 17-minute mark, the result of a wonderful tackle on Pies captain Nick Maxwell, and celebrated with gusto in front of the Members' stand. The Cats were seemingly in complete control of the preliminary final but, as it had done the previous week, Collingwood found a way back with quick goals to Tarkyn Lockyer and Didak. Both goals came from Geelong mistakes and reduced the margin to just two goals at the main break.

Despite the late opposition flurry there was an air of calm in the Geelong rooms at half-time. The coach, in particular, was surprisingly relaxed. "Even before the game I, along with the other coaches, had a chat and none of us believed the season was going to end on that night," Thompson said.

"Even when it was close at half-time it wasn't really aggressive down in the rooms. It was just 'this is where we are at and this is what we need to do to fix it up'. And the players basically went out and did that."

Steve Johnson, who had moved well in the first half, snapped truly at the four-minute mark to get the Cats' first. Cameron Mooney, who had sprayed two shots in the opening quarter, got the confidence boost he desperately needed from a 40-metre set shot. Goals to Corey and Byrnes soon followed and by midway through the third quarter the lead passed six goals.

With momentum and confidence in place, and the lead billowing, Geelong's place in another Grand Final was secure. "Our third quarter was as good as we have played all year," McCartney noted.

At three-quarter time, the theme in the huddle was simple: *Let's send a message.* "We just wanted to keep the foot down and finish the job," Scarlett said. "Throughout the year we had played some good footy in patches but we just wanted to finish the game off."

The message was not as much for the Magpies as the Saints. Harley thought it was important to let St Kilda know what was coming in a week's time. "We were really keen that, if we did get the ascendancy at any stage of the game, we wanted to make not only a statement to Collingwood but make a statement to St Kilda, who was sitting back watching."

Chapman played chief messenger. He kicked three goals in the final 30 minutes, including the final two of the game, to make it five for the night. Geelong piled on six goals to Collingwood's return of two behinds for the term. The desired message was writ by the final score: 17.18 (120) to 6.11 (47).

It had been a complete performance, yet the main post-match topic quickly swung to the likelihood of another selection nightmare. Stokes would be available, but whose spot would he take? Shannon Byrnes, who had enjoyed the best season of his life, had that night kicked two goals and looked lively while Travis Varcoe had also booted two majors and shown flashes of brilliance.

Thompson then fuelled the speculation when he was effusive in his praise of Stokes' decision to remove himself from selection.

"If he is right to play, he probably deserves to get a game," the coach said. "That's one tough decision."

While there was obvious excitement in the rooms, it was reserved. Geelong players quickly clicked into recovery mode, a critical phase given they had one day less to prepare than St Kilda. Ling, who had been brilliant in keeping Swan to just 17 possessions, summed up the feeling in the MCG rooms: "We weren't too keen on just making another Grand Final."

chapter 30

The countdown begins

"I was looking around thinking how good it was that I was sitting here drinking water knowing I have a game to play, rather than drinking."

– Paul Chapman enjoys Brownlow Medal night

"Three votes, Geelong, *G Ablett.*" Tom Harley looked up at the big screen inside the Crown Palladium Ballroom. It was only Round 5 in the 2009 Brownlow Medal count and his teammate already had 12 votes. He then leaned over to Mark Thompson and said: "It's taken me 13 years to get 12 votes."

Votes in each of the first five games, including three best-on-ground outings, had the favorite out of the blocks and running. As Harley scanned the *Herald Sun* form guide on the table, he realised his teammate was going to finally get the honour he so richly deserved. "I knew then he was a pretty good thing," Harley said. "I sat back and you knew he was going to be pretty hard to peg back. I so wanted it to happen because for him to win three AFL Player Association MVPs and three coaches awards but not to get a Brownlow in that period would have said to me that the umpires have got it wrong.

"You have got the players and coaches voting for their best player and that's who it is. It would have almost been an indictment if he had walked away from this three-year period without a Brownlow."

Back in Geelong, Cameron Ling knew there would be no "early to bed" opportunity this night. "I went around to my mum and dad's house to watch it," he said. "I usually go to bed very early and I said to them, 'Right, if he is struggling by about Round 10 I'm going home to bed but I will be shattered if he comes storming home and wins it. If he is in with a chance at around Round 10 I will stay up and watch the whole thing'. Of course, he just polls votes galore in the first 10 rounds, so I knew I was in for a long night."

In Torquay, Corey Enright visited Matthew Scarlett's house to watch the count. The pair were hanging off AFL boss Andrew Demetriou's every word as he read out the votes. "I was just hoping he would win as it would take the pressure off him and people would stop talking about why he hadn't won one," Scarlett said.

By the end of Round 11, Ablett had moved to 19 votes. St Kilda's Lenny Hayes had emerged as the main danger, sitting within striking distance on 16. It was then that Brian Cook turned to his wife, Annette, and declared: "He's going to win." The CEO had been confident from the beginning. "I sort of worked on the theory that he had won the most valuable player by the coaches three years running and he had won the most valuable player by his own peers three years in a row, so the only group left were the umpires," Cook said. "I was thinking after three years these guys will get the hint; they'll get the message that this guy is definitely the best player."

As he sipped on his water in the Palladium, Paul Chapman's confidence was growing, and not only regarding the chances of his teammate. "I was looking around thinking how good it was that I was sitting here drinking water knowing I have a game to play, rather than drinking," he said.

"Initially I'd been a bit worried about Collingwood's Dane Swan (winning the Brownlow), maybe because of the media build-up as he'd had a great year and had touched the ball more than anyone else. But he wasn't really getting votes so I figured Gazza was going to win pretty easy."

As the count moved into its second half, there were rumblings at Mark Thompson's table. Ablett missed a game through injury and the Cats present knew he hit a relative form slump just as Brisbane captain Jonathan Brown and former winner Chris Judd started to gather momentum.

"I knew he was injured there for a period and everyone around our table was saying, 'Oh, I'm not sure'," Thompson said. "I said, 'Nah, he's got the votes at the end, for sure'. I knew the last three games of the season he played were outstanding. I was praying for him because I thought he thoroughly deserved to win a Brownlow Medal after the three years he had played. It would have been really hard for him if he hadn't won it because he had won everything else."

The man himself had arrived at the count in a far more relaxed state than previous years. "I was actually a lot less nervous coming in," Ablett said. "I got there and thought, 'Well, whatever happens, happens'. I had been the favorite the last two years and I just didn't want to expect too much, that was the way I was looking at it."

Still, his grip on girlfriend Lauren's hand started to tighten as the count headed towards the final four games. "I started to get a little bit nervous because I was thinking, 'Oh no, I don't want it to be one of those years where I just get pipped at the end or something like that'. I knew I couldn't do any more, you can only go out there and do your best and if you get the votes, well, you get them. In the end we had another shot at the premiership, which meant a lot more to me."

Jimmy Bartel, the 2007 Brownlow winner, was sitting across from Ablett. He knew the hardest part was how confusing it can become sitting there under the spotlight. "We were doing the math and just telling him what was happening," Bartel said. "Once he got seven or eight votes up we were telling him that someone needed to have three best-on-grounds just to catch him."

As the count hit Round 20, Ablett was starting to shift around in his seat. "One of the blokes at the table said just before that round, 'Three votes here and you have won it'," Ablett said.

"I was still thinking to myself, 'Let's just get to the end and if I have won it, well, I've won it'. Someone could have added it up wrong in their head and I didn't want to look up at the screen and add it up. I didn't want to think about it at that stage."

Everyone in the room knew "Charlie" was going to the Geelong champion. In Round 20 against Sydney – the game on the back of criticism from media commentator Tim Watson – Ablett had put on a clinic, collecting 44 possessions.

To add to the theatre of the occasion, Demetriou threw in a long pause before delivering the killer blow: "Three votes, Geelong … G Ablett."

A microphone was quickly handed to Ablett as host, Channel 7's Sandy Roberts, crossed down to him. "It means, Gary, you can't be beaten," Roberts said.

It hadn't yet sunk in for Ablett. "Thanks mate," he said. "I can't add up too well so if you just read out the next two rounds that would be good."

He wasn't going to believe he'd finally won it until all 22 rounds had been done and dusted. Another three votes came is way in Round 21 against the Bulldogs – his eighth best-on-ground performance – and a vote in the final game against Fremantle pushed Ablett's total to 30. For all the nerves, he had cleared out on his opposition, winning by eight votes from Judd with Hayes third on 20. Brisbane pair Simon Black and Brown were tied for fourth on 19. The best-performed Cat behind Ablett was youngster Joel Selwood, who polled 16 votes. The 1200-strong crowd rose as one to applaud a popular winner, who made his way to the stage, where last year's winner, Adam Cooney, was waiting for him. The Western Bulldogs star planted a kiss on Ablett's bald head, much to the amusement of everyone, as he handed over the 2009 Brownlow Medal.

Ablett was then put through a five-minute interview on stage where Roberts asked him a variety of different things, including his thoughts on winning the Norm Smith Medal, the demeanour of his coach and whether he'd like to hook up with Tiger Woods when he was in town in a couple of months. One sensible question was about his father's reaction. "He would be stoked for me," Ablett said. "I'll give him a call after this. It will be great to talk to him."

He was then whisked away to the winner's press conference where it was obvious an enormous pressure had just been lifted from his shoulders. Ablett smiled and joked about how he now had bragging rights in football's most famous family. "It's fantastic. I can at least say that I've done something that he hasn't done," he said. "He's away in Queensland at the moment and he gave me a call (before the count) and just told me to enjoy myself and have fun, that it's not everything and there's a lot more to life than awards.

"He's always been so supportive of my football and always tells me that he loves me no matter what I do and that footy is just a game … and there's lots to life afterwards."

Ablett finished the press conference by making it clear what was next on the list. "A premiership means more to me than this."

In Geelong, Ling was tired but pumped for his little mate. "It was a late night, they stretched it out a bit but in the end it was worth it," he said. "I was just so happy for him. He's a champion player, an absolute superstar and such a nice bloke."

Further down the coast, Scarlett was already predicting more to come. "It was fantastic for him that he got his first one as I'm sure he will win another five."

Ablett's best friend, David Johnson, and VFL teammate, James Podsiadly, had driven up from Geelong to join in the celebrations, which were understandably low-key. After an hour or so, the Brownlow Medallist escaped upstairs to his room at Crown with "Charlie" still safely around his neck.

For the third year in a row, David Wojcinski had a lot on his plate in Grand Final week. In 2007, he had been sick all through the lead-up; 12 months later he had experienced the heartache of being dropped from the side. Now, he faced another dilemma.

Wojcinski received some surprising news following a visit to the obstetrician with his heavily pregnant wife, Casey. Their second child, due on October 11, was ready to come. Now. Given what had happened in the past and the fact he knew Mathew Stokes was again fit and pushing for selection, Wojcinski was concerned about the impact this could have on selection, given he would need time away from the club to be with his wife. His fears were soon eased when he went and saw his coach and explained the circumstances.

"Don't worry, you're in," Thompson said. A relieved and excited Wojcinski then trained in the main session on the Wednesday before going to hospital that night, where Monty Max was born.

One of his teammates not feeling as much joy was Steve Johnson. After his miracle return in the preliminary final, he had pulled up extremely sore. As part of his normal routine he was not required to do much in the first few days following a game, but the Wednesday session was when he was expected to step it up. He took only four or five steps before stopping, while assistant fitness adviser Mike Snelling kept encouraging Johnson to extend himself.

"I just couldn't get my body going at all, I literally couldn't jog," Johnson said. "He was like, 'Try it again, try it again', but I got up to maybe 40 or 50 per cent just running on the square and I was like, 'F..cking hell, this is not right'."

The pair walked to the gym to do some exercises to loosen Johnson's muscles. It worked to a degree but after just two stridethroughs he pulled up again. "Can you just give me until tomorrow to try and prove my fitness?" Johnson pleaded to 'Smelly'. "I'll try anything." Johnson knew that after the debacle of playing unfit players in the 2008 Grand Final there would be little leniency no matter the status or reputation of the player in question. "And I didn't want to go in really sore because I knew what the side had done in the past, how it had happened with Stokesy and Chappy," Johnson said.

After training, he went straight to the beach to get his legs moving in the salt water; he was then in and out of ice baths, on the massage table and back to the beach again. That would be his life for the next 48 hours. "I didn't want to think about the game," he said. "I wasn't getting excited about it because all I was worried about was my body, getting it right and at the same time not showing how sore I was either."

The Cats' other comeback story, Brad Ottens, was in much better shape to the point that he was pinching himself that he was actually preparing for the Grand Final. By his reckoning, he had been a week away from missing out. "If I didn't play when I did, it probably would have been over," he said. "I would have really battled to just get my spot because it was going to be hard to bring someone in underdone to play in finals. So if I didn't play when I did, I was going to be in trouble. I probably would have been a liability as much as anything if that (Round 22) had been a final."

Ottens admits there were several times when he thought he was no chance. "There were a couple of months there where it just didn't improve," he said. "It was frustrating to train really hard and not feel like you are getting anywhere."

For Cook, the sight of No.6 preparing to play in the biggest game of the year was "a bit of a miracle".

"I remember I saw him at training one day and he looked like a chicken with a broken leg, like it was swinging in the breeze," he said. "But he just kept at it and found something internally and that is probably the thing we have loved about this year – against the odds we have actually come good."

Signs of how tough the year had been were all around him. The stadium's redevelopment work had meant major upheaval for the administration and football departments.

All offices, including the CEO's, were now portables in the park outside the ground, while the players had spent the season training in a makeshift gym behind the Doug Wade Stand.

"We have been nomadic," Cook explained. "You have got the players working out of a shed. What we have been using as a gym will be the maintenance shed for the tractors once the redevelopment is finished. Our sports science area has been housed in this tiny shoebox of an office, the marketing and administration are in temporary offices in the park. The football department remained in the Brownlow Stand, so we have been de-centralised. Calling a staff meeting for everyone is nearly impossible.

"Plus, we couldn't train at the ground until February because of the turf so it has been quite a turbulent and challenging year in many ways."

The coaches were certainly finding things challenging with the crucial team selection.

After lengthy discussions they had narrowed down the 22nd spot to a battle between Shannon Byrnes and Mathew Stokes. It was essentially a speed versus toughness discussion, with the forecast for wet weather playing on their minds.

Travis Varcoe had been considered on the fringe but there was a feeling that, because he could also play a role in the midfield, he had leg speed and was a bit of an X-factor, he deserved a spot.

Two years earlier, Byrnes got to enjoy the Grand Final preparation because he had been told early in the week that he was in the team. This time he didn't know what to do with himself. The situation was made clear to him after training. "It's between you and Stokesy. You'll know tomorrow," Thompson said.

Which made for a long 24 hours.

chapter 31

Nothing to do but prepare

"I don't look too far ahead and I don't look too far back. This is the moment, isn't it?"

– Mark Thompson, 2009 Grand Final eve

Mathew Stokes was doing his regular check of what was making news back at home, scanning the *Northern Territory News* website on a computer in the players' lounge. Shannon Byrnes was mucking around next to him on another computer, and it was Byrnes who first saw Mark Thompson approach.

"You got a minute, Stokesy?" the coach said.

As Byrnes watched the pair walk off, he couldn't decide if this was a good or bad thing. "I didn't know if that meant, because he'd gone in first, that he was playing and I wasn't," Byrnes said. "It was a long few minutes."

It turned out to be a good thing but Byrnes had to temper his excitement given that, when he received confirmation that he was playing, Stokes was standing alongside the coach.

"It was such a tough situation but that's footy I suppose," Byrnes said.

Leg speed held sway; in the end it came down to Thompson's gut. In the previous year's Grand Final, on a fast track under warm conditions, they had been exposed for pace by Hawthorn after leaving David Wojcinski and Byrnes (who, admittedly, wasn't in the form of 2009) in the stands.

This year, the theory centred on the likes of Byrnes and Travis Varcoe, with their skill and pace, being a factor late in the game when the physical, contested style of football both clubs played would start to take its toll. It was easily the toughest decision the coaching panel had faced.

"Whoever was going to miss out was going to be more unlucky than the other years," Thompson said. "Blake missed out on form (in 2007) and Wojo missed out on form (in 2008) but this year someone was going to miss out and not on form. It was going to be because we had 23." The coach couldn't have been more impressed by the 24-year-old's handling of the biggest disappointment of his career. "I had no doubt Stokesy deserved to play so it made it a really tough decision," he said. "But I thought he handled it probably better than anyone has over the last five or six years. He was just outstanding and gained a lot of respect."

Brendan McCartney agreed. "Some players sometimes say, 'It is not me, it is about the team', and they are saying it because they have to say it. Mathew Stokes meant it. The things he spoke about was what was in his heart."

After hearing the news he had suspected was coming his way all week, Stokes rang his parents in Darwin. He then felt like he had to get away from the rooms. "As soon as I left the club I wanted to be my myself," he said. "But I actually had to pick up some furniture, which was a bit of a problem because I got hassled the whole time there."

A couple of hours later he was back at Skilled Stadium for a press conference. He had been the one who pushed the idea to Thompson and media manager Kevin Diggerson. "I just thought it would be good to get it over and done with so the boys, and everyone, can move on and prepare for the game," he said.

Stokes handled himself impeccably in front of the cameras. There was not a trace of bitterness as he talked about how much he loved his teammates and the football club. There was also bit of humour. "I saw something in the paper which was pretty funny. It said, 'Did Matty Stokes get a five grand fine for being a spectator on the field last year?' Last year that would have hurt but this year I can look at it and laugh."

He explained how he had no regrets about pulling out of the preliminary final side, which ultimately cost him a shot at another premiership. "I've moved on, I've dealt with it," Stokes said. "I knew the consequences of me not playing in the preliminary final if the boys played well and unfortunately the worst case scenario happened. To be honest, the whole reason I didn't play last week was because of last year and letting the boys down. I played two games I shouldn't have, when my groins probably weren't strong enough and I shouldn't have played.

"I let my pride get in the way. This year I didn't want to make the same mistake, so I pulled out."

Every time Steve Johnson kicked the football, it felt like a knife was being driven into his hip. Johnson had just started the warm-up for the captain's run on the Friday morning at Skilled Stadium.

He knew the eyes of the coaches and fitness staff were on him but because he was able to run freely – the pain only hit when he kicked – everything looked fairly normal.

"It seemed okay when I was running but when I kicked there was a really sharp pain," Johnson said. "I just thought to myself, 'Well, if it means I get 10 kicks in the Grand Final, I can put up with the pain'. And, hopefully, I'm not going to have a set shot from 45 or 50 to win the game, because then I might be in trouble."

In the previous two years, the Friday session had been held at the MCG following the Grand Final parade. A change in routine provided an opportunity for players to stay in their own beds that night. With nothing organised after the parade they could be back in Geelong by around 2.30pm – the majority of the team took that option, with only a handful deciding to stay at the hotel in Melbourne.

The early training session meant the Cats were cutting it fine to arrive at the Arts Centre by midday for the start of the parade. A regulation traffic jam on the West Gate Bridge had AFL officials in a panic but, with just a couple of minutes to spare, the bus arrived.

With hoods and beanies on and umbrellas in tow due to the rain, the players climbed off the bus and straight into the waiting cars. While for some the third consecutive parade may not have been as exhilarating as other editions, that certainly wasn't the case for Tom Harley. The Cats' skipper had his own reasons for taking in as much as possible given he knew he would never be in this position again. Though he kept it to himself, Harley knew he was playing his final game – No.198 – of AFL football the following day.

There had been speculation in the media about his future. One report had him playing with the Swans in 2010, given he was getting married to his Sydney-based girlfriend, Felicity, in October. But 31-year-old Harley had deliberately avoided the topic.

Midway through the season, Harley and fellow veteran Darren Milburn had met with Thompson, Brian Cook and Neil Balme and were told any decision about their futures was totally the players' call. It was a great show of faith by the hierarchy but, as far as the captain was concerned, this week was not the time to be talking about individuals. This was about the team and the football club winning its eighth premiership, not about Tom Harley.

"I had been thinking about it a lot, you can't really sort of help it," Harley explained. "The fact that we were going into a Grand Final meant I couldn't worry about send-offs and those sorts of things as there were bigger fish to fry."

The first retirement seed was planted even before he'd played a game this year, for pre-season battles with his knee had told him a lot about the state of his body.

"I find footy really challenging all the time but in particular this year. You realise when you see other players from other clubs who are physically struggling, their form struggles," Harley said. "I am the first to admit that my form this year wasn't great but I can honestly say it was the best I could manage. People see that you are selected in a side so you must be 100 per cent fit when, really, you are miles off it.

"I have trouble jogging across the street or walking down stairs. In your day-to-day living you are thinking about your body and knee 24/7. I look back on the year from a personal point of view and I'm really proud that I even played at all. It certainly wasn't my best year output wise and it was probably never going to be but to go through it all and get on the park was something I was pretty satisfied about."

Now, all he needed was the fairytale ending.

He first had some more pressing captain's duties. Harley had to pose for the traditional photo, holding up the premiership cup with St Kilda skipper Nick Riewoldt, before entering the Treasury Building for the Grand Final Eve press conference.

It evoked memories of the previous year, which he admitted to the large contingent of football media present. "Losing a Grand Final is exceptionally heart-wrenching and it's even tough to watch highlights, when you saw the brown-and-gold ticker tapes throughout the whole advertising campaign, even for this game," Harley said. "So if you need that as motivation, we've certainly got that. I think, as players, we've got the onus to do whatever it takes."

He was then asked about the debate on how the events of the following afternoon would define where this Geelong team sits in history. "We're not going to define ourselves as a great team (based on this result), I don't think. As a club we've built a reputation as quite humble and respectful. That's for all you people sitting here to define what we are with the result."

Thompson was also asked about the role last year's loss would have in this year's Grand Final. "They're pretty recent memories, so you'd hope that, when the players are going through a tough period in the game, they should be able to find something from the hurt that they felt last year," he said. "Because it's a very hurtful thing to occur in a person's life and it was quite recent. It's been a tough year, we've had a really good first half, we had to scramble home and we got our act together and we're really excited about being here. I don't look too far ahead and I don't look too far back. This is the moment, isn't it?"

Later that afternoon, when Thompson finally got home, the pressure and stress of the week hit him like a sledge hammer. "It was the busiest week I have had in footy and that's even with trying to minimise what you do," he said. "I remember driving home from the parade and I was totally exhausted. I thought to myself, 'This is not right, you shouldn't be like this. You should be really fresh and looking forward to the game, excited about the game'. But I was just tired. I got home by 4pm and I was in bed by 9pm."

His vice-captain was staying at the Holiday Inn in Flinders Lane but, for much of the afternoon, he'd wished he was at home in Torquay indulging in his other passion. "When we were stuck at the parade, the surf was pumping so I was a bit annoyed about that," Cameron Ling said. "I'd surfed the first few days of the week but unfortunately it had died down a bit until coming good on the Friday. I'd stayed in Melbourne the previous couple of years, mainly because I didn't want to bother with the traffic again, so I was happy to do it again and by 9.30pm I was in bed."

Cameron Mooney was at home looking after his two young children, excited by the rain which was falling outside. "Seona went out and met some family and friends because they all came down from interstate, so I had the kids by myself, which was nice," he said. "I was feeling good because I felt like it was going to happen for us because of the weather. I was so excited about it being wet because no one plays as much wet weather football as we do. To be honest, I thought we were going to win by six goals."

Gary Ablett was also in Melbourne, staying at his girlfriend's house, but he wasn't giving the Grand Final much thought at all as he kept to his normal routine.

"You hear about a lot of people before a game who can't sleep," Ablett said. "I can't remember the last time I got nervous the night before a game. I am one of those people who find it pretty easy to forget about footy until I get to the game. I just kind of muck around and do my own thing, take my mind off footy. I think sometimes players might do their heads in a bit because they think about it too much. I was pretty good and prepared how I normally would."

Brian Cook got nervous, which was why, at 7am on Grand Final day, he was swimming in the bay with the Brighton Icebergers. "I got up and went for a 2.5km swim," he said. "It got me tired which I needed to be so I wouldn't be too jumpy."

It had been a strange week for the CEO as he tried to balance the demands of his marketing team and that of the football department. In the post mortem of last year's loss, there was a feeling, particularly from the coaching staff, that the players had been caught up in peripheral issues such as organising the post-match celebrations.

At his mid-week press conference, Thompson had raised this point: "This year, especially, the whole focus has been on playing the game rather than the event. I can see a significant difference in the playing group, they are really focussed on the game."

Cook understood the concerns. "In 2007, it was our first Grand Final for a long, long time and so you have to find out how you prepare, what functions do you put on before the game, what functions after the game, what about the supporters day, what about the parades," he said. "It is all new so you have to find out how to do all this and in doing that there is a lot of energy used by a lot of people, a lot of discussion with players and coaches to make sure it is all in line.

"Then in '08 we basically rolled out a similiar plan and everyone got involved again. It was ultra-organised and there seemed to be so much effort in making the whole Grand Final week, pre and post, excellent, precise and beautiful.

"This year we hardly spoke to the players because the only thing that we were really concerned about was them winning the Grand Final. What that meant was that we were not that organised for some of the events, it created a lot of issues with our marketing team but we just tried to make sure that for the players it wasn't about the week, it was about the day."

The day brought a refreshed and relaxed Thompson after 12 hours sleep. He had organised a car to drive him up to Melbourne, which allowed the coach to sit in the back listening to his iPod tunes as he did some notes on the match board.

Brendan McCartney should have done the same. "I might have been a road rage candidate on the way," he said. "Someone cut me off so I was a little bit wound up but once I got to the ground I was fine."

Scarlett and Enright, whose turn it was to drive, were a lot more relaxed as they set off together from Torquay, with Harley and his fiancé not far behind them. "She gets quite excitable, Flip, that's just the type of person she is, so throughout the week I had to tell her to calm down," Harley said.

"And I had to do it again on the drive down. It was actually bucketing down with rain when we set off but it was great to see all the flags hanging out of the car windows.

"There were kids waving out their windows which was great and I was surprised with the lack of traffic. I thought it would be a standstill and you'd be stressed but we got a pretty sweet run."

While they were winding their way down the Princes Highway, Ling hadn't even stirred. At 10.30am he finally rose and started preparing himself for the Grand Final. "I always prefer to sleep basically right up to the time I have get up," he said. "I still had time to have a shower, a bit of brekkie and then jump on the bus. There's nothing better than a good night's sleep before a big game."

It was a simple edict. "We have to play as a team," Mark Thompson stated with authority as he looked around at his players in the meeting room under the MCG grandstand. "We're not worried about who wins the Norm Smith, are we?"

Everything was about the team structures for the Cats, about the players not straying outside the team framework as they had 12 months earlier. Thompson stressed that if they got that focus correct then the opportunity for individual talents would flow from there. "The number one key is we need to have that selflessness as a team for it all to work," the coach demanded.

There was an air of calmness about the two-hour build-up in the rooms. "It was unbelievably relaxed," Jimmy Bartel said. "I know blokes who come from other clubs just shake their heads at how everyone is very cruisy before the game. I didn't do much as it was pretty cold, so I stayed in my tracksuit until about 10 minutes before the warm-up, then I threw the boots on and went out for a kick.

"It was good knowing that it was going to be flogging rain all day because I think it just got straight in the guys' heads that it was going to be a tough old battle."

Mooney had noticed a distinct change to the previous Grand Final. "I think last year there were more nerves in the rooms as I think everyone thought, 'It is just going to happen a bit'," he said. "This year it was more relaxed because we knew it just wasn't going to fall into place, but we knew what we had to do."

The heart-breaking 2008 loss was also in the back of Ablett's mind as he went through his preparations.

"We knew we had another opportunity at it and it was definitely in the back of our mind that, 'Shit, if we lose another one here, it is going to be a tough thing to take'," he said. "You don't want to look back at the end of your career and say, 'Wow, we had three shots at it and to only win one with the team we had …

"The reason you play is premierships and you don't want to be known as a great side that couldn't finish on the last day of September. I'm sure a few guys felt that pressure and we were as ready as we were ever going to be."

In the kitchen area, a video had been playing showing the Players' Spirit Award winners from each round – the players voted each week for their teammate who best represented the team's values for that game. It was on continuous rotation, so players could wander in and out and have a look at any time as they went through their varied individual preparations. And they were all very different.

David Wojcinski had gone through the routine last year, taking part in the warm-up in case of any last-minute withdrawals before getting dressed again and heading up to the stands. This time around he couldn't stop smiling.

By contrast, the ultra serious Harry Taylor had spent time sitting down reading his notes on Nick Riewoldt. For the second consecutive year he had been identified as the exposable defensive link despite his good record on the Saints skipper. "The media really jumped on my back and said that I might be the weak link in the Geelong defence," Taylor said. "I cut those articles out and put them on the wall to use them as motivation for me. That criticism from last season has been a driving force."

Mark Blake also had some special motivation in his much-hyped match-up with his former teammate Steven King. After last year's Grand Final loss, he had received inflammatory text messages from someone whom he had been led to believe was King's brother.

Tom Harley had spent most of the pre-game endlessly stretching as he tried to get his body up and going, while Matthew Scarlett had wandered around in his full kit which he had on from almost the moment he arrived. As usual, Ablett spent most of the time with football in hand practising his bags of tricks. The odd one out was Darren Milburn.

"Dasher is really laidback and he would probably prefer if he could rock up 20 minutes before the game, whack his gear on and get out there," said Ling, who spent a lot of time in the doctor's room just having a chat to anyone who was up for one. "It was a lot of waiting around for him. Bomber (Thompson) is really good because he isn't a coach who has to have it a certain way. He is happy for some guys to be relaxed and happy with guys who really get themselves fired up."

Ling's focus for the week had been Nick Dal Santo. He had been told on Wednesday that Dal Santo was the No.1 target, and yet he had also studied tape of Lenny Hayes and Leigh Montagna in case a move had to be made during the game. Sending Ling to Dal Santo and not Hayes – who had raised his game to a new level in the finals – had been discussed at length in match committee.

"Hayes was a great player and we had great respect for him," Hinkley explained. "At match committee I said to Bomber, 'Lenny is the bloke you would want in your team because of what you love'.

"The discussion was if Dal Santo gets 20 he might punch through us a bit too much. If Lenny gets 20 there might be a chance he might not be as damaging. Ling has a good record on Dal Santo over the time so we figured if we put Dal Santo away then Montagna has to have a big day and we have got Enright to cover him.

"We have to take a risk with one of them and it's Lenny. We felt Corey and Selwood can play off and on him a bit."

A match-up which needed little discussion was Max Rooke playing as a defensive forward on Sam Fisher. Back in Round 14, Fisher had 11 to quarter-time before Rooke was moved to him. He had just nine more for the game, with St Kilda even forced to move Fisher to the wing in the last quarter. "We knew he didn't like having Rooke on him," Hinkley continued. "We had watched Fisher in the preliminary final and the Bulldogs had left him alone. You just can't do that, so there was never any debate about Rooke on Fisher."

Just before it was time to run out, the players were called back into the meeting room where they were shown a 90-second motivational DVD. It showed football being played "the Geelong way" – players demonstrating the hard, tough ruthless footy which was expected over the next two hours.

"Let's start well," Harley said to his teammates as they came together for a final time. "We need to be 100 per cent committed and we all need to be able to come in at quarter-time and look each other in the eye and say you have delivered on your word."

And with that, the captain turned on his heels and started up the race. Next to him was Ling, with Mark Blake and Steve Johnson, ball in hand, both eager to get things happening. Down the back of the line a relaxed Thompson was having a chat to Scarlett and Andrew Mackie, who always liked to be the last ones onto the ground each week.

"Let's stay calm," Harley was urging. "We're the best team so we'll get the job done."

A clap of his hands signalled it was time, and the captain burst onto the MCG – for the last time – with purpose.

The roar from the 99,251 supporters sent shivers down Harley's spine as he again waited for his teammates before charging through the banner as a group. The Cats were first onto the ground, with the traditional team photo taken straight away ... Milburn again standing out as the only player with his tracksuit top on.

A number of sprints and stretches were followed by some kicking drills before the players broke away for shots at goal. The adrenalin was certainly doing the trick for Johnson, who felt the best he had for a week, although his mindset was dramatically different to the previous two Grand Finals. "Mate, I honestly don't care if I don't get a kick today, as long as we win," he said to Paul Chapman as they completed one final stretch.

His forward partner, with whom two years earlier he had joked about winning the Norm Smith Medal, was taken aback.

"Shit. That's the best thing I have heard all week," Chapman said.

If anything summed up the concept of "the Geelong way", Steve Johnson had just voiced it.

chapter 32

Game on

"I wasn't too sure how bad it was and then I went for that long kick from 50 and felt it even more," he said. "I thought then, 'I'm in some trouble here'."

– Paul Chapman considers his hamstring tear in the Grand Final

It couldn't have been scripted better. Two minutes into the Grand Final, St Kilda defender Raphael Clark had marked at half-back. With no options immediately available, he wandered off the mark and was looking to shift play to the outer wing when suddenly he was stopped in his tracks.

Max Rooke had flown in from behind and nailed Clarke with a brilliant tackle which stunned the Saints defender and earned a free kick. As the Geelong hard man lined up for goal, up in the coaches' box Thompson was ecstatic.

The tone for the day had been set.

Ten weeks earlier, Rooke had seen a psychic who had told him Geelong would defeat St Kilda in the Grand Final. The same psychic – she was a friend of Corey Enright's girlfriend – had last year told him that Hawthorn would win the premiership. "She said it would be a Geelong-St Kilda Grand Final and I was obviously curious to see how we would go. She flipped over a card and said, 'Yeah, it looks pretty good'," Rooke said.

With the spirits on his side, Rooke unloaded from 50 metres to kick the opening goal of the Grand Final.

The match-ups went largely as expected. Clint Jones shadowed Gary Ablett, and Jimmy Bartel started in the middle for the first bounce on Luke Ball before moving out to the wing to play on Brendon Goddard. Tagger Steven Baker lined up on Steve Johnson, with the much taller Sam Gilbert taking Paul Chapman. The inexperienced Zac Dawson, who had kept his spot in the St Kilda side ahead of veteran and favourite son Max Hudghton, was assigned Cameron Mooney, leaving Jason Blake to play in the goalsquare on Tom Hawkins.

At the other end, Matthew Scarlett had Justin Koschitzke with Harry Taylor standing alongside Nick Riewoldt. Harley was playing on goalsneak Adam Schneider in one back pocket; James Kelly took Andrew McQualter, given Stephen Milne had surprisingly started on the bench.

The Cats had started Darren Milburn on the interchange, alongside youngsters Joel Selwood, Travis Varcoe and Mark Blake.

The early signs were good for the Cats with Andrew Mackie, who was being tagged at half-back by Sean Dempster, repelling St Kilda's first two forward entries and Tom Harley's first attack on the ball being low and hard, upending Sam Fisher in the process.

At the seven-minute mark, one of the most significant moments in the game arrived. A brilliant Scarlett handball released Kelly, who kicked long to centre half-forward. Mooney marked on the second attempt, diving to the ground. Everyone in the stadium knew the importance of the next 30 seconds. The man himself was relieved by the fact he was 45 metres out from goal... not 25. "I remember taking the mark and thinking, 'Thank Christ I am 45 out because, if I miss, no-one will really care'," Mooney said.

At least he was comfortable taking the shot, something he actually shied away from on occasions earlier in the season before he sought help from a sports psychologist. "At times I maybe could have gone for a mark inside 50 but I didn't go because I didn't want the shot on goal," he said. "At least now I wanted the shot on goal."

Without spending too much time over the kick, Mooney went through his old goalkicking routine, which he had re-introduced mid-season. From the second the ball hit his boot he knew he had executed an almost perfect kick. "I hit it as sweet as I have hit any kick in my entire life," he said. "From the moment it left the boot it didn't deviate, it didn't move. I was like, 'Thank God that went through'.

"From that moment on I felt really good."

His 45th goal of the season was a perfect 30th birthday present. In the Channel 10 commentary box, Robert Walls summed up the feelings of all Cats fans: "That is *such* an important kick for the Geelong Football Club."

A jarring miss from Schneider, running into an open goal from 15 metres out, at least got St Kilda its opening score of the game. Several minutes later, Goddard marked, uncontested, 40 metres out to register their first goal. Five minutes later, Selwood showed everyone why, after just three years in the game, he is already rated one of the best in the land. After winning a free kick for a high tackle, the Cats youngster kept going, bulldozing through Jones in the process and then running forward to nail the goal from 40 metres.

Three goals to one after 17 minutes, and Mooney was excited. "I thought, 'Gee, we are flying here. We're going to belt them'," he said.

That confidence wasn't shared by those in the coaches' box. They sensed St Kilda was mounting something, inspired in particular by Hayes, who was becoming a major problem. He seemed to be everywhere and, at the 19-minute mark, he kicked his side's second goal after accepting a Nick Dal Santo pass which crept over the outstretched hand of Selwood.

Plus, the Saints seemed to dominating Geelong around the ball, with a 12-6 advantage in clearances plus a significantly higher number of forward entries. Hayes already had 11 touches, including five clearances and a goal, and Cameron Ling sensed he might be getting a tap on the shoulder. "Lenny was just running amok and I wouldn't have been surprised if the runner had come out," he said.

Yes, the runner appeared. But he headed to Bartel, not Ling.

During the season, assistant coach Brendan McCartney, who was in charge of midfield rotations, had used Bartel half-a-dozen times in "run-with" roles at various stages of games, as much for the experience as the situation. "We had prepared Jimmy earlier in the year as we just thought for a rainy day if we ever needed two to be kept quiet, we would know what to do and he would know something about the role," he said.

Putting Ling onto Hayes was discussed but Thompson had pencilled in a lesson he witnessed the previous week. He noticed the Western Bulldogs had reacted to a slow start against St Kilda, changed their initial structures and it had thrown them out substantially.

"As a team we don't like to jump on too many situations where you become too reactive," he said. "But you still have to show initiative and Hayes was flying so somebody had to do something. Hence, we asked Jimmy."

Thompson and McCartney both made a beeline for Bartel at the quarter-time huddle to explain the job he had done for the last couple of minutes was now his for the rest of the afternoon. "I'd done it for a quarter here and there, as had Joel Corey and Joel Selwood, in case one day we needed to lock down on more than one or two," Bartel said. "I guess that turned out to be the day. The way we play is usually 50-50 attack-defence for our midfielders, so I had to probably change that to 70-30 with more defending, although still try and push off every now and then."

Apart from not controlling Hayes nor having the lead – Schneider had kicked a goal in the final minute of the first term, which put St Kilda two points to the good – there were several other problems presenting themselves.

Johnson hadn't earned a clear possession in the first 30 minutes. "It was a bit like that Carlton game from earlier in the season," he said. "Normally when I get the ball I can change direction and get out of trouble. When I got the ball I just felt slow and got tackled a couple of times early."

And Chapman was hobbling, having copped a nasty corked thigh just before the quarter-time siren. "Rookey kicked a ball to me and it sat up a little bit," he said, "and I tried to put out my leg to stop Dawson from coming through. But he got me right on the quad."

Chapman was still trying to get his leg working properly at the start of the second quarter when he was called into action. His opponent, Gilbert, had the ball; as he tried to lay a tackle, Chapman felt a tightening in his right hamstring. "Oh shit, not again," he thought as he picked himself up off the ground. He tried to walk around to assess the damage when he again found himself in the middle of the play, receiving a handball from Hawkins and letting fly off one step with a shot at goal from 50 metres.

"I wasn't too sure how bad it was and then I went for that long kick from 50 and felt it even more," he said. "I thought then, 'I'm in some trouble here'." Chapman immediately went off and down into the medical room. "There's not much we can do," Geelong's doctor Chris Bradshaw said, "except strap it up and see how we go."

Up in the box, an exasperated Thompson was asking the bench for an update. "Can we get anything out of him?" he asked.

When Chapman re-appeared and did some sprints along the boundary line, the coach got him on the line and said: "Just stay deep inside 50."

While the mini-crisis was unfolding, an even bigger one was taking place on the ground. St Kilda took control of the game but, fortunately for the Cats, it was shooting itself in the foot as Milne and McQualter missed easy shots.

"Another miss from St Kilda and it's shades of the Cats in the second term last year in the Grand Final," Channel 10 commentator Stephen Quartermain said of the Saints' conversion issues.

Still, it seemed the damn was about to burst, as the ball seemed trapped in St Kilda's half with the Geelong defence under siege. "We kept getting messages, 'Guys, you have got to take the game on, you have got to run and be risky'," Harley said. "But we were absolutely buggered as the ball just kept coming in there."

Against the run of play, the Cats manufactured a score: a Selwood handball allowed Ling to squeeze a right-foot snap towards goal, which rolled into the arms of Shannon Byrnes, alone in the goalsquare. Goal.

Another Schneider miss followed before one of Thompson's Plan B scenarios came off. Ablett headed to the goalsquare and immediately earned a free kick against Gilbert for a hold. He converted the shot from 30 metres and, in an instant, the Cats were back in front by a point.

Five minutes later, Hawkins made his mark on the Grand Final in controversial circumstances. After brilliantly smothering a Dawson kick, the youngster gathered the ball and instinctively slammed it onto his boot for a goal. Slow motion replays showed the ball clearly hit the post, but the goal was awarded, a crucial decision in the context of a game which had settled into a captivating wet weather slog.

The Cats ensured there was no dwelling on their stroke of fortune. They broke clear from the next centre bounce, Corey handballing to Ablett, who found Travis Varcoe for one of his rare touches in the first half. He then handballed to Chapman, who tested his hamstring out with a one-step shot from 40 metres for a goal.

Despite being out-played for most of the quarter, and with the weather turning ugly again, the Cats now found themselves 12 points clear with less than five minutes remaining to the long break. That was still the case with 52 seconds remaining on the clock until Jones managed to manufacture a lucky goal out of nothing.

The Saints then won the ball from the centre, Sam Fisher going long to a two-on-two in the goalsquare. Koschitzke read it best, managing to soccer through the goal despite the desperate lunge from Milburn, who was convinced he had touched the ball. On the bench, an exasperated Mooney turned to his captain: "We always let in goals at the end of quarters."

Upstairs, Thompson had been handed his stats sheet and was about to get out of his seat when he noticed field umpire Stephen McBurney standing in the goalsquare talking to Milburn as Schneider lined up for a shot at goal.

Milburn had been penalised for being demonstrative towards the goal umpire – he raised two fingers to let him know that, in his opinion, that was the second error the umpire had made. McBurney took the finger salute to mean something completely different.

"It was just a silly, silly mistake," Milburn admitted. "I shouldn't have said anything. I was saying, 'That is two you have missed', as there had been a decision earlier when Joel Selwood said he'd touched it. I should have just shut up but in the heat of the moment you get frustrated and you want to do everything to win."

Milburn's brain fade awarded the Saints a second shot from the goalsquare. Mooney was right – St Kilda had kicked three goals in the final minute of the second quarter and led by a goal at half-time, 7.7 (49) to 7.1.(43).

Milburn was gutted. The veteran defender was last player into the rooms, where he found a seething Thompson waiting for him. "If we lose by less than a goal Dasher, it is on you. It is on you."

Steve Johnson had barely noticed his coach's tirade. He had his own problem to deal with, specifically that he was still without a possession in the Grand Final.

"I felt like my co-ordination was not there so I got (player development manager) Ronnie Watt and took him into the boot room to do some boxing with me, just to get my hands going a bit," Johnson said. "I was feeling different to what I normally did and we did a couple of minutes of boxing and I thought, 'Okay, I'm a bit more alert now'."

Ken Hinkley had come over for an encouraging word. "Just do what you need to do for the team and things can happen because of you," he said.

Johnson had already decided there would be no repeat of 2008, when he had gone wandering for possessions in the biggest game of the season. "I said to myself, 'Don't go chasing easy kicks', which I had done the year before," he said. "I probably could have gone up (the ground) and got five or 10 kicks in the first half but I thought, 'I don't care, I'm going to play my role for the team'."

In the medical room, Taylor, who had been brilliant on Riewoldt, was getting some attention to his hand, which he suspected he had broken in a marking contest in the second quarter. Next to him, Chapman was getting more strapping applied to his injured hamstring.

Mooney didn't know about the injury to his fellow forward until he walked past the open door.

"I saw the bandage and thought, 'Jesus Christ, he has gone again'," he said. "The thing is, we'd been talking during the week and I said, 'If you do you f...king hammie this week, I am going to kill you'."

There was also concern in the room about several areas of the game plan which were clearly not working. Ablett, in particular, was talking to his fellow midfielders and coaches about setting up differently in the second half.

"I was pretty nervous," Ablett said. "I knew we hadn't played as well as we could and I knew they had played really well with their structures and shut down what we wanted to do. There were quite a few things I wanted to say to the boys at half-time that I had been thinking about towards the end of the second quarter. I thought there were quite a few things that had to change."

Scarlett knew what had to change: the ball needed to get up the other end every once in a while. He wasn't surprised when he asked defensive coach Brenton Sanderson for the inside 50-metre zone stats for the first half. "It was 37 to 15, St Kilda's way. Usually we try to keep a team under 45 for the whole game so I thought we'd actually stood up reasonably well down there on the scoreboard," he said.

Hinkley agreed. He had actually mentioned to the other coaches on the way down to the rooms at half-time about the similarities between this year's Grand Final and what had happened to the Cats the previous year. "You know it's almost the reverse of last year," he said. "We are a goal down and we are probably a bit closer than we should be."

It was a sentiment shared by Brian Cook.

"I thought we were going to be three or four goals down at half-time the way it had been going," he said.

"I was absolutely exhausted at half-time and went inside (the AFL luncheon) and met (St Kilda's chief executive) Michael Nettlefold. We had a little chat and I said, 'God, mate this is too hard to take isn't it? Anyone is going to win'. We were quite honest because we were in awe of the effort out there."

The Geelong theme was all about persistence, rather than coming up with something new for the second half. "No panic" was the thread of Thompson's half-time address.

"Boys, you are playing okay, they are playing okay," he said. "It is going to get down to the point of who is going to wear out first. So that means it comes down to how much you are prepared to give. You are going to have to give more than them. It might take until the last minute, but you are going to have to be prepared to give more and just do the basics well.

"History will judge you on what you do in the next hour."

He then urged some of his senior players to give him more, including his captain: "Can you lift?"

"Absolutely I can lift," Harley responded.

Just before the players were about to run out for the second half, Thompson pulled Mooney aside and said: "Make sure you don't come off this ground again without a medal."

chapter 33

60 gruelling minutes

"I figured if you get the ball to Gaz, good things happen most of the time."

– Matthew Scarlett on a toe poke that decided a Grand Final

After an hour of zero impact football, Steve Johnson took just 30 seconds of the third quarter to register his first possession, a hurried kick into the Cats' forward line. It was one of five entries to St Kilda's zero in the opening seven minutes of the third quarter, and it resulted in Cameron Mooney getting his second goal of the game, having outbustled Zac Dawson at the top of the goalsquare.

The lead was Geelong's again, although the Cats had it for only a minute. Jason Gram, who had been busy on the wing in the opening half with 14 possessions, pumped the ball in long to Nick Riewoldt. For the first time, Riewoldt had the better of Harry Taylor in a one-on-one contest. The St Kilda skipper converted from 15 metres out; he had another two attempts shortly after, Taylor coming up with a brilliant smother to save the second chance.

St Kilda again seemed to have locked the Cats into their defensive half. It wasn't until the 17-minute mark that Paul Chapman was able to run onto a loose ball and, with a brilliant block by Max Rooke, easily nail one of his trademark "snap over the shoulder" goals. The move inspired Tim Lane in the commentatory box.

"He's a killer around goal, can he kill them here? *Yes he can!*" was Lane's description of Chapman's second goal of the game.

It was immediately obvious both on the ground and in the coaches' box that Geelong was playing much more as it wanted in the third term. "We thought we were playing the right way even if we weren't scoring," Brendan McCartney said. "We were getting more of it and winning more contests. Every time there was a contest there seemed to be Geelong blokes heading to the area to tidy it up and give us possession."

Scores remained level for more than eight minutes late in the quarter before Leigh Montagna ran onto a boundary throw-in deep in the forward pocket, his freakish snap sailed through to break the deadlock. Being so close to the final change, it looked to be one of those critical opportunistic moments in a gripping match; indeed, while Geelong had steadied its ship, the Saints had appeared to have the edge for much of the day.

At three-quarter time, their lead was seven points, 9.11. (65) to 9.4 (58). Key Saints playmaker Brendon Goddard was in the wars, having copped a broken nose courtesy of friendly fire from teammate Steven Baker, then having his collarbone smashed in a bruising tackle by James Kelly. The Cats also had concerns, with Tom Harley's knee giving him some problems although, remarkably, Chapman seemed to be moving freely.

Lenny Hayes was no longer causing problems, thanks to a remarkable blanket job by Jimmy Bartel – the Saints vice-captain, comfortably best afield in the first 30 minutes, had just eight possessions in the second and third quarters. "It's a big thing to go out and ask one your star players, your Brownlow Medallist, that we need you to sacrifice your game for the team," Cameron Ling said. "It's not about you getting the footy, it's not about you being the superstar, it is about playing your role for the team and Jimmy just accepted that and did it straight away."

Despite the scoreboard, Mark Thompson remained confident. He had been so throughout what had been an epic struggle and he saw the next 30 minutes as an opportunity of a lifetime for the 22 players wearing the blue and white hoops. "This next quarter of footy can set you up for the rest of your life," he said calmly to his players. "It is going to take all your knowledge, all your experience and toughness to get us over the line but it is an opportunity to do something really special in your football career.

"Imagine how good the feeling will be if you win this, it will be the quarter of your lives and you will never forget it."

Throughout the game, many of the Geelong players had been using the pain of the previous year to motivate each other. It was now the dominant mood inside the huddle.

"We're not going to lose this game," Cameron Mooney said.

Matthew Scarlett joined in. "We never want to feel like that again."

And then Kelly echoed his teammates. "Remember that feeling in the pit of your stomach when the siren goes, and you're behind? That's the worst feeling in the world and we aren't going through that again."

Thompson waited until just as the huddle broke to repeat the challenge he had put to Mooney at half-time: "Make sure you don't come off the ground again without a medal."

It was strong, passionate and simple, but it struck a chord with his players.

In the opening few seconds of the final quarter of the season, Travis Varcoe, who had been quiet, flashed onto a spillage at half-forward and very nearly created a scoring opportunity. The opening came 45 seconds later, when Gary Ablett put on a wonderful shepherd for Chapman, allowing the latter to find Tom Hawkins, who took two bites to take the mark at centre half-forward.

Like his colleague, Mooney, the 21-year-old had been criticised heavily for his wayward goalkicking throughout his brief career. That was going through his head as he lined up from 50 metres out ... so too was the fact the wind was swirling around inside the MCG.

Bartel was standing behind his teammate when Hawkins let fly. He was at first convinced it was going out on the full. The ball then corrected and split the big sticks. "That was amazing," he said. "It started out on the full and then came back. I was absolutely pumped for him because all year you hear this crap about how bad he and Moons kicked for goals but they'd both kicked the crunch ones when it really mattered."

Thompson was pleased that the coaching panel's faith in the "Tomahawk" had paid off at just the right time. "The match committee and coaches, everyone, thought that this year we are just going play him and try and find another key forward," he said. "We knew there would be times where he would doubt himself and there were going to be some weeks where it worked and some difficult weeks until the point came that he knew he could play. I think by the end of the year he reached that point. There is nothing more than playing well in a final and he had a pretty impressive final series."

Hawkins celebrated his 34th goal of the season with a double-bicep pose. The kick brought the margin back to one point, but it would be another 22 minutes before the next goal.

The Saints again missed golden opportunities. After easily side-stepping Tom Harley at the 13-minute mark, Schneider pushed wide his running shot from directly in front. Sean Dempster missed another chance to convert soon after, and when no free kick was awarded to Schneider for a clear hold several minutes later, the football gods seemed to be smiling on the Cats.

A courageous touch on the line by Baker, who crashed into the goal post, saved what looked like a certain Max Rooke goal. Then Joel Selwood's set shot from 50 metres was wide; the scores were again level with the clock ticking into time-on. Suddenly, the spectre of a draw loomed.

"I kept looking up at the scoreboard thinking, 'Wow. If it's a draw today we have to come back next week'," Ablett said.

Chapman also kept looking at the scoreboard. "You just wanted something special to happen, someone to do something."

Ironically, but not surprisingly, that someone was Johnson. The Norm Smith Medallist from 2007 had then spoken of living for Grand Final day. So the fact he had endured a career-worst afternoon on the game's biggest stage perhaps hinted that he might cleanse his soul before the game was out. Johnson found himself in space on the wing at the 23-minute mark.

"Bomber brought me back on and I wanted to pretend that I was going to a half-back flank," Johnson said. "I don't know why a St Kilda player would think I was going to a half-back flank as I've never been there in my life. But I was pretending I wasn't going forward, which had them looking around for a few seconds and I thought that might get me into a little space.

"Luckily, Boris (Enright) got it and I put my hands in the air and he spotted me beautifully."

Ablett was watching this unfold from the middle of the ground where he found himself all alone after electing not to follow his shadow Jones into the contest.

"I was actually chasing Clinton Jones and he took off and I missed him," he said. "He got 15 or 20 metres of space on me and I thought he was going to get the ball but I also realised we had players there so he wasn't going to be able to run a long way with it. I thought there is no use me running over and chasing him as he is going to get the ball no matter what, so I took off to the middle of the ground and luckily enough it turned over."

A number of his teammates saw him open but they weren't sure if Johnson did. "Gazza's free," Ling started screaming, although he was too far away to be heard in the din.

Harley was on the bench and went to do the same thing. "I was watching the play unfold and was thinking to myself, 'I can't believe Gary Ablett is in the middle of the MCG by himself'."

Johnson eventually spied Ablett. He initially thought the 30-metre pass from the wing was perfect but, as it got closer, it seemed to hold up.

"I remember thinking, 'I've kicked that alright but it's hanging in the air for a long time'," Johnson said. "Then I thought this could be the worst day of my life ... if this ball turns over and they kick a goal, it's on my shoulders."

He could see Zac Dawson charging at Ablett, who was blissfully unaware the Saints defender was closing.

"Normally you can hear the crowd making noise so you know someone is coming," Ablett said. "I didn't hear anything so I thought I must be completely free. Then when he got a punch on it I remember thinking for a split second, 'Oh, no, if this bounces the other way...'"

Scarlett, who was at centre half-back, had seen Dawson leave his man. He realised he had to help Ablett. "Stevie kicked it a little bit too high. Gazza was by himself but Zac Dawson came off his man to spoil," he said. "I thought then, 'Shit, I've got to go and help Gazza out here'."

What Scarlett did next will go down in Grand Final history forever – he somehow managed to "toe poke" the ball back to Ablett.

"I don't know why I kicked it but it was some good Pele work," he laughed. "I was probably too buggered to bend over and pick it up. I thought I will just get it to Gaz any way possible and something will happen. Luckily I just timed it right but there was a bit of luck involved. I figured if you get the ball to Gaz, good things happen most of the time."

A loud "*YEEEEAAAAAHHHH*" erupted in the coaches' box.

"We don't normally barrack but it was very exciting having Gary with the ball, by himself about to run inside 50," Thompson said.

McCartney said: "If there is the ball in the area and you want two Geelong players near it to decide an outcome they are probably the two."

Hinkley was thinking goal as he watched Scarlett run alongside Ablett towards the 50. "I thought he would take them on and keep going and kick the goal."

Ablett was thinking the same thing. "There was a bloke running at me from the front so, for a split second, I was thinking about taking him on," he said. "But then it kind of just came into my head that if we could get a point, it is going to be enough. So I kicked it as long as I could and the wind actually held it up a bit."

Mooney had been on Dawson but had run backwards to get in position for the chip over the top, only for Raph Clarke to cover him. He then sprinted for the goalsquare and appeared to have timed his run to perfection. "When Zac had gone to Gaz and spoiled it I was like, 'Oh no, what have I done?' but then I saw the toe poke," Mooney said. "Then when Raph Clarke manned me up I wasn't happy but as the ball was coming down in the goalsquare I thought, 'I'm going to get this and then everyone is going to forgive me for last year'."

Unfortunately, Max Rooke also had his eyes on being the hero. The pair, who both had their eyes on the ball, bumped as they attempted the mark with the ball luckily spilling back towards the top of the goalsquare.

Waiting for it was Shannon Byrnes. He managed to tap it towards Varcoe, whose quick handball found Chapman.

"I was 40 metres out when Gaz got it and I started to run back to the goal," Chapman said. "I was running along and I couldn't find my man, I didn't know where he was. I tried to find him, I think it was Gilbert, but figured he must have dropped back and was being an extra number in the marking contest.

"Then when it came down and I got the handball from Travis, at that stage I thought there was someone on my tail too. Lenny Hayes was in front of me so I had to go left. Then someone dived across my boot but the kick was always good. It was always definitely going through but I knew I had to get it up there and over their hands."

Johnson was a relieved man. "We can't lose."

For the first time, Bartel was starting to believe. "That was the first feeling of, 'We've got them here'," he said. "I knew because of the experience we'd had during the year, we had half-a-dozen games where there was only a kick in it, that we knew what to do. As guys were running back to the centre bounce, everyone was adjusting on the field. We knew where to 'hit' it in this situation and it was all business."

Of course, there was at least seven minutes remaining and it was again going to need something special to lock away the premiership.

Enter Rooke again. The man who had started it two hours earlier managed to bounce off several St Kilda defenders and soccer through a behind to extend the Cats' lead to seven points at the 27-minute mark. It was enough to get Cook out of his seat; on the ground, Ablett and Johnson were convinced it was game over, although the coaches' box refused to concede just yet.

And for good reason. Just 90 seconds later, Justin Koschitzke won a free kick for a ruck infringement and immediately played on, bombing the ball 60 metres straight down the middle. Stephen Milne ran onto the spillage and got off a left-foot kick which was running dangerously towards goal.

Scarlett sprinted after it, Schneider on his tail. The Cat defender expertly managed to fall to the ground and at the same time punch the ball over the line for a behind.

"I just thought get it through for a point, it's not a bad result even if it makes it only one kick," he said. "I just didn't want them to get a goal."

The behind brought it back to six points and had Ablett and Cook both thinking draw again. Johnson was still confident but confused. "I remember seeing Scarlo rush the point and I had to look at the scoreboard about three times," he said. "For some reason I thought we were only five points up so I had to look at it three times to add up the difference. I'd never had trouble doing that before."

Hinkley was concerned as kick-outs, which Milburn was about to take, hadn't been the Cats' strong point all day. Then when the umpire called play on because the Saints' zone had cut off any easy options, Riewoldt went within a whisker of smothering Milburn's kick.

Luckily, he missed. The ball sailed long and wide towards the half-back line, where Bartel was wrestling with Hayes to get position. Alongside both was Harry Taylor.

"I could see him (Taylor) coming flying in so, if I'd gone for it, he would have poleaxed me," Bartel said.

In scenes reminiscent of Leo Barry in the 2005 Grand Final, Taylor plucked the ball out of the sky. "It was relatively easy because I'd practised it so often at training," Taylor said.

Brenton Sanderson had seen him do it 500 times over the past couple of years as the pair had worked on the proper way to mark the ball which made it hard for opposition to spoil.

As Taylor walked back, pretending to rub his head to milk the clock, Thompson finally relaxed for the first time. It was only fleeting, however, as the umpire quickly called "play on", forcing Taylor to handball to Brad Ottens. Selwood, Ling, Byrnes and Mooney were involved in the passage of play before it finally landed in the hands of Rooke, 30 metres out from goal in the forward pocket.

Ling had just been told by the runner there were two minutes to go and was trying to compute in his head how much time might be left. "I thought it had almost been two minutes, it had to be close and I started screaming out to the boys to set up the zone when I heard it," he said.

"It" was the siren.

The coaches' box erupted. The normally controlled Thompson was jumping on his chair, banging on the glass and hugging everyone around him. "You can't script that," he said. "That wasn't false or made up, that was just pure emotion from a pretty stressful day, a long year and then winning a premiership in that manner."

Neither Thompson nor Cook saw Rooke kick the goal after the siren – they found out when they read the next day's papers – which took the winning margin out to 12 points, 12.8. (80) to 9.14 (68).

No one had bothered to man the mark, with distraught St Kilda players slumped to the ground but Rooke decided to dribble the ball through because he knew it might be worth a free beer for someone. "A mate of mine told me the Birregurra pub (Royal Mail Hotel, near Colac) was shouting free pots whenever I kicked a goal, so I thought I'd help them out," he offered.

When the siren sounded, Ling dropped to his knees with his arms raised to the sky.

"I'm not the world's most emotional bloke, I don't really cry," he said. "But I just remember getting very, very emotional. It was just a magical time, one of the greatest feelings ever."

Group hugs were breaking out everywhere. Scarlett had bear-hugged Taylor, who was delirious with his first premiership win. Chapman, the goalkicking hero, was swamped by Byrnes and Selwood. Ablett was struggling to hold back tears as he embraced a relieved Milburn, who had played a sensational second half following his half-time horror.

Mooney embraced Harley as the latter was doing a television interview. "The cameras were on us but I didn't want to let him go because I was bawling my eyes out," Mooney said. "You just don't get that feeling every day, I can tell you."

Cook plucked Sir Donald Trescowthick, the former No. 1 ticket holder at Geelong, from the crowd and brought him onto the ground for the celebrations. He also grabbed Billy Brownless, whom security were not allowing on because he didn't have the correct wristband.

"Sir Donald couldn't believe he was on the ground and he looked around and said, 'I can die happily now'," Cook said. "It was a great feeling down there and this time around I felt a real part of it. I don't know why I say that but maybe it was just that the players had been very accommodating, particularly the leaders whom I had spent a bit of time with, so I felt like a partner. In many ways it was meant to be, somehow. It was a great achievement because of the bravery and because of the hunger to win it."

As the players gathered near the stage with the club's VFL players, staff and board all part of the festivities, thoughts turned to who would receive the Norm Smith Medal. Mooney had it pegged as his fellow forward Rooke. "His toughness was unbelievable," he said. "He would crash into a pack, get up and go again, plus Fisher had no impact."

Commentators were rightly "talking up" Chapman's 26 disposals and three goals. Taylor's job on Riewoldt – he kept him to just 13 possessions and one goal – had him in calculations.

Others in the running included Joel Corey, who had a great last quarter to end with 29 touches; Ablett was again superb with 25, while Bartel shut down Hayes and had an incredible 16 tackles. St Kilda's Jason Gram was the leading possession-winner on the ground with 30.

Brad Ottens, who led the hit-outs for the afternoon, asked Chapman whom he thought would win it, just as 1991 Norm Smith Medallist, Hawthorn's Paul Dear, was announced on stage.

"I have got no idea," Chapman answered. At that moment, AFL media manager Patrick Keane rushed up alongside him. "Make sure you don't swear and thank your supporters," Keane said.

Chapman wasn't sure what was happening.

"Does that mean... ?" said Ottens.

"I don't know," replied Chapman, daring to think the dream. Twenty seconds later he indeed knew he was adjudged best afield.

In many ways, Chapman encapsulated Geelong's journey. Twelve months earlier he had left the MCG shattered at his own failings and that of his body – now he had been voted the best player on the ground in one of the great AFL Grand Finals in history.

"I was so rapt for him," Ling said. "He put in such a big year and really found a new level of professionalism in the way he went about things. The off season he put in to come back in good nick and then not having any groin problems, getting through a full pre-season and then a full home-and-away season. It's just reward for his work."

Ling shared a priceless moment with Joel Corey and Corey Enright as they waited for each player to be called up on stage to receive their premiership medallions.

"It's a long way since November '99 and that draft when the three of us came from different parts of Australia to start training together," Ling said.

Corey laughed and as he looked around at the sea of blue and white in the stadium. "Yeah, how good is this!?"

With the captain called up last, Harley, who had sat on the bench for the final eight minutes, had time to gather his thoughts. A mixture of emotions ran through his head. Relief was the primary one, but he was also proud, satisfied, frustrated and a little sad at the realisation that his journey was over.

"It was just pure relief when I heard the siren," he said. "I really wish that I had been able to contribute more on the day but I realised that this was not about just what had happened in the past two hours. The whole journey with this team over the past three or four years, that was what was overwhelming for me."

He decided he would single out a couple of people in his speech, including Mathew Stokes, Josh Hunt and his good friend, Matthew Egan, who was looking more and more unlikely to play football again.

And he had a plan with the premiership cup. He wanted to break with the tradition of the captain and coach holding it up before the rest of the team came on stage.

"Because it had been a real struggle for me and the team I thought it would be self-indulgent to accept the cup by myself," Harley said. "I had only played a handful of games so it was really the boys who won it so I spread the word amongst them about coming up early."

Geelong's 1963 premiership coach, Bob Davis, had the honour of handing over the cup and the players were already on the dias waiting for him, even helping the old-timer up the stairs. Davis managed to hand it over to Thompson before the players grabbed hold. Harley had slipped around the back and actually didn't touch the cup until half-way around the celebratory lap.

After making it back into the rooms, the players were directed into the meeting room, where Thompson placed the premiership cup in the middle and nominated players to speak about what this day meant.

Harley jumped up first and did everything but tell them he was hanging up the boots. "I just want to say what an honour it has been to play with you all," he said.

Mooney was next. He revealed the depth of the pain he'd carried around since last year. "You guys have no idea how bad I have been feeling for a year," he said. "I just want to thank you all for letting me hold the cup once more. If I'd lived with (2008) being my last Grand Final I probably would have been miserable for the rest of my life."

The first-time premiership players – Blake, Varcoe, Taylor and Hawkins – were called upon to say a few words, with Mooney jumping in to do an introduction for his fellow forward. "Remember everybody what he (Hawkins) did at the start of the last quarter. It was unbelievable."

Darren Milburn was next, and he was quick to apologise for his umpire abuse debacle. "There was a chance of me jumping off the West Gate if we lost," he said. "I promise I'm not going to talk to umpires ever again."

The most moving of all the speeches had come from Mathew Stokes. "I'm so proud that I was a part of this and you guys made me feel like I was," he said.

After about 10 minutes, the players drifted out to see family, friends and a waiting media pack. Ablett stayed behind and ended up being alone for a few minutes.

"I sat down by myself and just thought about what we had just done, what we had achieved," he said. "The thing that makes it the most special is the ups and downs you go through as a playing group. A lot of people on the outside don't see the amount of meetings we have, we challenge each other, there is a lot of honesty in the footy club and the injuries we go through. The pressure and the sacrifices, all that kind of stuff. Not that it's something to complain about, I love it, but when you sit down with the group after you have achieved what you have achieved ... there is no better feeling, you just feel like hugging every one of them."

Thompson was feeling a lot different to two years earlier. "In 2007, I was so emotional, I basically cried and I couldn't hold myself back," he said. "This year I was a bit more excited, I was happy, there were lots of man-hugs and after I got over that phase it was really peaceful for me. It didn't matter what happened, it was just a nice peaceful feeling." He was then whisked away to a press conference with Chapman, where he revealed to the media that his half-forward had won the Norm Smith Medal on one leg.

"Do you want to tell us how you played, and got best on ground, with a torn hamstring?" Thompson asked.

After a laugh and a brief explanation, Chapman put the medal into perspective.

"The Norm Smith's great, but you don't catch up with other blokes who have won Norm Smiths, or anything like that. You catch up with your teammates you win premierships with," he said. "This is something we're going to have forever."

Harley's celebration was delayed by a drug test. He then had to ring fiancé, Felecity, to bring back his suit, which was in the car in which she had departed the MCG. By the time he got out of the changerooms, the bus was almost ready to take the team to its post-match functions at Federation Square and Melbourne Park.

However, the captain still had one more thing to do, something he had not got the chance to do in 2007.

"I wanted to go out on the ground and have a look around for one last time," Harley said. "It was just coincidental that Dasher and Moons were out there with me. I walked arm in arm to the middle with Dasher, my oldest teammate, and we had a bit of a moment.

"I said to him as we walked off, 'The next time I'm out here in an official capacity for Geelong, hopefully it will be presenting a cup to the next premiership captain'."

Already out there on the ground, on the other side, was Harley's vice-captain, who was also making up for not having enjoyed the experience two years earlier.

"There was no one there and the night had got really nice," Ling said. "The stars were out, the moon was out and it was all really quite peaceful. It was weird because an hour or so earlier there had been 99,000 people going completely nuts. I remember walking around and having a bit of a laugh to myself because I still couldn't believe I'd done it. I'd always dreamt as a kid of just being able to watch a Geelong premiership as a supporter but then to play in one in '07 was amazing and more than I could ever have hoped for. Now, to be a two-time premiership player, it was almost funny."

The cocktail party was jumping by the time by the players arrived at Melbourne Park and as they were introduced on stage they were all high-fived by the club's mascot, Half-Cat. Frank Costa watched with admiration as his warriors appeared but his favourite moment for the day came when Half-Cat removed his mask.

It was Mathew Stokes.

"I reckon Stokesy showed so much team ethos and team spirit and it was an example to the rest of the club," he said. "It is an example to the boys in the future, the way he accepted what happened and it's an example to everyone."

The president summed up the overwhelming feeling for football followers everywhere on Saturday September 26, 2009 when he said, "If you look at the three years – 2007-08-09 – this team won more games than any team in the history of senior football since 1897 in that three-year period. They had 15 All-Australians in those years, two Brownlow Medallists and two Norm Smith Medallists. It was a pretty awesome performance and it would have been really, really unfair had they lost that one."

Epilogue, 2009

Two days after winning the premiership, Ken Hinkley bid farewell to Geelong after six years as an assistant coach. He took up an offer to be the senior assistant coach at the new Gold Coast franchise, working alongside former West Coast champion Guy McKenna.

"This is an opportunity to challenge myself and when you're a coach you look for opportunities to do that," Hinkley said. "I thought for me to develop as a coach was to go back and have an opportunity to work with some young kids, and certainly the Gold Coast provides me with that."

Within a fortnight, his position had been filled by former Essendon premiership player and Collingwood assistant coach, Blake Caracella.

There were several other key departures in the wake of the 2009 premiership success, with Brian Cook losing his right-hand man, chief operating officer Stuart Fox, who became chief executive at Hawthorn.

In the playing ranks, rookie ruckman Shane Mumford received an extraordinary $1 million-plus offer from Sydney which he couldn't refuse – not bad for a kid from Bunyip.

Mumford went to the Harbour City in exchange for selection No.28 in the national draft.

The premiership success was celebrated with gusto at the best and fairest night at Crown Casino, with a club-first tie in the Carji Greeves Medal between defender Corey Enright and Brownlow Medallist Gary Ablett. Ablett drew level after receiving one more vote (30 to 29) in the Grand Final, but it was an emotional Enright who captivated the large crowd. In a moving speech, the All-Australian defender paid tribute to Matthew Egan, describing his teammate as an inspiration.

"He's a really special person that has had some hard times and his outlook and the way he goes about life (I admire)," Enright said. "He probably goes unnoticed now that he's had those setbacks, but I just think he's a really special person and someone that does inspire me."

Egan was officially delisted by the club at the end of the season but will continue his rehabilitation from a foot injury and hopes to be re-drafted for 2011.

On Thursday, October 22, Tom Harley announced his retirement. Surrounded by Cook and coach Mark Thompson, the two-time premiership captain admitted his body no longer allowed him to play AFL football. The CEO said there was "no one I respect more in this organisation than Tom Harley", while Thompson described the 31-year-old as "one of the great captains in the history of the Geelong Football Club".

The newly married Harley rejected an offer from his coach to assist him to play on in 2010 in search of 200 games – he finished two short.

"That's my lot, I had my chance to play 200 games this season and didn't get there," he said. "It's game, set and match for me with the Geelong footy club as a player and I couldn't leave more content with my career at the club, where the club is right now and where the club's going in the future."